HIGH ROLLERS

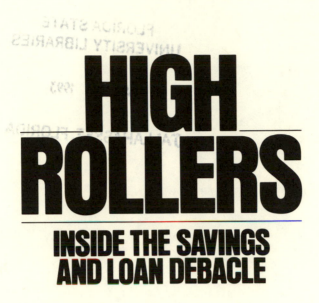

HIGH ROLLERS

INSIDE THE SAVINGS AND LOAN DEBACLE

MARTIN LOWY

New York
Westport, Connecticut
London

Library of Congress Cataloging-in-Publication Data

Lowy, Martin E.
    High rollers : inside the savings and loan debacle / Martin Lowy.
        p.   cm.
    Includes bibliographical references (p.   ) and index.
    ISBN 0-275-93988-X (alk. paper)
    1. Savings and loan associations—United States—Corrupt
practices.   2. Savings and loan associations—United States—
Deregulation.   3. Savings and loan associations—United States—
State supervision.   I. Title.
    HG2151.L68   1991
    332.3'2'0973—dc20   91-8344

British Library Cataloguing in Publication Data is available.

Library of Congress Catalog Card Number: 91-8344
ISBN: 0-275-93988-X

First published in 1991

Praeger Publishers, One Madison Avenue, New York, NY 10010
An imprint of Greenwood Publishing Group, Inc.

Printed in the United States of America

The paper used in this book complies with the
Permanent Paper Standard issued by the National
Information Standards Organization (Z39.48-1984).

10 9 8 7 6 5 4 3 2

For Joe Taffet

Contents

Preface		ix
Introduction		1
Chronology		7

Part I: How It Happened 11

1	Fixed Rates in a Volatile World	13
2	How Insured S&Ls Fail	27
3	Dick Pratt Figures Out How to Run a Bankrupt Federal Insurance Fund	35
4	The False Spring of 1983	58
5	Real Estate Lending 101	64
6	Permissive Loan Fee Accounting—The Linchpin	77
7	Mammon Against the God of Home Ownership	86
8	Ed Gray Tries to Cope and the World Goes Galloping By	100
9	The Big Texas Disaster	126
10	The Laws Trash the Trash	136
11	Silverado, Lincoln and CenTrust	140
12	The Junk Bond Connection	155

13	Fraud and Misconduct 101	160
14	Wall Street Remakes the Mortgage Business	165
15	Politics as Usual—Everybody Fiddles While the FSLIC Burns	176
16	Danny Wall and the 1988 Deals	198
17	FIRREA	222
18	What Caused How Much of the Losses?	229
19	High Rollers	238

Part II: The Lessons of the Piece — 241

20	Evaluating Deregulation	245
21	Because Banks Are Where the Money Is	250
22	The Importance of Counting	254
23	Avoid Complexity That No One Can Understand	263
24	Supervision and Enforcement	267
25	Regulation Can't Tame Technology or Market Forces	271
26	Deposit Insurance Reform	273
27	The Future of Thrift Institutions	283

Postscript	287
Appendix: Dynamics of a Broke S&L	291
Glossary	295
Notes	301
Selected Bibliography	311
Index	317

Preface

A book like this one requires the author to make a great many judgments about people and the policies they pursued. It thus necessarily involves a kind of arrogance, because nobody appointed the author to judge other people. But judging has to be done by somebody. I hope that my experience has prepared me to be judicious and understanding.

A book like this one also involves help from so many people that the writer ends up embarrassed at the length of the list. I conducted more than fifty interviews, was provided with many documents by dozens of law firms and libraries, and was given data by Salomon Brothers, Ferguson & Co., and Cates Consulting. My friends at Coopers & Lybrand were extremely helpful on technical accounting issues. My former partners at Gibson, Dunn & Crutcher provided stacks of documents, as did Tom Vartanian. Almost every interview or document involves somebody doing you a favor, with no more reward than the hope that you will use the information responsibly. Many former regulatory staffers consented to be interviewed only because they believed that I would keep their confidences, which I have tried to do, while at the same time conveying to the reader the substance of what they told me. Dick Pratt, Ed Gray, and Danny Wall, former chairmen of the Federal Home Loan Bank Board of whom I am critical, were particularly generous with their time. I'm sorry that some of my judgments may give them pain.

People who assisted me include Ed Barber, Phil Bartholomew, Jeff Bilsky, Jim Butera, Larry Connell, Bill Crawford, Bill Davis, Bob Eager, Bert Ely, Ed Etten, Ann Fairbanks, Bill Ferguson, Tom Gochberg, Roy Green, Mary Grigsby, Merrikay Hall, Michael Herrick, Roger Hood, Paul Horvitz, Don

Hovde, Jane Isay, Doug Jones, Barry Kolatch, Len Lapidus, Art Leiser, my sons Chris and Peter, Bill McKenna, Chuck Muckenfuss, Penny Murphy, Ron Murray, Lou Nevins, Jim Pledger, Bob Pomeranz, Curtis Probst, Romelle Roeske, Wendy Samuel, Dick Schapiro, Joe Selby, Jim Sexton, Tony Shulte, John Stone, Angelo Vigna, Roger Watson, and Larry White.

Of course there were many others, including those who gave me confidential interviews.

Three people deserve special thanks: First, my wife, Louise, who read every word many times and gave me constructive criticism. Second, my assistant, Maryann Schembri, who slogged through thousands of documents and dozens of drafts, without ever complaining. She is definitely a candidate for sainthood. And third, my friend Gerry Rosenberg, who encouraged me and helped me to find a publisher despite the plethora of books on my subject. My special thanks also to Bill Seidman for his support and encouragement.

At Praeger and Greenwood I want to thank Jim Dunton, whose confidence in the face of so many other books made this one possible, and the many other fine people who have helped me so much in turning a manuscript into a book.

Joe Taffet, to whom this book is dedicated, was Professor of Economics at CCNY; he was my parents' friend and my advisor, and we all miss him. If he had written this book, it would have had more jokes in it.

Any errors, as one is bound to say, are my own. That is the fate of those who have the arrogance to judge.

HIGH ROLLERS

Introduction

On a day near Christmas in 1984, Edwin J. Gray, Chairman of the Federal Home Loan Bank Board, sat in his twenty-by-thirty-foot office at the corner of 17th and G Streets and agonized over new regulations to put a brake on the growth of S&Ls. He knew the regulations were necessary, but the head of the U.S. League of Savings Institutions, the industry's largest lobbying group, had just warned him that the regulations could cost him his career. He had been Chairman for a year and a half, and practically everything he had done had caused controversy.

David Paul, the head of CenTrust Savings in Miami, had different concerns that day. He had just decided to build a forty-seven-story headquarters office tower overlooking Biscayne Bay that would put the name CenTrust on the Miami skyline. But he desperately needed to keep growing in order to outrun the $2 billion of debt that he had acquired along with CenTrust's $1.5 billion of assets. He also had to keep reporting profits even though profitable operations didn't seem possible with a half a billion dollars more of debts than of assets. He needed new, higher yielding investments.

Meanwhile, Charles Keating, who was rapidly turning Lincoln Savings of California into an Arizona real estate company, had just gambled Lincoln's whole capital account on a takeover play for Gulf Broadcasting. Lincoln, a staid S&L until 1984, was on its way to becoming a pure speculation vehicle.

At the same time, Tom Gaubert, Don Dixon, and Ed McBirney were flying high in Texas—meaning that they were skiing in Colorado or sunning on the beach in southern California. Their S&Ls had grown tenfold in the last two years and had recorded huge profits on land loans and construction loans.

They had paid themselves big bonuses and dividends, and they were basking in the reflected light of their own brilliance.

The world didn't know it, but by Christmas 1984 a savings and loan crisis already was in the can. It was only a two-reeler then but it was ready for sneak previews around the country. Ed Gray would adopt his regulations—somewhat too little, somewhat too late. David Paul would build his CenTrust office tower, now a monumental symbol of the greed and egotism that gripped the industry. He would find his high-yielding investments in junk bonds. Keating would prove himself a genius in his own mind by making $50 million on the Gulf Broadcasting play. Then, when things started to go bad, he would loot Lincoln and cheat depositors. And Gaubert, Dixon, and McBirney would fly along, progressing from aggressive, speculative lending to fraud after fraud to cover up the bad investments they had made. Eventually CenTrust, Lincoln, Sunbelt, Vernon, and Independent American would cost the government about $10 billion to liquidate, but that wouldn't come to light until 1987, 1988, and 1989. Keating, Gaubert, Dixon, and McBirney would be indicted. David Paul is still under investigation. Ed Gray is president of a small S&L in Miami.

A great deal more would happen after 1984 to make the crisis worse than it had to be. Insolvent S&Ls were allowed to continue in business even though they were guaranteed to lose money. The price of oil dropped from $28 a barrel to $10. President Reagan's 1986 Tax Reform Act made real estate investment unattractive to individuals and knocked down the value of commercial real estate by about 20 percent. Lower real estate values made failed institutions cost more and caused more institutions to fail. Eventually, the sheer size of the problem made it unmanageable. But the crisis really began in 1978—or even in 1966, when spending on the Vietnam War and President Johnson's Great Society programs triggered an increase in inflation. For a while regulations kept a lid on the problem, but in 1978, unchecked inflation overcame the regulatory apparatus put in place in 1966.

Except for an interim period in 1982–83 when declining interest rates restored some of the value of fixed-rate loans, the savings and loan institutions of the United States steadily lost money from 1978 to 1990. They reported profits from 1983 to 1986, but there really weren't any. Inflated loan fees, purchase accounting anomalies, skimmed loan and securities portfolios, and low loan loss reserves gave S&Ls an appearance of profits when in fact they were going backward. If all the weak S&Ls had been liquidated at the end of 1981, when interest rates were at their highest point, the loss would have been something on the order of $100 billion (about $140 billion in 1990 dollars). The amount would have been less than half that figure a year later, after interest rates had come down.

From 1978 to the middle of 1982, the losses came strictly from interest rate risks, as inflation depreciated the value of S&Ls' assets while they had to pay more for deposits. In the second phase, from mid–1982 to 1985, the S&Ls made risky loans that resulted in losses that they didn't report until 1986 through 1989. In the third phase, the government's failure to close insolvent S&Ls caused huge operating losses; the 1986 tax law increased embedded real estate losses; and legislation designed to end the S&L problem depreciated S&Ls' franchise values, caused more of them to fail, and made investment in them unattractive.

At the end of 1982, the stock market boom, interest rate deregulation, new asset powers, the 1981 Tax Act, and a spirit of free markets and entrepreneurship came together to transform the savings industry. New lending patterns developed; new owners came into the small Texas, Florida, and California institutions; and supercharged growth fueled by deregulated deposit rates became commonplace. S&L deposits—and therefore the FSLIC fund's potential obligations to the nation's depositors—grew from $567 billion at the end of 1982 to $724 billion two years later. The FHLBB (which some people called "Flub" but most people called "the Bank Board"), which managed the FSLIC (which everyone called "Fizz-Lick"), couldn't keep up. It moved slowly to reinject discipline into the system to replace the straitjacket discipline that deregulating interest rates on insured deposits had removed.

Speculators and fraud artists flourished. They used every rule and accounting practice to their advantage, while the accountants and the regulatory apparatus struggled to catch up.

The FSLIC became bankrupt sometime between 1982 and 1985, and that's what cost the taxpayers money. All the S&Ls could have failed and it wouldn't have cost anything if there had been enough money in the insurance fund to pay the depositors. The FSLIC—a federal agency—is what we're bailing out, not the S&Ls.

Almost everybody missed the S&L crisis as it was happening because the FHLBB first fuzzed up the numbers, then postponed doing things so that the public wouldn't lose confidence. This fooled the press, the Congress, and even most of the S&L industry.

When the Bank Board woke up and began telling Congress that something was seriously wrong, it temporized because it foresaw that if Congress had to use tax dollars to bail out the FSLIC, Congress would exact a serious price, most likely the end of the FSLIC as a separate insurance fund and the end of subsidized housing finance through the Federal Home Loan Banks and S&Ls.

Then the Congress, lulled by lavish campaign contributions and befogged by Texas politics, went along with the S&Ls and tightly rationed the FSLIC's money in 1987.

So to most people the problem seems to have come up in 1988 or 1989, when by 1984, in fact, the FSLIC already was mortally wounded and we didn't stop the bleeding after that. Many of the efforts to cure the problem just made it worse.

This is a hard story to tell, and many of us are to blame for it. If it wasn't only the bad guys who did it, then it must have been the Congress, the administration (or several administrations), or the regulators, who failed to deal with the consequences of economic and technological change. The emphasis on fraud and criminal prosecutions is a cover-up that panders to the anger of the American people, who demand someone to blame. In most cases, the insider fraud didn't cause the insolvency. It came afterward, to conceal the failing institution's true financial condition. The real causes of the S&L crisis weren't the bad guys. The real causes were *and are* far more fundamental and far more frightening. This wasn't a bank robbery; it was a fundamental economic failure of a substantial part of our financial system, and the same forces are threatening other parts of the system today.

I have spent twenty-five years as a lawyer and as a banker learning about banks, S&Ls, accounting, economics, bank regulation, real estate lending, and politics in the banking business. I have represented thrift trade associations and thrift institutions, some of which have failed; I have represented the FDIC in bank liquidations and the Superintendent of Banks of New York on failing banks and S&Ls; I have been a member of senior management and I have done "workouts" of troubled real estate loans; I also have been part of the lending process—approving, I am sorry to say, some loans that didn't turn out just right as well as some that did. I have investigated great frauds such as IOS, Penn Central, and Equity Funding. In the course of these professional activities, I have had many wonderful teachers, whose perspectives I will try to share. I want to tell you the S&L story the way the professionals see it.

It will help us to understand the story, if we first look at where the money went:

Some of the money—but not a large percentage of it—went to S&L executives and owners who committed fraud. Bad management cost a lot more money, but that's not fraud. I don't think we will trace $2 billion to insider fraud.

Most of the money went to people like you and me. It went to everyone who had a fixed-rate mortgage in the 1960s and 1970s. It went to everyone who bought a bank or thrift CD in the 1980s. Some of it went to investment bankers, lawyers, and accountants whose business benefited from the overheated market that S&L lending created in the 1980s. Some of it went to all of the construction workers and suppliers of all the surplus buildings that S&L money built in the 1980s. Some of it went to the developers of those buildings, who got the best deals ever—but many of them lost it all when the bubble burst. Some of it went to speculators who got out in time—but most of them didn't. Some of it went to borrowers who defrauded lax S&L managements. And a lot of the money went up in the smoke of the Southwest depression that destroyed property values, fortunes, and careers.

What unifies all of us is that we acted in our own self-interest to take advantage of a deposit insurance system that the FHLBB and the administration managed ineptly.

To understand how the S&L problem could fester for ten years, we will need to investigate how the S&L business and its regulatory system were set up, how the accounting rules gave a false picture of financial health, how the economics of the S&L business changed, how real estate markets work, how the regulators and the accountants couldn't keep up with the changes, how greed and fraud were permitted to take over, how the time value of money makes it impossible to stand still in the financial world, and how the political process made matters worse.

We will cover these subjects as efficiently as we can, but it can't be done in ten-second sound bites. Chapters 1 through 6 teach some technical basics you need to know (if you know them already, please bear with me), but after that you can follow the story like a pro.

At the end we will explore deposit insurance reform ideas and ask about the future of specialized housing lenders. Deposit insurance and preservation of a specialized housing finance business are what made the losses possible—should we therefore end them? This book will give you the tools to understand and participate in the debate even if you disagree with my particular policy choices. It is hard to think logically about this greatest financial scandal of all time, but we should make the effort to do so.

When President Bush proposed the FSLIC bailout law (called FIRREA— pronounced "FI-REE-AH"), he promised "never again." Regarding the thrift industry, he will be right, because—although he didn't quite ask for enough money the first time—there won't be much of a thrift industry in a few years. The same kinds of troubles that crippled the S&Ls and bankrupted the FSLIC can, however, afflict other businesses—such as the commercial banks that now are failing at a record pace—that come under the federal guarantee umbrella. Interest rate risk, credit risk, dodgy accounting, and the potential for long delays before problems get dealt with can cause other devastating taxpayer losses unless Congress can come to grips with technical as well as purely political issues. Most people are easy to fool on technical matters. They just want the right to get mad as hell when things go wrong. But if we don't understand the technical subjects, we are doomed to manage the process of change badly.

The story has no beginning and no end—yet. Of necessity we pick it up in progress. The thrifts had prospered for most of the 1970s, but at the end of that decade inflation became a threat to them as well as to the economy in general. Interest rates shot up to historic highs.

Chronology of Significant Economic and Regulatory Events

1965 Vietnam War and Great Society program

1966 Interest rate regulation applied to thrifts

1972 Bank Board permits five-year averaging of assets to permit more growth with less capital

    Money market mutual funds introduced

1978 Inflation and interest rates rise

    June—Regulators authorize thrifts to offer six-month money market certificates at market rates

    Secondary market for mortgages begins to grow rapidly

1979 Bank Board increases amount of loan fees that S&Ls may recognize as income from 1 percent to 2 percent (2½ percent for construction loans)

    October—Fed changes monetary policy to choke off inflation; interest rates rise further

1980 March—Congress passes Depository Institutions Deregulation and Monetary Control Act to deregulate interest rates, expand S&L powers, and increase deposit insurance to $100,000 per account

    Bank Board reduces S&L capital requirement from 5 percent to 4 percent

1981 First interest rate failures

New purchase accounting rules promote mergers with failed institutions

Tax Act creates incentives for real estate development

Deferred loss accounting rules adopted by Bank Board

1982   Oil boom ends

August—Stock market boom begins and interest rates begin to decline

Banks increase real estate lending in response to decreased business lending opportunities and tax incentives for real estate development

Bank Board reduces S&L capital requirement from 4 percent to 3 percent

85 percent of S&Ls lose money

DIDC removes 5 percent cap on brokered deposits at S&Ls

October—Garn–St Germain Act increases S&L powers, speeds interest rate deregulation, and provides for net worth certificates

October—California passes Nolan Act to permit S&Ls to invest in anything, effective 1/1/83

1983   S&Ls report record growth

Number of S&Ls declared to have failed declines

Loan-to-value regulations repealed

S&Ls increase real estate lending on commercial properties and condominiums

50 percent of S&Ls still lose money

December—Bank Board adopts de novo charter regulations

1984   S&Ls record second year of record growth

February—Empire of Mesquite fails

April—FDIC and FHLBB adopt brokered deposit regulations

June—Deinsuring of brokered deposits ruled beyond powers of FDIC and FHLBB

1985   January—Bank Board adopts new capital rules to reduce growth to 25 percent a year, as well as regulation to limit direct investments to 10 percent of assets

Need for FSLIC recapitalization seen

July—Examination force switched to FHLBs

Management Consignment Program begun

December—Oil prices begin to collapse

Loan classification regulation adopted

1986   More new capital rules to reduce growth further

Oil price collapse continues

August—Tax Reform Act depreciates real estate

December—Financial Accounting Standards Board adopts FAS 91, curtailing loan fees, effective 1988

1987   FSLIC declared insolvent

FSLIC recap passed, giving FSLIC $10.8 billion borrowing authority

Arizona real estate values decline

1988   Southwest Plan deals

Yield curve inverts; interest rates rise

Northeastern real estate values begin to decline

1989   FIRREA passed, doing away with FHLBB and FSLIC, and putting S&Ls under regulation of Office of Thrift Supervision and FDIC. Full faith and credit given to deposit insurer obligations. Resolution Trust Corporation created to liquidate failed S&Ls. Money appropriated. New capital requirements imposed on S&Ls.

Part I
How It Happened

1 Fixed Rates in a Volatile World

THE GREENWICH SAVINGS BANK FAILS

When the prime rate went over 20 percent in the summer of 1981, American newspapers carried stories about possible failures of S&Ls and mutual savings banks for the first time since the 1930s.

Despite the advance publicity, the first major failure, the demise of the Greenwich Savings Bank, a New York City mutual* that had over $2 billion in assets and had been in business for almost 150 years, shocked the public. The FDIC had decided that the Greenwich's net worth was too low to allow it to continue in business so, after obtaining the consent of Muriel ("Mickie") Siebert, the Superintendent of Banks of the State of New York, the FDIC invited several healthy banks to bid for the Greenwich. Under the law, the FDIC couldn't take Greenwich over without the Superintendent calling them in. But Mickie Siebert's perspective was "He who has the gold makes the rules," and the FDIC had the gold, so she went along despite her public preference for nursing sick banks back to health. Before the FDIC was ready to sell the Greenwich, however, a reporter came across draft bid documents that had been left in a conference room. The next day the New York papers reported that the Greenwich was about to fail. Lines formed in front of its branches, and the six o'clock news featured the first New York bank run since the 1930s.

The FDIC and the Superintendent had been bickering about the details of how the Greenwich should be handled, but the run convinced them to set aside their differences and act quickly. Siebert told the Greenwich board of

*Terms marked with an asterisk (*) are defined in the glossary.

trustees that if they didn't vote for the merger arranged by the FDIC, she would be forced to take the institution over and merge it as a closed bank. That threat wouldn't have scared bank directors a decade later, perhaps, but in 1981 it was enough to induce the board to vote for the merger, and on November 4, 1981, the Greenwich was merged into the Metropolitan Savings Bank (a Brooklyn-based bank now called CrossLand) with FDIC assistance estimated to cost $400 million. The banking offices of the Greenwich never closed, no wrongdoing by anyone was alleged, substantially all of the Greenwich's loans were collectible (they were just at low interest rates), and the assistance package provided by FDIC to facilitate the merger protected the acquirer from the interest rate problems that had buried the Greenwich.

The Greenwich's deposits were insured by the FDIC, not the FSLIC, which insured savings and loan associations, so its failure isn't, strictly speaking, a part of the story of how FSLIC became bankrupt. But the failure of the Greenwich illustrates the mechanics of the early 1980s interest rate failures and how they could be dealt with expeditiously.

INDUSTRY-WIDE LOSSES

The interest rate mismatch that killed the Greenwich afflicted the whole thrift industry—S&Ls and mutual savings banks—in 1980 through 1982.

Whereas in a typical year in the 1970s only about 200 out of the approximately 5,000 thrift institutions in the country lost money, in 1980 about 1,800 of them were in the red. By 1981 over 4,000 thrifts (80 percent of the industry) were losing money, and the *average* thrift *lost* 76 cents for each $100 of assets. The 200 worst performers lost over $2.00 for each $100 of assets, and the thrift industry as a whole lost over $6 billion for the year. The 1982 numbers looked about the same as the 1981 numbers.

The Mismatch

These losses were unavoidable, given the way thrifts were structured. Because of the type of assets that thrifts owned at the end of the 1970s, the high interest rates of 1979–82 *had to cause* enormous losses, regardless of what thrift institution managements did. The high interest rates made losses inevitable because at the time interest rates shot up there was a "mismatch" between the "interest rate sensitivity" of thrift institutions' assets and the "interest rate sensitivity" of their liabilities. In plain English, the thrift institutions had borrowed short to lend long.

They owned assets (e.g., mortgages) that paid them low fixed rates of interest for a long term, usually thirty years. There was nothing wrong with these assets except that they had been bought with borrowed money (deposits) that could be withdrawn by depositors anytime they didn't like the interest rate the bank was paying them. When open market interest rates went up, depositors predictably demanded higher rates from their banks and S&Ls or went elsewhere. The S&Ls couldn't raise the rates on the fixed-rate mortgage loans that they had made years earlier.

Why the Mismatch?

The interest rate sensitivity mismatch that devastated the S&L industry in the early 1980s was built into its basic design. The two roles that society had assigned to S&Ls were to provide long-term credit to home owners at stable rates and to get the money to lend by taking deposits from individual savers. The savers' money could be withdrawn at any time because that was good for the public; the mortgages had to be fixed-rate and long-term because that also was good for the public. The S&Ls weren't allowed to borrow long, and just about the only investments they were allowed to make were long-term mortgages.

Amazingly, for many years what was good for the public was good for the S&Ls. Provided that interest rates didn't go up too fast, the S&Ls would benefit from the mismatch because long-term rates usually are higher than short-term rates. That is, usually you can get a higher rate of interest if you are willing to lend your money for a longer period of time. In fact, S&Ls did benefit from the mismatch for many years because most of the time long-term rates were higher than short-term rates and interest rates generally were stable (albeit with an upward bias) from World War II until 1966, when interest rates started to rise more significantly in response to forecasts of inflation.

INTEREST RATE REGULATION

The unraveling began in 1966 when, in order to protect thrift institutions from having to pay the rising market rates of interest that they couldn't afford, Congress put interest rate controls on savings deposits at all federally insured institutions. No bank or S&L, Congress decreed, could pay more interest on a depositor account than the regulators permitted. In effect, by interest rate regulation, Congress artificially corrected the mismatch by fixing the rate on savings deposits and thereby making them act as if they had locked-in, long-term rates, just like the mortgages owned by thrifts. Thus the policy of rate regulation permitted S&Ls to flourish again without depriving home owners of long-term, fixed-rate mortgages. Savers, unaware that the system was cheating them, were made to foot the bill.

The imposition of rate ceilings in 1966 was typical Johnson administration policy. The inflation had resulted from Johnson's determination that the nation could afford "guns and butter" (the Vietnam War and the Great Society program). The inflation had created higher interest rates that thrift institutions apparently couldn't pay and still earn a profit; if thrift institutions couldn't pay rates that would attract funds, housing would suffer because thrifts still supplied the lion's share of housing the nation's credit. The administration solved this problem by imposing interest rate controls on deposits rather than by dealing with the causes of the problem.

At the end of the 1970s, the hitherto apparently successful policy of interest rate regulation unraveled. It no longer worked because inflation had driven interest rates so much higher than the 5.5 percent regulatory ceiling on passbook accounts at thrifts that depositors began moving their money out of those accounts.

By 1978, Treasury bills were paying over 9 percent, and money market mutual funds, which had been invented earlier in the decade, were paying almost 9 percent. Many depositors couldn't resist moving their money out of thrift institutions and into these higher-yielding instruments.

In response to this threat to thrift institutions' liquidity, in June 1978 the regulators tried the expedient of letting thrifts pay higher interest rates on six-month CDs while retaining the old ceilings on passbook accounts; they let six-month CD rates go up when the Treasury bill market went up. The new ceiling for six-month CDs became ½ percent over the T-bill.

That helped keep money in the thrift institutions, but it cost them a lot. By the end of 1979, over 20 percent of their depositors' money was in six-month accounts at rates over 10 percent. On a deposit base of half a trillion dollars, that 20 percent shift from passbook to six-month accounts would cost the S&Ls $5 billion a year—exactly the amount that the industry had made in its *best* year. The situation was desperate in places like New York and Chicago, where usury laws had kept down the rates that thrifts could charge to borrowers and sophisticated depositors quickly moved their money to the higher-yielding accounts.

The problem got worse at the end of 1979 when the Federal Reserve Board,* acting under the leadership of its new chairman, Paul Volcker, radically changed its way of conducting monetary policy. Previous policy had aimed at keeping interest rates reasonably stable, even in times of inflation. The new policy abandoned interest rate stability and focused instead on the size of the money supply. The theory said that by shrinking the supply of money, the Fed would choke off inflation.

In the long run, Volcker's strict control of the money supply may have been good policy, but in the short run it sent interest rates to historically high levels. Rates already were high because of high inflation, but the deinflationary medicine caused them to go higher. Whereas the prime rate had fluctuated between 2 percent and 12 percent during the period from World War II to 1978, in the last three months of 1979 it reached almost 16 percent, and in 1981 it hit an all-time high of 21 percent.

Interest rates stayed at historically high levels through 1980, 1981, and 1982, with disastrous consequences for American thrift institutions. Either depositors withdrew their money from thrift institutions and bought T-bills and money market mutual funds, or they moved their money from 5.5 percent savings accounts to 15 percent six-month money market accounts. If the money flowed out, the S&Ls had to borrow from banks or investment banks at 15 percent or even 20 percent, or they had to sell mortgages at a loss. Either way, they lost money and their net worth eroded.

The Greenwich Savings Bank was just one of the first of many casualties of this inexorable process.

THE MARKET COMPELS INTEREST RATE DEREGULATION

As early as 1979, the industry, the regulators, *and* the economists agreed that in principle and in the long run, deposit interest rate regulation was a bad idea. It caused dislocations in markets; it prevented savers from getting a market rate of interest; it provided an indirect subsidy to home owners but it also caused mortgage credit to dry up when high rates prevented thrifts from attracting funds; and it promoted general inefficiency. But since thrifts couldn't afford to pay market interest rates, anyone concerned had to ask whether the immediate consequences of removing the ceilings would be worse than the deposit outflows that the ceilings made inevitable.

Thrift institution executives mortally feared quick deregulation of interest rates because they believed that it would lead to immediate and substantial losses. They also believed that the government couldn't permit a liquidity crisis at S&Ls, so they lobbied for retaining the interest rate ceilings, working to reduce inflation, and having emergency liquidity provided by the Federal Home Loan Banks* and Federal Reserve Banks* at below-market rates of interest.

The Carter administration didn't agree with the strategy of continued regulation. They already had deregulated trucking and the airlines; they didn't believe in rate regulation; and they didn't want the thrift industry on the dole.

They were supported by a 1978 presidential commission that had concluded that deposit interest rate regulation fails to promote housing, is unfair to small savers, and is inefficient.[1] So the Carter administration continued gradual deposit rate deregulation during 1979 to maintain thrift institution liquidity and the availability of funds for housing.

At the same time, Congress was holding hearings on interest rate deregulation. What had once been an arcane subject, debated only by academicians and a few regulators, became a national cause célèbre. Everyone wanted to testify about what was wrong with rate ceilings. "Equity for the small saver" became a Congressional priority after the small saver had been a doormat for thirteen years.

The Gray Panthers testified most effectively. They showed how older Americans were being hit by high inflation while their savings dwindled in real dollars. For elected members of Congress, it was powerful stuff and showed the clout that older people could have.

The thrift industry found itself fighting a rearguard action to prevent immediate deregulation. The "housing card," which had won the thrifts Congressional extensions of the interest rate ceilings four times since 1966, didn't do them any good, because even Congress could tell that S&Ls couldn't increase their loans to housing if they couldn't get funds from deposits.

The Gray Panthers' testimony, a generally prevailing theory of deregulation, and skyrocketing interest rates caused a consensus to form: Interest rates had to be deregulated gradually, and thrift institutions should get powers to make additional types of more interest rate sensitive* loans and investments. Everyone knew that if interest rates stayed high, deregulating the asset side of the balance sheet wouldn't save a lot of thrift institutions; it was too late for that. But there didn't seem to be any better policy.

A policy of giving thrifts some commercial bank* powers seemed obvious in 1980 because commercial banks, which didn't have the same lending and investment restrictions as thrifts, hadn't been mismatched and hadn't failed as a result of rising interest rates. It therefore looked beneficial to give thrifts some of the powers that commercial banks had to make the types of loans that could be tied to the prime rate and that therefore earned a rate of interest which changed as the market changed. It also appeared that the loans which fit this description were consumer loans, such as installment loans and credit card loans, and commercial loans, most of which would be safer if secured by something solid like real estate rather than being unsecured by collateral.* The commercial banks, which had always opposed these powers for S&Ls even though national commissions had been recommending for years that they be granted,[2] bought into the consensus in order to get interest rate deregulation.

Congress Deregulates

In March 1980, Congress passed the Depository Institutions Deregulation and Monetary Control Act of 1980 (which we will call the 1980 Act). It called for a gradual phaseout of deposit interest rate regulation over six years and established the Depository Institutions Deregulation Committee (known by its initials DIDC and pronounced "DIDDICK"), composed of federal bank regulators and the Secretary of the Treasury, to implement the phaseout.

The 1980 Act also gave federal S&Ls expanded powers on both sides of the balance sheet. On the liability side, it empowered federal S&Ls to offer NOW accounts.* On the asset side, it gave federal S&Ls power to invest in consumer loans and expanded their powers to make various kinds of mortgage loans.

The 1980 Act also attacked the problem of state usury laws. These laws, which had been enacted by many states to protect individuals from being charged exorbitant rates of interest, set ceilings on the rates of interest that lenders could charge on nonbusiness loans. Over the years, most states had created exceptions to their ceilings for loans made by small loan companies and credit card loans. But in many states, such as New York and Illinois, the usury ceilings still governed mortgage loans on single-family homes. As a result, thrifts in those states not only were mismatched, they also were required to make their mortgage loans at rates of interest that were below the market.

The 1980 Act did away with the usury problem by saying that, with respect to residential real estate loans, state usury laws were "preempted" by federal law and, therefore, were null and void. Since 1980, thrifts and banks all over the country have been able to charge market rates of interest on their mortgage loans.

This elimination of usury ceilings was enormously important because the ceilings not only had prevented thrift institutions from making loans at market rates of interest; they also had prevented adjustable-rate mortgage lending. It was clear that S&Ls in states which allowed adjustable-rate mortgage lending (notably California and Wisconsin) could survive high interest rates far better than S&Ls in states that did not allow such lending.

The 1980 Act also increased the deposit insurance ceiling from $40,000 to $100,000. Extraordinarily, this significant increase in federal government exposure was never the subject of hearings; was never debated in Congress; was not in the bill passed by the House or the quite different bill passed by the Senate; it was slipped into the Act in the conference between the House and the Senate that was supposed to resolve differences between the two bills. $100,000 of deposit insurance was inserted by a few powerful Congressmen so that S&Ls could compete for deregulated deposits of $100,000 on a fully insured basis.

Consequences of the 1980 Deregulation

Not surprisingly, although deregulated deposit accounts permitted thrifts to attract deposits, deregulation didn't help thrift institutions' earnings in the face of high interest rates. Although deregulation made theoretical sense for the public and for healthy banking institutions, it couldn't prevent mismatched thrifts from losing money in the short run. Indeed, many thrift executives contended that interest rate deregulation made the problem worse.

The 1980 Act and the regulatory efforts that immediately followed it probably were good policy, but they couldn't stem the tide of loss and, ultimately, of failure.

REAGANOMICS MEETS DISINTERMEDIATION

When the Reagan administration took office on January 20, 1981, Donald Regan's Treasury Department formulated a simple set of policies to deal with the wave of thrift failures that could be clearly seen on the horizon. The Regan formulation said:

1. The current problem is interest rates. High interest rates are due to inflation, which the administration is going to cure. Therefore the problem is temporary.

2. The problem is basically a liquidity problem caused by interest rate regulation. If rates are deregulated, the S&Ls will be able to attract funds. Therefore, rates should be deregulated.

3. There is no money in the budget for bailouts. (Reagan had been against the bailouts of New York City and Chrysler.) Therefore, if S&Ls need assistance, it must be purely paper assistance that has no budgetary cost.

4. The important thing is to get real deregulatory legislation to give S&Ls the same powers as commercial banks.

The administration didn't believe that balance sheet insolvency (negative net worth) was significant. As long as an S&L could get enough deposits to continue in business, the Treasury people believed, it didn't need to be closed.

Dick Pratt Comes to Town

President Reagan appointed Richard Pratt as Chairman of the Federal Home Loan Bank Board (FHLBB) in February 1981. An intelligent, energetic, chain-smoking, confident (stuck on himself, some say), tough-minded professor of finance from Utah, Pratt came to the Bank Board well prepared. He understood the issues—he had been chief economist for the U.S. League of Savings Institutions—and he brought in competent staff, largely from his home state (known as the "Mormon Mafia"). Dick Pratt believed in progress and free markets.

Dick Pratt didn't like to bend to ordinary party politics. Instead of hiring his staff through the White House Appointments Office, he put together a group that consisted mostly of lawyers and professors who didn't have any political clout. In fact, some of them weren't even Republicans, a shocking thought in the early days of the Reagan administration. They were a collection of Mormons and an Armenian from Brooklyn. But they were vigorous and intelligent, even if Pratt didn't help his White House relations by hiring them.

Dick Pratt's first major rule-making served notice that he would be an active regulator. The S&Ls needed the right to make adjustable-rate mortgage loans, and the FHLBB had power to give them that right. But Congressional opposition had persuaded prior chairmen not to do it, and at his confirmation hearing, Pratt testified that he didn't know whether he would adopt regulations to override state laws and permit federal S&Ls to make adjustable-rate mortgage loans.[3] He knew that several powerful Senators didn't like adjustable-rate loans because they made people's mortgage payments uncertain. But just a few weeks after being confirmed, Pratt plunged ahead because he was convinced that the S&Ls needed variable-rate assets to survive. He got questions from the Hill and was called back to testify, but no one seriously tried to reverse his decision. Members of Congress often bluster about things they don't like; but laws are hard to pass.

This experience proved Pratt's theory about how an independent regulator should deal with Congress: Listen attentively, be courteous, provide information, but make it perfectly clear that you will do what you think needs to be done and that you will not play politics with policy. Pratt felt—probably correctly—that the worst thing that can happen to a Congressman when he intercedes on behalf of a constituent is to be too effective, because then he is on the hook for the decision. Thus when Senators and Representatives complained to Pratt about his taking over and liquidating or merging local S&Ls, he just said he was sorry, that was what he had to do, and explained why.

The thrift industry was in a state of crisis, and Dick Pratt knew he had to deal with it. He agreed with Treasury that liquidity had to be maintained; he agreed that S&Ls should have the same powers as commercial banks, and he drafted and supported legislation to accomplish that; he even agreed that the rules had to be bent so that S&Ls could survive the period of high interest rates, principally because the FSLIC didn't have the money necessary to deal with all of the failures that he would have to declare under normal rules. But Dick Pratt and his staff did not agree that balance sheet insolvency was meaningless. At the same time that they changed and bent the rules to permit S&Ls to survive, they liquidated or merged almost 400 S&Ls in their two years at the Bank Board, and they fought the Treasury's efforts to accelerate the pace of interest rate deregulation because they believed that faster interest rate deregulation would result in higher losses and more balance sheet insolvencies so long as high interest rates persisted.

The political role of the FHLBB Chairman was delicate. The President appointed him, but by statute he was supposed to be independent. He was the guardian of the insurance fund, but he was dependent on the Office of Management and Budget (OMB)* for money. Historically, he also had been a cheerleader for the S&L industry.

The DIDC Games

Don Regan thought that in its first year the DIDC had been deregulating interest rates too slowly. He also thought that, as Chairman of the DIDC, Paul Volcker's donnish deliberateness had been getting in the way of pursuing the true cause—free markets. Congress, Regan believed, really wanted the DIDC to do its job quickly, not to take the allotted six years to deregulate interest rates. So he took over as Chairman of the DIDC.

Don Regan believed that competition cured everything. Whereas Volcker and Pratt were willing to review facts and listen to arguments, Regan had an almost religious belief in free competition. He *knew* that the trouble with the thrift institutions was that they weren't allowed to compete for deposits. He knew that if you removed deposit rate ceilings, all the thrifts would have big inflows of deposits that they could invest profitably. Thus the thrifts would return to profitability and they would help to finance the coming economic boom.

Volcker and Pratt, because they believed that S&Ls needed capital to operate safely, had a short-run problem with interest rate deregulation. As long as interest rates stayed up, the thrifts would suffer greater losses the more interest rates were deregulated. They therefore sought to steer a middle course in the DIDC until interest rates moderated. Regan thought Pratt, who had been, after all, the U.S. League's economist, was too close to the industry.

The Treasury saw no reason for the bewildering array of different types of accounts that the DIDC had created—accounts that had different minimum amounts, maturities, interest rate ceilings, and differentials. But the complexity of these accounts had been fashioned intentionally to permit thrifts to compete for marginal dollars without all of their funds immediately flowing out of lower-yielding passbook accounts. Although the Fed is peopled by economists who loathe the kind of complex regulation that deposit ceilings produced, they thought it prudent to wait until rates declined before eliminating the complexity.

The battle between the Fed/FHLBB and the Treasury was played out in the "Cash Room" of the Treasury Building, a baroque chamber with nine kinds of marble and a magnificent coffered ceiling, in which the five DIDC members and their staffs sat in the front of the room and lobbyists for the thrift and banking industries and dozens of reporters crammed into the remainder of the room in a crowd of 300 or so. The DIDC decisions made big news.

The confrontation between Regan and Pratt over the ceiling on the passbook rate illustrates how the DIDC worked. The ceiling on passbook accounts was 5.25 percent for banks and 5.5 percent for thrifts (the differential having been designed to promote housing). The commercial banks didn't care about passbook accounts, but those accounts provided the low-cost funds that kept many thrifts alive. Any increase in passbook rates would have a significant impact on S&L earnings—at least a $1 billion annual loss for every 1 percent increase in the rate.

The 1980 Act required the DIDC to "consider" a quarter percent increase in the passbook rate by September 1981, but in June, Regan orchestrated a proposal to increase the passbook ceiling by 5 percent—to 10.25 percent for commercial banks and 10.50 percent for thrifts. Regan began the meeting by saying, "I believe it is essential that the committee act to permit depository institutions, and thrift institutions in particular, to offer savers a better rate of interest so they can be as competitive as is economically feasible." The Fed staff and Dick Pratt then gave reports on the financial status of the thrift industry. Then, seemingly out of the blue, FDIC Chairman Irvine Sprague (supported, he said, by his soon-to-be-successor William Isaac) proposed a 500-basis point (5 percent) jump in the passbook rate. Volcker and Pratt, taken by surprise, agreed to put it out for comment, believing that after consideration no one would want the thrift industry to lose $11–$15 billion for the year rather than the forecast $6–$10 billion.

At the next DIDC meeting in September, its staff reported that 4,751 comments had been received, mostly from retired persons who liked the proposal and from thrift institutions that didn't like it. The commercial banks were about evenly divided. Mr. Regan, on behalf of the Treasury, then proposed a 150-basis point increase (to 6.75 percent and 7 percent) instead of the previously proposed 500-basis point increase. "Now, why are we suggesting this and why are we doing this?" he asked. "I'm convinced that from a purely marketing point of view, the thrift institutions are losing deposits very rapidly. I think that we ought to strike a blow for the little guy."

Volcker and Pratt wouldn't go along. Volcker said the "impact on earnings . . . seems so severe in a situation in which the safety and soundness of these institutions would be jeopardized" that the proposal should not be adopted. Pratt went on at greater length with arguments and statistics.

When Regan called for a vote, he and Isaac (who by then had replaced Sprague) voted in favor, while Volcker, Pratt, and Credit Union Administrator Larry Connell voted against, defeating the motion.

Isaac then proposed an increase of 50 basis points (½ percent), which engendered a little gallows humor:

> *Mr. Isaac:* I would move that we move the passbook interest rate 50 basis points now.
>
> *Mr. Regan:* Any discussion of that one?
>
> *Mr. Pratt:* I would move that we amend the motion to extend a half billion dollar credit line from the Treasury to the Federal Home Loan Bank Board at the same time.
>
> (General laughter.)
>
> *Mr. Regan:* I think that one is out of order at this point.
>
> [Pratt had privately asked for a larger line of credit, and Regan had turned him down.]

Regan then called for a vote, and Larry Connell switched from his "no" on 150 basis points to "yes" on 50 basis points.

Ironically, after all this maneuvering, commenting, staff work, projecting, and posturing, the fifty-basis-point gesture never went into effect because Jake Garn (Chairman of the Senate Banking Committee) and other Congressional leaders, acting at the behest of the thrift lobbies, convinced Don Regan that it would be better for deregulatory legislation if he backed down. Thus, without a meeting—by "notation," as they call it—the DIDC reversed itself on the passbook rate and it stayed at 5.5 percent until complete deregulation in 1986.

Dick Pratt remembers the DIDC as being a lot like his favorite musical, *A Funny Thing Happened on the Way to the Forum*. You know the opening song, "Something for everyone, a comedy tonight."

FEDERAL ASSISTANCE PROPOSALS

Even though the pace of deposit rate deregulation roughly balanced the liquidity needs of the thrifts against the damage to earnings and net worth caused by paying higher rates, the thrift executives knew that the erosion of net worth was threatening the long-term health of their industry. The administration was offering to paper over the problem and effectively ignore it, but thrift executives wanted more: They wanted real relief from their low-rate mortgages as long as high rates persisted. The Treasury staunchly opposed any real assistance with a simple dictum: no bailouts.

The Treasury thought the FHLBB and the industry were unduly alarmist. The Treasury summarized its opinion in its 1982 report to Congress on behalf of the DIDC in these words:

> The eroding net worth of a well managed institution is not in itself a reason to close or merge the institution. Similarly, the problems caused by eroding net worth, although serious, should not be the cause of public concern about the viability of the thrift industry. Most institutions can cope successfully with the current high interest rate environment. Those that need some help can get assistance from the Federal deposit insurance agencies. The few institutions that are not viable long term can be merged into stronger organizations. . . .
>
> . . . The administration has adhered to certain basic policy goals in formulating its views. First, any program should be designed to minimize the impact on the Federal budget. Second, it should minimize government intervention in the thrift industry's business. Finally, where possible, government programs should encourage free market solutions to the thrift industry's problems.
>
> As interest rates decline, the vast majority of thrift institutions will return to profitability. Accordingly the task has been to design an assistance program to prevent or slow the decline in thrift institutions' net worth by granting them assistance without governmental cash expenditures. . . .

This policy led to the "net worth certificate" program at the end of 1982 and, later, to other measures whose watchwords were "no governmental cash expenditures." But not everybody thought the thrifts could survive without governmental cash expenditures.

Probably the most workable assistance proposal was a "mortgage warehousing" concept that was championed by Senator Daniel Patrick Moynihan of New York. Under this proposal, the federal government would buy all of the single-family mortgages held by banks and S&Ls that had interest rates under a certain benchmark rate, such as 8 percent. The government would pay for these mortgages with notes having floating interest rates tied to the market. This would cost the government the difference between the 8 percent or less earned on the mortgages and the market rate on the notes as long as rates stayed high, but it also would protect the banks and S&Ls from the same amount of losses. When short-term market rates declined to a specified level such as 10 percent, the banks and S&Ls would be obliged to reverse the exchanges of paper. This proposal would have worked especially well in states like New York and Illinois, where usury ceilings on mortgage loans had made thrift institutions especially vulnerable.

The problem with the mortgage warehousing proposal—as with other assistance proposals—was that it cost a lot of money, probably between $3 billion and $7 billion for each year that interest rates remained high. The Treasury therefore decried it as a "hidden subsidy" and a "budget buster." The U.S. League found that it couldn't get the mortgage warehousing program moving in Congress over the administration's opposition. Congress had no stomach for another Lockheed or another Chrysler.

The warehousing proposal probably would have cost about $10 billion if the program had been introduced in June 1981 and had been carried out until short-term rates reached 10 percent in 1983. That $10 billion would have left the S&L industry strongly capitalized going into the deregulated world and would have permitted the regulators to impose normal capital and accounting standards on the industry. Instead, the regulators had to temporize in 1981 and 1982, which had disastrous consequences when the temporizing wasn't reversed in 1983 and 1984.

2   How Insured S&Ls Fail

Chapter 1 set up the dilemma that public policy faced in 1981–82. This chapter will discuss how banks and S&Ls fail and how the accounting that S&Ls used gave a misleading picture of their financial health. It also will explain why a broke S&L is doomed to lose money forever, no matter who runs it.

A bank or S&L fails when its "chartering authority" — the state or federal agency that gave it the right to do business as a bank or S&L — "declares" that it has failed. The failure laws aren't self-executing, and the normal bankruptcy laws don't apply to banks and S&Ls. If no one declares that a failure has occurred, a dead S&L that is doomed to lose money forever can stay open and operating.

The FHLBB could declare that a federal S&L had failed when (1) the S&L was insolvent, (2) it was engaged in serious violations of law, or (3) it was in an unsafe and unsound condition to conduct business. (The FSLIC's lawyers usually were afraid to use any ground except insolvency.) State-chartered S&Ls are governed by state laws. All of those laws permit state S&L Commissioners to declare an S&L to have failed on grounds of insolvency and sometimes on other grounds, such as being in an unsafe and unsound condition to conduct business.

When a chartering authority — state or federal — declares that a bank or S&L has failed, it "takes possession" of the corporate entity — that is, it kicks out management and counts everything on hand, down to the pencils — and usually it immediately hands the corporate entity over to the insurer of deposits. The insurer can liquidate the bank or S&L or run it even though it has been declared to have failed.

Until the FSLIC started running failed S&Ls in the 1980s, the deposit insurers almost never ran failed institutions. (The FDIC did run Continental-Illinois National Bank in Chicago at about the same time that the FSLIC was beginning to run failed S&Ls.) Insurers didn't run failed banks and S&Ls because (1) the insurer shouldn't be in the business of competing with institutions it regulates; and (2) private enterprise is better at running businesses than the government is. Instead of running them, insurers liquidated failed banks and S&Ls.

The public may not have seen that banks were being liquidated because regulators tried to hide the liquidation by making sure that branches didn't close and service wasn't disrupted. The conventional regulatory wisdom said that, to protect public confidence in the "banking system," the public shouldn't be inconvenienced by bank failures. Therefore, in almost every failure, the bank was open for business continuously—maybe with the same name, maybe with a different name. However, from a legal point of view—and from the point of view of stockholders who lost their investments and senior managers who lost their jobs—failed banks were being liquidated.

What the press calls a "bailout" or "rescue" neither rescues nor bails out anyone except the depositors. "Interment" or "burial" would be a better term to use to describe what happens to the failed S&L. The failed S&L's stockholders are wiped out. Top management is out of a job. Middle management is an endangered species. Often only branch personnel such as tellers and branch managers go to the healthy bank along with the deposits—and they have to learn a new system and sink or swim in a new (and often hostile) environment.

"INSOLVENCY," "CAPITAL," AND "NET WORTH"

Whether the regulators will declare a bank or S&L to have failed usually depends upon whether they say it is solvent or insolvent. The concept of insolvency therefore is crucial to understanding S&L failures. There are two kinds of insolvency: "liquidity" insolvency and "balance sheet" insolvency.

An enterprise is liquidity insolvent when it doesn't have enough cash to pay its debts as they come due and can't get that cash from any source. In the case of a bank or S&L, this usually means that it doesn't have the cash to pay its depositors when they ask for their money *and* can't borrow that cash from some other source or sell assets to generate it. Old-fashioned bank runs used to cause liquidity insolvencies, although the reason for a run usually was a public perception that the bank was balance sheet insolvent first and therefore couldn't repay all of its depositors. Deposit insurance was designed to prevent bank runs, which it does successfully because depositors know that even if the bank fails, their deposits are insured. As a result, liquidity insolvencies of federally insured banks or S&Ls are rare.

Balance sheet insolvency is the key concept in the thrift crisis, and it is somewhat more complicated than liquidity insolvency. To understand balance sheet insolvency, it will be useful to understand a little accounting – not a great deal, just some basics that can be learned in a few minutes.

Here is a simplified balance sheet of an S&L:

Balance Sheet No. 1

ASSETS		LIABILITIES	
Cash	$ 100	Due Depositors	$1,700
Mortgages	1,800	Due to Banks	200
Plant, Property		Total Liabilities	1,900
and Equipment	100	Net Worth	100
Total Assets	$2,000	Total Liabilities &	
		Net Worth	$2,000

The S&L represented by this balance sheet is "solvent" as defined by accounting conventions because its Net Worth (sometimes called "capital") is a positive number – that is, $100. (We will use "net worth" and "capital" interchangeably even though sometimes there is a technical difference between them.) The Net Worth in Balance Sheet No. 1 is $100 because the Total Assets exceed the Total Liabilities by $100. If the Net Worth number were less than zero, then the S&L would be *in*solvent. The concept is that simple.

We also should understand how a solvent S&L can become insolvent. It won't become insolvent just by depositors' drawing money out, because deposit withdrawals won't by themselves change the Net Worth number. The $100 of Net Worth could remain the same even if $300 of deposits (much more than the S&L's $100 of Cash) were withdrawn, so long as the S&L had $200 of Mortgages (or other assets) on its balance sheet that it could sell for $200 – that is, assets that it could sell without taking a loss. The entries on the balance sheet would be as follows: The $300 of withdrawals would wipe out the $100 of Cash (the Cash would go down to zero) and the sale of $200 of mortgages would reduce the $1,800 of Mortgages to $1,600 (reflecting the sale of $200 of mortgages for cash that was paid out to depositors). But since the amount Due Depositors would now be reduced from $1,700 to $1,400 by the withdrawal of $300, the Net Worth would remain $100. The balance sheet now would look like this:

Balance Sheet No. 2

ASSETS		LIABILITIES	
Mortgages	$1,600	Due Depositors	$1,400
Plant, Property		Due to Banks	200
and Equipment	100	Total Liabilities	1,600
Total Assets	$1,700	Net Worth	100
		Total Liabilities &	
		Net Worth	$1,700

It is easy to see that this S&L is still solvent. Moreover, not only is the S&L represented by Balance Sheet No. 2 still solvent, but its "net worth percentage," sometimes called its "capital percentage," has *increased* as a result of the deposit outflow. It still has the same *amount* of net worth or capital—$100— but because it has fewer assets, its capital percentage has gone up. Whereas that percentage was 5 percent at the time of Balance Sheet No. 1, when the S&L had $2,000 of Assets ($100 of Net Worth divided by $2,000 of Assets), it is now almost 6 percent ($100 of Net Worth divided by $1,700 of Assets) at the time of Balance Sheet No. 2. Many regulatory issues hinge on capital percentages.

Of course most sales of assets result in a gain or a loss against the price at which they are carried on the books. And of course over time an S&L has income or loss from its operations. These income or loss items *do* cause the S&L's net worth to change, as we can see if we pursue our example a little further. Let's go back to Balance Sheet No. 1.

Again assume that depositors withdraw $300; but this time let's change our assumption about the value of the mortgages that the S&L has on the asset side of its balance sheet. For purposes of this example, let's assume that, because of changes in interest rates, the mortgages are only worth 50 percent of the dollar amount listed on the balance sheet.[1] Therefore, when we have to sell $200 of these mortgages, we will get only $100 from the buyer and will have a loss of $100. Moreover, when we sell that $200 of mortgages, we will get only $100 of cash against the $200 of cash we needed to satisfy the deposit withdrawals. Therefore we will have to sell *another* $200 of mortgages (a total sale of $400 of mortgages) to raise the $200 of cash that we need to pay depositors. As a result, we now have the money we need to pay withdrawing depositors but we also have an aggregate loss of $200, which is a direct consequence of the interest rate sensitivity mismatch.

This loss of $200 will get reflected in the Net Worth number on the balance sheet. We begin again with Balance Sheet No. 1 and make the following entries to create Balance Sheet No. 3: On the liability side of the balance sheet, the withdrawal of $300 of deposits reduces the amount Due Depositors from $1,700 to $1,400. On the asset side of the balance sheet, we reduce Cash from $100 to zero and we reduce Mortgages from $1,800 to $1,400, reflecting the sale of $400 of mortgages and the use of the $100 of cash. We will now have a negative net worth of ($100) rather than a positive net worth of $100. (Accountants use parentheses around a number to indicate that it is negative—here representing a loss or deficit.) The balance sheet now looks like this:

Balance Sheet No. 3

ASSETS		LIABILITIES	
Mortgages	$1,400	Due Depositors	$1,400
Plant, Property		Due to Banks	200
and Equipment	100	Total Liabilities	1,600
Total Assets	$1,500	Net Worth	(100)
		Total Liabilities &	
		Net Worth	$1,500

Now our S&L is *in*solvent. It has a *negative net worth* of $100—which, as we can see, results from having only $1,500 of total assets against $1,600 of total liabilities.

After this explanation you may naturally ask why the S&L was carrying mortgages on its books at $400 when they were worth only $200. Wasn't the S&L just as insolvent before the sale as after it?

The very unsatisfying answer to this question is that American accounting conventions—whether under generally accepted accounting principles established by the accounting profession (known as GAAP) or rules established by a bank regulatory agency (known as regulatory accounting principles, or RAP)—provide that assets such as loans are to be carried on the books of a financial institution at the value at which they were made unless there is a "permanent" impairment of their value. Under these principles, the decline in the value of our S&L's mortgage loans isn't deemed to be "permanent" because it resulted from an increase in interest rates and the value could be fully restored if, at any time during the remaining lives of the loans, interest rates in general fell back to the rates at which the loans were made. The S&L's accounting was correct even though it didn't reflect *market* value. This is a hot topic among bankers, regulators, and accountants; we will come back to it later.

Using historical accounting principles (that is, nonmarket-value accounting principles), it doesn't seem difficult to know when a bank or S&L is insolvent.

We can just look at the net worth entry and see whether it is positive. Thus, although reasonable people might have differed about whether an S&L was in an unsafe or unsound condition (which is the finding that Mickie Siebert would have had to make to take over the Greenwich before it was insolvent), or whether laws are being violated (another common ground on which a regulator can take over an institution), the question of solvency or insolvency under GAAP was pretty cut and dried.

WHAT GOOD IS GAAP?

At this point reasonable people ask why it is necessary to take over an S&L just because its GAAP capital is negative. GAAP insolvency doesn't prevent the S&L from taking deposits, making loans, paying its bills, and going about business as usual. If the problem will reverse itself when interest rates go down, why not just let it run?

In addition, our reasonable person points out that GAAP insolvency doesn't provide the "right" or theoretically optimal time to take over an institution and liquidate it. As we have seen, if we are trying to protect the deposit insurance fund, the GAAP insolvency test doesn't work because the market value of the assets may be very different from their book or "carrying" value. That's why it cost FDIC about $400 million to induce another bank to merge with the Greenwich even though the Greenwich was "dealt with" before it was insolvent under GAAP.

As we will see, those obvious shortcomings presented plausible explanations for why GAAP insolvency could be ignored—indeed, plausible excuses for why many people thought it was acceptable to stop keeping books that would have made it possible to know when GAAP insolvency may have occurred.

In Defense of GAAP

GAAP accounting is, as its name implies, "generally accepted" despite its shortcomings. It provides the numbers that accountants will attest to, and therefore it provides a measure of consistency and certainty when we are trying to measure insolvency. Therefore, until we have a good system of market-value accounting—which we don't yet have—GAAP deserves a presumption that it is the right tool to use.

The most important point in defense of using GAAP as the starting point for an insolvency test is that we have to have *some* insolvency test, because after insolvency, bad things happen to the insurance fund. Insolvent S&Ls usually don't recover, and managements that don't have any financial stake after net worth has been wiped out will take bigger and bigger risks to try to recover. Recovery takes extremely good management and even better luck. There's no margin for error. Moreover, beyond a certain amount of negative net worth, an insolvent S&L *cannot* recover—*ever*. The process becomes absolutely irreversible because a bank or S&L *must* lose money if its interest-paying liabilities exceed its interest-earning assets by very much.

A BROKE S&L WILL CONTINUE TO LOSE MONEY FOREVER

Conceptually, we can think of an S&L's income as depending upon four factors (in addition to taxes): spread (which is reflected in net interest income), the ratio of interest-earning assets to interest-paying liabilities (which also gets reflected in net interest income), noninterest income (usually in the form of various fees paid by depositors and borrowers), and operating expenses.

"Spread"—a key concept in the banking business—is the difference between the interest rate a bank pays on average for its liabilities and the interest rate it makes on average on its assets. The normal spread of a healthy S&L is between 2 percent and 2½ percent. The normal spread of a healthy commercial bank is over 3 percent. We usually talk about spread in "basis points," each of which is one hundredth of a percent. Thus, 225 basis points equal 2.25 percent, which is a healthy S&L's normal spread.

In 1981–82 the savings banks and S&Ls failed because their spreads declined to well below 200 basis points—indeed, in many cases, even to a negative number. Since it costs an efficient thrift institution more than 1 percent of assets to pay operating expenses (most operating expense ratios were over 200 basis points in the 1980s), and since historically most thrift institutions have had very little noninterest income, the institutions with very low spreads lost money. Eventually, these losses caused many institutions to fail.

A healthy institution has more earning assets than paying liabilities. A marginal institution with slightly less earning assets than paying liabilities still has a chance. But with about a 10 percent deficit, that chance disappears. The S&L will make riskier and riskier investments to try to recover, but it will end up losing more and more money no matter what management does.

The losses will grow in each succeeding year, and the process won't stop even when the S&L runs out of assets. When there are no more assets, the S&L will still have obligations to pay interest to depositors, and those obligations will have to be funded by taking in more deposits and paying old depositors with new depositors' money. Unless the S&L is closed, the losses will, *by definition and without fail, grow forever.* And this really happened. Several S&Ls

that the FSLIC operated under government auspices were doomed to lose money forever, as a consequence of which they eventually lost more than their prompt liquidation *could* have cost, even if their assets had been totally worthless. The dynamics of this process are further explained in the Appendix.

THE ROLE OF DEPOSIT INSURANCE

Without deposit insurance, the example of the S&L losing money forever couldn't happen because, if deposits were uninsured, depositors would withdraw their money as soon as they saw the S&L running out of capital. Indeed, the depositors might not wait that long, because they would be concerned with the market value of the S&L's assets rather than their book value under GAAP. But with deposit insurance, depositors will leave their money in an insolvent S&L, up to the insured limit, so long as the S&L pays them a good rate.

For this reason, the S&L problem could not have grown to anything like its current magnitude without deposit insurance. Without deposit insurance, virtually all S&Ls would have been insolvent *in the liquidity sense* before 1982 because depositors would have seen that they could not repay all of their deposits and there would have been a nationwide run. The S&Ls therefore would have been said to have failed and would have been liquidated. *All* the S&Ls would have been closed. The public might have lost 20–30 cents on the dollar, or a total of $100 to $200 billion, if the run had come at the worst time. If the run had started in 1966, the cost would have been very small.

Deposit insurance saved us from those runs (and perhaps from an ensuing depression), but it imposed duties on the deposit insurers to stand in the shoes of the insured—the public—and take steps to impose the discipline that an insured depositor has no reason to impose. Economists have warned again and again—even before 1980—that an insolvent firm which is kept afloat by deposit insurance will roll the dice to try to get back to solvency.

3 Dick Pratt Figures Out How to Run a Bankrupt Federal Insurance Fund

In mid–1981, a few months after Dick Pratt took office at the Bank Board, the world he regulated looked something like this:

- The average S&L earned 10 percent on assets but had to pay 11 percent on deposits, and this negative spread was getting worse as deposits migrated to deregulated accounts.

- 75 percent of all federally insured S&Ls were sure to lose money in 1981.

- About 50 S&Ls were insolvent, and unless interest rates turned around fast, another 300 were sure to become insolvent in the next year.

- Over 1,000 S&Ls couldn't meet traditional 5 percent net worth requirements; 500 couldn't meet even a 3 percent requirement, and most of these were losing net worth at a rate of close to 200 basis points per year.

- The healthiest S&Ls would be insolvent in less than two years if interest rates didn't go down.

- For these reasons, it was quite foreseeable that if traditional regulatory practices were followed, FSLIC would have to liquidate $300–$400 billion out of $750 billion in industry assets, at a net cost (after getting paid for franchise values) of 15 percent to 25 percent, for a grand total of $45 billion to $100 billion.

- The FSLIC fund had $6 billion and a $750 million line of credit with the Treasury.

The Treasury said it wouldn't increase the line of credit unless it was "really" necessary; and the administration wouldn't support a move to get the Congress to give full faith and credit backing to the FSLIC.

A bank regulator's first worry—what the regulator sees as job no. 1—is maintaining the public's confidence in the system. A regulator's worst nightmare is that the public loses confidence on his or her watch, which Dick Pratt and his people reasonably believed could happen if the newspapers—and therefore the public—knew the facts. The facts showed not only that the S&Ls were broke but also that the FSLIC was broke, even though its published balance sheet looked healthy enough.

Pratt was in a box. He believed that as the substitute for the market in an insured banking industry, he had to declare insolvent institutions failed and to liquidate or merge them into healthier ones. Indeed, he believed that institutions which fell below net worth requirements *should* be merged or liquidated, because insolvent institutions have incentives to take increased risks. But he had neither the money nor the staff to liquidate all the insolvent institutions, much less all those which failed to meet their regulatory capital requirements.

The Treasury's view was that S&Ls didn't have to be liquidated when they became insolvent. The Treasury believed the S&Ls merely had an "accounting problem"—that GAAP net worth was a flawed concept and, therefore, meaningless. OMB agreed with Treasury. Although Pratt kept asking for more personnel to deal with the problems of the industry, OMB kept ordering cuts. At one point OMB went so far as to threaten Pratt with criminal sanctions if he didn't obey its spending restrictions. On another occasion, OMB cut off FSLIC funds for liquidations. (Even though the FSLIC fund came from the industry, FSLIC was an "on-budget" agency.) David Stockman, then head of OMB, was apoplectic about the budget deficit and didn't care about S&Ls' accounting net worth as long as they had cash flow from deposits. Smaller government was the order of the day in the Reagan White House, and nothing could stand in its way, especially not a crybaby industry that needed more nursemaids.

Nevertheless, Pratt and FSLIC Director Brent Beesely liquidated, merged, or otherwise dealt with almost 400 insolvent S&Ls between February 1981 and April 1983, when they left. The total cost to the FSLIC was estimated at less than $3 billion, a small number for resolving so many failures. Their methods often were innovative and took advantage of discontinuities in the system; they also often involved risks of nonresolution—that is, risks that the acquiring institutions would fail in the future—and many of them did. But given the limited resources, it would be petty to criticize the deals they did even though a substantial number of the acquirers eventually failed.

MINIMIZING THE COSTS OF LIQUIDATION

In an ordinary liquidation, the liquidator sells all of the assets for whatever they will bring and pays off the creditors whatever percentage of the debts is covered by the cash generated from selling the assets. If anything is left over (there usually isn't), it goes to the stockholders.

When a deposit insurer liquidates an institution, it has to pay all the insured depositors, regardless of whether the assets are sufficient to do so. Under its contract with each depositor, the insurer *must* make the depositor whole, that is, repay the full amount of the deposit, including interest—up to the deposit insurance limit, which has been $100,000 since 1980. The depositor, not the bank or the S&L, is the insured party.

In order to realize the maximum net amount of money (and therefore to have to pay out the least amount), the insurer has to try to get paid for the failed institution's "franchise value"—the value of its competitive position in the market, which another bank or S&L may be willing to pay for. This franchise value usually inheres (paradoxically) in the *liabilities* of the S&L—its deposits—rather than in its assets. The deposits have value because (1) they represent *customers* and (2) they usually bear a rate of interest that is below what a borrowing in the open market without deposit insurance would cost. Thus a banker will ascribe a value to deposits that will be measured as a percentage of the deposit liability, usually ranging from 1 percent to 10 percent, depending upon the market and the type of deposit, such as checking account, savings account, or CD.

Because of franchise value and the value of deposits, a bank or S&L insurer usually ends up costing itself less on a liquidation if it sells the bank or S&L as a going business rather than if it simply pays off the depositors and sells assets. That's why the public often doesn't see that the old bank has gone out of business and it appears to customers that the failed institution has been "bailed out" or "rescued," when in fact no bailout or rescue usually is occurring.

In many cases, even after taking franchise value into account, the FSLIC would have to pay a healthy S&L to take over a failed S&L's liabilities because the value of the assets was so much lower than the amount of the liabilities. The FSLIC could, of course, pay cash for this shortfall to induce the healthy S&L to take over the failed one. But even in 1981, the FSLIC was short of cash. Moreover, cash payments would be on-budget, and that would mean a fight with OMB. So Pratt and Beesely developed substitutes for cash. They used FSLIC notes (IOUs issued by the insurer), FSLIC guarantees against loss on sales of assets or from unknown liabilities, tax benefits (Congress passed a law that FSLIC payments to acquirers were tax free and that an acquiring S&L could shelter its profits with the failed S&L's losses), and something called "spread maintenance," which was especially useful in interest rate failures if the insurer assumed that interest rates would come down in the not-too-distant future.

Spread Maintenance

When the FSLIC sought a buyer for a failed S&L, the buyer looked at the assets and liabilities and concluded that if it took those assets and liabilities without any assistance from FSLIC—even if it purchased the assets for no payment except the assumption of the liabilities—it would continue to lose money on the package, just as the failed thrift had done. The low or negative spread of the failed institution was locked in and would continue no matter how well the acquiring institution managed the assets. Nevertheless, the assets eventually would pay off at full value, so the acquirer usually was willing to take the assets as long as someone else was willing to make up the spread differential between what the assets earned and a market rate. Therefore the FSLIC guaranteed the acquiring bank a normal spread of 200–250 basis points between the interest cost of the assumed liabilities and the interest earned on the acquired assets. This assured the acquiring S&L a normal profit margin on the type of assets being purchased (usually mortgages).

More Money-Saving Techniques

Even notes, guarantees, and spread maintenance would eventually cost the FSLIC cash. These techniques just defer the cash payments to later years. Because the FSLIC needed to conserve its obligations to pay cash in the future as well as its present cash reserves, Pratt, Beesely, and company developed three more strategies to save money: purchase accounting techniques, interstate sales, and "phoenix" plans. In the process of saving money, however, the new accounting rules not only fooled the press and the public about the true state of the industry and the FSLIC fund but also confused the industry and the regulators who followed Pratt and Beesely. As a former regulator put it, "Dick Pratt changed the rules so you couldn't count. That was a mistake, because if you can't count, you don't know where you are."

Purchase Accounting

Healthy (or even reasonably healthy) S&Ls didn't want to acquire insolvent ones without assistance because their earnings (and eventually their net worth) would suffer from the negative spread on the assets and liabilities acquired. This was simple arithmetic. To get around this arithmetic, the FSLIC called on "purchase accounting."[1]

There are two ways of accounting for business acquisitions: "pooling" and "purchase." These two types of accounting for similar transactions were governed by accounting rules which said that business combinations should be treated as "purchases" unless "continuity of interest requirements" for pooling treatment were met. These rules made it easy to treat a transaction as a "purchase" if you wanted to.

The difference between a "pooling" and a "purchase" is that in a "pooling" the assets and liabilities of both parties to the consolidation are accounted for in the same way they were before the deal, except that they are combined — these are referred to as "historical" values — whereas in a "purchase" the assets and liabilities of the *acquired* party are *revalued* at the date of the deal and are reflected on the balance sheet of the new combined enterprise at the new fair market values.

Now we will have to learn a little bit of more complicated accounting, but since losing count is one of the causes of the eventual large cost of bailing out the FSLIC, it is worth understanding *how* we lost count by attempting to save the government money. It will only take a few paragraphs, and it will show how the FHLBB permitted S&Ls that acquired other insolvent or failing S&Ls to *create* accounting income without adding any new cash flow.

When you value the assets and liabilities of an insolvent S&L on the date of acquisition by a solvent one, what you find in every case is that the assets are worth less than the liabilities. The accountants assume that this difference represents a kind of going concern or franchise value inherent in the acquired institution — otherwise why would the *acquiring* institution do the deal in the first place? So the accounting rules say to put this shortfall number on the balance sheet as an *asset* called "goodwill" (actually the accounting literature refuses to use the word "goodwill" and calls it "excess of fair value of liabilities acquired over fair value of assets acquired," but because that's such a mouthful no one calls it that). The accounting rules then say that this asset — goodwill — is to be "amortized" against earnings over its "useful life" — a period not to exceed forty years. Thus, for example, $100 of goodwill amortized over *ten* years would result in a charge to (reduction of) earnings of $10 per year in each of the ten years.[2]

So far so good, but how does this charge against earnings become an *inducement* to a healthy S&L to buy a sick one? It looks like the opposite of an inducement.

The inducement came about because when the accounting profession designed the purchase accounting rules in the early 1970s, they didn't anticipate the case of insolvent thrift institutions with low-yielding assets in a high-yield world. The rules for that situation were simply unclear until September 1982.

The FSLIC accountants took advantage of a counterentry to the goodwill number described above. They saw that mortgage loans which today were worth, say, 80 percent of their face value because they had low interest rates were good loans that on date of maturity would be worth 100 percent of face value because they would pay off. That meant that, for accounting purposes, the acquiring institutions would be permitted to recognize noncash *income* as the loans got closer to maturity—and the total amount of this noncash income recognized over time would be about the same as the amount of goodwill.

Noncash income of this sort is not strange, nor is it unique to S&L accounting. It is called "discount," which comes about whenever a financial instrument is bought for less than its eventual face value. This discount is said to "accrete" into income over the life of the financial instrument. The extreme example of discount is the zero coupon bond.

Applying these discount and accretion concepts to the mortgages acquired by healthy S&Ls when failed S&Ls merged into them, the discount was said to accrete into income "over the average life of the mortgages acquired." That average life might well be twenty years or less.

Now we are ready to see the advantage to the acquiring institution.

If you allowed the acquiring S&L to amortize the goodwill over forty years and to "accrete" the discount over twenty years, you created income to the acquirer for the first twenty years because, by definition, the goodwill and the discount started as similar numbers. For example, if the goodwill was $100 million and it was amortized over forty years, there would be an annual charge to earnings of $2.5 million; but in the same example the discount also would be $100 million, and if it were accreted into earnings over twenty years, there would be an annual increase in earnings of $5 million. The resulting $2.5 million of *net* annual earnings increase might be enough to convince the acquiring S&L to do the deal. So although the FHLBB had proposed to outlaw this type of artificial earnings creation in 1980, in 1981 it repealed that proposal in order to save money when selling failed institutions.

Of course the purchase accounting gambit didn't repeal the laws of nature: At the end of twenty years the acquiring S&L in our example still has $50 million of goodwill left to be charged to earnings over the *next* twenty years, when its earnings will be *reduced* by $2.5 million per year.

But twenty years is a long time, most S&L managements reasoned, and by doing purchase accounting transactions they were doing a favor to their regulators, who would protect them. There could be little wrong with a transaction not only approved, but also encouraged, by the FHLBB. It was especially easy for mutual institutions (over 80 percent of S&Ls were still mutual) to reason this way because they cared more about asset growth and long-term survival than about real profitability.

Thus in 1981–82 over 200 supervisory transactions and many other privately negotiated transactions were approved that created total goodwill on S&L balance sheets of $16 billion. As a result, at the end of 1982, $16 billion out of S&Ls' total regulatory accounting capital of $25 billion was goodwill—an intangible asset worth nothing in liquidation. By December 31, 1985, S&Ls had $23 billion of goodwill, which represented half the industry's total regulatory capital of $46 billion. In other words, at the end of 1985, based on this factor alone, the S&L industry had half the capital that it and its regulator pretended it had. In addition, about another $3 billion of apparent net worth had come from the income effects of purchase accounting. The FSLIC had saved money, but the numbers the Bank Board published on S&Ls were getting more and more fuzzed up and the stronger, acquiring institutions were being weakened.

Interstate Acquisitions

Another way the FSLIC reduced the cost of disposing of failed S&Ls was to permit interstate acquisitions. By creating a loophole, the FSLIC used the federal prohibition against interstate banking that was contained in the Bank Holding Company Act (BHCA)* to induce healthy banks and S&Ls to acquire insolvent S&Ls in other states. This required great creativity because American politics long had been hostile to interstate banking.

In the United States we have had independent banks and S&Ls in just about every town of any size, whereas in most other countries a few big banks dominate the business. In Britain and France, for example, the top four banks have more than a 50 percent market share. In the United States we had 14,000 banks and 4,000 S&Ls in 1981. No bank then had a meaningfully large share of the U.S. national market, and today even Citicorp has only about a 5 percent share.

Our large number of banks and S&Ls has been fostered by numerous laws and policies that made it easy to start banks and hard to compete outside one's local market. Branch banking, for example, has always been restricted. Until recently, very few states permitted statewide branching; and many states, including populous states such as Texas and Illinois, permitted no branching at all well into the 1980s. Under the 1927 McFadden Act, Congress prohibited national banks from branching anywhere that state banks couldn't branch.

The big banks sought ways around the state branching restrictions by forming holding companies that could own banks in many towns even if branching into those towns wasn't permitted. Indeed, some of the early holding companies owned banks in several states.

To prevent interstate banking and preserve states' rights, Congress enacted the Bank Holding Company Act of 1956, which under its "Douglas Amendment" (named for its sponsor, Senator Paul Douglas of Illinois) prohibits a company that owns a bank in one state from acquiring another bank in another state unless the laws of both states *specifically permit* the acquisition. A similar prohibition was written into the Savings and Loan Holding Company Act (SLHCA)* when it was passed in 1968.

These restrictions on branch and interstate banking reflect America's populist values and assumptions: Banking is money, money is power, power should not be concentrated. The local bank, we have traditionally believed, will lend to the local business. The giant bank from the big city only wants the big business customer; it will drain deposits from the small towns for the benefit of big city businesses and will not finance the entrepreneur.

In recent years these populist assumptions about banking have been giving way to the march of technology and foreign competition, which seem to favor big banks. The failures of S&Ls in the 1980s and interstate sales by the FSLIC contributed strongly to what now seems like an inexorable drive toward open interstate banking in the early 1990s. FSLIC took some of the first steps toward interstate banking when it created First Nationwide and sold large failed S&Ls in Florida, California, and Illinois to Citicorp. The rest of the banking world couldn't let Citicorp and Ford (which owns First Nationwide) have the only interstate franchises, so interstate banking became almost inevitable.

In the first interstate S&L sale, the FSLIC merged failing S&Ls in New York and Florida into Citizens Savings of San Francisco to create First Nationwide. The SLHCA, unlike the BHCA (which prohibited any other kind of business corporation from owning a bank), permitted an industrial company, such as Ford, to own an S&L—but only one S&L. The FHLBB then stretched and bent the S&L branching laws to permit merging insolvent S&Ls from one state into a solvent S&L in another state, so that Ford ended up owning one S&L with branches in California, New York, and Florida. Later they added failed S&Ls from other states to enlarge the franchise still further.

Using the same interstate branching inducement, the FSLIC quickly convinced two sound New York mutual savings banks to convert to federal savings and loan charters, change insurance funds from FDIC to FSLIC, and merge into failing S&Ls in other states ("reverse mergers"). Again interstate banking institutions were created, today called Empire of America (in liquidation) and Northeast Savings (in trouble but may be turning around). Other large S&Ls, such as the California giants Home Savings of America, California Federal, and Great Western, followed the pattern and had failed S&Ls in states such as New York, Florida, and Texas merged into them. The resulting immediate savings to the FSLIC fund were substantial.

To save even more money, the FSLIC needed to be able to sell S&Ls interstate to bank holding companies, which the Fed's rules clearly prohibited. First, the Bank Holding Company Act prohibited a holding company from owning banks in more than one state, and second, the Fed had interpreted the BHCA as prohibiting a bank holding company from owning an S&L at all, on the ground that the S&L business wasn't closely related to banking (a nonsense position of ancient lineage).[3]

Nevertheless, the Fed understood the FSLIC's predicament: not enough money to do the job assigned to it. So the Fed did some fancy footwork to help out. It said that S&Ls aren't "banks," so the interstate prohibition doesn't apply; and that when an S&L is failing, its operations can be deemed a proper function for a bank holding company, subject to numerous conditions that had nothing to do with the matter. The Fed's decision wasn't wonderful logic but it was powerful policy-making because it broke the interstate banking log jam.

Phoenixes

To save even more money, Brent Beesely invented another method of temporizing: He merged several failing S&Ls together, brought in new management and a new board of directors, and let them continue in business. These merger creations were known as "phoenixes," having arisen from the ashes of their defunct predecessors.

Beesely intended the five phoenixes that he created to be temporary. The consolidation would achieve economies of scale, the hand-picked managements and boards would act responsibly and not take undue risks, and eventually the institutions would shrink and gradually liquidate, or would be sold to a healthy bank or S&L when the market was better. Today two of them are still hanging on.

KEEPING THE EGGS FROM FALLING OFF THE TABLE

If you now have the impression that bank and S&L regulation was being contorted in an attempt to deal with the S&L problem without spending money, you are correct. At this point we have only scratched the surface of the complexity that eventually became part of the problem rather than the solution.

Even with the fancy footwork, there were too many insolvent institutions for FSLIC to handle with its limited resources. The industry was aghast at the rate of failure (over 800 institutions were merged or liquidated in 1981 and 1982, over 200 of them requiring monetary assistance from FSLIC, compared with 30 supervisory mergers or liquidations in the worst earlier year); they called Brent Beesely "Dr. Doom" and pleaded with Pratt to stop dealing with the failures. But Pratt believed it was right to stand in the shoes of the marketplace and declare and enforce failure and its consequences when net worth was depleted. He also largely ignored OMB, which believed that everything would be fine when interest rates moderated, and that declaring failures and taking the consequences wasn't productive.

But because FSLIC couldn't deal with all the insolvencies as they were occurring, Pratt and his team decided (with support from both the administration and the industry) to change the definition of net worth so that fewer institutions would have to report that they were insolvent. This would prevent public confidence from being impaired while FSLIC dealt with the problems over a longer period of time. If reported numbers showed insolvencies, the regulators reasoned, the press would destroy confidence in institutions, there would be runs, FSLIC would have to deal with more cases than it could handle, and everyone would be in deep trouble. They had to "keep the eggs from falling off the table."

Capital Rules Shenanigans

As part of this strategy to fool the public, the Bank Board changed the capital rules in two ways:

1. They reduced the capital requirement to 3 percent from 4 percent.
2. They permitted "appraised equity capital" to be counted.

(This was on top of counting goodwill as capital.)

To put these changes in context, S&L capital requirements had been 5 percent until the 1980 Act gave the FHLBB power to regulate them between 3 percent and 6 percent. The FHLBB had lowered the requirement to 4 percent in 1980. Thus 3 percent was historically a very low requirement, but it could be justified as a temporary expedient to give S&Ls some breathing room at a time when they had no way to raise more capital and had a liquidity crunch as well.

But even this 3 percent requirement was illusory, because under a five-year averaging concept adopted in 1972 to promote growth of S&Ls, an institution could grow faster than its capital would have permitted because it could average its assets over five years in applying the test. Thus a $10 million institution could grow to $100 million in one year and its capital requirement would be $840,000 (less than 1 percent) [(4 × $10 million + $100 million) / 5 × .03] rather than $3 million. The five-year averaging provision therefore intentionally encouraged high rates of growth so that an S&L could, in effect, have old assets that lost money because they were mismatched at negative spreads and new assets that made money because they were matched at profitable spreads. Virtually no one outside the industry knew about this. Nor did outsiders know that for new institutions there was a twenty-year phase-in, so that a new S&L was allowed to have even more minute capital in its early years. The Pratt Bank Board didn't invent these averaging provisions, but they left them in place. They didn't seem important in 1981, when the S&Ls' problem was that they couldn't get enough funds to operate without selling assets at a loss.

"Appraised equity capital" meant that if an S&L had a bank building that had a market value higher than its book value (usually historical cost), it could count the higher market value without selling the building. It also could appraise and "write up" various other kinds of assets. But under the rules of this particular Wonderland, an S&L never had to "write down" an asset that had depreciated.

The best that can be said for appraised equity capital is that it didn't have a very material impact. (It inflated reported S&L capital by a total of about $2 billion.) Appraised equity capital just made it hard to count. The more adjustments you have to make to figure your way back to somewhere near reality, the less likely it is that you are going to do it.

These rules were designed to fool the press and the public (for the public's benefit) and were successful, since the press didn't understand the changes and its source of information on S&Ls was the FHLBB, which provided data on the new basis.

Deferred Loss Accounting

The FHLBB also took various actions designed to increase reported earnings of mismatched S&Ls, most materially by permitting "deferred loss accounting," under which an S&L could sell low-yielding long-term assets and set up the loss as an asset (and therefore part of capital) — a "deferred loss" account similar to the goodwill balance sheet entry used in purchase accounting. This deferred loss then would be amortized over the average remaining life of the mortgage loans sold. Income would increase in the early years because the cash could be reinvested short term at high rates in 1981–82 (leaving a deficit when rates came down in later years). In addition, the S&L could qualify for tax loss carrybacks (recapture of taxes paid in prior years) on the losses. Under pressure from the industry — and with a push from a blue-ribbon academic study that concluded it was "firmly rooted in economic and financial theory" — the Pratt people reasoned that you shouldn't have to do a merger to use purchase accounting and restructure your assets.

Deferred loss accounting, for which the S&L industry lobbied long and hard before its adoption, was a bad idea. Not only was it bad accounting, but it also promoted bad management by encouraging S&Ls to sell their long-term holdings at a time of very high rates when they had depreciated most, and to invest the proceeds of the sale in shorter term instruments, thereby effectively "locking in" the loss even if interest rates came down.

Several hundred S&Ls used deferred loss accounting, creating $6 billion of deferred losses that (because it was an accounting asset) contributed to the growing difference between GAAP and RAP net worth. By the end of 1984, goodwill, deferred losses, and other regulatory accounting intangibles amounted to $34 billion out of total industry RAP capital of $37 billion. In other words, the industry as a whole was broke at the end of 1984 but almost nobody knew it.

IMPROVING THE THRIFT FRANCHISE

The third leg of the Pratt strategy for getting the S&Ls back to solvency was to make the thrift franchise more attractive to investors so they would buy whole S&Ls, buy S&L stock in public offerings, and buy subordinated debt and other capital instruments that S&Ls could offer. Luring new private capital was the only way to recapitalize the industry without enormous government assistance. Improving the franchise also coincided with the Treasury's goal of equalizing the powers of S&Ls and commercial banks, so as to create a "level playing field."

Pratt and some of his colleagues got a bit carried away with the idea of improving the franchise. Imbued with an entrepreneurial spirit, they seem in retrospect unintentionally to have encouraged some of the speculative excesses that characterized the most expensive failures.

The administration had early on entrusted Pratt with the task of leading the way on a financial deregulation bill. Pratt and his staff created the new legislation, and Jake Garn, Chairman of the Senate Banking Committee, introduced the bill in late October 1981. But the bill got nowhere. The big city commercial bankers weren't getting enough. The securities industry didn't like what the big city commercial bankers *were* getting. The country commercial bankers—the "independent banks"—didn't want the thrifts as competitors. Some members of Congress were concerned that they didn't yet understand what they had done in the 1980 Act. In various forms, the bill floundered around for a year.

Congress wasn't unaware of the national thrift institution crisis; it just wasn't ready for another big deregulatory banking bill. So it tinkered a little. In October 1981 Congress passed the "All-Savers Act," which created a short-lived certificate of deposit called the "all-savers account" that could earn tax-free interest. This placated the thrift industry, made constituents happy to receive tax-free interest, and helped the thrifts by providing an inflow of deposits at below-market rates because of the tax-exempt feature—sort of a token subsidy.

More to the point, in March 1982 both houses passed a "sense of the Congress" resolution stating that the full faith and credit of the United States stood behind the deposit insurance funds. The administration didn't want a "full faith and credit" law, but the industry convinced Congress that public confidence would erode if it wasn't made clear that the government stood behind the insurance funds. A sense of the Congress resolution isn't binding, but it's very hard to go back on because the public doesn't make such fine distinctions between Congress's laws and its mere resolutions.

The catalyst that finally got the deregulation bill moving wasn't deregulation or any other long-term theory or political motive. It was the short-term expedient of a "net worth certificate" program—a paper-for-paper swap that the accountants wouldn't recognize under GAAP—that would keep S&Ls and savings banks from looking insolvent, even if they were. The members of Congress didn't like the mail they got when institutions failed, and they didn't want to swell the deficit by providing a direct subsidy, so they embraced Treasury's paper swap proposal, which was supported by the industry, even though it was opposed by the FDIC and, less vigorously, by the Bank Board.

The net worth certificate plan got the Treasury the kind of "big deregulatory bill" that it wanted. When finally passed, the Garn–St Germain Act, as it became known, gave S&Ls new investment powers, authorized new types of deposit accounts at S&Ls, enabled conversion of mutual institutions to stock form, allowed emergency interstate mergers, sped up deregulation of interest rates on deposits, preempted state laws prohibiting "due-on-sale" clauses in mortgages, permitted S&Ls to borrow more from Federal Home Loan Banks, authorized all S&Ls to write adjustable-rate mortgages (ARMs),* and dealt with a host of matters related to commercial banks, credit unions, and the securities business. The Act sought to transform S&Ls from weak mutuals into strong and diversified stock institutions that could raise new capital by public offerings in the emerging stock market boom.

Mutuality

About 80 percent of the 3,779 federally insured S&Ls that were in business at the beginning of 1982 were organized in mutual form. By definition, they could not issue stock.

Tracing its roots to Scottish savings banks of the late eighteenth century, the

mutual movement in the United States was largely a nineteenth-century phenomenon. The savings banks in New England and the Middle Atlantic states,
and most of our life insurance companies, such as Prudential, Metropolitan
Life, and New York Life, were established in mutual form. The mutual savings banks offered the working class places to save and encouraged "thrift"; the
mutual life insurance companies issued small policies and returned part of the
profits to the policyholders in the form of dividends. There were no owners
except the savers and the policyholders; the institutions were managed by self-
perpetuating boards of "trustees" who were prohibited from receiving any re-
muneration for doing any business with the mutual institution they served,
and the savers and policyholders had no say in management.

Mutual S&Ls had a different background. Most of them were founded in
small towns after 1900, and were established to provide home loans as much
as to provide places to save. Their models were the English building societies.
Also, rather than being founded by local Brahmins for the benefit of the
working classes, mutual S&Ls were started by the local lawyer, the local insurance agent, and the local real estate developer or broker, all of whom could
profit substantially from their association with the institution. Mutual S&Ls
didn't have rules that prohibited their directors (not called "trustees") from
profiting by dealing with the institution. Indeed, although most people picture
S&L managements as warm-hearted local heroes based on Jimmy Stewart's
portrayal in *It's a Wonderful Life*—and doubtless many were—in fact mutual
S&Ls had a *tradition* of self-dealing that was kept within bounds only by detailed regulation.

Today you can't tell an S&L from a savings bank. The institutions call themselves anything they want. But historically there was a big difference.

Mutuality and Capital

By their nature, institutions organized in mutual form—meaning without
stock ownership—can't raise new *capital*. A mutual institution can acquire
funds through taking deposits, but it cannot obtain *capital* (the excess of assets
over liabilities) except by accumulating it through earning profits, which of
necessity is a slow process. Therefore, when the mutual S&Ls (and savings
banks) lost money in the early 1980s and substantially depleted their capital,
they had nowhere to turn for more capital. Even if they had a franchise value
that the market would pay for, they couldn't tap the market because they
couldn't issue stock.

Since 80 percent of the federally insured S&Ls and all of the FDIC-insured
savings banks were mutual, this limitation was a serious impediment to re-

plenishing the industry's capital. Converting to stock form was perceived as a solution.

For over ten years, substantially all economists who had studied mutual thrift institutions had concluded that their inability to issue stock would arrest their growth and threaten their survival. Most of the officers and directors or trustees did not agree with this conclusion, however. Mutuality had served the country well, they said. Thrift institutions had paid depositors higher rates of interest and had made socially useful investments. If you allowed them to convert to stock form, you would replace the community service motive with the profit motive of stockholders; society thereby would be diminished. Mutuality therefore had strong support in Congress and in state legislatures. The philosophical position in favor of mutuality was even embodied in the New York State Constitution, which forbade any New York savings bank or S&L to issue stock.

By 1982, however, mutuals clearly needed capital more quickly than they could build it through earnings. (It is especially difficult to build capital through earnings when you are losing money.) As a consequence, the Garn–St Germain Act included provisions that authorized conversions of federal associations regardless of state law.

The Garn–St Germain Act of 1982

When he signed the Garn–St Germain Act in October 1982, President Reagan said proudly that it was the most significant piece of banking legislation since 1933. It was in fact a bold exercise of federal power that swept away state laws and even state constitutional provisions with a flick of Congress's magisterial hand, revealing the shallowness of states' rights sentiments.

To enable mutuals to convert to stock form, the Congress said, "Notwithstanding any other provision of Federal law or the laws or constitution of any State . . . the Board may authorize . . . the conversion of a mutual savings and loan association . . . into a Federal stock savings and loan association." As a result, between 1983 and 1989, over 300 mutual S&Ls insured by the FSLIC converted to stock form and raised an aggregate of about $5 billion of capital, an amount greater than the whole industry's tangible capital* at the end of 1982.

Many of the books and articles written about the S&L mess condemn the Garn–St Germain Act as irresponsible deregulation. The Act's deregulatory thrust is portrayed as having opened the floodgates to bad loans, fraud, and further failure. I believe that even though, like most legislation, you would rather not know how it was made, Garn–St Germain was basically good legislation that looks bad because after it was passed the FHLBB didn't do its job, the industry obstructed the FHLBB in its attempts to do its job, the administration didn't understand the FHLBB's job, and the Congress, thinking it had done all that was required of it, hid its collective head in the sand for seven years.

The detractors most often decry the expanded asset powers that Garn–St Germain gave to federal S&Ls. These new powers were indeed permissive compared with the powers federal S&Ls had been able to exercise five years earlier, but insured *banks* had long exercised substantially all of the newly granted powers. It wasn't Congressional or regulatory safety and soundness considerations that had limited S&L asset powers, but rather the ability of the commercial banking lobbies to forestall competition. Since interest rate deregulation had leveled the playing field on the liability side of the balance sheet, it was good policy to make it level on the asset side as well, and the commercial banks' desire for interest rate decontrol persuaded them to stop opposing the new competition.

In substance, the new asset powers for federal S&Ls did the following:

- Eliminated the statutory loan-to-value (LTV) tests* for making home loans and apartment loans, but gave the FHLBB power to establish these tests.

- Eliminated the requirement that commercial real estate loans be made on the security of first liens.*

- Increased the percentage of assets that an institution could invest in commercial mortgage loans from 20 percent to 40 percent.

- Authorized the making of unsecured business loans with up to 10 percent of an institution's assets.

- Increased consumer lending authority from 20 percent of assets to 30 percent of assets.

To go along with these asset powers, the Garn–St Germain Act added power to take demand deposits, the most profitable traditional commercial bank service.

The bad loans that S&Ls made in 1983–85 were almost all real estate loans, not the newly authorized commercial and consumer loans which were the central product extensions that commercial banks had fought for years. And most of the bad real estate loans could have been made under pre–1980 law. Even the power to make second mortgage loans on commercial real estate— which S&Ls such as Sunbelt abused at great cost—can be defended on the basis of the history of real estate lending in big cities, where second mortgages on stable office buildings were common as inflation increased rents and, therefore, cash flow. The Congress and the regulators thought S&Ls knew real estate, and that with expanded real estate lending powers, they could diversify their assets, which theoretically would increase their stability.

State-chartered S&Ls in many states, including Texas, had had some or all of the expanded real estate lending powers for years. Commercial banks all over the country—both national banks and state-chartered banks—had exercised real estate lending powers, as well as commercial and consumer lending powers, as part of their normal lending businesses, although before the 1980s their real estaste lending powers were limited by loan-to-value ratios. Real estate lending powers are not inherently unsound powers for banking institutions to exercise, although their exercise requires prudence and risk management.

Indeed, a study done for the Bank Board in July 1982 had compared the performance of federally chartered Texas S&Ls with the performance of state-chartered Texas S&Ls, which already had all of the powers that Garn–St Germain later gave to federally chartered institutions. It concluded that additional asset powers would permit institutions to reduce exposure to interest rate risk and provide significantly higher returns on assets. It also opined that "S&Ls would probably move cautiously to use the alternative asset powers should they be granted."[4]

Net Worth Certificates

The "net worth certificate" program was far more radical than asset deregulation. It effectively set aside traditional capital standards to save failing institutions and prop them up until they could utilize the new powers to restructure and become profitable. The program authorized the FDIC and the FSLIC to buy from a failing thrift a form of subordinated debt that they would count as regulatory capital, thereby preventing the failing institution from becoming technically insolvent for regulatory purposes. The agencies were authorized to pay for these net worth certificates with their own promissory notes—and the statutes directed that the net worth certificates issued by the banks or S&Ls and the promissory notes issued by the agencies bear the same rates of interest. The net effect of issuing net worth certificates therefore was curious: No money changed hands; no interest ever had to be paid; but by operation of law regulatory capital had been created. The accounting profession refused to give any credence to these paper transactions because they lacked substance. As a consequence, audited balance sheets showed neither the net worth certificates issued by the savings banks and S&Ls nor the promissory notes issued by the agencies. As far as the accountants were concerned, they didn't exist.

The major problem with the net worth certificate program was not that assisted institutions later failed—they already had failed, and some were saved—but that *by its adoption Congress blessed expedient accounting and gave a signal to the regulators that the old rules didn't have to be applied.* Both Congress and the administration seemed to be saying that insolvent institutions didn't have to be liquidated.

STATE LEGISLATURES EXPAND THRIFT INSTITUTION POWERS

The dual banking system has always generated competition between the federal regulatory agencies and their state counterparts. The legislatures also compete because banks and S&Ls are rich sources of political contributions, which are given to the legislatures that have the biggest impact on the institutions—and no governmental authority has a bigger impact than the legislature that grants statutory powers.

This situation has created what some see as a competition in laxity and others see as a climate of healthy experimentation. Whichever characterization you prefer, the fact remains that many state legislatures responded to the 1980 Act and the Garn–St Germain Act by enacting deregulatory statutes themselves.

It was fairly easy for state-chartered thrifts to obtain "parity" legislation to give them the same powers that had been given to federal S&Ls. The local commercial bankers had been able to prevent S&Ls from getting commercial banking powers for many years, but when an S&L could get those powers just by converting to federal charter, state legislators' interest in keeping their S&L constituents overpowered the commercial bankers' arguments and political power.

Many state legislatures went beyond Garn–St Germain in granting new powers. They wanted to provide positive incentives for thrifts to stay in or return to the state system. The legislators weren't very sophisticated about financial institutions; they saw that deregulation was working; the stock market and real estate were booming. Why not give the thrifts a chance to participate? In several states the power to invest in real estate ventures as an equity participant, not just as a lender, was added to the commercial banking powers granted by Garn–St Germain. A few states went further and permitted other kinds of equity investments as well.

California went the whole hog. In the Nolan Act it said that after January 1, 1983, an S&L could invest in anything it wanted, no holds barred. Texas S&Ls had been able to invest in almost anything for years, but everyone said, "Texas, well, you know, that's Texas; it's different." California was a real surprise.

At last count, over 80 percent of the S&L losses have been in state-chartered institutions. We will try to evaluate as we go along the factors that made 80 percent of the losses come from the 50 percent of the industry that was state-chartered. And we will have to question whether the dual banking system is still viable.

THE STATE OF THE INDUSTRY WHEN DICK PRATT LEFT

When Dick Pratt and most of his key aides left the Bank Board in April 1983, most of the world had the impression that the thrift industry had recovered from its problems. It was off the front page; it was even off the front page of the business section, back in the "executive changes" section, where it belonged.

But the facts didn't support complacency. At the beginning of 1983, over 130 S&Ls had a negative net worth even after using all the RAP accounting gimmicks. Another 1,048 (about a third of the industry) had less than 3 percent RAP net worth.

Estimated GAAP figures—which no one used at the time and weren't published until years later—would have shown about 237 insolvent but open institutions and 1,166 with less than 3 percent net worth. Thus there were between 1,200 and 1,400 institutions open and functioning with a net worth level that would have required that they be closed, or at least severely restricted, if the regulators applied pre–1980 standards. If, in addition, you knocked out the GAAP goodwill, as the FDIC would have done for banks under its jurisdiction, you could have added another 100 or so S&Ls to the list, which then would have included almost half of the industry. Between 1980 and 1982, the industry had contracted from 4,000 institutions with $32 billion of tangible capital to 3,300 institutions with less than $4 billion of tangible capital. The $28 billion difference was the realized part of the loss. An even larger loss was embedded in the depressed value of the old mortgage portfolios.

The *Agenda for Reform*

Dick Pratt left the Bank Board in April 1983 to join Merrill Lynch and make a lot of money selling mortgage derivatives to S&Ls. Before he left, he and his staff published their legacy, a document called *Agenda for Reform*, in which they intended to present a blueprint for future S&L regulation.

Agenda for Reform is long enough and contains enough statements on S&L regulation that one can find support in it for a wide variety of positions.

The principal thrust of *Agenda for Reform* is that the U.S. deposit insurance system, in which FDIC and FSLIC insure deposits for a flat fee based solely on the size of the deposit base, is unsound because it encourages excessive risk-taking. The solution that the *Agenda* proposed is "risk-based" insurance under which a bank or S&L would pay larger insurance premiums if it took on larger risks, as defined by the regulators.

This was not a new idea. Academic economists had seen the disparity between deposit insurance premiums and hypothetical private insurance premiums for years, and had suggested that excessive risk-taking should be curtailed by risk-based premiums. The importance of the *Agenda for Reform* is that it placed the risk-based premium discussion in the context of the S&L industry as it existed at the beginning of 1983:

> Under the system in place today, the federal government shares in any losses while gains accrue entirely to those who have [equity] interests in depository institutions. A rational course of action in these circumstances is for the firms to engage in activities that may be excessively risky.[5]
>
> The current system of uniform premiums does not discourage risk-taking; regulations have been used for that purpose.[6]
>
> Although the deregulation of depository institutions may enable them to be more competitive, it also significantly broadens the government's exposure to risk.[7]
>
> The current system is unstable; without reform, it threatens the viability of federal deposit insurance.[8]

The *Agenda* warns that low net worth S&Ls present special problems:

> Moreover, this [deregulation] has occurred at a time when there are a number of insured institutions that are operating with impaired capital and have strong incentives to engage in very risky investments. In light of the competitive pressures that the industry will face in the next few years, this deregulation could result in substantial losses.[9]
>
> Many institutions are simply too weak to restructure their operations toward new business endeavors without assuming undue risks. Some S&Ls may take these excessive risks because they believe that their weakened financial condition leaves them no choice—that is, they believe that they must restructure to survive.[10]
>
> The Bank Board believes that adequate capital must be maintained in thrift institutions if risk to the FSLIC is to be limited to prudent levels. The existence of risk capital . . . is mandatory if the risk exposure of the FSLIC is to be contained to a manageable level.[11]

I have taken these statements out of context to make Pratt and his colleagues look prescient. Other statements can paint them as advising that nothing really *needs* to be done to prevent institutions from taking undue risks:

[T]he size of the fund is more than adequate to handle even severe problems as long as the FHLBB's regulatory powers are used skillfully. More importantly, the recent experience revealed that the powers to arrange mergers and prevent failures are fundamentally more significant than the size of the fund.[12]

There are legitimate considerations that argue for allowing some S&Ls to continue operating even if they are losing money on a current basis, and even if they have negative net worth. Many S&Ls with negative net worth can be expected to be profitable in the future, on the basis of yields and costs currently prevailing in the market, given their existing location, organization, and management.[13]

Disappointingly, the *Agenda* doesn't point out the need to repeal some of the excesses of regulatory laxity that the Bank Board had had to adopt to get through 1981–82 in order to prevent fruition of the *Agenda*'s risk-taking prediction before Congress could act on risk-based deposit premiums – if it ever would.

Opening the Door in the Name of Improving the Franchise

Having a dual banking system – a system in which we have both federally chartered and state-chartered banks with federal and state regulators and legislatures free to offer different powers – traditionally has imposed restrictions on the types of regulations that federal deposit insurance regulators could impose on state-chartered institutions. Because the (sovereign) state legislatures are permitted to grant powers to state banks that are different from – and can be greater than – the powers given to national banks, Congress did not give the FDIC the right to restrict those state powers except on strict safety and soundness grounds.

Congress copied the dual banking system when it authorized federal S&Ls in 1933 and federal deposit insurance for S&Ls in 1934. Thus the states were free to give their S&Ls the right to engage in whatever activities the state legislatures thought proper, and the FSLIC had little direct power to curtail those activities. The FSLIC had only four big sticks: capital requirements, loans-to-one-borrower rules, conflict-of-interest rules, and any other regulations it could show to be necessary to protect the safety and soundness of institutions and the insurance fund.

Loans-to-one-borrower regulations are designed to promote diversification of loan portfolios and to make sure that a bank or S&L doesn't take too much risk in any one loan or on the signature of any one borrower. Commercial bank regulatory agencies* use these rules as primary tools in making sure that banks diversify their lending risks. But loan-to-one-borrower rules had always been a low-priority subject at the Bank Board because single-family lending didn't involve big loans, and loans secured by larger real estate projects seemed to the Board not to present the same risks as unsecured lending by commercial banks. The Board's regulations only said that an S&L could not make loans to one borrower that exceeded the S&L's total net worth.

After passage of Garn–St Germain, a number of aspects of the lending limit had to be reviewed. The Bank Board adopted rules for the newly authorized unsecured lending that conformed to rules for national banks (as required by Garn–St Germain). These rules imposed a lending limit of 15 percent of net worth. The Bank Board could have imposed the same limit on commercial loans secured by real estate. That would have been consistent with National Bank regulation. But the Bank Board didn't impose those more stringent rules on commercial real estate loans "because . . . insured institutions have expertise in assessing the risks involved in real estate loans." This left S&Ls free to risk their entire net worth on a single commercial real estate loan even though most S&Ls had no expertise in large-scale construction lending. Even Real Estate Lending 101 would have taught that large-scale construction lending entails very different risks from traditional S&L lending.

This naiveté carried over to the conflict-of-interest regulations that were adopted or proposed at the end of the Pratt tenure. The Board had appeared to proceed from a sound premise when it proposed new regulations in September 1982: "The Board believes that transactions between an insured institution . . . and an affiliated person present the risk of insider self-dealing." It therefore proposed to require that prior notice of insider transactions be given to the regional Supervisory Agents* of the Board and that the Supervisory Agents should have an opportunity to approve or disapprove any transaction.

But a few months later, at the same time that Pratt and his team were writing the *Agenda* and warning that weakened institutions would take risks, they had a change of heart:

> The Board . . . has decided to propose a different approach to regulating transactions involving affiliated persons. The Board believes that the starting point of its regulatory analysis should be the recognition that the vast majority of insured institutions avoid conflict-of-interest situations on their own initiative as a matter of prudent management policy.
>
> Consequently [consequently?], the opportunity cost resulting from a prohibition of a particular class of business transactions outweighs the benefit of preventing abuses unless the specific types of prohibited transactions are ones likely to involve abuse in a majority of cases.

Using this reasoning, the Board proposed only to prohibit transactions that were not on "prevailing terms" and substituted S&L board of directors' approval for the previously proposed Supervisory Agent approval, unless the transaction involved more than 25 percent of the association's net worth. (These proposals were withdrawn in part later in the year, after Pratt and his staff had left the Bank Board.)

The Board also exempted from the conflict-of-interest rules any transaction between the S&L and a partnership in which insiders had less than a 10 percent limited partnership interest. The Board reasoned that a limited partner has no management role (true in theory but not always in practice), and that "If a limited partner has less than a 10 percent interest in a partnership, there is little likelihood that an indirect benefit to the partner from a transaction between the partnership and the insured institution generally would give rise to a material conflict of interest." That is a very naive statement. A 5 percent interest in, for example, a $10 million project would give most people a very substantial conflict of interest. These rules weren't fixed until FIRREA was passed in 1989.

THE IMPORTANCE OF CONTINUITY

Dick Pratt's last months deserve our attention because control of the situation was lost in 1983. Of the mistakes that he made, the one that Pratt says he regrets most was having too much faith in "the continuity of the process." If he had focused on what had to be done, he feels he would have made the three or four crucial moves to prevent extreme difficulty from turning into disaster.

Deregulation and regulatory flexibility heighten the need for good regulators. Regulators need to know which problems are real and which ones are shadows.

4 The False Spring of 1983

In August 1982, with inflation finally under control, the Fed eased its monetary policy and made more liquidity available to the American economy. As a result, interest rates tumbled, releasing pent-up consumer demand that had been depressed by years of stagflation and tight money. The stock market, predicting an economic boom, broke out of its five-year (some would say thirteen-year) doldrums and took off. Finally, Paul Volcker's monetary policy, combined with the Reagan tax cuts and the "benefits" of a recession, had been successful in stanching inflation and getting the economy moving.

The world again looked hospitable to S&L operations. S&L spreads that had been negative in 1982 turned positive in 1983, and the strong economy generated plentiful lending opportunities. The U.S. League wrote a paean to home ownership that began, "The sun shone brightly on home buyers in 1983. . . . Savings institutions emerged from the interest rate storms of the preceding years and the disruption of deregulation flush with cash and a renewed dedication to housing finance."[1]

Andrew Carron, who had written a pessimistic book called *The Plight of Savings Institutions* in 1982, wrote another book, *The Rescue of the Thrift Industry,* in which he said:

> This crisis was resolved by a potent combination of lower market interest rates, engineered by the Federal Reserve Board, and landmark legislation, for which many can share credit. Few realize how close the thrifts came to complete disarray; fewer still appreciate the difficulty of the challenges ahead. Substantial failures can be expected in the next few years, from both the lingering effects of

the 1980–82 crisis and the inability of some thrifts to adapt to the new, less regulated environment. . . .

The best reason for optimism about the future of the thrifts is the expansion of their asset and liability powers. The problems of the thrift institutions were severe but manageable.[2]

The results of S&L operations that the Bank Board reported for 1983 seemed to bear out this optimism. Whereas FSLIC-insured S&Ls lost in the aggregate over $6 billion in 1981 and slightly under that figure in 1982, in 1983 they made over $2.5 billion. At the same time, the S&Ls were growing at a rate of 18 percent in 1983 and the number of failures declined from 247 in 1982 to 70 in 1983, almost all early in the year.

Moreover, as a result of deregulation, S&Ls had the most attractive charters in the financial field. With deposit insurance they could attract virtually unlimited funds at below market rates; they had low capital requirements that permitted rapid growth; they had expansive asset investment powers that, at least in California and Texas, were advertised by experts as permitting investments in anything, including "cat houses" in Las Vegas. To top off these attributes, whereas the Bank Holding Company Act prevented business corporations from owning commercial banks, the Savings and Loan Holding Company Act permitted any kind of business entity to own an S&L. With all of these advantages, it seemed apparent that the industry would attract the new capital it needed and would flourish in a deregulated world. The major worry was whether S&Ls could restructure their assets to get better matched before interest rates went up again.

The policies and steadfastness of the Treasury and OMB appeared to be vindicated. Interest rate deregulation had cured the S&Ls' liquidity problems; and with declining interest rates and new asset powers, it was apparent that S&Ls would be profitable and healthy again. The alarmists who had contended that the industry required massive federal assistance of billions of dollars had been proven wrong. Moreover, the administration believed that, with deregulation now accomplished, the market could govern the thrift industry; the government could get off its back.

PRESIDENT REAGAN APPOINTS A NEW BANK BOARD

In this climate, President Reagan named Edwin J. Gray Chairman of the FHLBB on May 1, 1983, promptly after Dick Pratt's departure. Ed Gray was a peculiar choice to regulate the S&L industry. A speech writer and public relations man, he was by background unprepared to formulate or understand the complexities of federal banking regulation. He knew no law; he knew no accounting; he knew little economics. Even worse, those who knew him in the White House, where he had served as one of Ed Meese's assistants, variously describe him as a nincompoop, a fool, and a buffoon; but Ed Gray was a loyal Reaganite who could be counted on to carry out the policy of getting government off the backs of the people, and Dick Pratt told the White House that he thought Ed Gray could do the job well. The U.S. League, the California League, and the Texas League, the three most important S&L organizations, all supported Ed Gray for the job. At the White House they reasoned that he must know something about S&Ls because he had worked for Great American First S&L in San Diego, (yes, all three: "Great," "American," and "First") and the S&L business wasn't very hard anyway. So "good old Ed" got appointed to what turned out to be one of the hot seats in American government, and although he turned out not to be the nincompoop a lot of people thought he was, he proved tragically unable to put together the technical and political forces that would have been necessary to keep the problem within manageable proportions. Ed Gray was Chairman of the FHLBB for over four years, from May 1983 to June 1987, and although we should not impugn his motives or his dedication, we will have to say that an awful lot happened on his watch.

One would have thought that the Senate might have trouble confirming a man of Ed Gray's reputation and limited qualifications as chairman of a federal agency. However, it never had to consider Ed Gray as chairman because he first was appointed as a member of the FHLBB in February 1983 (after Dick Pratt had said he would be leaving soon) and was confirmed for that position. Once he had been confirmed as a member of the FHLBB, the President was free to appoint Gray as chairman without further Congressional review.

The other two members of the FHLBB for most of Ed Gray's four years were Don Hovde and Mary Grigsby. Hovde, a real estate man from Minnesota who most recently had been HUD Under Secretary, was appointed in May 1983 and confirmed in June. Mary Grigsby, the retired head of an S&L in Houston and a former chairman of the Texas League, was appointed in November 1983 and confirmed in February 1984. The administration thus had appointed three Board members from the industry they were supposed to regulate.

1983 THROUGH OTHER GLASSES

The aggregate figures for 1983 quoted above were the type given out by the U.S. League and the FHLBB. They are what the press printed. But the impression of relatively robust health for the S&L industry as a whole masked what was going on in the bottom half of the industry. Despite positive earnings for the industry as a whole, almost 50 percent of S&Ls lost money in 1983; and despite the declining interest rates, over 35 percent of institutions lost money in the second half of 1983, after the positive impact of declining rates should have been fully recognized. Moreover, even at many of the profitable firms, an analysis of the industry's positive earnings for the year shows that they did not result from normal operations. On the contrary, because the industry's spread for the year was barely 130 basis points—not enough to cover operating expenses—operating income would have been negative without income from gains taken on loans and securities that appreciated when interest rates came down.

More alarming, the decline in the number of failures resulted not so much from fewer problem institutions as from a change in policy whereby the FSLIC liquidated insolvent institutions only when it thought management was extremely weak or where they found significant fraud. At the end of 1982, 130 S&Ls (with $17 billion of assets) were insolvent even under liberal RAP accounting principles, and about half of them were liquidated or merged in the first third of 1983. But by the end of 1983 the number of RAP-insolvent institutions was back to about the end-of-1982 level. If we take out the RAP funny money and look at GAAP (which still includes a lot of funny money, many people would say) the number of insolvents at the end of 1982 would be a much higher 237 (with $68 billion of assets) increasing to 297 (with $84 billion of assets) by the end of 1983. Further demonstrating the industry's weakness and the FSLIC's peril at the end of 1983, 900 institutions with $263 billion of assets (almost one-third of the industry) had under 3 percent GAAP net worth. Shockingly, if goodwill generated by mergers (which counted as net worth under both GAAP and RAP) was removed from the aggregate industry balance sheet, the industry as a whole would have had almost no net worth (0.4 percent of assets) at the end of 1983.

Even the strong deposit growth figures for 1983 have an alarming underside: Over 20 percent of the S&Ls in the country grew at a rate of over 25 percent in 1983. Dozens of the S&Ls that later failed grew over 100 percent in 1983. Regulatory experience has shown that banks or S&Ls that grow at rates of 25 percent per year or higher almost always encounter significant problems with the assets they acquire because they lack the infrastructure necessary to select or generate sound assets on such a steep growth curve. Moreover, it should have been clear that only high-risk assets could provide a spread against the new deposits, because in 1983 the S&Ls were growing fast by paying over 75 basis points more than the commercial banks for CDs. They were attracting hot money. How were they going to earn the extra yield that they needed in order to pay the high rates to depositors and still make a profit? The obvious answer is that they would have to take extra risks. And a few centuries of banking experience show that when bankers take extra risks, they usually end up in trouble.

But if you had been the manager of an S&L with low net worth in 1983, what would you have done? Wouldn't you have "gambled for salvation"? Wouldn't you have tried to "grow your way out of the problem"—that is, add new assets at good spreads to overcome the burden of the old low-yielding assets? Wouldn't you have grown as much as you could within the existing net worth restrictions? If you didn't overcome your old low-yielding portfolio, chances are that sooner or later you would be merged out of existence. If you could have valued prudence and caution more highly than your job, you are an unusual person—and would have been even more unusual in the go-go, everything-goes-up climate of the greatest bull market and real estate boom in history.

Moreover, growing with variable-rate assets was what everyone was telling S&L managements to do. Interest rates won't stay down forever, regulators and economists kept saying; lengthen your liabilities and generate variable-rate assets in order to cure the historical interest rate mismatch. Therefore many S&Ls revamped their strategies to make bigger spreads, to better match the interest rate sensitivities of the new assets and new liabilities, and to grow so much that the old problem assets would become a small part of the balance sheet.

Beverly Hills Savings & Loan, one of the first big bad-asset-generated S&L failures, revamped its strategy to accomplish these goals and failed very quickly. "We could not survive if we continued to do business in the traditional fashion," testified Dennis Fitzpatrick, a long-time S&L manager who had been Chairman of Beverly Hills.[3] He outlined five components of a survival and profitability plan adopted in late 1982:

1. To raise funds wholesale

2. To become a full-service real estate financial concern, which included having 10 percent of assets in construction loans, originating permanent commercial property loans, investing 7 percent in real estate joint ventures, and buying real estate for syndication

3. To match maturities

4. To grow in order to reduce the significance of the existing low rate portfolio and thereby facilitate matching

5. To earn higher fees to offset the expected lower spreads on matched fundings.

Although Beverly Hills failed at great taxpayer cost after adopting this policy, it was not a farfetched or irresponsible policy to adopt in late 1982. Most industry consultants at the time would have said that it was a sound strategy— maybe not the only sound strategy, but one that could work. The regulators were nagging at the S&Ls to get more matched. The regulators also were saying that S&Ls should stick to real estate because that was what they knew best. Dick Pratt had said it; Ed Gray said it; even the academic experts said that, while they would have a hard time competing with banks for commercial loans, S&Ls had a comparative advantage in real estate lending—and they didn't distinguish between different types of real estate lending.[4] The problem at Beverly Hills, as at many other S&Ls, was that the assets they invested in didn't pan out, and their controls were so lax that they became prey to kickbacks and fraud artists.

Policies like the one that Beverly Hills adopted created a historic increase in construction lending by S&Ls. Texas S&Ls, for example, which had made $1.8 billion in construction loans (90 percent for residential construction) in the good but preboom year of 1978, made $10.3 billion in construction loans in 1983 (and $16.4 billion in 1984). Well over half of this new lending was for commercial construction and another big chunk was for condominium development, which, although it was residential, turned out to be just as risky as commercial development. But at the time, increased construction lending looked good for the S&Ls. Real estate was supposed to be their business.

THE BOTTOM LINE ON 1983

In 1983 the S&L industry lost about $4 billion from operations but showed a profit of $2.5 billion based on about $2.5 billion of gains from sales of appreciated assets and income of about $4 billion from loan fees. Without liberal purchase accounting, operations would have shown a loss of about $5 billion rather than $4 billion. In addition, the S&Ls made about $25 billion in construction and land loans, much of it of questionable value. On the surface, 1983 looked good for the S&Ls, but if you probe the numbers and look at the loans they made, it was a disaster.

5 Real Estate Lending 101

S&L managements and their regulators failed to fully appreciate the enormous gulf between S&Ls' real estate experience in the single-family-home business and the experience necessary to participate in other parts of the real estate business. Construction loans on condominiums, office buildings, shopping centers, and hotels require entirely different expertise from single-family lending or even from lending on occupied office buildings, shopping centers, or apartments. Here's a look into the world of real estate lending.

TYPES OF LENDING

Single-Family-Home Lending

Underwriting loans to people to buy their own homes is simple. All the lender has to do is (1) check the applicant's credit with a credit agency such as TRW (which maintains a file on just about everybody's prior defaults, bankruptcies, etc.), (2) check the applicant's earnings, (3) make sure that a percentage of the earnings (typically 25 percent to 33 percent) will cover the interest and principal on the loan, and (4) get an appraisal of the property. The appraiser will compare the house with similar recently sold homes in the area and will determine a value based on those comparisons. The lender will make the loan only up to a specified percentage of appraised value (LTV), typically 75 percent to 80 percent; above that guideline it may make the loan but will buy mortgage insurance from an insurance company that specializes in that field. Variable-rate loans add some complications, but the process remains essentially the same.

Servicing the single-family mortgage loan is a mechanical task of making sure that the payments are made every month. If a loan gets into arrears, foreclosure actions are fairly routine in most states.

Single-Family Construction Loans

Making loans for the purpose of *constructing* single-family homes is a bit more complicated. Most homes are built by tract developers who buy a large parcel of raw land, obtain subdivision approvals, put in roads, water mains, and sewers, then build homes they hope to sell to individuals. The developer's goal is to spend as little of his own money as possible, and therefore he seeks to borrow the whole cost from the bank. The developer's dream is to borrow 110 percent of cost and live off the 10 percent while building the project. Gone is the stable homeowner whose salary will pay the mortgage; gone is the simple appraisal based on comparables—here the homes haven't even been built yet. We are dealing with projected costs and a projected market. Can the houses be built for the projected amount? Can they be sold for the projected amount? Is there a demand, as some market study says there is?

The lender can't rely on the appraiser alone to answer these questions. Since the appraiser will have to guess about the relevant factors, just as the S&L's lending officer will have to guess about them, the appraisal is no better than a second opinion that has no better chance of being right than the first one. A construction lender who relies on appraisals rather than his or her own experience and analysis is an amateur asking for trouble.

If the lender finances the land before governmental approvals, the lender is taking additional risks: governmental risks, environmental risks, longer-term cost and market risks. Before the 1980s, almost no one would lend more than 50 percent against the value of land. The S&L standard used to be one-third; but in the 1980s, somehow 75 percent and 80 percent seemed okay. S&Ls lost billions of dollars by lending on raw land. Many S&Ls in Texas, Colorado, and Arizona lent a third of their assets or more on raw land, much of it at 100 percent LTV. With raw land, there's no cash flow to pay the interest or the taxes. If the market goes south, as it did in those states, the lender ends up owning the land and the land has very little value. Land loans accounted for a significant part of the losses in over half of the costliest S&L failures.

Administration of construction loans must be assiduous. Construction draws are based on estimated percentages of completion, which often are a source of disagreement between the bank and the builder. The builder claims to be 50 percent complete; the bank says "no, you're only 40 percent complete." If 40 percent of the money has already been advanced, the developer doesn't get more money. If the lender isn't careful, the borrower really can have a 110 percent loan; and if the borrower defaults, the lender won't have enough money left in the budget to finish the job. Moreover, because the borrower may operate through a corporation or partnership, there is an intervening entity to put into bankruptcy to make foreclosure difficult in the event of default. Foreclosing on an unfinished project is no fun—and it almost always ends in a loss for the bank.

Because of these significant uncertainties, not all S&Ls have engaged in single-family construction lending. Some have made it a specialty, however, because the pricing is better than for "end loans." Construction loans usually yield 100 to 200 basis points over prime, as well as an up-front fee. But to be successful in this field, the lender must become as expert as the developer at estimating costs; the lender also must know the local markets well and be able to estimate what types of homes will sell well and how long it will take to sell them. When construction loan interest is running, time really *is* money.

Most S&Ls that have really become expert in the single-family-home construction business have made money at it—at least in good times. Those who have dabbled in it usually have lost money.

Occupied Apartment and Commercial Property Lending

Making loans on occupied apartment buildings or occupied commercial properties is again an entirely different business. Historically, it has been less risky than single-family construction lending but more complex, and S&Ls that have made a specialty of this "income producing property" lending usually did well from a safety perspective, until the Texas real estate crash of the mid-1980s and the crunch in the northeast five years later, when even conservative income property lenders lost money. Except in these extreme markets, S&Ls' main problem in income property lending was that they had to compete with insurance companies that could offer borrowers long terms at relatively low fixed rates.

The key to lending on occupied commercial structures is the cash flow that comes from rent paid by tenants. The lender wants to make sure that this cash flow is sufficient to cover the payments on the mortgage as well as taxes, insurance, and operating expenses. In addition, because income property loans usually are not completely self-amortizing—that is, the payments of principal during the term of the loan are not sufficient to pay it off—the lender wants to make sure that at the end of the loan term there will be enough cash flow to refinance the remaining principal even if interest rates are somewhat higher.

The underwriting process begins by finding out how much rent is being paid and how much it costs to run the building. By subtracting the cost from the rent, the underwriter can figure out how much net operating income (NOI) the property generates. Of course the property may generate a given level of NOI today but not tomorrow; tenants may move out or they may be unable to pay; or rents in the area may decrease or expenses may increase. The underwriter therefore will evaluate factors such as market rental rates and trends in the area, lease terms compared with the loan term, credit quality of tenants, and environmental and structural factors affecting the building. If the results of these investigations are satisfactory, the lender usually will apply a standard of "debt service coverage," that is, the ratio of the amount of fairly certain NOI (as determined after investigation) to the payments called for under the loan. Conservative lenders may require a debt service coverage ratio of 1.25 to 1; more aggressive lenders may use debt service coverage guidelines as low as 1.10 to 1.

Income property lenders also require appraisals, but sophisticated lenders will use the appraisal only as a check on their underwriting. They will not make the loan just because the appraisal is adequate, but if the appraisal comes in significantly lower than the in-house underwriting would suggest, they will question their own process and either will not make the loan or will reduce its size. Almost every real estate lending organization has loan-to-appraised-value (LTV) guidelines,* and the loan should not be made if those guidelines are exceeded.

Less sophisticated lenders tend to rely almost entirely on the appraiser's view of value and on the LTV test in deciding whether to make a loan. These lenders fall prey to optimistic or co-opted appraisers.

Appraisers were not regulated and, although their professional associations administer tests and provide "designations" that indicate competence, the old saw has it that the highest designation, MAI, stands for "made as instructed."

Startlingly, income property lenders typically make loans without recourse, which means that the owner of the property is not obligated to pay the debt if the cash flow from the property is insufficient to pay. The owner thus limits potential loss to the amount invested in the property but retains the full benefits of any appreciation of the property. Some form of guarantee is usual only if there is an NOI shortfall at the time the loan is made.

Administering income property loans usually is not extremely complex, but it is very different from administering single-family loans. Income property loans can lose value quickly if, due to inadequate rents or high vacancy levels, owners allow properties to fall into disrepair. The owner may be able to milk the property for immediate cash flow while the building deteriorates, leaving the lender with an expensive repair bill at the end of the loan term. Monitor-

ing of rent rolls and expenses and periodic inspections—and occasional remedial actions—therefore are required.

In addition, because of the bankruptcy laws, it often is impossible to gain
control of a building through the foreclosure process in less than two years,
during which time the property almost always will deteriorate further. Our
bankruptcy law, as revised in 1979, is friendly to the bankrupt. It makes even
secured creditors wait for their money and puts the burden of proof on them
to show that they need protection. These aspects of the bankruptcy law inflate lenders' real estate losses because the losses continue to build up during
the proceeding.

Big-Time Construction Lending

Construction lending on income-producing properties presents all of the
analytical difficulties and practical contingencies of lending on occupied buildings plus the added complexities and risks of the construction process and the
vagaries of the leasing market at a future date that may be years after the loan
is committed. Neither key ingredient—the building or the income—exists
when the lender gives its legally binding commitment to make the loan. This
is not a business for the lazy, the inexperienced, or the unlucky. But many
S&Ls went into it with inadequate preparation.

A construction loan begins with a "piece of dirt," a set of plans, and projected income. All of the approvals necessary to build the building, provide
access to it, parking for it, sewers, water, electricity, and so on may not yet
have been granted by the many municipal departments that need to approve
the project. The architect may not have finished the plans. There may be no
contractor selected; usually there is no fixed-price contract to build and no
insurance bond to protect the bank and the developer if the contractor or a
subcontractor goes bankrupt or simply walks off the job. The developer asserts to the bank that the unbuilt space can be leased at a specified price per
square foot, but it may be that no leases have been signed. At this early stage,
it often is the case that the building will be built if—and only if—the developer
can find a bank that will say "yes" and put up almost all the money for construction. Indeed, at this stage the developer may not even own the land but
may have an option to buy the land. The option will be exercised only if a
bank says "yes." Many S&Ls said "yes" and later learned about the pitfalls.

Banks engage in big-time construction lending because the loans bear relatively high rates of interest. Whereas a loan to, say, General Motors might be
at a rate below the prime rate, construction loans typically cost prime plus 1½
percent and carry a substantial (again, typically 1½ percent but in riskier cases
2 percent, 3 percent, or even 6 percent) up-front commitment fee. For the
thrift institutions that went into construction lending in the mid-1980s, this

pricing was irresistible, not only because they were able to recognize the up-front fees as income and earn a good rate but also because loans tied to the prime rate adjust as market interest rates change, and therefore provide protection against the mismatch between assets and liabilities that had caused the thrifts' problems in the first place.

Of course, most lenders won't make construction loans with just the borrower's assurances about costs, approvals, and markets. They not only will investigate those matters for themselves, but they also will structure the loans so that they do not fund anything until approvals have been obtained, acceptable contractors have been hired (often at a fixed cost for the entire job and sometimes bonded), and some level of preleasing or guarantee of debt service coverage during a lease-up period or a committed takeout* by a permanent lender has been arranged. These all are hotly negotiated issues between the lender and the borrower—and as the lender gets more security, the amount that the borrower will be willing to pay decreases. Unfortunately, many S&L managements that were inexperienced in construction lending couldn't resist the high fees and high rates, and therefore didn't work hard to get more security. If they had, a lot of loans wouldn't have been made and a lot of surplus buildings wouldn't have been built.

Construction loan administration needs to be far more intensive than permanent financing administration. Whereas in a permanent loan the money is advanced on day one and then paid off over time, in a construction loan the money is advanced in stages as the construction goes along, and the lender expects to be paid back in a lump sum when another lender makes a permanent loan on the property. Intensive administration is required at every "draw" of funds under the loan, including an engineering report, so that the lender can satisfy itself that after advancing the money, there will be enough left in the loan budget to finish the project. If the projected cost to complete is higher than the amount in the budget, then the loan is said to be "out of balance" and the lender is not obligated to fund.

In practice, however, a lender may not have any choice but to continue funding an out-of-balance loan because (1) an unfinished building has little value, (2) the borrower won't (or can't) put in the money necessary to bring the loan back into balance, (3) the bankruptcy laws make it almost impossible for a bank to take over an ongoing construction project without suffering significant losses, and (4) market factors such as preleasing, which are the lender's ultimate way out, may be such that the delay involved in foreclosure will result in greater loss than providing the excess funding. This pattern is especially usual when the borrower has little equity in the project.

Despite these complexities—perhaps because S&L managements didn't understand them—many S&Ls went into big-time construction lending in 1982, 1983, and 1984.

Hotel Lending

Many S&Ls made loans on hotels (construction and permanent) based upon LTVs, as if hotels were merely real estate projects. Of course, in a sense they are; hotels are buildings that sit on land. But hotels don't get rented up and stay stable. They are businesses that have to be managed intensively; they have to be rerented every night; they have to serve food and liquor. The real estate deteriorates *very* fast if it is not kept up. And the public is fickle; a hotel that's a hit today can be a flop tomorrow. Too many institutions (many of them S&Ls) financed hotels in the mid-1980s, so now we have a hotel room glut.

Condominium Lending

Condominium construction lending was especially insidious for S&Ls because it looked so much like single-family-home construction lending—the only difference was that the homes were stacked instead of each being on its own piece of ground. But the dynamics of the condo market were completely different. You couldn't build one or two homes on spec and wait for them to be sold before going further. You had to build a whole section of maybe twenty or forty units. And often you couldn't sell those unless you showed that you were going to complete the project, because the area would be unsightly until completion. So before you knew it, there was a supply of hundreds—or even thousands—of unsold condos in an area. The estimated selling price may originally have been enough to take the lender out and have a profit for the developer. But with a big supply the price plummeted. Rather than reducing the prices and taking a loss, the S&L and developer would leave the prices up, the units would sit empty, and the interest reserve would continue to make the loan look like a good performing loan. "We're just having a little absorption problem," they'd say when the examiners came around.

LOAN PARTICIPATIONS

Big-time construction lending requires not only customers for the loans but also participants—other lenders—who will take part of the loan. Even though S&Ls' loan-to-one-borrower regulations on real estate loans were not very stringent, few S&Ls could, on their own, make a $50 million or $100 million loan. They needed networks through which they could sell pieces of the large loans.

Commercial banks have had participation networks for many years, usually growing out of "correspondent banking" relationships. Lacking these networks, the fast-growing S&L lenders put together new groupings of similarly situated S&Ls that needed up-front fees and high income and that, by reason of their low capital, were in a risk-taking mood or that, by reason of their abysmal ignorance, didn't understand the risks they were taking. These S&Ls bought construction loan participations after very little investigation. They were used to lending at a specific LTV based on an outside appraisal. They would review the appraisal and some projections, then sign on. Without these participants, the process wouldn't have worked.

In particular, S&Ls in midwestern states that didn't have booming economies in the early 1980s fell prey to the sharp Texas lenders. Dozens of midwestern S&Ls failed at least in part because of buying participations from Vernon, Sunbelt, and a few others.

How could the participating S&Ls have been so misinformed? Where was their prudence? Weren't they bankers? Well, no, they weren't bankers—or hadn't been bankers—they had been "association managers" who played the game prescribed by the Bank Board, which was not a bad thing to be, but it wasn't the same as being a banker. (And by 1983 even many of the bankers seem to have lost their prudence.) Besides, for those who had been listening, the regulators had been saying that an S&L could buy commercial loan participations without actually having a department devoted to the field.[1] We shouldn't lay the blame on the regulators—they didn't make the loans—but their speeches do show how little the field was understood, not only among S&Ls but also in their regulatory agency. Probably no one in any authority at the FHLBB had ever actually *made* a construction loan.

HOW CONSTRUCTION LENDING INCREASED THE COST OF LIQUIDATING THRIFTS AND NOBODY KNEW IT

Although the majority of bad construction loans were committed by S&Ls in 1982, 1983, and 1984, the outside auditors and examiners from the Bank Board usually didn't learn that the loans couldn't be repaid until 1985, 1986, or 1987. To some extent these delays in discovery were caused by concealment, overoptimism, and an antiquated examination system; but even before those factors delayed discovery, the normal construction lending process made it hard to say that a loan had gone bad for several years.

The normal construction lending process begins with an agreement in principle between the lender and the borrower, after which, over a period of one to three months, the lender and the borrower hammer out the details of the construction project and the various terms and conditions of the mortgage loan; then the lender issues the commitment. (Some of the Texas high flyers probably committed to make loans over lunch or dinner, but that's not how it's supposed to be done.) More paperwork, and usually physical work, to satisfy commitment conditions must be done before a closing takes place and the first draw is made. Construction of the building may take twelve to twenty-four months, if it proceeds on schedule. But typically, the loan does not come due even when construction is completed, because the building may not be rented when construction is complete. The lender and borrower anticipate that another lender may not be willing to provide the funds to take out the construction lender until there is sufficient cash flow from the property to support the loan. The construction loan therefore often provides for a "mini-perm" or "lease-up" period of eighteen to thirty-six months for the property to become fully leased or "stabilized."

All this time, of course, from the beginning of construction through the lease-up period, the property is not generating cash flow. But the interest on the loan has to be paid every month. This is typically provided for in the loan commitment by creating an "interest reserve" from which interest is paid monthly—*by the bank to itself*—and added to the loan balance. Therefore, as long as construction is proceeding approximately as planned, the loan cannot go into default until the end of the mini-perm period, which will be two to five years after the date the bank or S&L originally decided to make the loan. (Many commentators on the S&L mess have spoken as if S&Ls invented the interest reserve to fool the regulators. Whatever its merits, banks, not S&Ls, invented the interest reserve to take account of what they perceived as reality, not to fool anyone.)

Because of this process, S&Ls that committed to make loans in 1983 often looked good through 1984 and 1985, even though there never was a market for the buildings they financed. Of course when the interest reserve ran out, the loan went into default because the building couldn't support the debt without tenants. However, until the reserve ran out, FSLIC examiners, independent auditors, and boards of directors failed to see that losses had occurred. Thus literally billions of dollars—perhaps $20–30 billion—of losses that were reported by S&Ls in 1986, 1987, and 1988 were really generated in 1982, 1983, 1984, and 1985 when the loans were committed.

At the weak S&Ls this delaying process was particularly pernicious. Remember, on a market value basis over 90 percent of S&Ls were insolvent in 1982. They had no capital; no owner had anything left at risk. Thirty-five percent of S&Ls were still losing money at the end of 1983, and a substantial proportion of these had no hope of ever making money if they stuck to their traditional businesses.

Construction lending seemed like a salvation to them. There was a building boom fueled by a bull market, and favorable tax provisions for real estate ownership enacted in 1981 had made equity money available. The lending

S&L could charge 2 percent to 3 percent up front (in extreme cases as high as 6 percent) and could take that into income at the time of commitment (or at the time of the first draw), even before any construction had begun and even though the S&L often paid itself the fee by adding it to the loan balance (another practice that S&Ls did not invent). The S&L then could earn a high interest rate, which it also would pay itself, and management would receive congratulations and big bonuses for having generated earnings and floating-rate assets. The S&L also could continue to grow without violating the capital rules because the apparent earnings created enough net worth to satisfy the capital rules. Construction and land loans made by S&Ls increased from $29 billion outstanding in 1982 to $102 billion outstanding on June 30, 1985. A large part of that $102 billion wasn't repaid because after the buildings were completed nobody rented them and the land that was supposed to support a continuing southwestern expansion became practically worthless when the economic contraction put development off into the distant future.

WINDOW DRESSING APPRAISALS

This system of paper profit creation was supported by appraisals that made the loans possible. S&Ls were used to making loans on the basis of LTVs. Their residential lending standards were based on LTVs; construction lending didn't look very different if all you focused on was LTV. Even S&L examiners from the FHLBB cared only about LTV—did it comply with the regulations? Senior management and directors were happy to make these profitable loans if they were told that the LTV was 75 percent or 80 percent. In Texas they were happy to lend 100 percent of appraised value.

The first problem with construction lending based on LTVs is that the appraiser is guessing. The appraiser is going through a part of the process that the underwriter should go through. The key to the appraisal will be the rent that the appraiser projects can be earned from the property. It will be a projection about a building that does not exist and about a market that also may not yet exist. The market that counts will exist only when the building is completed—in about two years. Since markets are not stable, the appraiser will try to project what the market will be. As part of the process, he or she will look at the optimistic market studies and projections prepared by the developer, which may be quite persuasive.

Once the appraiser has determined the market rent and has arrived at a conclusion that the building can be rented, the rest is fairly automatic: Multiply the rent times the number of square feet, subtract projected expenses, and divide by a "capitalization rate" to determine value. There are ways to try to check that value against costs of other buildings or sale prices of other buildings, but basically the "income approach" to appraisal tells the story. No other building ever seems quite comparable or has been sold recently enough.

Obviously, the problem with the resulting appraisal is that it is only as good as the appraiser's guess about the market, which is at least influenced by the developer's carefully prepared brief on why the market will be wonderful. Often the problem is worse because the appraiser knows what value is needed in order to sustain the loan; the real estate community is pretty tight-knit, and even if an appraiser is not dishonest, it is tempting to shade an appraisal in the direction of getting the deal done, because business breeds business.

A dollar or two of rent per square foot swings the value tremendously. For example, if you project that a 500,000-square-foot building will rent for $20 per square foot and will cost $5 per square foot to operate, and if you assume a 10 percent capitalization rate (that is, you assume that owners buy real estate for ten times annual cash flow), you can compute the value as follows:

$$\$20 - 5 = \$15 \times 500,000 \times 10 = \$75 \text{ million.}$$

If we reduced the key variable—rent per square foot—by $2, the value of the building would decline to

$$\$18 - 5 = \$13 \times 500,000 \times 10 = \$65 \text{ million.}$$

Since no one can know with precision what a building will rent for two years hence, our hypothetical situation does not involve atypical swings. Yet a $70 million loan on the building would be under water if the $18 rent figure is correct, would have a very tight 93 percent LTV if a $20 rent figure is correct, and would have a somewhat more comfortable 82 percent LTV if a somewhat more optimistic $22 rent were correct. You can bet that the developer's study will say the rent will be $22.

Many S&L boards of directors didn't understand how subjective the appraisal process is. They didn't understand the market risks; and they didn't want to inquire too closely, because making construction loans and taking in fees was the way they hoped to make money. Most S&L directors, after all, were local doctors, insurance agents, and small businessmen who ran hardware stores or sold farm equipment or cars; or they were local lawyers who represented local people and businesses. To all of them, an appraiser was a professional who said what the value was. The appraiser gave them a turnkey test. They didn't have to know how the appraisal was made any more than they had to know how an engine worked in order to be able to drive a car.

The Texans carried appraisal lending to extremes. We've talked about lending up to 80 percent of appraised value, but the Texas statute said that S&Ls

could lend up to 100 percent of appraised value or the purchase price, which-ever was lower, and Texas S&Ls regularly went to the limit. When the FHLBB eliminated LTV tests in May 1983, the Texas S&Ls stopped paying attention to purchase price because Texas had a "parity" statute that permitted them to use federal rules if they were more lenient. Loans at 100 percent of appraised value became routine. In addition, several Texas borrowers and S&Ls began constructing "land flips" and similar devices to provide inflated "comparables" in order to get higher appraisals. The bigger the appraisal, the bigger the loan. The bigger the loan, the bigger the loan fee. The developers loved it; they not only got 100 percent financing; they got "walking around money," too.

What did the Texas S&L managers think they were doing? Didn't they know that when the loans came due, they wouldn't be repaid and the bad loans would kill the S&Ls? No one admits to that knowledge. Fraud, greed, and Texas-sized optimism seem to be the answers.

ENTERTAINMENT, SPORTS, AND SEX

Few S&Ls made any great changes in personnel to prepare for the new, more complex lending. Officers with no prior construction loan experience were expected to enlarge their capabilities overnight to handle the more com-plex loans. So-called experts were hired away from commercial banks, but they usually turned out to be people the commercial banks wanted to get rid of. (Did that matter? The commercial banks were making aggressive construc-tion loans, too.) Sometimes even worse, people with construction experience on the developer side were brought in. They understood construction but had none of the cautious instincts necessary to be successful construction *lenders*. They automatically believed the developer's hype.

Moreover, most of the S&Ls that embarked on construction lending pro-grams lacked relationships with established builders. The S&Ls hadn't done any business in the field and needed a type of customer they didn't have. Enter the loan brokers.

Not all loan brokers are sinister or unscrupulous people. However, their job is by its nature a high-pressure sales job with millions of dollars of loans and potential profits for developers at stake and hundreds of thousands of dollars in fees for themselves on the line. The developer is their client; the bank is their target. Not surprisingly, loan brokers entertain lavishly; bank loan offi-cers become their best friends. At the least, bank officers are treated to lunches, dinners, and golf outings at the finest clubs. (All loan brokers belong to golf clubs rated in the top 100 and most belong to a club that every golfer has heard of and wants to play.) In many cases, loan brokers arranged shooting parties at private hunting lodges or preserves, junkets to Las Vegas, and prostitutes for the loan officers whether they said they wanted them or not.

Loan officers usually react with gratitude to this treatment. They form close personal bonds—relationships of trust—with the loan brokers. A man who earns maybe $50,000 a year—a loan officer, for instance—usually enjoys it when someone spends a few thousand on him for a single weekend.

Many of the loan participations were sold through brokers. But whether they were sold through brokers or directly by lenders, the bonding process was the same. Entertainment, sports, and sex easily cloud the eyes of middle management male executives (and this was an almost exclusively male world) who are tired of dealing with normal domestic problems. A respite of a few hours or a few days when they can feel like millionaires does wonders for the executives' views of their hosts' judgment.

Ironically, it is just a footnote that Congress passed in 1984 (and repealed in 1986) a law that made it a crime to give a thing of value to an employee of a federally insured bank or S&L in order to gain a business advantage. Under this law, a bribe could be anything of value, so in theory the golf games, dinners, and shooting parties could have sent both giver and recipient to jail.

Prosecutors know that a jury won't convict someone for having eaten lunch or played a round of golf. And there was a way to legitimize entertainment by sharing expenses. But the U.S. League thought the theory was outrageous; its efforts got the law repealed.

Where does relationship building leave off and bribery begin? We don't have a good answer, but we should know that the transition takes place earlier and more often than most people in business would admit. A well-run company has a code of ethics to guide its employees; but few of the S&Ls had codes of ethics. They let their employees take the chicken-feed gifts and made the big loans.

6   Permissive Loan Fee Accounting – The Linchpin

Permissive accounting for construction loans was the linchpin of the boom-and-bust process. Among the fastest growers, loan fees accounted for substantially all net income in the crucial years 1983 and 1984.

By 1983, S&L managers had access to an almost unlimited supply of funds because, after interest rate deregulation, they could pay whatever it took to bring the money in. With the federal insurance guarantee, depositors didn't worry about the safety of putting their money in S&Ls with no capital, so attracting funds was just a question of willingness to pay a high rate. The S&Ls could grow out of their interest rate mismatch problems by making large amounts of variable rate loans.

Under regulatory accounting rules, construction loans provided a quick fix in the form of big up-front fees that S&Ls could immediately take into income just for *making* the loan. Consequently, construction lending provided the best use of the new funds for S&Ls that needed quick income either to shore up their depleted net worth or to sustain rapid growth. Up-front fees were the drug – the crack, the heroin – on which S&Ls binged in the mid–1980s. The bigger the up-front fee, the better the loan; and, perversely but quite naturally, developers of projects would agree to pay higher up-front fees if they didn't actually have to put up any of their own money. Thus, there were clear incentives for S&Ls to pay 100 percent of the cost of building a project in exchange for a promise of large up-front fees, a good rate of interest, and, often, a "kicker" arrangement that gave the S&L a percentage of the profits from the venture. (Remember, paying 100 percent of cost – even including paying itself the fees and interest out of the loan proceeds – would not necessarily result in a 100 percent LTV because the appraiser would base the appraisal on projected rents or sales prices rather than costs; thus the typical LTV on a 100-

percent-of-cost loan was 80 percent.) If the project was profitable, the S&L made out very well and so did the developer. If there were losses, the S&L took the losses and the building; the developer walked away with no further obligation.

Obviously, an S&L shouldn't be able to record income just for making a speculative loan and paying itself fees by lending more, regardless of how the fees are packaged. Nevertheless, fine-line decisions on three accounting aspects of these transactions permitted this immediate up-front recognition of fees, thereby permitting managements to inflate S&L earnings, which in turn encouraged them to take excessive risks. The rules on these points were changed in 1985, 1986, and 1987—after a lot of horses had left a lot of barns.

Under the accounting rules, in order to call the fees current income (1) the transaction had to be deemed a "loan" rather than an "investment in real estate" by the S&L; and (2) the fees had to be deemed immediately recognizable as income rather than being deferred and taken into income as an adjustment to the yield* on the loan over its term. In addition, (3) in order for the immediate income not to be offset by loan loss reserves based on the riskiness of the loan, those reserves had to be smaller than the fees.

THE "LOAN" OR "INVESTMENT" QUESTION

The accounting distinction between a loan and an investment in real estate was well recognized in the early 1980s. In a "loan" transaction, interest paid could be taken as income at the rate agreed upon between the lender and the borrower, and fees could be recognized as income in accordance with special rules applicable to loan fees.[1]

"Real estate investments" were treated differently from loans in that, regardless of whether there was a stated rate of interest to be paid on the investment made, the investor could record as income no more than its cost of funds, and therefore could derive no profit from the deal until the investment was sold or was earning money from unrelated sources. (Indeed, even the ability to record income at the cost of funds rate was controversial.) Any fees paid to the S&L for making a real estate investment also could not be taken into income until sale or the establishment of independent income status.

The line between an "investment" and a "loan" had not, however, been very clearly drawn in the accounting literature. This lack of clarity was compounded by the fact that most of the accountants who audited S&Ls were not familiar with the kinds of complex transactions that led to questions of "loan" or "investment" treatment. They tended to be quite lenient when they considered the question. As a result, in audited financial statements for 1982 (prepared and released in 1983), it is clear that a great many transactions made by

S&Ls which should have been accounted for as investments in real estate, and therefore should *not* have resulted in any income, were treated as loans and *did* result in immediate income.

Leaders of the accounting profession quickly recognized that there was a problem and that the line between loans and real estate investments had to be made clearer. To do so, the American Institute of Certified Public Accountants (AICPA) published a "guidance for practitioners" in the November 1983 issue of *Journal of Accountancy.* This guidance was, however, significantly less than direct. It discussed a new category of loans called "acquisition, development and construction (ADC) loans" and said that *"in some instances* accounting for such arrangements as loans *may* not be *appropriate"* (italics added). It then went on to discuss a laundry list of factors that an accountant should consider in deciding whether a loan was an ADC loan, and therefore should be treated as an investment rather than a loan. Even for accountants, the language was unduly subtle and diffuse, undoubtedly the product of a series of compromises made in committee and therefore lacking force or clarity.

This November 1983 guidance had little impact on the way S&Ls prepared their financial statements for 1983 or the way in which accounting firms audited those statements. Not only was the guidance mealymouthed; it also wasn't clearly authoritative.

Generally accepted accounting principles (GAAP) are in constant evolution. They are not written down in a single place or established by a single body. Statements by the Financial Accounting Standards Board (FASB)* are authoritative, as are certain kinds of statements put out by the AICPA. But the authoritative AICPA *Audit and Accounting Guide for Savings and Loan Associations* didn't even mention ADC loans. The status of commentary such as the November 1983 guidance was, in the view of many accountants and the Bank Board, unclear. Thus, even if an accountant read and understood the guidance, it wasn't clear that he or she had to follow it.

With all this uncertainty, when, in early 1984, an S&L management prepared its 1983 financial statements treating loans as plain old "loans" even though a suspicious accountant might have deemed them to be "ADC loans," most accounting firms went along with their clients' treatment. This complaisance was facilitated by the lack of clarity and the uncertain status of the guidance; but it also reflected the natural tension between an accounting firm's desire to satisfy its client—the S&L—and its responsibility to the public to make sure that the financial statements are fairly presented.

Theory says that the client prepares the financial statements and the accounting firm reports on them and, after performing audit tests, says whether they are prepared in accordance with GAAP. Thus, as a matter of formality—

and usually as a matter of practice—the client will first present its idea of proper accounting treatment and, if the accounting firm wants to change the presentation, it will have to say that the proposed treatment is not permitted by GAAP. Indeed, to get a client to make a major change, such as accounting for a major group of loans as investments, the accounting firm may well have to risk losing the client. Naturally, when the accountant can find a basis for not jeopardizing the client relationship, the accountant usually will go along with the client's position. In the context of this kind of accountant–client relationship, the November 1983 guidance didn't give accountants much backbone. As a result, few loans were classified as ADC loans in S&Ls' 1983 financial statements, and the incentives to make "full loans"—a euphemism for 100 percent financings—in order to earn big fees continued.

Leaders of the accounting profession again recognized that ADC loans were a problem after they reviewed the 1983 financial statements, so they took the subject to a committee of the FASB, the profession's most authoritative rule-making body. After two meetings on the subject, that committee decided in July 1984 that the November 1983 guidance was adequate, "though some variations in application of the guidance were noted." The AICPA followed up on this conclusion by publishing a second "guidance" that basically repeated what the November 1983 guidance had said.

The accounting staff of the Bank Board, alarmed by this professional complacency, got the Board to propose a formal policy on the subject of ADC loans in October 1984. But the proposed policy, like the November 1983 guidance, was somewhat confusing; after discussing the problem, the Board's statement said that the Board expected transactions to be accounted for in accordance with GAAP, which left its commentary confusing because it eventually referred back to the two confusing AICPA statements. The Bank Board adopted this policy in April 1985 and made it retroactive to November 1983, but by then the 1984 financial statements were out, so retroactivity appeared to be punitive rather than clarifying.

Again in 1985 leading accountants (most notably senior partners at Peat, Marwick) saw problems in the 1984 treatment of ADC loans. They went back to the FASB and practically pleaded for "more definitive" and "authoritative" guidance. Finally, in March 1985 the FASB agreed that more guidance was needed and assembled a group of accountants to deal with the issue. This led, after almost another year of discussion, to the publication of another notice to practitioners from the AICPA in February 1986. That notice *did* clarify matters considerably and led to almost all 100 percent-of-cost financing schemes, with kickers, being treated as investments rather than as loans. But by its terms, the 1986 notice applied only to transactions entered into in 1986 and thereafter. Thus, the accounting profession permitted perverse incentives to persist for three years after they had been discovered. And during those three years, S&Ls made a very large amount of ADC loans that were improperly accounted for.

THE LOAN FEE RECOGNITION RULES

An accounting decision to treat a loan as a loan, rather than as an investment, did not necessarily result in immediate recognition of loan fees as income. The timing of when loan fees could be taken into income under GAAP was the subject of a great deal of confusing language in the literature. For example, the November 1983 guidance referred to above said that even if loan treatment was appropriate, the lender should "consider" whether immediate recognition of fees is appropriate. The AICPA *Savings and Loan Accounting Guide* had six confusing pages on the subject.

Probably GAAP said that you could only recognize the *costs* of origination, plus any fees received on loans that you sold to another institution or into the secondary market. However, the FHLBB had a simpler rule on the subject for RAP accounting, which allowed a fee of up to 2 percent of the loan (2.5 percent in the case of a construction loan) to be taken into income immediately and required any greater amount to be deferred. Most S&Ls adhered to this 2/2½ percent formula, which was explicitly permitted by the Bank Board's rules. Many accountants went along for GAAP purposes because it was hard to say what GAAP required.

A 2 percent fee may not sound like a big deal, but if we remember that a typical S&L's spread is little more than 2 percent and that most of that spread is eaten up by expenses, we can see the major boost to earnings that is given by the ability to recognize 2 percent of a loan as income on the day it is made. In fact, on an industrywide basis, if we took loan fees out of S&L income for the years 1983 through 1987, we would wipe out all of the reported earnings of the industry. Yes, that's right: The amount of loan fees recorded as income in those years (a fraction of which was properly recorded because the loans had been sold) equaled or exceeded the total net earnings of all S&Ls.

(The Bank Board knew it would create earnings when it permitted recognition of 2 percent fees in 1979. It increased the permitted amount from 1 percent precisely in order to increase S&Ls' reported earnings at a time when their spreads were being squeezed by high interest rates. And everybody in the business knew that you could create a 2 percent fee on *any* loan just by lowering the interest rate—which damaged future earnings in order to pay for immediate accounting profits.)

The accounting profession didn't think it was appropriate that these fees were creating earnings where otherwise none were present. But, as with ADC loans, it took years to tighten the rules because the S&Ls and the Bank Board didn't want S&Ls' income to be wiped out. Even though the problem was identified in the early 1980s, the FASB didn't come out with a final rule on the deferral of loan fees until December 1986, and that rule, because of notions of fairness and good lobbying by the S&L industry, was not effective until 1988. As a result, nearly all S&Ls continued to count fees of up to 2 percent as income until 1988. For 1988 and later years Statement of Financial Accounting Standards No. 91 (known as FAS 91) requires that all loan fees be deferred and taken into income over the life of the loan unless the loan is sold, in which event the income can be recognized at the time of sale. The Bank Board didn't change the RAP accounting rule—the one that really counted—until after FAS 91.

LOAN LOSS RESERVES

If the S&Ls had had to establish meaningful loan loss reserves as they put risky loans on their books, they would not have had such a perverse incentive to make 100 percent-of-cost construction loans. The loan loss reserves, which are accounted for as an expense, and therefore reduce income, would have wiped out the profits from the loan fees. In fact, however, most S&Ls established little or no reserves for possible loan losses in the 1981–85 period.

The subject of reserves for possible loan losses is arcane but important. Unfortunately, all formulations on the subject are, in practice, defective.

Bank auditors say that, in theory, the loan loss reserve should tell the reader of the financial statements the amount of losses that he or she can assume will result from the loans currently on the bank's or S&L's books. The problem with the theory is that in practice nobody can know what this number really should be. We only know that it must be *some* number because, as Alan Greenspan, current Chairman of the Federal Reserve Board, has told bankers, "If you have zero loan losses, then you aren't doing your job."[2] But how can we know what those losses will be? They are dependent not only on the types of lending businesses the institution is in and not only on the types of lending judgments it makes, but also on the economic future of the markets in which the institution lends.

Since most of us are better at predicting the past than the future, the accounting profession tends to look to historical results to evaluate the adequacy of the loan loss reserves proposed by management. Thus, for example, if a bank has been in the credit card business for ten years and has had a loan loss experience of between 1 percent and 3 percent of the portfolio, the accountants probably will agree with management's judgment that a 2 percent reserve is appropriate. But this simple historical method will not work when an institution goes into a new type of lending business. Then what benchmark should it use for establishing reserves? Will its experience in the new business be the same as its experience in other businesses? Will its experience in the new business be the same as the experience of other institutions that have been in that new business for a long time? Even more problematical, did the new lending business exist before?

For most S&Ls, the matter of loan loss reserves had always been pretty simple. They made single-family loans on which loss experience was minimal (almost always well under 1 percent and sometimes very close to zero) except in times of absolute economic crisis. (In Texas there had been no downturn since before World War II, so there had been no loan losses.) Therefore most S&Ls established *no* loan loss reserves. This was reflected in, and basically blessed by, the AICPA *Savings and Loan Accounting Guide*, which does discuss some loan loss reserve theory but puts the emphasis on management's judgment. The AICPA *Industry Audit Guide for Audits of Banks* is far more stringent on the subject of loan losses, but as anyone who reads the newspapers knows, when a bank's loans go bad, there still are never enough reserves.

Against this background, S&Ls established almost no reserves against the new loans they were making—even commercial mortgage loans on which they were lending 100 percent of cost. The S&Ls showed their auditors their historical results—a history of almost no losses on their traditional single-family lending—and contended that it was all just real estate lending ("100 percent secured"), and therefore no reserves were required. Again, in the absence of authoritative guidance to give them backbone, most accountants went along. Theory allowed them to do so because they could point to the *S&L Accounting Guide* and accounting literature which said that loss reserves should be established only if the losses could reasonably be estimated. The auditors felt that they couldn't make an estimate they trusted.

CONSEQUENCES

The ability of an S&L to create immediate income by making 100 percent-of-cost-of-development loans on large commercial projects was responsible for several disastrous consequences.

1. Loans were made without sufficient underwriting. They later went bad to the tune of billions and billions of dollars.

2. The immediate income (about $4 billion in the key year, 1983) created apparent net worth that permitted institutions to continue to grow even after the FHLBB had adopted regulations to put a stop to excessive growth by low net worth institutions. Without the fee in-

come, the industry as a whole would have lost money in 1983 and 1984. Without the fee income, the fast growers couldn't have continued to grow, couldn't have paid big dividends to stockholders, couldn't have paid big salaries and bonuses to management, and couldn't have built up fleets of airplanes.

3. The excessive lending for office buildings, condominiums, and shopping centers led directly to the devaluation of the properties that were being built. Some of the loans involved fraud and some involved dishonest appraisals. But even honest appraisals will be totally wrong if the amount of property built in the marketplace significantly exceeds demand, because without demand, prices will fall precipitously, as they did in Texas, Colorado, and Arizona, wiping out substantially all of the S&Ls in those states. We can't blame all of this on permissive accounting, but if the accounting had been done right, the problem would have been much smaller.

Some of the Texas and California high flyers, such as Vernon and Independent American, added a little fraud to the aggressive accounting by having borrowers pay additional fees to "service corporation" subsidiaries, usually in exchange for fictitious "mortgage banking" or other services. This could bring the total fee to 6 or even 10 percent. Of course the S&L financed these fees as well—and what did the developers care, if they were getting a loan of 110 percent or 120 percent of cost without recourse? They already had their profit without having invested a penny.

SKIMMING

Loan fees weren't the only way that S&L income was being inflated. You will recall that the form of purchase accounting whereby the goodwill is amortized over forty years while the "discount" is accreted into income over a lesser number of years (such as twenty) also inflated reported income. But purchase accounting also created another opportunity to inflate income by selling written-down assets at a profit.

The mechanism worked like this: When an acquisition was made, all of the assets of the acquired S&L were written down to market value in the interest rate climate of the date of acquisition. The deficit was put into the goodwill number. If interest rates later went down, the value of the assets would increase. The acquirer then could sell the appreciated assets and achieve a gain against book value (and, even better, a loss for tax purposes to shelter other income, because the IRS doesn't permit purchase accounting for tax purposes). The accounting convention said that it was legitimate to take this gain as income, and not to reduce goodwill by a corresponding amount, because the goodwill account is "closed" and cannot be adjusted after one year from the date of acquisition. Thus the sale of appreciated assets would create both income and net worth.

In later years, the S&L's earnings would be reduced by these sales of written-down assets because after the sale, the "discounts" that had resulted from the purchase accounting valuation of the sold assets *would* be written off (unlike the goodwill) and, as a result, they would not accrete into income in the future. But for S&Ls starved for income and net worth—as the vast majority of them were—mortgaging the future in exchange for current income was irresistible.

Purchase accounting wasn't necessary, however, for a second form of skimming that inflated S&L earnings at least through 1988. This form of skimming could be done by any institution when interest rates went down even a little bit. It could sell assets that it had purchased in a higher rate environment and record an immediate gain. After all, management reasoned, they made a good investment, the market went their way, they sold the investment and got a cash profit; that's income. What they ignored was that they didn't sell the assets which didn't have gains. They held onto the assets that didn't have gains, thereby increasing with each sale the negative difference between the book value of their assets and their market value. Eventually, they were left with the "dog" investments, all carried at original cost. When these institutions failed and everything was marked to market, the FSLIC took the losses. The stockholders may have taken out the gains as dividends. CenTrust was the master of portfolio skimming.

The accounting literature says that if you trade securities or loans rather than holding them to maturity, you have to record them at market value (mark them to market)* every quarter. But management always affirmed its intention to hold to maturity and excused the sales as "portfolio adjustments" resulting from "changed circumstances." Compliant auditors went along. If they hadn't gone along, the alternative was to mark the S&L's entire securities portfolio to market, which *in almost every case* would have resulted in deep and apparent insolvency, and therefore would have caused the S&L's owners to sue the accountants for causing the institution to fail. It's much easier to take management's assurances at face value.

7 Mammon Against the God of Home Ownership

In August 1982, economist Henry Kaufman of Salomon Brothers, who had been bearish on interest rates for years, finally predicted that rates would come down. The Fed eased its monetary policy and interest rates started to decline. The stock market, which had been waiting for a signal, heard the starter's gun and took off on the greatest bull market in history. Real estate values, which had been depressed by stagflation and high interest rates, also responded with a boom of historic proportions, propelled in part by tax legislation passed in 1981 that permitted investors in real estate to take accelerated depreciation and to deduct interest paid on their personal tax returns. Equity money for real estate ventures became plentiful as syndicators sprang up all over the country to put together real estate deals for doctors, dentists, and even schoolteachers. Pent-up demand after years of high interest rates made fortunes for single-family-home developers.

The great god mammon was on the loose, as greed became socially acceptable, investment banking became the most popular professional aspiration for college seniors, and everyone thought that he or she not only could but *would* and *should* be rich. If there ever had been strong morals in American business—which had a spotty record at best—they gave way to the urge to take advantage of the moment.

THE MIRACLE OF LEVERAGE

Leverage—using other people's money to work for you—fueled the boom. In the new world of 1982 and 1983, real estate developers—always the masters of leverage—were able to get more leverage than ever before. They could get a syndicator to put together the equity money that the bank insisted on and could get the bank to lend the rest. As a result, they had "infinite leverage," with no money in the project and maybe 20 percent or even 50 percent of the profits. In many S&L deals, the developer didn't even need a syndicator to raise equity money; the S&L lent the whole thing. It was nirvana.

The industrial world also used leverage as never before. The leveraged buyout (LBO) became the favored business transaction. Entrepreneurs were building "LBO funds" to put up the small amount of equity required. Drexel Burnham—and later others—lent the "bridge mezzanine," then found the mutual funds, pension funds, insurance companies, and S&Ls to "take them out" by buying high-yield subordinated debt. And major banks such as Bankers Trust and Manufacturers Hanover led international syndicates of banks to put up the remaining funds to buy major corporations that had been thought impregnable to takeover. You could finance almost anything with this tripartite scheme, as long as there were pigeons to put up the "mezzanine" money.

Consumers jumped on the leverage bandwagon by running up their credit card debts and, as their homes grew more valuable, borrowing against them through home equity loans to finance the family Mercedes, a child's college education, or a speculative real estate investment that was itself highly leveraged.

In this climate, the potential of the enormous leverage offered by owning an S&L was especially obvious to real estate developers. They saw that with a very small investment you could command an enormous pot of assets, because with deposit insurance and deregulated rates you could raise as much money as you wanted. With relaxed capital standards, an S&L could have hundreds of millions of dollars of assets with almost no capital. The 3 percent net worth standard implies a debt-to-equity leverage ratio of 33 to 1—far surpassing even the 6 to 1 leverage provided by some LBOs. But with five-year averaging, a growing S&L easily could have a ratio of over 100 to 1 without violating the capital requirements. That means that by putting up $1 of their own money, entrepreneurs could raise $100 of deposits to invest. After interest on the deposits, all the profits were theirs. If they developed a property themselves, they had only maybe 10 to 1 leverage and paid a bank or S&L prime plus 1½ percent for borrowings; if their S&L supplied all of the funds, their leverage was at least 33 to 1 and they paid barely more than U.S. Treasury rates for money raised as insured deposits.

Dick Pratt and his staff assured potential owners that S&Ls had the best charter in the world, with the broadest powers and the most leverage.

States like Florida, California, and Texas had many small stock-form institutions that had little value left after the interest rate ravages of 1979–82. Established—albeit weakened—S&Ls in those states could be bought for a million or two.

Entrepreneurs filed for new S&L charters in record numbers. Several hundred new charter applications were filed in California in 1983 and 1984. With a new charter, you got not only five-year averaging but also a twenty-year "capital phase-in" that allowed even greater leverage. Theoretically you could get to 666 to 1.

Mammon loves leverage.

ENTER ED GRAY

Into this exploding S&L world stepped Ed Gray, who had been given the job of regulating it. The Bank Board information systems were rudimentary, so there was no way for him to know immediately what was going on in the industry. As one industry consultant put it, if Ollie North had been at the Bank Board, he wouldn't have had to shred documents to conceal anything. Everyone in the industry told Ed Gray that things were fine.

The California Connection

Ed Gray's wife and children didn't move to Washington with him (they had lived in Washington before, and his wife hated it), and he wasn't rich enough to support two homes on a government salary, so even after borrowing from banks and friends, he lived in Washington in a small apartment with a few sticks of furniture. He liked to go home to California, so he attended and arranged meetings there as often as he could. He lived very well on the Federal Home Loan Bank of San Francisco's budget.

Gray's two key aides, Chief of Staff Shannon Fairbanks and General Counsel Norman Raiden, also were Californians, as was Gray's chief outside adviser, Los Angeles S&L lawyer William McKenna, who had been Raiden's senior partner.

His California connections strongly influenced Ed Gray's view of the business. California was the leading S&L state (accounting for about a quarter of the industry's assets), and the leaders of the industry there were influential in state politics as well as social and financial circles. Whereas in most states *real* bankers looked down on S&L executives as a lower life form, in California, where real estate was king and the leading S&Ls were almost as big as the banks, they had power and respect.

These major California S&Ls had survived the high interest rate period better than their counterparts elsewhere in the country because California kept growing and they had been able to make variable-rate home loans. Led by Home Savings and Great Western, they stuck to the business of gathering deposits through extensive statewide branch systems and making residential mortgage loans. They made as many loans as they could with monthly variable rates tied to the 11th District (FHLB of San Francisco) cost of funds (cof) and sold excess loans (called "coffee ARMs") into the secondary market.

This California model was what Ed Gray and his key advisers thought an S&L should be—a specialized housing finance institution that managed its interest rate risk by making variable-rate mortgages. If they had stayed specialized housing finance institutions, many S&Ls would have failed but the cost of each failure would have been much smaller. Nevertheless, Ed Gray's theological approach to the housing finance question deprived him of credibility in many circles and on many key regulatory issues. Cutting back on nonhousing powers was seen as "reregulation"—a dirty word in 1983.

Ed Gray's Theology

Many commentators believed in 1983 that the Garn–St Germain Act had transformed the S&L business from a single-family loan and thrift business into a full service banking business very much like the commercial banking business. Ed Gray rejected this view.[1] S&Ls, he maintained, were intended to be dedicated to home finance and, while Garn–St Germain gave them some powers of diversification, those powers were to be used sparingly. He took this position consistently and made it the philosophical centerpiece of his tenure. It was based not on considerations of safety and soundness but on his belief that S&Ls existed for the purpose of supporting housing and were needed for that purpose. He supported this theological approach with a keen political observation of the ground rules for S&L privileges. For example, he said to a group of S&L executives in Hawaii in October 1983:

> [T]he Federal Home Loan Bank system is part and parcel of a national housing component and to the extent this fact of life is ignored; to the extent that Congress were ever to come to believe the fundamental purpose of the system had been so compromised that institutions the Home Loan Banks assist no longer strongly emphasize home ownership opportunities, then the system would no longer be able to count on the Congress for its continued support. The system, itself, would be in jeopardy and the day of its demise would accelerate. As I have said on a number of occasions in recent weeks, and as I want to emphasize again today, you simply cannot have it both ways.[2]

As events would show, Gray was right. If the Federal Home Loan Bank system involved a government subsidy whereby S&Ls were able to borrow at

below market rates, then Congress would support that system only so long as
it served a national housing goal.

But Gray's position was an anachronism as far as the Treasury, the administration, and academic commentators were concerned. The Treasury saw no
need for specialized housing institutions. The idea of deregulation was to level
the playing field so that people could compete with each other. Institutions
with restricted charters would be at a disadvantage and eventually would die
out. The official administration position was similar. In mid–1983, as Ed
Gray was making speeches exhorting S&Ls to stick to housing, the Cabinet
Council was preparing for additional deregulatory legislation to level the playing field further among S&Ls, banks, securities firms, and insurance companies. One suspects that if Ronald Reagan himself had focused on the issue, he
might have agreed with Ed Gray—their California populism overcoming deregulatory theory—but there is no evidence that Ronald Reagan ever focused
on the subject.

In the academic community, Gray's position was laughable. Whatever other
differences economists who studied the banking scene may have had, they
almost all agreed that changes in technology had rendered specialized housing
finance institutions unnecessary. The academic observers saw that with the
evolution of the secondary mortgage market, mortgage bankers could spring
up anywhere overnight—and in fact were springing up everywhere overnight.
Some S&Ls indeed would be efficient producers of mortgages and, like Home
Savings and Great Western, would be profitable and growing institutions
based on housing finance. But even if these institutions were efficient, that
didn't suggest that all S&Ls should be restricted to housing finance. Mortgage
pricing was being driven down by the growth of the secondary market. Duration-matched spreads* had practically disappeared from the single-family
mortgage business. S&Ls that were not efficient at housing finance, the conventional academic wisdom said, should pursue other businesses.

THE REGULATORY PROCESS SLOWS TO A CRAWL

In the Pratt years, on average the Bank Board proposed or adopted a new
set of regulations every other week and took over or merged an S&L every
other day. By contrast, in the second half of 1983 the process came almost to
a halt. "You haven't been appointed to make massive changes," says Ed Gray
seven years later. "You're appointed to run what's there."

No More LTV Requirements

In early 1983 the Bank Board did clean up the end of the Pratt deregulatory
agenda, for instance by finalizing the regulation that removed maximum per-

missible LTV ratios. This regulation, which the Texans turned on its head, made many bad loans easier to make, but its theory was defensible. Theory said that S&Ls should be encouraged to use prudent underwriting methods rather than being regulated to the "lowest common denominator." *Of course* no one should make 100 percent LTV loans—those aren't loans—but removing the limits didn't mean that the regulators believed 100 percent LTV loans were prudent. It meant only that the regulators thought S&Ls were run by adults, which proved to be a naive assumption. (The comptroller of the currency seems to have made a similar mistake in regulating national bank LTVs.)

Insolvent S&Ls Stay in Business

The major decision the Bank Board took in Gray's first six months (without announcing it) was not to merge or liquidate institutions as they became insolvent. Ed Gray didn't see himself as having had a choice. The FSLIC fund had only $6 billion of reserves to insure $750 billion of deposits. Nobody would want to deplete that $6 billion of reserves.

The S&Ls had just come through the interest rate crisis and were said to be recovering. They should have a chance to recover.

After Congress had enacted the net worth certificate program as part of the Garn–St Germain Act, Ed Gray believed he would be impeached if he started closing S&Ls left and right all around the country. (Ed Gray had an impeachment complex.)

The pundits would not have agreed that leaving insolvent S&Ls open was a good idea. They would have said that an insolvent S&L will gamble for its salvation and, if it loses the gamble, will be doomed to lose money forever. They would have said that this was a "moral hazard" risk that the insurance fund could not afford to run. As Professors Horvitz and Pettit said in 1981, "The longer an institution losing money is allowed to continue in operation, the greater the ultimate cost to the insurance fund."[3] The academic commentators' bottom line would have been that if the FSLIC didn't have enough money to do the job, then it would have to get a larger line of credit from the Treasury, as the regulators had proposed in 1981. But the academicians didn't have to report to Congress and live with the industry. Today Ed Gray says, "If even as late as January 1, 1985, we could have got the money to close down institutions and pay off depositors when the institution got to zero RAP capital, the size of the problem would have been relatively minuscule compared to what it is now. Operating losses are responsible for the lion's share of the cost that the taxpayers are going to have to pay."

Educating the Industry

From a supervisory point of view, the Board and its staff were primarily concerned with getting S&Ls to use the better interest rate climate to get the interest rate sensitivities of their assets and liabilities better matched. Ed Gray traveled all over the country, making speeches to S&L groups. Some months he was in Washington for only a few days. Educating the industry was his most important role, he said—and in almost every speech he talked about adjustable-rate mortgages. He exhorted all S&Ls to match their assets and liabilities by using ARMs. ARMs, he kept saying, were the way to future S&L profitability. S&L executives got tired of hearing him.

New Rules for De Novos

The Bank Board undertook two important initiatives in 1983. First, in October the Bank Board and the FDIC put out a "joint notice of proposed rule making" that solicited public comments on a proposal to restrict deposits gathered through money brokers. This subject became Ed Gray's principal focus for the next six months.

The second initiative dealt with the risk to the FSLIC fund caused by all of the new California institutions applying for federal insurance. The big California S&Ls didn't like the Nolan Law and didn't like all of the new potential competitors. They saw that these competitors would drive up the price of deposits and drive down their efficiency by decreasing average branch size. They explained to Ed Gray what could happen if these new institutions used all of the powers that California had given them. They showed that many of the applicants were entrepreneurs who really wanted to use government-insured money to engage in their own speculative ventures. Ed Gray saw the risks and liked the politics, and he acted promptly to tighten the insurance rules, putting out proposed regulations early in November and adopting a final regulation on the subject early in December.

The new regulations used two key elements to control risk to the FSLIC: (1) capital requirements and (2) federal restrictions on the unusual powers of state-chartered institutions. On the capital front, the new regulations required that a new S&L start off with capital of at least 7 percent (as opposed to the 3 percent being permitted for established institutions) and that it not be eligible for the five-year averaging and twenty-year phase-in. Thus any growth of new S&Ls would have to be margined by proper capital and, although that capital could be allowed to decline from 7 percent to 3 percent over a period of three years, the runaway growth that otherwise would have been possible would be significantly restricted. The regulation also provided that a newly chartered institution applying for insurance of accounts would have to agree to restrict its equity investments to 10 percent of its assets.

These new de novo rules were good regulations because they were precisely aimed at their targets and well designed to protect the deposit insurance system.

The Secret Committee

The new de novo rules had been recommended by a secret committee that the Bank Board had appointed to advise it. The committee, headed by Bill McKenna and including representatives from the industry, the Federal Home Loan Banks, Wall Street, and academia, had presented a report to the Board in October but the report, although printed, was never released by the Bank Board.[4]

The de novo rules recommendation came out of the secret committee's study of risk-based deposit insurance. The committee, having concluded that risk-based insurance sounded good in theory but wouldn't work in practice, recommended instead that the FSLIC protect itself by taking several steps, one of which was the de novo rules. Other recommendations included the following:

> Net Worth Requirement—. . . the Bank Board should immediately initiate a formal long-run program to phase upward the existing net worth requirement. Net worth requirements should be an important policy instrument used by the FSLIC to control its risk exposure.
>
> Examinations—In light of changing economic and financial conditions, the Bank Board . . . should increase the frequency of focused examinations of identified high-risk institutions. . . . Early treatment of problems is an effective means of controlling FSLIC payouts.
>
> Accounting Practices—The Bank Board should have an ongoing program to reexamine regulatory accounting practices promulgated during the emergency conditions of 1981–82. . . . [T]he continuation of such accounting policies may, in some instances, enable problem associations to conceal financial difficulties and thereby delay FSLIC detection and cure.

Missed Opportunities

If at the end of 1983 the Bank Board had enacted capital rules for existing associations similar to the rules imposed on de novo institutions, a large part of the eventual asset problems would have been avoided. But apparently the Bank Board wasn't yet prepared to tell S&Ls that they couldn't fast-grow their way out of their problems.

The Board also missed the opportunity to repeal the liberal purchase accounting rules. Deals still were being done that were creating phony capital and earnings—and they continued to be done until the Bank Board changed the rule in 1987. The FSLIC had no money, and perhaps it needed this mechanism for supervisory transactions. But it could have been limited to supervisory transactions.

The Board didn't repeal the rule permitting deferral of losses on loan sales. That also wasn't done until 1987.

And the Board didn't change the rule allowing income recognition for loan fees of 2/2½ percent even though it wasn't consistent with GAAP and was fueling the most dangerous growth. That, too, waited until 1987.

These proved to be costly omissions.

Some Difficult Decisions

There were some supervisory decisions that *had* to be made in 1983, including fateful decisions that led to the takeover of CenTrust by David Paul and the formation of American Savings in California as the largest S&L in the country.

The approval for David Paul to purchase CenTrust (then the insolvent Dade County S&L) illustrates the extreme difficulty of being an insurer with no money. Dade County was about a $2 billion S&L that, on a mark to market basis, had liabilities of $2 billion but assets of only $1.5 billion. It was a typical case of an S&L that is doomed to lose money forever, but it had a good franchise in Miami. And, just as horse racing had always been the sport of kings, S&L buying had become the sport of real estate entrepreneurs. So David Paul wanted to buy Dade County and was willing to put in $37 million in new capital. Of course $37 million was not enough new capital to make any real difference in Dade County's operations, and of course David Paul didn't really want to put in $37 million. He was, however, prepared to put in a piece of property that was *appraised* at $37 million—which later turned out to be worth a lot less.

The Federal Home Loan Bank of Atlanta understood that this transaction was no good: It didn't think that David Paul was qualified to run an S&L; it didn't think that there was enough capital going into the institution; and it didn't think that the deal would solve any problems. The Division of Supervision in Washington agreed, and they both recommended against approving the transaction. Nevertheless, the Bank Board approved it in October 1983 after it had been pending for almost a year.[5]

Why, we might ask, would a conservative person like Ed Gray, who was afraid of looking bad, override the recommendations of his staff and approve an acquisition for very little capital by a man like David Paul, whom he never would have trusted? Ed Gray doesn't remember, and insists that he wouldn't have approved the deal over the staff's objections. But there were no other offers on the table; and if you can't spend any money, you have to accept whatever offers you have. Eventually CenTrust will cost something approaching $2 billion to liquidate. It probably would have cost about $300 million to deal with the old Dade County back in 1983. Ed Gray says he never heard of CenTrust until after he left the Bank Board in June 1987.

A second hot potato that burned Ed Gray early on was the merger of two California S&Ls—American Savings and Loan and State Savings and Loan, the S&L subsidiary of Financial Corporation of America (FCA)—to form American Savings, the largest S&L in the country, with FCA's management surviving as the acquirer. FCA was controlled by a well-known maverick named Charles Knapp. Many people said Knapp was a genius and that although he ran his business by taking lots of risks, he always managed to hedge those risks so that his upside was better than his downside. Others, including the California S&L establishment, thought Charlie Knapp shouldn't be running an S&L.

Knapp's State Savings had a low net worth and a lot of both interest rate and credit risk. He had been ahead of his time, growing State from $500 million in 1978 to $10 billion in 1982 by buying wholesale funds when the rest of the thrift industry was treading water. Like his Texas counterparts after him, Knapp invested a lot of the expensive purchased funds in ADC loans to earn high loan fees. By 1982, some of the loans were looking shaky. But, as David Paul did later at CenTrust, Knapp also had purchased large amounts of mortgage-backed securities* in the high rate environment of 1980–81, which he sold when they went up (as they did at the end of 1982). This profit skimming and the loan fees covered over the deteriorating loans in 1982.

American, which Knapp had agreed to buy for almost $300 million in cash to be paid to its principal stockholder, plus paper for American's public stockholders, was a strong institution. Ed Gray and his California advisers certainly did not want Charlie Knapp to run the biggest S&L in the country, nor did they think that State Savings was financially strong enough to make a major acquisition. But the staff saw the merger as the way to strengthen State, which would be in trouble if the merger didn't go through. They apparently weren't so worried about Charlie Knapp. Moreover, after several months of temporizing, it became clear that Mark Taper, the major stockholder of American and a powerful man in California, wouldn't rest until he got his money. The Bank Board lawyers were afraid of being sued. So on a day in August 1983, after Charlie Knapp had given some pallid assurances about running a "traditional S&L," the Bank Board approved the acquisition of American by State Savings.

The merger approval was conditioned on the new American maintaining 4 percent capital, but the 4 percent was permitted to include the goodwill created by the transaction (which amounted to about $1 billion) and, under the terms of the approval (which Bank Board sources say was misdrafted), even though the capital was computed as of year-end, as it should have been, it was measured against the assets that had existed at the *beginning* of the year. Consequently, growth during the year didn't reduce American's capital percentage.

Using this lovely capital arrangement and a nationwide telephonic deposit gathering system, the new American eventually grew to $32 billion. American proved to be the Bank Board's number one problem. It required constant attention from August 1984, when a deposit run first would have made it insolvent without government assistance, to 1988, when it finally was sold to the Robert Bass group at a cost to the FSLIC variously estimated between $2 billion and $5 billion. FCA/American is another case we'll follow.

Changes in Control

Other apparently more routine approvals also permitted sales of stock S&Ls to entrepreneurs—sometimes even to crooks.

The big banking bill of 1978 had given the Bank Board power to deny a person the right to control an S&L. Anyone who wanted to buy 10 percent or more of the stock of an S&L had to file in advance with the FHLBB, which could deny the application if either

- The financial condition of the controlling person was weak
- The applicant failed to supply any information that the FHLBB requested or
- The FHLBB did not approve of the competence, experience, or integrity of the applicant or a proposed member of management of the S&L.

Unfortunately, the Bank Board had never established a very sophisticated mechanism for investigating and ruling on change-in-control applications. Before 1981 there had been relatively few applications, and in 1981 and 1982 most of the applications were in connection with failing institutions. Spending almost all of its energies wrestling with failures and implementing its deregulatory agenda, the Pratt Bank Board put a low priority on change-in-control applications. On their watch, people like Don Dixon, who bought tiny Vernon S&L in Texas and grew it into a billion dollars of mostly bad loans in two years, were approved. To be sure, there was nothing strange on the face of Dixon's change-in-control application, but vigorous investigation would have shown that Dixon and his associates were unsuited to manage a large pool of money with government guarantees. Vernon eventually cost over a billion FSLIC dollars.

Tom Gaubert took over Independent American, another little Texas S&L, in 1983. Again, he had no trouble with his change-in-control application. Eventually he ran the high-flyingest of the Texas high flyers—growing fast and using loan fees as the engine to show Independent American as one of the most profitable S&Ls in the country. When Independent American was finally interred as part of the Southwest Plan in 1988, it, too, cost the FSLIC over a billion dollars.

Spencer Blain, who took over Empire S&L of Mesquite, Texas, in 1982, didn't even file an application. When his law violation was noticed in 1983, he filed an application that was approved on the basis of his representation that he was going to sell out promptly. He never did, and he was still in control when Empire failed nine months later.

In 1984 Charles Keating and his American Continental Corp. (ACC) filed an application to control Lincoln Savings in California through ACC. ACC's change-in-control application disclosed that Keating had signed a consent decree with the Securities and Exchange Commission (SEC) after an SEC complaint had accused Keating and another Ohio entrepreneur, Carl Lindner, of securities fraud. Basically, Keating had signed a consent order admitting to insider dealing through an elaborate series of machinations. To meet the regulatory concerns raised by this background, ACC represented to the Bank Board that it would retain current Lincoln management, that it would not engage in any affiliate transactions, and that it would emphasize traditional home lending in California and fund Lincoln through retail deposits, not brokered funds.[6] With these reassurances and without imposing any special controls, the Bank Board approved ACC's acquisition of Lincoln. Ed Gray does not remember approving the change in control. He says he didn't know about Keating's consent decree until he read about it in a newspaper two years later.

Almost immediately after acquiring Lincoln, Keating and ACC began violating the representations that had induced the approval from the Bank Board. Old management was phased out, deals were done between Lincoln and ACC, and Lincoln became the leading opponent of the Bank Board's proposal to prohibit state-chartered S&Ls from investing over 10 percent of their assets in direct investments.* It didn't take Charles Keating long to show his colors. ACC was leveraged 3.4 to 1. By owning Lincoln through ACC, Keating's leverage became more than 100 to 1.

"The change of control procedures that we had back in 1983 were not effective—period," said Deputy FSLIC Director Bill Black in 1987 testimony. "But more than that, it was just plain things that could have been done but weren't, and are done now."[7]

In both the 1983 and 1984 Annual Reports of the FHLBB, activity under the Change in Control Act was summarized as follows: "Since the savings institutions industry remains predominantly mutual rather than stock in organization, administration of the Act generally has been uneventful. . . . for the most part, the notices presented no difficult informational problems. In addition, post-acquisition experience generally has been unexceptional." By the time the 1985 Annual Report was written—sometime in the middle of 1986—the Bank Board had changed its tune on the Change in Control Act:

> . . .[I]t has been the Bank Board's experience that the perceived attractiveness of thrifts unfortunately also has led to efforts by financially weak or unstable companies and unqualified and dishonest individuals to acquire and exploit thrift institutions. As a result, substantive as well as procedural weaknesses in the regulations implementing the Control Act too often have been abused, in some cases leaving the FSLIC to pay the price for such shortcomings.

As Bill Black testified, proper procedures could have been implemented under the law as it stood. The Board's Deputy General Counsel, Juile Williams, tightened up the process considerably, but procedural changes weren't implemented until 1986.

The Change in Control Act was designed to give the regulators a tool to prevent unscrupulous individuals from gaining control of banks and S&Ls; it was enacted because buying control of banks in order to get insider loans or otherwise to funnel money out the side door was not a new game. The history of banking is filled with failures caused by loans to owners, directors, and officers. Willy Sutton wasn't the only person to observe that banks are where the money is.

INSIDE THE BELTWAY

Some Washington pundits suggest that the Bank Board could not change course and tighten up in 1983–84 because the system was set up to prevent changes that the savings institutions didn't want. The U.S. League had connections with the Board members and with practically the whole staff of the Bank Board. The U.S. League had power in the Congressional committees that the Bank Board had to go to for appropriations, oversight, and powers changes. The industry itself controlled the Federal Home Loan Banks. In this climate, some insiders say, Ed Gray could not have effected meaningful changes.

I have never lived inside the Beltway. My observation from afar, however, is that members of Congress storm a lot about regulatory actions that they don't like; but laws are hard to pass. I believe that skillful agency chairmen have the right and the power to create staffs of which they are not prisoners. Thus, although change would not have been easy to effect in the face of U.S. League opposition, I do not believe it would have been impossible.

8 Ed Gray Tries to Cope and the World Goes Galloping By

About six months after he became chairman, Ed Gray saw that S&Ls' rapid growth was dangerous. His solution—to stop providing insurance for brokered deposits, which were a major engine of fast growth—did not succeed. William Schilling, then Director of Examination and Supervision, has written, "Under the Gray administration, we wasted a year on brokered funds. Brokered funds were a device; they were not the illness."[1]

GRAY AND ISAAC FIGHT BROKERED DEPOSITS

No question, fast growth was a problem. Little Texas S&Ls such as Vernon and Independent American were growing at rates like 400 percent per year. Twenty percent of *all* S&Ls were growing at a rate of over 25 percent per year. Such rapid growth leads to problems because the new assets usually are acquired haphazardly. The growing institution doesn't have the infrastructure and the discipline to avoid making bad investments, especially when the owners have little capital at stake and accounting techniques permit immediate income to be made on risky loans.

The way the risky loans are funded can be symptomatic of the asset problems that are likely to result. Hot money—money bought by paying high interest rates—leads to hot investments.

Most of the fast growers' new money wasn't coming from increases in local deposits. Most of it was coming from jumbo (over $100,000) CDs and other deposits gathered nationally, in some cases through direct advertising in national newspapers or, in the case of FCA/American, through a boiler room of employees "dialing for dollars," but more often the hot money was coming through deposit brokers. For S&Ls growing at over 50 percent a year, brokered deposits already accounted for over 15 percent of liabilities on average, and the percentage was growing quickly. Many of the Texas fast growers were getting more than half of their deposits through brokers. If you could cut down on the availability of funds through brokers, it appeared that you could cut down on the growth.

Deposit brokers were nothing new, but until interest rate deregulation they were a minor factor. Before deregulation they were limited to placing "jumbo" CDs whose rates were not regulated. In September 1982, however, over Dick Pratt's dissent, the DIDC quietly permitted banks and S&Ls to pay deposit brokers even if the payment, when combined with the interest rate paid on the deposit, would otherwise have violated interest rate restrictions. The DIDC also, since S&L liquidity was its first concern, repealed the rule that for twenty years had prohibited federally insured S&Ls from having more than 5 percent of their deposits represented by funds obtained through brokers. There was no great debate about these rule changes; the Treasury proposed them and they were adopted. It was all part of the administration's program to let the S&Ls compete. Money brokers were another competitive tool.

Money brokering was an easy business to get into: There were no regulations and no barriers to entry; no enormous capital was needed to be a player. Thus, although Merrill Lynch, the largest brokerage firm in the country, was also the largest money broker in the country, there were dozens of little shops that advertised in the newspapers that they would get their customers the best rates. Finding those best rates wasn't hard, either, because the fastest-growing S&Ls (most of them in Texas) consistently were paying the highest rates.

For a healthy institution, raising funds through a broker may be the most efficient way to fund specific new assets. The money raised through the broker doesn't have to influence the more general rates paid by the S&L because the S&L can offer brokers a special product, such as a CD with an unusual term. Major brokers such as Merrill Lynch can raise a designated amount, such as $100 million, in a matter of a few hours. The broker's fee often is far lower than the anticipated advertising cost to generate the same amount of deposits without a broker. But there is no question that deposit brokerage (combined with deposit insurance) made it easy for *any* insured depository institution to raise *as much money as it wanted regardless of whether it was financially strong.*

The little-noticed regulatory changes that the DIDC made in 1982 came on the heels of an even more subtle but equally momentous (and less-noticed) change in deposit insurance policy that had been implemented in the late 1970s. Until then, although pension funds and similar pooled accounts had been eligible for deposit insurance based on their beneficiaries' interests—that is, each beneficiary's share of the deposit was insured up to the full deposit insurance limit—each beneficiary was insured only for the proportion of his or her deposit that was vested* under the plan in question. This meant that if a bank or S&L failed, pension fund and similar pooled fund deposits in excess of $100,000 were never *fully* insured because there always were partially un-vested beneficiaries.

The FDIC and FSLIC had nice reasons for deciding to protect unvested pension amounts. The distinction seemed like discrimination. Younger work-ers and others—such as minorities—with less seniority (and therefore less vest-ing) would be the ones who got hurt. No policy reason suggested that that made sense. Besides, under the old policy, no one could figure out which deposits were protected and which weren't.

So they made this technical change. Nobody paid much attention to it. But the pension managers, especially the union pension managers, did. It meant that they didn't have to worry any longer if they put pension money in banks and S&Ls that failed. Now they could simply go after the highest interest rates and whatever else they could get.

Now that all the money was insured, a corporate or union pension fund could place millions of dollars in a single institution and have the full amount insured by the FDIC or the FSLIC. That made the money broker's job easy. He didn't have to gather the funds from hundreds or thousands of individual depositors; he only needed to have relationships with a few money managers or unions in order to have many millions of dollars to place with insured institutions. Naturally this invited abuse, particularly in placing union funds, with respect to which abuse is almost traditional.

Although most money brokers were normal agents of market forces, the case of Mario Renda and the First United Fund, his deposit brokerage firm, illustrates the potential for abuse.[2] From 1980 to 1987 Renda, with little capital and no special expertise, managed to broker $6 billion of CDs. His First United Fund acted mostly on behalf of unions (prominently, the Team-sters). Renda made sure he kept the business by kicking back a part of his brokerage fee to union officers.

But Mario Renda wasn't satisfied with what he was making from brokerage fees. He saw that he had power over the little banks and S&Ls where he placed the deposits. He apparently began with a little bank outside Kansas City called Indian Springs State Bank, where, in cahoots with a sad and unsa-vory bunch of characters, Renda arranged for Indian Springs State Bank to make loans to straw borrowers* in Hawaii who in turn would give most of the loaned money to Renda and his confederates. It was a sordid little scheme that sent Renda and others to jail. In fact, Renda repeated the scam a number of times, even advertising for straw borrowers in the *Wall Street Journal*. Several of the victims were small, now-defunct S&Ls.

This was the kind of problem that Ed Gray's instincts readily identified. He believed in local institutions with local deposits, and it was instantly clear to him that bad people could abuse the deposit brokerage system very easily. He and FDIC Chairman William Isaac saw eye to eye on brokered deposits — they saw them as a perversion of deposit insurance.

At one of their first meetings on the subject, Isaac told Gray that the FDIC could restrict deposit brokerage only if it enacted a rule which limited deposit insurance for all deposits placed by the same deposit broker in the same bank to $100,000. Isaac's plan would end the deposit brokerage business *entirely* because a broker could place only one insured client in any single bank or S&L. It was an extreme solution.

Gray went along with this "deinsuring" plan even though his legal advisers were dubious about it. Some of his advisers said that the Bank Board should merely reinstitute the 5 percent rule that for twenty years — before being lifted by the DIDC in 1982 — had limited the amount of deposits an S&L could obtain through brokers. The 5 percent rule would have solved the problem of excessive growth through brokered deposits. But Ed Gray believed that the two deposit insurance agencies had to act in concert on this issue, so that the solution would be fair to all depository institutions.

The FDIC and the Bank Board formally proposed the deinsurance regulation in January 1984. It wasn't popular because it was so extreme. If adopted, it would put deposit brokerage out of business. It would cost Merrill Lynch, where Treasury Secretary Don Regan had come from, a ton of money. The brokers had to fight hard and lobby any way they could. The deinsuring proposal raised a big cloud of dust that distracted everyone from the real problems.

Gray was determined to convince people he was right about deinsuring brokered deposits, and the subject took the place of ARMs at center stage in his speeches.[3] No matter what group he talked to — and he continued to talk a lot — brokered deposits were the central point for months and months. He satanized deposit brokerage, speaking of it time after time as "a spreading cancer on the Federal Deposit Insurance System." But the speeches were devoid of logic. They were filled with colorful words and expansive conclusions but, although they identified a real problem, they never explained why deinsuring (rather than a reasonable limitation) was necessary to cure the problem. Here is a sample from testimony before the Senate Banking Committee:

Indeed, these money brokering operations have sought to leave the impression
in too many instances that such money brokerage has wrought no harm on the

Federal Deposit Insurance System at all. Those at fault, they say, were not the money brokers, but rather insured institutions which invested the funds poorly. The money brokers and the brokered funds, they claim, were simply innocent bystanders, harmless participants in the death dance of failed and failing institutions.

Those who believe such stories are likely to believe in fairy tales. The fact is, in far too many cases it was the easy, instantaneous, access to very willing money brokers, willing to provide high-priced federally-insured money to any institutions which sought it—in virtually unlimited amounts—which fueled the rapidly-made investments and loans that have become very bad assets in some of the most significant thrift failures we have seen.[4]

Nice rhetoric. But why not put a limit on brokered deposits rather than prohibiting them?

Gray and Isaac persisted, and in April 1984, the Bank Board and the FDIC adopted a final rule deinsuring deposits placed by brokers, effective October 1 of that year.

Immediately, a deposit broker sued the FDIC and the FSLIC on the ground that adopting the deinsuring regulations was beyond the scope of the agencies' powers under their respective deposit insurance statutes. Congress, the lawsuit asserted, had enacted deposit insurance to protect *beneficiaries* and by explicit language had not given the insuring agencies the power to restrict that insurance by deinsuring selected deposits. In June the Federal District Court in Washington ruled in favor of the deposit brokers, and the Court of Appeals upheld that decision in January 1985.[5] Deinsuring thus never took effect, and while the controversy and lawsuits raged, excessive S&L growth continued.

With hindsight it is very clear that—at least for S&Ls—the deposit brokerage problem could have been dealt with simply by reimposing the 5 percent limit. Deinsuring was unnecessary. (The Bank Board did impose the 5 percent limit on insolvent institutions in 1984, and in 1985 made it applicable to institutions with less than 3 percent capital. But those rules didn't catch the high fliers who stayed in compliance with capital requirements until the examiners declared that their loans weren't worth anything.)

The Bank Board never reimposed the 5 percent rule on everybody. Apparently, Ed Gray thought he *had* to act in concert with the FDIC—and since the FDIC thought it didn't have power to impose the 5 percent limit, the Bank Board didn't do it, either. "Politically it would have been impossible, take my word for it," Ed Gray says. "We had to treat insured depositories the same way. Otherwise the Congress and the administration would have removed me from office." He asked Congress to impose a 5 percent limit. But laws are hard to pass.

The brokered deposits deinsurance fiasco was very costly. It distracted the Bank Board's efforts during vital months of 1983 and 1984. It presented a picture of an agency acting extremely and without logic. It depicted the agency as vindictive rather than regulatory. It convinced many in the administration, in the industry, in academia, in the legal profession, and in the Congress that this Bank Board was a little off the wall. These perceptions made it very difficult for Ed Gray to be taken seriously later on, when many of his instincts were right.

EMPIRE OF MESQUITE

Although Ed Gray says that he "saw the problem" six months after he became chairman, other observers date the Bank Board's understanding to a day a few months later, in March 1984, when Empire Savings & Loan Association of Mesquite, Texas, failed.[6] Empire was an early version of what became the classic Texas failure. A little S&L from outside Dallas, it grew at a rate of over 500 percent per annum in the second half of 1982 and through 1983. It grew by funding its liabilities through a variety of wholesale sources but predominantly through brokered deposits, which accounted for 75 percent of deposits in 1983. It invested these rapidly gathered funds in construction loans to build condos in the "I-30 corridor" outside Dallas, which allegedly was going to be a new boom town in Dallas's ever-expanding future. Empire failed when there were no buyers for the condos.

The raw data on Empire of Mesquite is astonishing. It grew from an average size of $13 million in assets in 1981 to $33 million in 1982 to (amazingly) $192 million in 1983, finishing the year at over $300 million—a total growth of over 1,000 percent in two years. At the end, jumbo CDs represented over 90 percent of Empire's liabilities; brokered deposits (including the jumbos) accounted for over 75 percent. Its construction lending grew at over 600 percent a year.

Until the examiners said Empire was insolvent because the buildings weren't worth nearly what Empire had loaned on them, Empire showed robust earnings that grew right along with its assets. It had a miraculous earning asset yield of 21 percent (including loan fees) in 1983, which gave it an astonishing spread of almost 10 percent (1,000 basis points). Of course it had no loan loss reserves.

Empire's auditors, Coopers & Lybrand, had taken until July 31, 1983, to report on Empire's fiscal year ended September 30, 1982; and when they finally reported, they reported that Empire's records were so bad that they couldn't evaluate whether there was a sufficient reserve for loan losses.

They also reported that loan fees taken into income—income for the period was just $7,000—had exceeded the amount permitted under generally accepted accounting principles by $1.2 million, which was more than Empire's entire net worth of $677,000. So on a GAAP basis, Empire had been insolvent at September 30, 1982. Empire was, as any bank analyst would have said, a foreseeable disaster. Nevertheless, Empire wasn't closed until March 1984, long after Coopers & Lybrand, the Texas S&L Department, and the FHLB of Dallas had identified its problems. Under the regulators' noses, Empire grew by over $200 million—it more than doubled in size—from the time it was identified as a problem to the time they declared it to have failed.

The examination staff had a videotape made of the empty freeways and wide open spaces around the Empire of Mesquite investments, as well as the emptiness of the buildings themselves. They showed the tape to the members of the Board and, if Board members hadn't recognized before that there were serious problems with many of the industry's new investments, they knew it then. It didn't take much further investigation to find out that the same pattern of growth and lending had been going on at many other Texas S&Ls. Many other Texas S&Ls were growing very fast, had made substantial investments in construction loans and land loans, and were showing absurdly high profits, just as Empire of Mesquite had done right up until its failure.

The House Committee on Governmental Operations immediately held hearings into how an apparently healthy S&L (its published reports—which included the $1.2 million of loan fees that GAAP had excluded—showed it to be the best-earning S&L in the country in 1983) could grow so fast and then so precipitously go under, leaving a tab of more than $100 million for the FSLIC. The obvious question was, Where had the Bank Board been?

Investigation showed that the Dallas FHLB chief had encouraged the rapid growth of the Texas S&Ls and that the Dallas region was far behind in examining institutions. The Texas S&Ls were being allowed to grow at unprecedented rates. Empire had been identified as a problem a year before it failed, but supervisory action had been slow and the Bank Board's procedures were cumbersome.

The Empire hearings also revealed several technical regulatory problems, including the ADC loan accounting problem, the disparity between GAAP and RAP accounting for loan fees, the excessive amounts that Texas S&Ls were lending, and the inability of S&L examiners to require reserves against loans that were in trouble but performing because of interest reserves. We have been over the ADC loan problem and the loan fees problem, but Real Estate Lending 101 didn't prepare us for what Empire and others were doing: lending 100 percent of appraised value even if the borrower had just bought the property for less than the appraised value (a contradiction within the proposition, but we'll have to assume that this happened regularly in 1980s Texas). As FHLBB General Counsel Norm Raiden explained it in the hearings, "If a person buys a piece of property for one price, has it appraised for a higher amount, it is possible for him to get a loan which gives him cash and so-called 'walking away' money." The Texas authorities blamed this excessive lending on the Bank Board's having removed LTV restrictions in 1983, which caused Ed Gray and the Texas S&L Commissioner a frank but incomprehensible exchange of views on the subject.

The inability of Bank Board examiners to require that S&Ls establish reserves against a loan unless (1) the loan was in default and (2) a new appraisal showed that the property wasn't worth the loan amount, looks bizarre in retrospect. (Bank examiners didn't have these restrictions.) General Counsel Raiden explained the reserves problem this way:

> Well, the classification of scheduled items is based upon whether or not the item is delinquent in payment, or whether it has been foreclosed or is otherwise in default. It is not based on an appraisal of the security. In these particular loans, they were arranged so the borrower has prepaid the interest on the loan for a substantial period of time, and the prepayment came out of the loan itself.

As a result, even though the examiners *knew* that the empty condos wouldn't bring enough to repay the loans, under the Bank Board's peculiar rules they couldn't force write-downs or require more capital or restrict growth based on these embedded losses because the loans were formally performing, with interest being paid from the interest reserve. The Bank Board blamed the problem on the interest reserves, which they said were designed to cover up bad loans. But interest reserves had a legitimate purpose. They had been designed by lenders who wanted to make sure they got the equity they bargained for up front. Did the Bank Board immediately change its examination rules? No. It changed them at the end of 1985, a year and a half later.

The Congressional committee that investigated the failure of Empire concluded that the Bank Board and the FHLB of Dallas had failed in their duties of supervision and regulation.

In 1983 and 1984 Vernon, Independent American, Sunbelt, Western, and all the other small but superfast-growing, recently acquired Texas S&Ls had statistical profiles that looked just like Empire of Mesquite. We'll follow their progress as we go along. (The Bank Board didn't follow their progress. Its problem book only had low net worth institutions in it. One nasty little fast grower called Western, for example, wasn't examined for three years. When it finally was examined, it was promptly taken over.) In all, about forty institutions, mostly in Texas and California, would have matched the Empire profile.

Those forty institutions later cost an estimated total of over $20 billion to deal with.

The regulatory problems that the Empire hearings disclosed were dealt with—eventually. For example, although the Bank Board had power to reimpose rules restricting or prohibiting 100 percent-of-appraised-value lending, it never did so until 1987. Reimposition of *some* LTV rules would have made sense in light of the abusive practice discovered at Empire. The restrictions had been taken off to let S&L managers exercise prudent judgment, not to permit them to lend 100 percent of anything. But so many things were happening so fast that the Board—which didn't understand the ways that the business was changing—couldn't keep up.

The world went galloping by.

NEW CAPITAL REGULATIONS

Under the five-year averaging rule, a growing association perversely needed a lower capital percentage the faster it grew. This rule needed to be changed to slow growth. The 3 percent basic capital requirement also was too low.

In February 1984 the Board proposed to phase out five-year averaging over five years and immediately to require 3 percent capital for any new growth. The proposal would have been effective immediately for all periods after December 31, 1983, and would have slowed several of the Texas fast growers.

This proposal was vital to protecting the FSLIC. It didn't go far enough (ideally, it should have required a higher capital percentage for new growth) but it would have helped a great deal. Nevertheless, the Board put the proposal on the shelf and took no further formal action on the subject until it reproposed somewhat different new capital rules in November 1984. It didn't adopt a new final rule until the end of January 1985. So instead of the new rule being effective December 31, 1983, it was effective December 31, 1984; meanwhile, the Texas high flyers had grown another 200 percent to 300 percent, and total Texas deposits went from $46 billion to $62 billion in that one year. Asked why it took so long to change the capital rule, Ed Gray says that the industry didn't want changes and he was "counting on the brokered deposit rule."

The world went galloping by. Whereas at the end of 1982 the S&Ls had $6 billion invested in commercial construction and $4 billion in land, by the end of 1984 they had $33 billion invested in commercial construction (and additional billions committed) and $19 billion in land.

The release accompanying the November 1984 reproposal of new capital rules showed that the Bank Board staff understood the problem well enough. The current rule, it said, places no limit on the rate of growth of institutions since it permits a debt to equity ratio as high as 666 to 1. . . . During the period from June 30, 1982 to June 30, 1984 retail deposits have increased 31.2% and jumbo deposits have increased 104.8%. Other borrowings increased 90.8%. . . . The industry has not yet had much experience with broadened investment authority under state law. Many of the investments made under these laws are too recent to have resulted in profit and loss. . . . A staff study indicates, in general, that faster-growing institutions have both riskier asset portfolios and less stable funding sources than do slower-growing institutions.

Instead of the simple phaseout called for in the February proposal, the November proposal provided for a complex combination of "factors" to calculate an S&L's net worth requirement. The minimum net worth requirement now would be comprised of a "base factor," an "amortization factor," a "growth factor," and a "contingency factor." The new rule was confusing to almost everyone. How it worked isn't worth explaining. Its complexity made it hard to enforce because violators could claim a lack of understanding. Moreover, the "growth factor" in this new rule restricted only growth of over 25 percent a year. Thus, although 1985 growth was significantly curtailed, rapid growth was still authorized. To anyone not inured to the 400 percent growth figures produced in Texas in 1983 and 1984, 25 percent growth for a financial institution is enormous. And 400 associations continued to grow at greater than 25 percent in 1985.

In 1986 the Bank Board recognized that it had been too lenient on growth in the 1985 version of its capital requirements and again tightened up on growth, but it still permitted growth of up to 10 percent without much capital support. Weak S&Ls no longer grew at 100 percent a year, but many of them still grew.

These new net worth requirements were the first meaningful steps the Bank Board took to curtail the escalating problems in the industry. They just came a couple of years late, and since they were indifferently enforced, they were less effective than theory would have said they should be.

DIRECT INVESTMENTS

At the same time that the Bank Board was working on new capital rules during 1984, it also was working on the regulation of direct investments. The state-chartered S&Ls, you will recall, had been given power under the laws of Florida, Texas, and California to invest in practically anything. At least in California, they appeared to be doing so, with many small institutions investing a substantial part of their assets in their own real estate ventures or other businesses.

There is nothing inherently wrong with investing in windmill farms and real estate. They can be successful ventures and, although windmill farms are a relatively recent invention, at least real estate can be shown to have been profitable for investment over a long period of time. It is easy to reason that banks and S&Ls give up the lion's share of the profits when they make loans to real estate entrepreneurs. If the property does well, this line of reasoning says, the bank gets a rate of interest and the real estate developer or owner makes the big bucks. If the property does badly, the bank gets the property and the real estate owner, who has a much smaller investment, walks away. The bank, we could reason, is better off owning and managing the property itself and thereby keeping all of the profits.

This line of reasoning, although in vogue in the mid–1980s, has several flaws. The first flaw is the assumption that the bank or S&L will manage the real estate well. This assumption usually turns out to be wrong.

Second, insured deposits shouldn't be used to make direct equity investments because, whereas a lender expects to be repaid, an entrepreneur making a direct investment in real estate sometimes will gain and sometimes will lose. The insurer shouldn't be left to pick up the much greater percentage losses that result from unsuccessful equity investments.

But even if it is bad policy to permit S&Ls to make direct investments, theories of federalism suggest that the federal government—in the form of the deposit insurer—shouldn't deprive state-chartered S&Ls of powers given them by the states, especially when studies showed they weren't dangerous.

For Ed Gray the issue wasn't that complicated. He saw that direct investments were relatively risky and that the FSLIC fund was too small to be able to afford additional risks. Therefore, in November 1984 the Bank Board proposed to prohibit FSLIC-insured S&Ls from investing more than 10 percent of their assets in direct investments without permission to exceed that level. This was a modest proposal that was *necessary* to protect the insurance fund. The only problem was that the Board didn't have much evidence that direct investments were risky. This made it easy to attack the proposal politically.

The Bank Board had often been easy to attack politically. Whereas the other federal banking agencies were merely guardians of the banking system, historically the Bank Board was not only the regulator of S&Ls but also the guardian of the S&Ls' special subsidies. As a result, Congress was used to a different kind of give and take with the Bank Board than with the Fed or the FDIC.

Charles Keating played on this relationship between Congress and the Bank Board to try to preserve his plan to use Lincoln Savings to build a vast real estate empire in Arizona and California. By using the power with members of Congress that lavish contributions gave him and combining this power with an alliance with the Texas high fliers, who also made lavish political contributions, Mr. Keating built political pressure on the Bank Board to back off the regulation. He also bought the best legal and consulting talent available—first to persuade the Bank Board and the Congress that direct investment really was less risky than making loans, and then to sue the Bank Board to overturn the regulation after politics and persuasion had failed.

The first big battles over direct investment were fought in late 1984 and early 1985. They took enormous energy from the Bank Board and particularly from thin-skinned Ed Gray, who held his ground despite brutal pressure. The U.S. League, the Texas League, and the State S&L Supervisors were all against the direct investment regulation. Only the California League supported Ed Gray's position. At one point, 229 members of the House of Representatives signed a statement generated by Keating urging the Bank Board to defer the effectiveness of the direct investment regulation.

The direct investment saga didn't end in 1985, however. The rule that the Bank Board adopted in January 1985 was temporary. Unless readopted, it would "sunset" twenty-four months later. Thus, all of Mr. Keating's political machinations continued. His campaign to prevent renewal of the rule in 1987 culminated in the famous meetings between Ed Gray and the "Keating Five"—Senators DeConcini, Cranston, Glenn, Riegle, and McCain. We will pick up on those meetings later when we discuss the transfer of supervision of Lincoln from San Francisco to Washington in 1988. We also will see how, if he couldn't prevent the rule, Keating just went ahead and violated it.

The bottom line on direct investments is that they are not suitable for insured banking institutions unless they are made with excess capital. Ed Gray's instincts on the issue were correct and, although he couldn't outlaw direct investments, at least he could, and did, restrict them to 10 percent of assets.

EXAMINATION AND SUPERVISION

Bank regulatory theory makes a distinction between "regulation"—the making of rules to govern bank or S&L conduct—and "examination and supervision"—the process by means of which the regulatory agency examines institutions for compliance with rules and general compliance with prudent banking practices in the interest of safety and soundness. The Bank Board, however, had always placed its emphasis on making rules and enforcing them through the examination and supervision process; it gave examiners little encouragement to comment on "prudent banking practices." Instead, examiners were expected to determine whether S&Ls complied with specific rules. This may explain why many S&L *managers* acted on the strange presumption that if something wasn't prohibited, it must be prudent. Thus, one can argue, S&Ls had too many regulations about minor matters, not too few regulations.

The Bank Board had four major examination and supervision defects that needed to be fixed in order to be able to supervise S&Ls in the postderegulation world: (1) not enough examiners, (2) not enough examiners trained to examine for prudent banking practices and safety and soundness, (3) a historical bifurcation between the examination and supervision functions, and (4) the inability of examiners to force loan loss reserves to be taken on a timely basis.

Bank Board examiners couldn't enforce their findings directly or through their superiors in the Office of Examination and Supervision. Instead, their reports were forwarded to "supervisory agents," who were employees of the twelve Federal Home Loan Banks. The supervisory agent in charge of the examined S&L would take over implementation of any recommendations made by the examiner.

This process not only deprived the examiner of any real authority, it also put the process of implementing examination findings into the hands of a supervisory employee of the local Federal Home Loan Bank rather than of the Federal Home Loan Bank Board. This distinction, which appeared meaningless to the outside world, was important because whereas the Bank Board is an agency of the United States whose members are appointed by the President and confirmed by the Senate, the local Federal Home Loan Banks are owned by the S&Ls themselves, and their directors are selected by the S&Ls. Thus supervisory agents who were employees of the local FHLBs had incentives to keep local S&L managers happy, not to tell them what was wrong with the way they were running their businesses.

The examination and supervision problems came to the fore in the wake of Empire of Mesquite. The Bank Board needed more money to be able to hire more examiners and to pay them more in order to prevent the excessive turnover that had hampered the examination force's ability to function.

The problem was especially acute in Texas because in 1983 the local Federal Home Loan Bank had been moved from Little Rock to Dallas. Many of the people who worked for the FHLB in Little Rock didn't want to move to Dallas; and thus, when it moved, it lost staff and continuity of supervision.

The Bank Board could not, however, just go out and hire the examiners that it thought it needed at the salaries it thought it had to pay. Even though S&Ls paid for their own examinations, the dollars spent—not enormous sums—were recorded as part of the federal budget. Therefore, although the *banking* agencies didn't have to answer to the OMB, the Bank Board—probably on the theory that S&Ls obtained subsidies from the government—did have to get budget clearance from OMB.

The OMB had been trying to *cut* the examination staff. It had ordered a RIF (reduction in force) at the end of 1983 and had rescinded it when the Bank Board complained. But OMB wasn't about to say "yes" when the Bank Board asked for more examiners and higher entry-level pay. At OMB they just plain didn't believe in examination and supervision; they believed in free enterprise. And they didn't believe Ed Gray when he told them that terrible things were happening in Texas. He didn't have a lot of credibility at OMB.

Gray tried going to Congress for the money, but there wasn't much sympathy for spending more than the administration wanted to spend on what seemed like an administrative issue.

The Bank Board needed more examiners, but it wasn't going to get them through the federal budgetary process. As a stopgap, the Board sent examiners from all over the country to Texas to help out. And it ordered the regional FHLBs to hire more supervisory personnel.

Finally, to get out from under the OMB, the Bank Board decided to transfer its examiners and the examination function to the twelve Federal Home Loan Banks, which were off-budget. A side benefit would be that the examiners now would work for the supervisory agents, and the Washington staff would concentrate on watching the supervisory agents.

The transfer began in July 1985, and in 1986 the Federal Home Loan Banks were successful in catching up with most of the examination backlog. Experienced supervisory personnel from the federal banking agencies whom the Bank Board brought in to supervise the examination force still thought the quality of examination was low, but at least the examinations were being done.

Transferring the examiners to the Federal Home Loan Banks was a radical solution to the budget problem—and it took a long time to implement. The Board knew it needed more examiners in April 1984. After being turned down by OMB, it formulated the plan to send the examiners to the Federal Home Loan Banks in the summer and got it approved by the Federal Home Loan Banks in the fall. But then the staff had to design mechanisms for moving federal employees to private employment status. Would the examiners be willing to give up their civil service status? What kind of pension and benefits arrangements needed to be made? There were six union contracts to renegotiate. The Bank Board "didn't want to lose half the crew in the middle of a hurricane." In the end, when the transfer took place in July 1985 (fifteen months after the problem had become obvious), almost all the examiners went along.

But in the meantime, the world went galloping by.

DEALING WITH THE LOAN
CLASSIFICATION PROBLEM

Examining institutions does little good if the examining agency can't order the proper remedies. The Bank Board argued in Congress that it needed better cease-and-desist order powers, better powers to order proper record keeping, and better powers to remove management—and maybe those better powers would have helped.

It is true that when an institution is growing too fast and making questionable loans, its records often are a mess. Senior management isn't concerned about records because it is focused on "the bottom line"—continuing to grow, continuing to make the numbers look good—not on putting things in order. Putting things in order is for the "green eye-shade guys."

The Bank Board's powers to order better record keeping were only so-so. But ordering better record keeping usually isn't very effective in a go-go situation. Nobody believes that he is going to get shut down just because his records aren't good.

On the most crucial supervisory issue—loan loss reserves—the Bank Board had tied its own hands. It didn't need Congress to change the rule.

The Bank Board needed to stop the rapid growth and the risky lending pattern. To do that, nothing works like writing down some loans, thereby reducing earnings, capital, and management bonuses. But Bank Board rules prevented supervisory agents from ordering specific loan loss reserves for problem properties without going through an elaborate process. The agencies that examined and supervised banks had long had a system under which problem loans were classified "substandard," "doubtful," or "loss." Loans (or parts of loans) classified "doubtful" had to be written down by 50 percent, and loans classified "loss" had to be written off entirely. "Valuation reserves" (which reduced earnings but still counted as regulatory capital) had to be held against loans classified "substandard." The Bank Board had no such system. Under the Bank Board system, as General Counsel Raiden had testified in the Empire hearings, without an actual default, an examiner couldn't order an appraisal of real estate standing as security for a loan, and without a new formal appraisal he couldn't order that the loan be written down. Thus, even if the Bank Board examined a Texas high flier and the examiners saw that the S&L's properties had no tenants, they couldn't force write-downs of the loans—and thus call a halt to the institution's growth of high-risk assets—unless the loans went into default, which they wouldn't do as long as they had interest reserves.

The Texas high fliers used these rules—were they ever good at taking advantage of regulatory defects—to prevent write-downs even after interest reserves had run out. They began by renewing the loans and "replenishing" the interest reserves, but when this proved transparent, they began swapping loans—"a rolling loan," they said, "carries no loss." Often it took examiners years to catch up with a "rolling loan."

The Bank Board saw the problem that its write-down rules caused at least as early as March 1984; it proposed a new regulation on the subject in June—

1985. The S&Ls didn't like the idea, of course. It wouldn't be natural for management to want low-level types like examiners to be able to classify their loans. Bankers don't like it, either, so the U.S. League's opposition was not surprising: "The U.S. League is deeply disturbed by the vast grant of discretionary authority which this proposal would confer upon the Bank Board's examiner staff, and strongly urges that the agency reject the proposed alternative to reevaluation by appraisal."[7] The Bank Board didn't put out a final regulation giving examiners authority to classify loans until December. Again, the problem should have been obvious in 1983. It clearly *was* obvious early in 1984. A regulation was proposed in June 1985. And a solution wasn't adopted until December.

Again, the world went galloping by.

THE REREGULATION BUGABOO

Not all the delays in regulatory reform were the fault of Congress or the OMB. Delay also came from the Board's being thin-skinned. The members read the trade press every day and were stung by articles calling them backward "reregulators." That was a dirty word in the prevailing deregulatory climate. Ed Gray would stay up nights carefully answering his critics rather than calmly pressing ahead despite them. Don Hovde and Mary Grigsby, who spent much of their time on the S&L lecture circuit, heard the reregulatory criticisms every day.

When the three of them couldn't agree, consideration of proposed regulations was deferred, meetings were postponed, and eventually they made compromises. Ed Gray reminds us that he had only one vote among three. Hovde and Grigsby deny that they held anything up.

THE RUN ON FCA

Meanwhile the problem was getting worse—and not only in Texas. It was getting worse at all of the risk-taking S&Ls.

The run on American Savings in August 1984 brought one major problem into the open. At that point the world knew about Empire of Mesquite—clearly an asset problem caused by bad lending practices, or worse. The world did not know that Charlie Knapp was gambling billions of dollars—effectively FSLIC dollars—on complex mortgage-backed securities transactions that had significant interest rate risk. That problem became public because FCA was a publicly owned holding company that reported to the SEC. It therefore had to file registration statements with the SEC when it issued securities.

The SEC questioned the way that FCA had accounted for transactions known as "dollar rolls," and insisted that FCA's American Savings subsidiary should have marked to market the billions of dollars of U.S. government-guaranteed GNMA ("Ginnie Mae")* securities that it owned as a result of these dollar rolls. The mark to market resulted in FCA's recording a $140 million loss. Whether the SEC's action was proper or instead was an improper retroactive change in GAAP, as FCA contended, we can leave others to argue about. (We'll see a later parallel in the Franklin Savings dispute.) The impact, however, was clear. Depositors—many with uninsured funds of over $100,000 on deposit—were scared by the $140 million loss; the big loss also made them focus on the relative weakness of FCA's financial condition in general. FCA, which had been gathering funds all over the country through its "dialing for dollars" program, began to lose deposits fast.

Angry with himself for approving the State–American merger, Ed Gray had long since decided that he had to get rid of Charlie Knapp. As part of his campaign, Gray explains that he had called Knapp to Washington in June 1984 and read him a "list of charges," concluding with the charge that Knapp was operating American in an unsafe and unsound manner. He told Knapp that he "would do everything in his power to remove" him.

So when the run began in August, Gray saw his chance to get Knapp out. When FCA couldn't fund its outflow, it went to the Federal Home Loan Bank of San Francisco for assistance. San Francisco declined to give assistance unless it was guaranteed by the FSLIC itself. Now Ed Gray had Charlie Knapp where he wanted him. We "squeezed him," says Gray, "we made life impossible for him."

But Ed Gray wasn't in Washington when the FCA crisis heated up. Nor were the other Board members, who were on vacation. Gray, Shannon Fairbanks, and Norman Raiden were in Europe on a road show selling Federal Home Loan Bank securities. They were on the phone to Washington between presentations, but they were afraid to come home for fear of precipitating a larger run by terminating their trip. So the staff struggled along with the problem and organized liquidity from a variety of sources including—need I say ironically?—brokered deposits. Prudential Bache and Salomon Brothers raised over $1 billion in brokered deposits to save FCA from a liquidity failure.

After the "road show," Ed Gray was supposed to go to his wife's parents' house in the French countryside for a week's vacation. When he got there and called Washington, however, the Bank Board staff and Preston Martin, Vice Chairman of the Fed, convinced him to come back as fast as possible. So in the middle of the night, his wife drove him to an airport in central France, from which he flew to Paris, took the Concorde to Washington, and went directly to Paul Volcker's office at the Fed.

FCA was trying to get additional liquidity from the Fed as the nation's "lender of last resort," but Gray convinced Volcker not to provide any funds until he got Knapp out of the picture.

After a tense and protracted negotiation — and after his board of directors had given him $2 million in severance pay — Charlie Knapp resigned as chairman of FCA and the FSLIC guaranteed all deposits in American regardless of whether they were over the insured limit. Thus the run was stopped and management was replaced.

The FCA problem showed how weak the FSLIC was. It began with a run on the biggest S&L in the United States. The Bank Board didn't trust its management and could have declared it insolvent. But the Bank Board didn't have the money to deal with FCA. Nobody knew exactly what the cost would be if American Savings had to be marked to market, but everybody knew that it would be more than a billion dollars and would unmask the fragility of the FSLIC fund. That in turn, it was feared, would result in a nationwide run on all S&Ls, because if the fund was broke, then people would doubt whether their savings were protected.

FCA ran in its weakened condition from August 1984 to December 1988, managed by William Popejoy, Ed Gray's handpicked president (he rejected the candidacy of David Stockman, then still head of OMB) who never made a move without consulting directly with the Chairman's office. Observers say that Bill Popejoy and Ed Gray took about the same amount of interest rate risk that Charlie Knapp took. At one point they had about a $6 billion mismatched mortgage-backed securities position that the Bank Board specifically approved so that FCA, despite its low capital (it didn't meet any relevant test), could try to grow its way out of its problem. The FHLBB of San Francisco, believing that FCA could not be saved, had wanted the new managers of FCA to conduct a quiet liquidation after Charlie Knapp had been forced out. Ed Gray and Bill Popejoy instead decided to make some big interest rate bets in an effort to save FCA, as vividly described in Michael A. Robinson's book, *Overdrawn*. I do not know whether in the end those bets paid off.

The eventual resolution of FCA will cost somewhere between $2 billion and $5 billion. Charlie Knapp's board and management still say that American wouldn't have failed if the Bank Board hadn't stepped in. That's what they all say.

WHISTLE-BLOWING

Ed Gray was first and foremost a public relations man. That was his job most of his life, and he thought almost entirely in terms of public image. In 1984 he saw that something bad was happening to the S&Ls, and he said,

"They're not going to pin this on me." He told Shannon Fairbanks that "Everything we do and everything we say is history."

At every opportunity, Ed Gray warned that something bad was happening. He railed against growth. He decried risky lending. Paul Volcker wrote to him in 1988, "You did more warning and alarm sounding than any regulator in my experience. You don't need to be defensive." Gray's hero is Winston Churchill. He saw himself as Winston Churchill in the 1930s, warning about the dangers of Hitler.

Gray's style of warning, however, became a part of the problem. Nobody wanted to listen to warnings in the first place—nobody ever does. Using too many words merely compounds the problem. As one senior staff member told me, Gray never used one word where a thousand would do just as well. Here is a very brief sample warning about the state of the FSLIC fund from Gray's testimony of March 13, 1985, before a subcommittee of the Senate Committee on Appropriations:

> Since December 31, 1982 almost all income received by the FSLIC has been expended to solve problem cases. While it is very difficult to project with precision FSLIC reserve levels at the end of 1985, we would be derelict in our duties as managers of the FSLIC in your behalf if we failed to inform you at this time that our caseload trends do suggest the possibility that such levels could be diminished significantly, both in 1985 and again in 1986, as a result.

By March 1985, Gray must have known that the FSLIC didn't have the money to do its job. Is that what he was saying? Why was his prose so prolix?

The world went galloping by.

DID YOU EVER HAVE THE FEELING THAT YOU WANTED TO GO, BUT STILL HAVE THE FEELING THAT YOU WANTED TO STAY?

On May 1, 1985, Ed Gray's wife reminded him that he had promised her not to stay at the Bank Board more than two years. He told her he would leave the government in the fall.

But in July, when Gray was in Europe again, this time selling Federal Home Loan Mortgage Corporation (FHLMC or Freddie Mac)* securities, Don Regan, by then White House Chief of Staff, let it be known that he wanted Ed Gray to resign. That stiffened Gray's resolve to stay. He wasn't going to be forced out—he would stay for the time being because "I could say 'til hell freezes over that this was my plan and nobody would believe it."

He worked harder than ever after he knew Regan wanted him out. Twenty-hour workdays weren't unusual. But what he worked on were his speeches and replying to critics. Staff members report that each day he was dominated by the day's clippings and the new actual or fancied slights from the press. As he says, he felt "beleaguered."

Gray also couldn't hire staff. He couldn't tell them how long he would stay, and the White House didn't want to approve his appointments. So when Raiden and Schilling left during 1985, Gray appointed an "acting" General Counsel and an "acting" director of the Office of Examination and Supervision (OES). By 1986 most of the top staff positions were "acting," so Gray sent out a memo telling the people in those positions to stop using the "acting" title — it didn't change their status, but it looked better.

The everyday processing of applications through the Bank Board practically ground to a halt.

BEVERLY HILLS

Although S&Ls in Texas and elsewhere were growing too fast and making investments that were too risky — and Ed Gray was warning everybody that this was going on — there wasn't much publicity about actual failures between the Empire of Mesquite hearings in April 1984 and the failure of Beverly Hills S&L a year later. The Bank Board simply didn't declare failures because it was trying to conserve the FSLIC fund.

The Beverly Hills failure caused a stir because of the name "Beverly Hills" and because Congress again held hearings.

Beverly Hills S&L looked a little bit like Empire.[8] It grew fast from 1981 to 1985; it made a large amount of construction loans; it took in a lot of loan fees that shouldn't have been accounted for as income under GAAP; it failed after Coopers & Lybrand found that $100 million of losses (more than its $40 million of RAP net worth) were embedded in its loan portfolio. Also like Empire, Beverly Hills had been criticized by the FHLBB's examiners for years.

Beverly Hills S&L had been practically out of capital when the interest rate ravages ended in 1982, so it had embarked on the new strategy described earlier, which quickly led to increased asset problems. As early as March 1983, the examiners reported high levels of nonperforming loans and no operating income.

But Beverly Hills was allowed to grow — from $950 million of assets at the end of 1982 to almost $3 billion at the end of 1984, based on almost no GAAP capital but on RAP capital composed largely of "appraised equity capital" and loan fees. The Bank Board didn't even classify Beverly Hills as a "supervisory case" until it had failed because it had always met its formal capital requirement. (Under the FHLBB's internal rules, an S&L wasn't a "supervisory case" if it met its capital requirement. And it didn't get any special treatment unless it was a supervisory case.) Ed Gray testified: "The problem of insolvency was created by that [$100 million] write-down [required by Coopers & Lybrand]. The institution had $40 million in net worth and the next day it had a negative net worth of $60 million after the write-down."

The Bank Board's assessment of its own performance in mid-1985 is reflected in the key sentence from Ed Gray's forty-seven pages of prepared testimony: "The Bank Board has taken all of the key regulatory steps it can under its existing statutory authority." Again, Congressional investigators didn't agree. Neither did the General Accounting Office (GAO), which concluded four years later: "We do not believe that the Bank Board lacked the necessary legal authority under the National Housing Act to promulgate regulations needed to ensure that all thrifts, regardless of their charter, operated in a safe and sound manner."[9]

DISTRACTIONS

The Bank Board and its senior staff could never get to concentrate on regulation and supervision for very long without something intruding on the process. Either it was Congressional hearings on failures like Empire and Beverly Hills, or the failure of state insurance funds in Ohio and Maryland, or a fight with OMB or Don Regan, or an FBI investigation of Ed Gray's $47,000 office renovation or travel expenses. The Gray Bank Board wasn't the most rigorously organized place to begin with—for example, one senior staffer described working for Gray as "chaos," and another described it as "nerve-racking"—so it got sidetracked easily.

Every Congressional appearance was a production. The Congress was always asking for information, and the Bank Board—never exactly a well-oiled information machine—had to spend enormous amounts of senior staff time preparing. What was worse, Congress didn't really care about regulatory problems. Most members have a kind of prurient interest rather than a serious legislative purpose. With some rare and notable exceptions, members of Congress are ignorant about the matters they are investigating and don't want to learn anything that might require more than a minute's concentration. Some of the hearings seemed to be aimed personally at Ed Gray or members of the Bank Board's staff. And Gray couldn't seem to resist verbally punching an antagonistic Congressman in the nose. He constantly fought with Representative John Dingell, the chairman of one subcommittee, and constantly misunderstood the questions asked by Doug Barnard, the head of another.[10]

As a result of all the Congressional investigations, the agency was constantly spending its time and resources looking backward and protecting personal reputations instead of focusing forward on the problem.

THE FREDDIE MAC DIVIDEND DISPUTE

Almost everything the Bank Board did got it embroiled in controversy. In early 1985 the Board imposed a special assessment on all insured S&Ls in order to beef up the FSLIC fund. The special assessment was entirely proper, even though it wasn't appreciated by the industry that had to pay it. (The U.S. League called it a "radical step that could well be counterproductive.")[11] At the same time, however, the Bank Board sought to soften the blow on S&L earnings by declaring a dividend of Freddie Mac preferred stock to the S&Ls. The Board had figured that the S&Ls already owned Freddie Mac through their ownership of the Federal Home Loan Banks that owned Freddie Mac's common stock, and therefore no one could complain if Freddie Mac issued preferred stock to the S&Ls.

OMB questioned whether Freddie Mac had the right to issue this stock to the S&Ls without legislation. It seemed to OMB that the S&Ls were being given something of value that belonged to the government. This OMB position led to a publicly reported vituperative exchange between Gray and OMB. The press enjoyed the members of two federal agencies calling each other names in public. Eventually the Attorney General ruled that the Bank Board was right.

Remarkably, all this (and Ed Gray's rejection of David Stockman as CEO of FCA) happened while the Bank Board was trying to get more money for examiners from OMB.

Freddie Mac as a Symptom

Even in concept the Bank Board's involvement with Freddie Mac was a distraction. What was the regulator doing in Europe selling securities? Isn't that role also inconsistent with being the regulator and insurer of S&Ls? Apparently nobody thought so. It was, somehow, a proper extension of the Bank Board's role as cheerleader for the S&L industry and its pro-housing role. And most Bank Board chairmen loved the perks of also being chairman of Freddie Mac and getting to do fun things like a European "road show." Ed Gray was always travelling.

THE MARYLAND AND OHIO CRISES

In the middle of 1985, two local crises added to the distractions from the Bank Board's focus on the problems of the institutions it already insured. First the Ohio insurance fund and then the Maryland insurance fund, both of which insured state-chartered S&Ls that had chosen not to be insured by the FSLIC, went under after depositor runs had overwhelmed the state S&L systems they insured. The FSLIC had to examine the state S&Ls and provide insurance on an emergency basis even though its resources were already severely stretched.

After the Ohio crisis, Congress held hearings on the FSLIC's response to Ohio institutions' need for federal deposit insurance.[12] Again a Congressional committee criticized Ed Gray for acting too slowly. If he had acted more promptly, they found, Governor Richard Celeste of Ohio wouldn't have had to declare the bank holiday that sealed the Ohio institutions' fate. Maybe the committee was right; maybe it wasn't. But its findings definitely distracted the Bank Board again.

CROSSCURRENTS

Thrift institution failures weren't the only financial institution issues arguing for public and Congressional attention. Commercial banks were seeking to peel back the industry barriers that prevented them from competing with securities firms and insurance companies, as well as the geographic barriers that continued to prevent nationwide consumer banking operations. The major banks and bank holding companies wanted to become diversified financial firms, but the Glass–Steagall Act and the Bank Holding Company Act stood in their way. The big banks saw things going their way when South Dakota permitted its banks to sell and underwrite insurance and the FDIC ruled that some banks could engage in securities brokerage operations. The big banks' lobbyists were all over Washington, clamoring for Congressional action to enlarge banks' powers.

Something called the "nonbank bank" also became a part of the banking powers controversy. A technical loophole in the Bank Holding Company Act was interpreted to permit banks that did not both take demand deposits (checking accounts) and make commercial loans to be treated as "nonbanks" for purposes of the Bank Holding Company Act, and therefore not to be subject to its bank ownership restrictions. As a result, the nonbank bank theory said that such a bank could be owned by a bank holding company in any state in the nation, despite the Douglas amendment. It also said that such a bank could be owned by any corporation without the corporation's having to be regulated by either the Bank Holding Company Act or the S&L Holding Company Act. These were heady times for creative lawyers in financial fields, and we kept inventing new ways around regulation every day.

THE GROWING MAGNITUDE OF THE PROBLEM

The number of insolvent S&Ls kept growing in 1984 and 1985. At the end of 1984 there were 103 operating RAP-insolvent institutions, 445 operating

GAAP-insolvent institutions, and 663 operating institutions with $336 billion of assets (a third of the industry) that would have been insolvent on a tangible basis—that is, if goodwill and deferred losses weren't counted as assets. At the end of 1985 there were even more insolvent institutions, many of which were dead institutions—"zombies" that the Bank Board couldn't afford to deal with.

MANAGEMENT CONSIGNMENT PROGRAM

The Bank Board had to do something about the zombies that it couldn't liquidate. It couldn't leave them operating under the old managements, so it designed a "parking place" program called the Management Consignment Program (MCP). Under the MCP, the Bank Board would take over an insolvent S&L whose management it didn't trust and would appoint a new board of directors who were independent and a management provided by a healthy institution for a fee. The new management was supposed to try to minimize losses until the FSLIC got enough money to deal with the institution properly. About 100 S&Ls were put into the MCP between the spring of 1985, when it began, and 1989, when it ceased to function.

The MCP accomplished something in that it prevented further looting or risk-taking by institutions that on average had over a 16 percent negative net worth and therefore never could recover. Nevertheless, institutions in the MCP—because they were doomed to lose money forever—continued to lose money at alarming rates, on average in excess of 10 percent of their assets per year.

The MCP seems to have disappointed even some of its proponents. They expected that, in the consignment program, insolvent S&Ls at least would stop paying the highest rates for deposits because they weren't making any loans. But the MCP S&Ls didn't stop paying up because they *couldn't* stop, no matter who managed them. Everyone knew the MCP S&Ls were broke, so the public demanded a premium for keeping deposits in them.

MCP institutions in Texas not only had to keep rates up to hold deposits but also had to *grow* deposits in order to pay operating expenses and to fund losses. Their managers—responsible people picked by the FHLBB and probably the most competent people who could have been found—had to inflate the loss to the insurance fund daily by using brokered deposits at high rates to pay salaries, electric bills, and rent, with no prospect of getting the money back. To maintain MCP liquidity, the FHLBB often had to waive its rule against brokered deposits for low net worth institutions.

It would have been far cheaper to liquidate the MCP institutions and fund the amount by which they were insolvent at government bond rates. But government money hadn't been appropriated. A GAO study summed it up this way in 1987:

> Allowing insolvent and unprofitable institutions such as those in the MCP to continue to operate has negative effects on FSLIC. The operating losses . . . which continue to be incurred by these institutions represent an additional liability for FSLIC to absorb that would not occur if they were not permitted to continue to operate.[13]

Later information indicates that the MCP was a disaster because the losses that these unresolved cases incurred over the years that the government ran them were astronomical—in many cases more than their total deposits when they entered the program. An S&L that is doomed to lose money forever will do so no matter who runs it.

HIGH SCHOOL CIVICS

In theory, the FSLIC *could* have spent money that it didn't have. It had done so in 1981–82 when it guaranteed acquiring institutions a spread on funding the assets of failed institutions, and it would do so again on a much larger scale in 1988 under a new Bank Board. But Ed Gray's scruples wouldn't let him transform FSLIC's obligations to depositors into obligations to acquiring institutions by giving acquirers guarantees against loss on assets of failed institutions. He strongly believed that such action would have been tantamount to imposing taxes on the American people and that constitutionally only Congress can do that.

This is high-sounding high school civics, but the fact is that the FSLIC already had the obligations to the depositors, and giving notes to others to undertake to pay those obligations would not have created new obligations. Transforming obligations to depositors into obligations to acquirers would reduce rather than increase the eventual FSLIC obligation. Moreover, although pretty much everyone assumed that the government would stand behind the FSLIC, no one knew absolutely for sure because the government hadn't obligated itself legally. Whether to do so was still up to the Congress. For these reasons, there was no serious constitutional question.

THE U.S. LEAGUE DIDN'T BELIEVE THAT
FSLIC WAS BROKE

At the Bank Board's Christmas party in 1985, the gallows humor said that FSLIC stood for "Nothing Left to Lose." The staff knew the FSLIC was broke. The U.S. League, however, refused to believe the problem was as big as they said it was at the Bank Board. In November the U.S. League's research director wrote to the League's Task Force on FSLIC Issues:

In testimony before the House Subcommittee on Financial Institutions on October 17, 1985 FHLBB Chairman Gray suggests that the problems facing the FSLIC and the low level of its unobligated balance presented a crisis for the insurance fund. This crisis statement directly contradicts the information we have spent many hours developing and the information we have received from the Bank Board staff.[14]

The League's eyes must not have been upon Texas.

9 The Big Texas Disaster

Texas failures accounted for almost half of the total damage. Out of 280 S&Ls in Texas before they started failing, only about 70 of them—mostly small, rural associations—have survived; and some of those are just hanging on. Honoring FSLIC's commitments in Texas probably will cost over $60 billion—present value. At the end of 1982, total S&L deposits in Texas were only $34 billion. To make a $60 billion loss, it took a combination of fast growth, overlending, fraud, lemminglike behavior, the Reagan administration's refusal to provide more money for examiners, Congress's failure to provide money to FSLIC when the Bank Board finally asked for it, the 1986 Tax Act, the 1985–86 crash in oil prices, the Bank Board's failure to close institutions when they were hopelessly insolvent, and a flawed bidding process for failed institutions.

Six fast-growing S&Ls accounted for over $9 billion of losses. Those six—Vernon, Independent American, Western, Stockton, State Savings of Lubbock, and Sunbelt—had aggregate deposits of only $450 million at the end of 1982. If they had failed right then, even if their assets had been totally worthless, they could not have cost more than that. By year-end 1983 they still had only $2 billion of deposits (note that they had grown 400 percent in 1983), and at year-end 1984 they still had a smaller amount of deposits than they eventually had of losses—$5.3 billion. Despite new growth rules in 1985, they continued to grow and to lose, reaching $9.4 billion of deposits before they finally were disposed of in 1988.

The regulators not only failed to stop the growth; in many cases they even approved it. For example, at the end of 1983 Independent American had six branches and only 1.8 percent net worth. The Texas Commissioner and the FHLBB approved the opening of another twenty-five branches in 1984. Eventually, Independent American ended its sleigh ride with forty-seven branches, almost all approved after the Empire of Mesquite failure. Sunbelt had twelve branches at the end of 1983, when it had barely 3 percent net worth, and it was allowed to open another thirty-seven (thirty-six in 1984), for a total of forty-nine. The *point* of having to get branch approvals is to give the regulators an opportunity to evaluate whether the proposed growth is sound. Apparently, they approved any branch application that came through the door. In all, they approved 173 new branches in Texas in 1984—at the very time Ed Gray was decrying fast growth. Who was running the Bank Board?

In order to grow so fast, Texas S&Ls had to pay premium interest rates for deposits. In 1983–84, Texas S&Ls were already paying about 100 basis points more than local commercial banks for CDs and a little more than S&Ls elsewhere in the country. By 1987, in order to keep deposits at prior levels, Texas S&Ls, many of which were in the MCP, were paying an *additional* 100 basis points (called the "Texas premium"). Of course, if you pay that much for deposits, you have to try to earn the extra amount on the asset side—unless you're the government, in which case paying up for the deposits merely increases the size of the operating loss and the taxpayers' eventual bill.

Several books have been written that detail the fraud and high living which the owners and officers of the high fliers like Vernon, Sunbelt, and Independent American enjoyed.[1] The stories are interesting, but they have been told many times. We will limit ourselves here to some analysis of how and why these S&Ls eventually cost so much to inter.

EVERYBODY LOVES A WINNER

The fast-growing little Texas S&Ls learned early that if you reported big earnings, nobody would bother you. You got the respect of your peers, your neighbors, and your government representatives. You could live high and pay yourself big salaries and dividends. You could be generous with your friends and could make life hard for anyone who opposed you. It all depended on showing big profits.

People like Tom Gaubert, Ed McBirney, and Don Dixon—all of whom bought their S&Ls in 1981–82, when they were small rural associations— lived for the moment. Tomorrow would take care of itself. So to make the big profits, they made big loans to people who couldn't get credit from the commercial banks. They lent to friends, they lent to friends of friends, and they lent to people with political connections. The loan terms would have been outrageous to any creditworthy borrower. Three or four points over prime plus a three-to-six-point loan fee, plus an equity kicker wasn't unusual. The borrowers accepted the terms because they were getting 120 percent of the cost of building. They put up no capital and got their profit up front. They borrowed through a corporation, so they had no personal liability. Heads they won, tails the S&L lost.

The people who ran Independent American, Sunbelt, Vernon, and the other fast growers (there were over twenty of them in Texas alone) made these loans over lunches and dinners, and instructed their employees to get appraisals that made the deals work. If they understood the risks they were taking, they didn't show it. If they understood Real Estate Lending 101, there isn't any evidence of it.

When the loans started going bad around 1984, these and other high-flying Texas S&Ls formed a ring that passed loans back and forth between them to conceal their problems and live to gamble some more.

The regulators saw the profits and don't seem to have worried about the process until it was too late. The regulators got to Independent American in 1984 and kicked Tom Gaubert out. But then they let his brother run it for another year, during which it grew another $400 million. They didn't crack down on Vernon until 1986—and didn't take it over until 1987. Sunbelt— which will cost the most money—continued to grow through 1987.

When the Texas high fliers started in business in 1981, 1982, and 1983, they didn't need to commit fraud in order to get big benefits from owning and running S&Ls. They could use big up-front fees to grow, show profits, and pay big bonuses and dividends based on those profits. Regulatory accounting rules made the scam legal.

Nevertheless, it was a scam—a Ponzi scheme that had to collapse because many of the loans had to go bad. When that happened, either the party was over, because the S&L would have to report the losses caused by the bad loans—which would put a stop to the bonuses and dividends—or they had to do something to conceal the losses.

Concealing losses is illegal. But it is not illegal to sell a loan to someone else or to refinance a loan when it comes due. The high-flying Texas S&L operators were all in the same boat by sometime in 1984, so about a dozen of them started buying loans from each other and refinancing each other's loans in order to cover up the losses. They kept the loans moving from one institution to another so that the regulators couldn't catch up with them. Apparently these S&Ls' accounting firms were too dumb or were paid too well to blow the whistle. Under GAAP, it is clear that reciprocal deals of this nature lack the substance necessary to be accounted for at face value.

Deputy FSLIC director Bill Black described the Texas "daisy chains" to Congress as follows:

"Daisy chains" of unscrupulous thrifts developed in the areas of the country where FSLIC suffered its worst losses. Two or more failing shops would refinance each other's ADC loans as soon as the interest reserves were depleted. The firms would claim new income immediately from the points and fees on the new loans and create new interest reserves and book further income—all self-financed, of course. The merry-go-round would start all over again. A variant was for thrifts to buy each other's bad projects. This was often called "I'll trade you my dead cow for your dead horse." By paying each other more than the book value of the projects, they could each convert a loss into a gain and declare new income. The most popular game, however, was a phony "sale" of the project to a shill or straw borrower, who would put no money down and get a loan with no personal liability on the debt for 100 percent of the inflated sales price. Again, the accountants frequently looked the other way and allowed these scams. These scams did not simply delay action, they led to increased outlays of cash to people who would default and cause FSLIC increased losses. By creating high, albeit phony, reported profits and net worth, such thrifts also made it far less likely that the regulator would crack down on them. Imagine the reaction of legislators and judges if FSLIC shut down the most profitable thrift in America![2]

The "daisy chain" S&Ls were already dead by the time the daisy chains were formed. If they had recognized the losses, they would have been deeply insolvent. The concealment significantly compounded the problem, however, because the dead S&Ls continued to grow and to speculate—gambling ever greater amounts in the hope of survival—and some of their managements began more active looting. Once a management has committed a few cover-up frauds, it speeds up its pace in order to stash away as much money as possible before the music stops.

The FHLBB examiners were overwhelmed by all this. There weren't enough examiners, and they were too inexperienced. The FHLBB didn't examine some of the worst cases for two or three years, even though they clearly fitted the well-known pattern of Ponzi scheme losers who later became looters.

LEMMINGS

From 1982 to 1985, Vernon, Independent American, Sunbelt and, for a time, Empire of Mesquite looked like the most successful S&Ls in the country. They were growing, their reported income was excellent, their reported capital was satisfactory, they had enough variable-rate loans to minimize their interest rate risk. They were paying their officers the best salaries and providing the best perks; their owners were getting enormous dividends. Hardly anybody questioned whether the loans they made would be repaid or whether their income was real. These institutions were envied and their business plans—high growth with purchased funds and high income from loan fees and high interest rates tied to prime—were copied by S&Ls all over Texas and other states in the Southwest.

S&L managers in the Southwest had never seen a downturn in real estate. Since 1945, real estate prices had always gone up and entrepreneurs had always been bailed out by inflation. Everyone knew that the Southwest would continue to attract people because it was the best place to live. There was still plenty of space. Growth was naturally ordained. One lawyer friend described it as "like being in love."

Everyone in the S&L business in the Southwest could see the success of the Vernons and the Independent Americans because everyone knew everyone else. They all went to meetings of the Texas League and meetings sponsored by the Federal Home Loan Bank of Dallas. They all talked shop in between tall stories on the golf course, at the cocktail receptions, and at late night bull sessions about how to run the industry, the state of Texas, and the country. They had all known each other for years, especially the many executives who had gone through the U.S. League's S&L school at Indiana University, where upwardly bound young S&L executives got degrees in a two-week-per-summer three-year course that was better at creating an old boy network than it was at teaching banking. Nearly every senior S&L executive in the Southwest, including the Texas S&L Commissioner, had gone through the U.S. League school at Indiana.

If the Vernons and Independent Americans could make a lot of money in construction lending and financing land plays, then so could everyone else—they thought. At least that's what the head of the Texas League said.

Almost everyone jumped on the bandwagon, causing S&L construction lending in Texas to rise from practically nil in 1981 to a high of $16.4 billion in 1984. Land loans shot up from about $1 billion (3.6 percent of assets) in 1982 to $15 billion (15.8 percent of assets) in 1986. At the most deeply insolvent institutions, land loans were over a third of assets—in some cases over half. And they weren't lending on the land at 75 percent LTV. The loans were at 80, 90, and 100 percent. Anyone who had taken Real Estate Lending 101 would know how much risk this entailed and that prudent management wouldn't do it. But commercial loan underwriting courses weren't the Indiana program's strong suit.

In a go-go climate like this, insider fraud is likely to occur. It is even more likely that a lot of institutions whose managements are not stealing from themselves will be defrauded by borrowers who will take advantage of obviously lax procedures. That happened in dozens of cases.

Lemmings were easily defrauded. Here's an example. A con artist named

Sam McConnell, who came to Texas from Florida and established a decent reputation that belied his seamy Florida past, became a customer of several S&Ls. Home Savings in Houston made several loans to McConnell and his associates, all secured by real estate (but much of it raw land). In each case, the title company gave Home a certification that Home had a valid first lien on the property. Home's senior management didn't know that its commercial loan officer (hired away from a local commercial bank) and Mary Smith of the title company knew about the fraud and were giving them false information. In fact, other banks already had liens on the properties that Home took mortgages on. So when McConnell went under, Home only had a suit against the title company. Ten million dollars went down the drain. McConnell was indicted but committed suicide before he could be tried. Mary Smith is in jail. Home's commercial lending officer was acquitted because, members of the jury said, he really didn't get anything personally from McConnell—just a ski weekend in Colorado.

It's hard to get a jury to convict someone because he took a ski weekend in Colorado. On most juries there will be enough people who have done "relationship" business that they won't think it is fair to convict for business-as-usual.

OVERBUILDING 101

In 1980 Dallas had more millionaires per capita than any other major city. It had the strongest influx of business headquarters in the United States. It had "America's team," the Dallas Cowboys. And it had 69 million square feet of office space. In the next five years Texas real estate developers built another 74 million square feet of office space, much of it excellent architecturally and well suited to corporate tenants. But 74 million square feet of space is too much for a 69-million-square-foot market to absorb in five years. As a consequence, total vacancy and space under construction went from 9 million square feet to 37 million square feet—over 25 percent of the total space available.[3] With that vacancy level, the market has to crash.

You could see it coming, too. Whereas in 1980–81 almost all the new office space was leased up before the buildings were finished, by 1984 about two-thirds of all construction was speculative rather than leased up before building. By 1987 Dallas had a big supply of see-through office buildings.

Dallas is a large example of overbuilding, but the same phenomenon occurred earlier in Houston and Denver, and later in Phoenix, Boston, Hartford, and several Florida cities, as well as in medium-sized towns all over the country that thought they could attract new businesses. Almost everywhere the commercial banks and S&Ls were anxious to lend on new real estate projects. The S&Ls needed the new business because the secondary market and interest rate deregulation had taken the juice out of traditional single-family lending. The banks needed the new business because sound industrial companies could go directly to the commercial paper market and had by-passed the commercial banks. The banks and S&Ls looking for profitable new business caused the overbuilding.

THE CRASH OF 1986

Bad underwriting, overbuilding, and fraud would have sunk a lot of Texas S&Ls and would have cost the FSLIC more money than it had, but the oil price bust and the Tax Reform Act of 1986 more than doubled the size of the problem. The overbuilding all over Texas was already in place. But if oil had continued to boom, the crash wouldn't have been so deep.

Experts trace the oil bust to 1982, but in November 1985 the price of Texas Intermediate Crude was still $28 a barrel. By February 1986 it had fallen to $10 a barrel. Almost overnight, people who took risks based on the value of oil in the ground got wiped out. Oil companies laid off people to cut costs. Exploration stopped. Finding oil wasn't worth what it cost to drill and re-cover.

But the buildings were completed or under construction. So the price of office space in Dallas, which was $18 per square foot for class A space in 1984, and had been projected to go to $25 by 1990, dropped to $16 in 1986 and to $14 in 1987—if you could get a tenant. Remember how real estate valuation works: You deduct the operating expenses from the income and apply a capitalization rate to the net cash flow. The operating expenses don't go down just because rents go down, so as rents decline, operating expenses take a bigger part of the pie. A drop of $4 per square foot (from $18 to $14) implies about a 40 percent loss of market value. So even if the S&Ls' 100 percent loans had been 80 percent loans (which they weren't), and even if there had been tenants for the buildings (which often there weren't), the loans would have been deeply underwater.

The process caught the single-family lenders in Texas, too. In Houston, where the depression was worst, single-family home prices dropped 40 per-cent to 50 percent. That led honest citizens to abandon their homes in order to reduce their mortgage payments because the arithmetic was compelling. If you bought your house for $100,000 and took an 80 percent mortgage at 10 percent interest, your interest burden was $8,000 a year. If the identical house next door was selling for $50,000, you could reduce your interest payments on an 80 percent loan at the same 10 percent rate to $4,000 a year—and your principal payments would go down, too. Then your S&L would get stuck with an $80,000 mortgage on a $50,000 property and have to take the loss. In theory, your lender could pursue you for a deficiency judgment, but in practice the courts weren't cooperative with lenders who sought deficiency judgments from people who had lost their homes.

This process caused even many of the more conservative Texas S&Ls to fail. If the tide ebbs enough, no anchorage is safe.

Tax Reform Act of 1986

To these factors, we have to add the Tax Reform Act (TRA), which was passed in August 1986. The TRA repealed the liberal depreciation and personal deduction provisions of the 1981 Tax Act and made it exceedingly difficult for individuals to take deductions for interest and depreciation. The 1981 Act had given these deductions and the 1986 Act took them away, an extremely costly policy switch. Real estate syndication dried up, which caused a lack of demand for properties. Old syndicates tried to sell, which caused an oversupply. Experts estimate that the TRA of 1986 caused commercial real estate values to depreciate 20–25 percent throughout the country. Thus, just as the government was accumulating commercial properties from failed institutions, it was deepening those institutions' insolvency and destroying the market for those commercial properties, thereby increasing its liquidation costs and causing still more S&Ls to fail.

The Domino Effect

The real estate crash devastated the S&Ls. If a problem property was worth 90 percent of the loan balance, the loss was 10 percent. If the property depreciated by 25 percent—to less than 65 percent of the loan balance—the loss didn't go up by a quarter, it more than *tripled*. If the S&L was insolvent after 10 percent losses, the FSLIC was looking at a loss to *it* that had tripled. If the S&L was still solvent with the 10 percent loss, it might well not be solvent after the additional 25 percent decline.

So a new category of S&Ls started showing up on the insolvent lists after 1986: institutions that had survived the interest rate devastation of 1981–82 in weakened condition but nevertheless had struggled through 1983–85 profitably. They weren't fraud artists, they weren't speculators; they may not have been the best lenders in the world, but they took normal lending risks. Their loans couldn't stand a 25 to 50 percent loss of value.

When the FSLIC started totaling up the costs of dealing with these institutions, it needed to add new factors. The older S&Ls that now were tipping into insolvency had grown since 1982, but not like the high fliers. They still had a large amount of old low-interest-rate mortgages and mortgage-backed securities on their books. To see what the FSLIC would lose, old mortgages had to be marked to market because acquirers weren't going to pay GAAP carrying value; they were going to pay the much lower market value. Thus the embedded losses on old mortgages that the FSLIC seemed to have dodged when rates came down in 1982 started to come home to roost.

The skimmed securities portfolios now were going to cost the FSLIC money, too. All those securities that the S&Ls carried at cost, but that had underwater market values because the portfolios had been skimmed for profits, now had to be marked to market for sale.

Acquirers weren't going to pay for goodwill or deferred losses or any other funny accounting entries. An institution might show a small RAP insolvency, but if it had nontangible items like goodwill on its balance sheet as a result of acquisitions, those had to be written off to see what FSLIC's loss would amount to.

The commercial real estate collapse thus caused a domino effect that destroyed a lot of the accounting values that had given the industry a robust appearance.

The Congress knocked down more dominoes when it passed FIRREA because the FIRREA capital rules caused more older institutions to fail. But that's getting ahead of the story.

They Were Still at It

Although the Texas S&L problems had come to light in 1984, growth and speculative lending continued at least through 1987. In a dead market, Texas S&Ls still made $8 billion of construction loans in 1987 and $5 billion in 1988. Many Texas S&Ls continued to grow by 15 percent a year when economics would have said they should shrink. The sixty-three biggest losers in Texas grew in size from $51 billion at the end of 1985 to $80 billion at the end of 1987. The situation basically stayed out of control until 1988.

Not Only the S&Ls Went Broke

The oil and real estate collapses in Texas killed off not only the Texas S&L industry but also its banking industry. The big Texas banks, a few years earlier rated among the nation's strongest, best capitalized banks, all failed between 1986 and 1989. They failed for the same basic reason as the S&Ls—bad real estate loans and the economic crash. But whereas the Texas S&Ls will cost us between $50 and $70 billion, the banks will cost only an estimated $12 billion, despite having been larger than the failed S&Ls.

The reasons why the banks cost less to deal with are

- Better management
- Slower growth
- Less fraud
- More capital
- Fairly prompt closure on insolvency.

But make no mistake about it: Banks, not just S&Ls, took greater risks in the 1980s and failed when regional economies turned against them. We will pay for the risks the banks took, as well as the risks the S&Ls took, in the 1990s and beyond.

10 The Laws Trash the Trash

We have seen how banks and S&Ls took excessive risks on real estate loans. But sometimes we can't fathom how the loss could be more than 50 percent of the loan amount. *Something* was built, after all. Doesn't it have value? The unfortunate answer is that often a lender can't recoup even the theoretical value of the real estate. The borrower doesn't just hand it over, and it can take years for the lender to get title. It seems as though all of nature has conspired to reduce the value of assets owned by failed S&Ls.

FORECLOSURE

The process of securing title begins with the foreclosure laws, which are state laws designed to balance the legitimate interests of the lender with the legitimate interests of the borrower in any equity that may be left in the real estate after a default. Texas is a creditors' state, where, after posting a series of notices, the lender can sell the property on the courthouse steps within ninety days after declaring a default. The lender doesn't even have to appear before a judge to have that right. Under this Texas theory, the debtor is adequately protected by the right to receive any amount over the debt that the sale brings. Almost always, that amount is zero.

Borrower Defenses

Many states require the creditor to obtain a court order before having the right to sell the property at auction. In those states, the foreclosure process takes much longer and the debtor has an easier opportunity to interpose a variety of defenses. (In Texas the debtor has to initiate a court action to stop the foreclosure sale.) The debtor may claim that the original loan violated usury statutes, that the default is temporary, that the default was caused by the lender's interference with the debtor's business, that the mortgage papers don't confer a valid lien on the property, or that the lender is an out-of-state institution that isn't licensed to make loans in the state. All these are common defenses that seldom are ultimately successful but that the court has to hear and take seriously. That takes time.

The usury allegation is particularly nettlesome in many of the Texas and Arizona cases involving ADC loans because the potential fees, interest, and kickers often would have violated those states' criminal usury statutes, which are still on the books. Whereas in the 1980 Act Congress preempted state usury laws that prevented lenders from charging market rates of interest, Congress did not override the criminal usury statutes that typically make it illegal to charge over 25 percent interest. Hundreds—perhaps thousands—of S&L loans in the Southwest are tied up in usury proceedings.

The allegation that the lender interfered in the borrower's business also frequently causes uncertainty and delay. These allegations involve intricate fact patterns, oral representations that can't be verified objectively, and charges that invoke dealings between the debtor and *former* employees of the lender who no longer have any particular interest in helping the lender collect the loan or obtain the property.

Worse still for the lender, in many of these cases the borrower asserts that the lender owes him money for having damaged his business. A few years ago that charge would have seemed farfetched, but a couple of court decisions—notably in California—have given substance to these allegations and have struck fear into the hearts of lenders.

Often the lender's documentation isn't very good, so it has a hard time proving its rights in court. Whereas experienced and sophisticated real estate lending institutions have detailed form documents for all the different types of loans they make—and typically won't agree to vary those forms very much, no matter how hard the borrower bargains—many of the S&Ls just getting into the business and growing at 100 percent a year were winging it. They entered into complex real estate transactions without adequate preparation. Their files were a mess, their documents were sloppy. Borrowers' lawyers are having a field day finding loopholes and omissions that buy their clients time, even if not eventual victory.

The Bankruptcy Law

If a lender overcomes all of these problems and is about to get the court to order a foreclosure sale, the borrower has another bag of tricks: the Bankruptcy Law. The Constitution declares that although most property matters are reserved to the states, the Congress has power to make laws affecting bankruptcy, a power it exercised most recently in a wholesale revision of the Bankruptcy Law in 1979.

This Bankruptcy Law revision proceeded from the basic premise that debtor "rehabilitation" should be a principal goal in dealing with business bankruptcies. Therefore, rather than encouraging liquidation of bankrupt companies, the Bankruptcy Law encourages them to keep going, with management attempting to develop a "plan of reorganization" as a "debtor in possession."

Whatever the merits of this theory in industrial company bankruptcies, it wreaks havoc in the real estate world because the borrower can zip into the Bankruptcy Court and gain its protection as a "debtor in possession" just before being ousted by a foreclosure. Under the Bankruptcy Law, the borrower now has an opportunity to prove to the court that the property can be run successfully if only the lenders will give a little more time to lease up, stretch out the loan payments, and lift the enormous penalty interest that has been building up since the default.

The lender will ask the court to order the foreclosure of the property while the bankruptcy proceeds, but the court often will be reluctant to do that, since it knows that the property *is* the bankrupt's business. If the bankrupt has any chance of rehabilitating the asset, the court wants to provide that chance. And the court has broad powers to "cram down" new interest rates and new terms as part of its decision on a "plan of reorganization." Often the lender is totally frustrated by its inability to enforce the clear provisions of the loan documents that permit it to foreclose and sell.

The bankruptcy proceedings can take another year or two on top of whatever time the original foreclosure proceeding took.

Property Deterioration

While all this is going on, the lender may not be getting paid interest, the lender and borrower are paying enormous legal fees, and the value of the property is changing—usually going down. Markets are changing, the property gets older, the debtor usually doesn't maintain the property well because that takes money and by definition there isn't enough of that. Current tenants are reluctant to sign new leases because they don't know who the landlord will be. New tenants are hard to attract because of all the obvious uncertainties. The delays almost always lead to greater losses.

Foreclosure Sales

When the lender finally overcomes all the defenses that the borrower can throw at him, he gets the right to have the sheriff or some other designated person sell the property "as is," without warranty, on the courthouse steps or at some less colorful spot, such as a title company's offices. Only very infrequently will that kind of sale bring a decent price, so now the lender has to "bid in" the property so it can organize a proper sales effort. That means that the lender itself, usually through a subsidiary corporation, has to buy the property at the foreclosure sale, spend money to rehabilitate it, and hire a real estate broker to sell the property. Until the sale, the lender—now the owner—has to maintain, lease, and manage the property.

Environmental Hazards

Before the lender bids in the property, however, it had better do an environmental audit. Recent laws and court cases hold the owner of a property liable for cleaning up problems such as asbestos in buildings and toxic wastes in the ground. It doesn't matter how you acquired the property, you're still responsible. In many cases the costs of cleanup exceed the value of the property—and the owner can be liable for the whole thing. If the lender takes title, the lender has to pay for the cleanup. The lawmakers thought they were getting a free lunch because lenders have deep pockets and nobody has any sympathy for them.

ENTER THE LIQUIDATORS

When the FSLIC, the FDIC, or the RTC takes over one of these loan situations, the problems get even worse. New people take over who don't have any memory about the case. The old employees who do have a memory turn hostile. The courts get confused by the multiplicity of parties, the name changes, and the potential overlays of federal laws that give federal liquidators defenses against borrower allegations of lender misconduct. The liquidators are government employees who can't profit; they are bound by the rigid rules that the bureaucracy has to impose to protect itself politically; so they don't take chances to get things to move along. Time, it seems, only feels like money if you're an owner.

Some of the federal laws make the liquidator's role even more difficult. The extreme case is a new federal rule that makes the government liable for the environmental cleanups, even after it has sold a foreclosed property. Some have estimated that that rule will cost the government a billion dollars.

And in the end, the sheer magnitude of what has to be sold hangs over and depresses the market so that even performing loans have to be sold at a discount.

11 Silverado, Lincoln and CenTrust

Three S&Ls outside of Texas have achieved the greatest notoriety. Each of them — Silverado, Lincoln, and CenTrust — will cost the American taxpayers in excess of $1 billion. Each of their stories is worth a whole book. We'll have to make do here with one chapter on all three. But you'll get the picture.

SILVERADO

The banks in Colorado stopped lending on big real estate projects between 1982, when the oil boom ended, and 1984, when the overbuilding was apparent. The S&Ls kept going. By 1986, despite the bloom having been so long off the oil boom rose, Colorado S&Ls were heavily invested in land and construction loans. And they were making more land and construction loans every day.

Silverado Banking, Savings and Loan Association now is best known for the involvement of Neil Bush as a director from 1985 to 1988 and for loans that Silverado made to Mr. Bush's business associates. Congressional Democrats predictably have been trying to make political capital from the President's son's minor role in a large and costly S&L failure.

The Bush involvement is, of course, beside the point. Neil Bush was just another pretty face who enabled a high-flying management to put a patina of respectability on a scandalously mismanaged operation. Michael Wise, Silverado's CEO, was a master of appearances. He was a leader in the U.S. League and a director of the FHLB of Topeka; he chaired their important committees and portrayed himself as a statesman of the industry while he gambled away Silverado's assets. He fooled Danny Wall and even his suspicious Board member Larry White. But he shouldn't have fooled *anyone* who was looking at the facts.

Silverado demonstrates so many key management and regulatory failings that we have to use it as a paradigm case.[1] Silverado had problems from 1980 until it finally got taken over by FSLIC at the end of 1988. The list of regulatory concerns over the years is staggering. Whereas institutions in Texas weren't being examined for periods as long as three years, Silverado, supervised by the FHLB of Topeka, was examined every year; and in between regular examinations, its loans and underwriting policies were specially examined. Silverado sailed along, getting in deeper and deeper, not because the supervisors in Topeka didn't know something was wrong but because they kept getting sweet-talked into granting permissions they should have known would lead to worse trouble.

Silverado was a fast grower. From 1980 to 1983 it grew from $83 million in assets to $371 million, largely by acquiring small S&Ls in transactions that the regulators approved despite their doubts about Silverado. In 1984 Silverado went into high-gear growth by going up to $953 million. With regulatory permission, it again grew by over 50 percent in 1985, to $1.5 billion. The regulations then somewhat restrained its growth so that it only went up to $2.3 billion by the time the party ended.

At all times until the end of 1987, Silverado was in compliance with its capital requirement despite the fact that it *never* made money from its interest income. First, the Silverado management were masters at earning loan fees and skimming profits from securities portfolios. With commercial real estate loans and land loans at one point reaching 66 percent of assets, they recorded more loan fees than net income *every year*. In every year in which they reported a profit, income from securities and loan sales also exceeded net income. In addition, they took lower loan loss reserves for RAP than for GAAP. As a result, when they were examined as of July 31, 1984 (they were in the midst of growing more than 100 percent for the year), GAAP capital was only 0.6 percent even though RAP capital was over 5 percent. And if you removed the goodwill from their mergers, Silverado would have been insolvent under GAAP as early as 1984.

Even under RAP accounting, however, Silverado had inadequate RAP capital for its growth aspirations, so beginning in 1984 it sought more creative ways to raise capital. Although it was a stock association, Silverado was privately owned, almost 90 percent by one shareholder. He and management didn't want to give up control, so in theory the best way for them to raise additional capital would be to sell nonvoting preferred stock, if you could find buyers for it.

Unfortunately, almost nobody will buy nonvoting preferred stock of a nonpublic entity controlled by one person. You get no control, you get no reporting safeguards. The risk/reward ratio doesn't work. But Silverado's management found a way around those issues: Give some people the money to buy Silverado preferred stock.

To get money into the right hands, Silverado began buying land at inflated prices from people who would use the excess proceeds to buy Silverado preferred stock. The land would go on Silverado's books at the purchase price, and the cash from the sale of preferred stock would be recorded as paid-in capital. As long as they could get an appraiser to say the land was worth what they paid for it—not too difficult—nobody would object. (The FHLB of Topeka *should* have objected.)

Sometimes Silverado varied the program. Instead of buying land, it would make a big loan for a real estate project and then accept an unrelated piece of land from the borrower as payment for preferred stock. Again Silverado's RAP capital was increased by the amount of the appraised value of the land. Nobody seemed to ask whether Silverado had overlent on the real estate project.

All this was going on *before* Neil Bush joined the Board. He must either have been a babe in the woods or hard up.

By 1985, the poorly conceived loans started to weaken and go bad. Like trying to count a six-deck shoot, Michael Wise had continued to finance Denver commercial real estate construction long after the boom was over. Vacancy rates all over town were growing by 1982, but Silverado kept lending to keep the fees coming in. Making loans in Texas at the same time didn't help, and all the loans began to go bad as the interest reserves ran out. The list of Silverado borrowers reads like a Who's Who of con artists and gamblers.

In 1986 Silverado tried an outrageous stratagem to conceal its bad loans. In Texas the S&L managers had induced developers to refinance their bad projects by doing three-cornered deals. This was bigger time. To conceal its losses, Silverado put all its bad assets—almost a billion dollars' worth, almost half the bank's assets—into one "pool" and offered to sell securities representing interests in the pool. To substantiate the supposed value of the pool, Silverado's management induced a few borrowers to buy interests in the pool at the offering price. This allowed them to claim that Silverado didn't need loan loss reserves for the pool. (For the borrowers, this meant that their loans didn't get called.) The FHLBB didn't go for the stratagem, but Silverado's auditors were partially taken in. That allowed the S&L to have GAAP earnings in a year when it had RAP losses. So Silverado's Board of Directors paid bonuses on the GAAP earnings—$2.3 million in bonuses to management.

Silverado's management kept plugging away. In March 1987 they lent

$73.8 million to a Texas developer. The loan was secured by a *second* mortgage on *vacant land* in *Fort Worth*, Texas (remember, this is 1987). The developer then bought interests in Silverado's troubled loan pool for $17.8 million (which Silverado claimed established the loan pool's market value) and pocketed $23 million. When the FHLB of Topeka got an appraisal a few months later, it came out over $40 million short.

Finally, the regulators made Silverado's Board sign a "supervisory agreement" in which they promised not to make any more commercial real estate loans or land loans. So in 1987 they switched their asset strategy to buying massive amounts of the most highly speculative mortgage-backed securities— residuals (in this case called STREMICS), IOs, and POs. We'll get into what they are later, but for the moment we can note that Silverado owned almost $600 million of these securities, which lost over half their value when the yield curve inverted at the end of 1988. The STREMICS, IOs, and POs were equity securities masquerading as government-guaranteed debt securities with a little extra interest rate risk. Talk about gambling for salvation!

Why didn't the regulators take more forceful action before 1988? This wasn't one of those cases where the examiners didn't see what was going on. They rendered accurate reports, and those accurate reports caused letters to be written, meetings to be held, and charges to be made and defended against. In the end, Silverado always prevailed. A former FHLB of Topeka employee charged that "they [Silverado] got preferential treatment. They [the Topeka regulators] refrained from taking action. Instead, they just sat there and watched it all unfold like a slow motion accident."[2] If they had stopped Silverado's growth at the end of 1983, it might have cost $100 million to deal with when it failed—tops. Now it is estimated that the Silverado failure will cost more than $1 billion. Is Neil Bush partly responsible? Sure he is. He's one of the directors who approved rolling the dice.

Did anyone do anything illegal at Silverado? I don't know, but colloquially you might call a lot of the deals they did "criminal."

CALIFORNIA

The S&L losses in California were second only to those incurred in Texas.

How could so many California S&Ls have failed? California has the best economy in the country, the best demographics, the best climate, and the best real estate market. The state also authorized ARMs several years before the interest rate crunch hit the S&Ls, so in California they had time to get at least a part of their portfolios matched. Nevertheless, California failures will cost at least $12 billion, plus the cost of Columbia.

The story of California failures is more complex than the story of Texas failures because in California the causes were more various. We can, however, analytically divide the California failures roughly into two groups: the smaller institutions, many of which were new, that failed because of fraud or the same types of fast growth and bad lending that we saw in Texas; and the bigger failures that started out as interest rate failures but may have ended up as asset failures when management sought to restore net worth by leveraging up and making riskier investments in condos, hotels, or junk bonds. Lincoln is a special case that illustrates almost all of the sins. If Lincoln will cost $2 billion, then it won't account for more than one-sixth of the total California cost. Let's keep Lincoln in perspective.

The California story illustrates the interrelationship between public policy and private decision-making. In 1980 Governor Jerry Brown appointed Linda Yang, an enthusiastic young academic economist, as California S&L commissioner. She believed in the community obligations of banks and S&Ls and in the aims of the Community Reinvestment Act (CRA), a vague federal statute aimed at putting political pressure on banks and S&Ls to invest more in inner city areas after studies claimed that they had been redlining minority neighborhoods in the 1960s. California had its own version of CRA that, like the federal version, was most effectively enforced by holding up merger or branch applications until the applicant agreed to a new lending program in inner city areas.

Probably nothing infuriates a bank or S&L's management more than having an application held hostage to credit allocation. Usually management will contend that it makes all the prudent loans that it can at a market rate of interest in the inner city area. It contends that the commitments the regulator seeks are commitments which will cost the lender money, through reduced pricing or increased credit risk or both. Although we have seen that many S&Ls took excessive credit risks in pursuit of high fees and interest, many other S&Ls continued to run their businesses prudently; they deeply resented being held hostage.

So when Linda Yang held up an application from Home Savings, then the largest S&L in the country, and made it known that her first priority was to force state-chartered S&Ls to make inner city loans, Home, followed by *all* of the other big California S&Ls, most of which had been state-chartered, converted to federal charter to escape her jurisdiction.

After all of the large S&Ls had converted to federal charter, the state legislature cut the S&L Department's budget drastically. The Department, after all, had nothing left to examine or regulate.

The examination force wasn't the only thing that got cut however; contributions by S&Ls to state legislators fell way off because federal S&Ls had less incentive to contribute to state legislative election campaigns. To restart the flow of contributions, the legislature decided that it needed to induce the S&Ls to reconvert to state charter. And the way to do that—clearly—was a state law that gave more powers to S&Ls than the federal law. That is how the Nolan Law was passed in 1982.

Seventy-one new state-chartered S&Ls started business in California in 1982–85, many of them owned by real estate entrepreneurs. (Linda Yang's successor, Larry Taggert, approved 215 new charters in 400 days, but under Ed Gray's 1983 de novo chartering regulations, they didn't all get deposit insurance.) Many of these new institutions paid up for deposits in order to grow quickly and made risky investments, many of which didn't pay off. Twenty of these new California institutions have failed and others are teetering.[3] Most of these weren't big-ticket failures, but they show that you didn't have to have an overhang of low-yielding assets or invest in the oil patch to fail. You could decide to risk your $3 million of original capital (the minimum amount to start business) right at home in sunny California and lose it there.

Another group of small institutions failed mostly because their managements engaged in fraud. It is hard to know exactly how many fraud failures there were, but informed estimates suggest that a dozen or fifteen out of a total of sixty California failures were caused by insider fraud. Included among the fraud failures are San Marino, North American, American Diversified, Golden Pacific, Centennial, Presidio, Consolidated, Ramona, Signal, and, probably the largest California failure involving insider fraud, Bell. In the aggregate, these institutions cost less than $2 billion, so they are not a big part of the story. But they show how entrepreneurs mistook deregulation for a permanent law enforcement vacation.

The California fast growers looked a lot like the fast growers in Texas. They were small institutions that grew rapidly, usually after being acquired in the early 1980s by an individual or group who milked the institutions by paying themselves high salaries and dividends, and in many cases siphoned off loaned money through kickbacks or straw borrowers. Many of their owners are in jail or have committed suicide. Some have been murdered by confederates. The illegal conduct that many of them committed was so obvious that it is hard to fathom what they thought they were doing, unless they believed that the press and law enforcement officials had gone to sleep permanently.

All of the *big* California S&Ls that failed—except Lincoln—started out as interest rate failures. American's predecessor State Savings, Imperial, Gibraltar, Santa Barbara, Mercury, and Columbia all had less than 3 percent tangible capital at the end of 1982. They hadn't converted to variable-rate lending when Home and Great Western did, and they were terribly mismatched.

They therefore embarked on a variety of methods to restore their net worth after 1982. American pursued interest rate risk and big-time construction lending. Imperial tried a potpourri of different kinds of loans, some direct investments, and a good-sized junk bond portfolio. Gibraltar went into mortgage banking, condo development, and almost everything else on at least a small scale. Santa Barbara, with the best retail banking franchise in that magnificent town full of rich people, pretty much stuck to traditional S&L business combined with some mortgage banking. Mercury tried traditional business, added mortgage banking, and then went into hotel lending, on which it lost a lot. Columbia became the largest S&L investor in junk bonds. Although each of these institutions seemed for a time to be coming back from near insolvency, eventually the risks they took caused losses that were inadequately reserved for, and FIRREA finished them off. California observers suggest that most of the managements weren't very strong. But I know of no allegations of insider fraud in these cases, except for claims against Columbia's management in connection with junk bonds.

All of these large institutions grew rapidly, with Columbia being the champion. It went from $381 million in 1981 (with only $9 million of RAP net worth) to over $9 billion at the end of 1989. They made maximum use of leverage to try to grow their way out of their problems.

Several of these institutions were hanging on the edge and might have survived or might have cost minimal amounts until FIRREA did them in by changing the capital rules, tanking junk bonds, and creating a climate in which a panicked Office of Thrift Supervision (OTS)* put institutions into conservatorships before anyone was ready with solutions.

Lincoln is another story.

LINCOLN

Although Lincoln was based in California, its story is more a story of Arizona, where all the S&Ls failed. The same forces that destroyed Arizona's S&Ls doomed Charles Keating's speculative Lincoln investments in Phoenix and Tucson.

The Arizona S&Ls should have been a great success story. The state's population was growing. Competition was modest, since there were only about a dozen financial institutions of any size in the state. Home building was brisk. But the Arizona S&Ls went crazy for growth, office buildings and land, land, land. It is true that Western and Merabank, the state's two largest S&Ls, didn't have much capital after 1982, but "slow and steady" would have won the race. Unfortunately, nobody used that strategy. Western grew 134 percent from 1982 to 1987, Merabank grew 166 percent, and Pima, the largest in Tucson, grew 320 percent.

The Arizona S&Ls, like the Texas S&Ls, got caught up in the Sunbelt optimism. The Arizona banks were more prudent, and they haven't failed. But three out of the top four Arizona banks are owned by Citicorp, Chase, and Security Pacific and bear their names. The fourth, Valley National, although weakened by the real estate crash, continues to be the state's leading financial institution.

The remains of Western and Merabank have been bought by Bank of America.

When Charles Keating acquired Lincoln in early 1984, his goal probably was to continue his home building business with more leverage and insured deposits. Although the business plan that Keating had submitted in order to gain approval to acquire Lincoln hadn't shown either rapid growth or direct investments in real estate, Lincoln immediately doubled in size and began direct investment in single-family home development.[4]

Lincoln's 1984 growth from $1 billion to $2 billion was legal under the FHLBB regulations. Although ACC (Keating's holding company) paid $51 million (raised by a junk offering through Drexel Burnham) for an S&L that had $31 million of net worth (and put no money into Lincoln), the transaction increased Lincoln's regulatory capital by creating goodwill of over $96 million. As a result, Lincoln started life with Keating at a $54 million net worth level ($51 million under "pushdown purchase accounting"* plus $3 million of appraised equity capital). Using five-year averaging, it could grow 100 percent in 1984, even though its tangible net worth was minus $40 million. (Remember how easy it would have been to fix the capital rules at the end of 1983 or early in 1984, when the problems already were clear? Keating's looting of Lincoln was a preventable offense—preventable many times over.) In 1985 and 1986 Lincoln's growth was moderated to about 25 percent a year. In growing fast, Keating looks a lot like his Texas counterparts.

He also looks a lot like them in taking larger and larger risks. Keating built in Arizona rather than Texas, but he seemed to believe that the boom there, as people believe everywhere before the bust, would never end. The projects got more and more grandiose, ending up with the Phoenician, a resort hotel complex of Brobdingnagian proportions and Babylonian excess whose cost overruns by themselves, including a million dollars worth of NFL football tickets (for whom? to pay off what?), would have funded a normal hotel. David Paul built his tower. Charles Keating built his Phoenician. Don Dixon's wife had her "gastronomique fantastique"; Keating's wife had her chance to buy marble and so forth in Italy to furnish the Phoenician. The Phoenician project eventually lost over $100 million.

Lincoln's diversified program of speculation included takeover stocks, junk bonds, hotels, financial futures, and high-risk loans. By mid-1986, these speculations accounted for 62 percent of Lincoln's assets.

When the FSLIC finally took over Lincoln Savings in mid-1989, they found vacant land in Arizona that wasn't worth half what Lincoln had paid for it, a weak junk bond portfolio, half-built hotels in overbuilt markets, and inventories of unsold homes. Yet Lincoln had reported profits in every quarter from 1984 to 1986 and had grown from $1 billion in 1984 to $4.7 billion in 1989.

Lincoln never made money from net interest income. All its income came from capitalized interest,* from trading in loans, land, and securities, and from tax benefits.

One 1985 transaction—the sale of Gulf Broadcasting stock after an aborted takeover attempt—resulted in a $50 million gain. That speculative transaction, on which Keating had bet more than 100 percent of Lincoln's capital in 1984, probably made Charles Keating think he was a financial genius. It emboldened him to speculate even more.

Another large part of Lincoln's so-called net income came from selling loans and securities that had been on the books before the acquisition and had been written down in the purchase accounting process. These clever transactions resulted in book gains but tax losses. They therefore increased net worth by the amount of the gain, plus the amount of the tax benefit, while the goodwill stayed on the books. It was all legitimate under GAAP, but it didn't reflect the underlying economics, which were that the future earning power of the enterprise was being seriously depleted.

Keating tried to intimidate everybody. He hired lawyers, accountants, and lobbyists in enormous numbers and discarded them when they became lukewarm about his tactics. He threatened suit whenever anyone questioned his position. He never cooperated. Keating used corporate money to buy politicians, regulators, anyone he needed. He even reportedly offered his archenemy Ed Gray a job to get him off the Bank Board.

Meanwhile, Keating piously insisted that he was a legitimate businessman who was being victimized by overzealous regulators. He gave money to Mother Teresa and other charities to solidify his image. Ironically he made a sixth(!) mortgage loan to Covenant House in New York, which his people defended on grounds of Father Bruce Ritter's dedication. (Father Ritter later was forced to resign because of accusations of an overzealous dedication to some of his young male charges.) In April 1987, Keating also convinced the "Keating Five" Senators to badger Ed Gray about the direct investment rule and the length of the 1986 examination of Lincoln. That meeting shows how contributions can pervert the political process, but it also shows how little impact Senators can have on independent regulators. The Senators didn't accomplish anything except to hurt their own reputations because Ed Gray, Jim Cirona (President of the FHLBB of San Francisco), Mike Patriarcha (Principal Supervisory Agent [PSA]* in San Francisco), and Bill Black (then General

Counsel of the FHLB of San Francisco) stood their ground. Mr. Cirona informed the Senators that Lincoln was a "ticking time bomb."

After the OTS finally seized Lincoln in August 1989, Keating had the chutzpah to sue OTS, claiming that the seizure was unlawful. A year later, after thousands of exhibits and twenty-nine days of testimony, Judge Stanley Sporkin threw out the case. Why he took so long when the challenge so clearly had so little merit, I am not certain. But Judge Sporkin's opinion lays to rest any shadow of a claim that Charles Keating was a victimized legitimate businessman—and maybe that's why he took so long. He wanted to make sure that nobody would ever again pay attention to Keating's sheep's clothing.

Judge Sporkin was Director of the SEC's Division of Enforcement and General Counsel of the CIA before President Reagan appointed him to the federal bench. Thus he had the right kind of background to understand Mr. Keating's machinations, even if he also had a bit of the "hanging judge" tendency that is natural to former enforcement officials.

Judge Sporkin based his opinion on a tax-sharing agreement* that American Continental (ACC, Keating's holding company) entered into with Lincoln, pursuant to which Lincoln agreed to make tax payments to ACC based upon its (Lincoln's) GAAP earnings, regardless of whether Lincoln owed any taxes. Under this agreement, Lincoln paid $94 million to ACC between 1986 and 1988, despite not having any taxes to be paid.

The opinion isn't very crisp on a key issue concerning whether the tax-sharing agreement had been approved by the FHLBB and therefore *couldn't* be used as a basis for OTS to take over Lincoln. This was an awkward point for the OTS, on which Judge Sporkin was more than charitable.

If the OTS hadn't approved the tax-sharing agreement, Lincoln would have violated the SLHCA when it made the first payment of over $100,000 to ACC. But the FHLBB (OTS's predecessor) *had* approved the tax-sharing agreement in 1986. OTS conceded that. What OTS contended was that when it approved the agreement, it understood that payments would be based on taxes payable by Lincoln as a stand-alone entity, not on GAAP earnings. The OTS contended that the Bank Board hadn't approved the agreement as Lincoln had implemented it.

To substantiate this contention that the Bank Board had approved a more limited agreement than Lincoln had implemented, the OTS supplied testimony by a fairly low-level employee of the FHLB of San Francisco, whom the judge believed. The language of the agreement doesn't really support the OTS contention, so Judge Sporkin didn't quote from the agreement.

Nor did the Bank Board's conduct help its contention about the tax-sharing agreement. If the Bank Board believed that the tax-sharing agreement was more limited than the construction that Lincoln implemented, why didn't it come down hard on Lincoln in 1986, when it made, and reported having made, the first payments under the agreement? Those payments were millions of dollars more than what OTS now claims would have been payable based on its understanding. Nevertheless, the FHLB of San Francisco didn't even *mention* the tax-sharing agreement in its 1987 report on the 1986 examination. "Asleep at the switch" would be the best explanation that the FHLB of San Francisco could give. "Had no understanding of the tax-sharing agreement in the first place" would be a less charitable explanation.

These cavils about how the FHLB of San Francisco and Judge Sporkin dealt with the tax-sharing agreement illustrate how weak the regulatory system was even as late as 1986, and how federal judges often seek ways to support federal regulatory authorities against scoundrels; but they shouldn't cloud what Judge Sporkin found in the rest of his opinion, which in my view would have been ample to justify taking over Lincoln, and some day should be ample to send Mr. Keating to jail if his personal fingerprints can be found on the deals that Judge Sporkin describes.

The four deals, which were engineered in 1987 and 1988, are typical frauds that occur late in the cycle of risk–loss–cover-up–fraud–failure that so many of the high flyers went through. Each deal resulted in a paper profit for Lincoln (and therefore money that could be upstreamed to ACC under the tax-sharing agreement). Each deal involved transactions between Lincoln and another party who made a down payment to Lincoln to buy land or securities but who in fact got the money to make the down payment from a third party who got the money from Lincoln as part of Lincoln's overfinancing of that third party's assets. The deals, however sophisticated, constituted fraud designed to cover up the true financial condition of Lincoln and to loot Lincoln by passing money upstream to ACC—and they all would be fraud even if the FHLB of San Francisco did approve the tax-sharing agreement as implemented by Lincoln.

Judge Sporkin says that the four deals he describes are just examples, and that there are additional similar transactions which account for almost all of Lincoln's 1986–88 reported income.

All of the deals that Judge Sporkin describes created paper profits that in fact had to be long-run losses for Lincoln because, while on one side of the transaction someone was paying Lincoln too much for a property, most of the payment for that property was made in the form of a nonrecourse note that would never be paid, whereas on the other side of the transaction, Lincoln was overpaying for another property *in cash*.

These are late-game deals because they cannot *by definition* succeed. They were merely attempts to stay one jump ahead of the law. Mr. Keating may have believed he could stay one jump ahead forever. But nobody can. Eventually the scheme collapses.

I wonder whether Judge Sporkin saw the parallels between Charles Keating and Robert Vesco, who looted IOS (an international group of mutual funds) of something like $200 million in 1972. Vesco, like Keating, was apparently an aggressive, risk-taking, sharp but legitimate businessman who in early 1972 "turned" when his empire started to crumble and the SEC began to delve deeply into his financial reporting and disclosure. I believe that Vesco "turned" while the head of the SEC's Enforcement Division—one Stanley Sporkin— was taking his deposition day after day, much the same way that he tried the Lincoln case. I read that deposition and thought I could feel almost the exact time when Vesco decided to start his looting campaign.

Vesco's deals looked a lot like Keating's deals. (Maybe all crooked deals look alike.) Vesco stole money from all the people around the world who invested in the IOS mutual funds. Keating (through ACC) stole from all the Lincoln customers (26,000 of them) who bought ACC subordinated debt—over $200 million of it—at Lincoln's offices, thinking that it was federally insured. Keating and the top Lincoln officers have been indicted for this offense in California.

Vesco didn't go to jail, and maybe Keating won't. Vesco fled the country and has been a fugitive for eighteen years. Keating learned a different lesson, maybe from Roy Cohn, who never had an official position anywhere and never carried any money. As a result, you could never pin anything on Cohn. Keating wasn't an officer of Lincoln and seems never to have signed the papers that did the deals. His subordinates, who did the dirty work, will be convicted. It will be too bad if Keating isn't. As Judge Sporkin summarized:

> What has emerged is not a pretty picture. It is abundantly clear that ACC's officials abused their positions with respect to Lincoln. Bluntly speaking, their actions amounted to a looting of Lincoln. This was not done crudely. Indeed, it was done with a great deal of sophistication. The transactions were all made to have an aura of legality about them.

Just when Keating "turned" criminal is still hard to say. He always had the tendencies; he always used his facade of piety to hide his absolute ruthlessness. But my guess is that he really turned in early 1986, when he began to see that Lincoln wasn't going to make money and that the regulatory system wasn't going to roll over and play dead; when he was confronted with his first real FHLBB examination and the Arizona boom started to fade, leaving Lincoln and ACC overextended. If he could stay one jump ahead, he probably felt, then maybe one of his big swings, such as the Phoenician, would be a home run—like Gulf Broadcasting—and save the empire. He probably was very good at self-deception.

The signs of trouble were there by the end of 1985. The examiners could see them. Better regulatory supervision and enforcement would have saved a very large amount of money, since Lincoln probably could have been liquidated at relatively moderate cost at that time. Instead, Lincoln kept on going and spent $1.6 billion on Arizona land in 1987 and 1988, most of it worth very little today. But hindsight is still 20/20.

You can be a bull or you can be a bear, they say on Wall Street, but pigs, they say, get slaughtered.

CENTRUST

David Paul, maybe Wall Street's best customer ever, behaved like a pig. He had CenTrust spend $40 million for a yacht, a sailboat, a Rubens, some impressionists, Limoges china, and Baccarat crystal; and he used it all himself, claiming that his home and his life were an extension of his business. All the while he was pocketing a total of $16 million in salary, bonuses, fees, and dividends between 1983 and 1990. He could do this because CenTrust *looked* like a successful bank—if you didn't look too closely. If you did that, you found that although CenTrust *reported* profits every year through 1988, its normal operations *lost* a total of $365 million between 1983, when Paul acquired it, and 1988, when it first reported losses. Let's go to the 1990 testimony of John E. Ryan, OTS District Director in Atlanta, for a quick overview of the story:

> Even though CenTrust reported substantial net income in every year from 1983 to 1988, it was, in our opinion, skimming the profits off the top, leaving substantial risk and future losses embedded in the balance sheet.
>
> First, the substantial gains reported in the early years resulted largely from the sale of the loans that were marked-to-market as a result of the acquisition and that subsequently increased in value with falling interest rates. In other words, the assets were sold at a book profit with the loss carried as a $525 million asset [goodwill] to be written off over a 25-year period.
>
> Second, there is considerable evidence of so-called "gains trading" by CenTrust. Gains trading is the device whereby CenTrust commits to take future delivery of securities at a price. If there was a gain on the transactions [when the delivery date came], CenTrust would take the profit by selling its position. If there was a loss, CenTrust would take delivery of the security and carry it at cost rather than market value.
>
> It was not until almost two years after the acquisition that additional capital was raised and then it amounted to only $17 million as opposed to the $35 to $40 million required [by David Paul's agreement with the FHLBB—reality would have required more]. An additional $12 million in high cost subordinated debt was also raised at the time. [CenTrust sold its own junk paper through Drexel.]

Although there is no clear cause and effect relationship between the capital sale [by CenTrust] and the [its] junk bond purchases, CenTrust began making significant purchases of junk bonds from Drexel around the time that Drexel was serving as lead underwriter for the [CenTrust] securities. From the beginning, the FHLB of Atlanta regulators had a strained and contentious relationship with CenTrust and its CEO, David Paul. Examinations were conducted under extremely adversarial conditions and the examiners reported being frustrated by inordinate delays in getting information and financial data.[5]

We are familiar with much of this—purchase accounting, skimming the profits as interest rates go down, selling the gainers and holding the losers at cost, growing the capital while the market value net worth treads water or declines, using the book net worth plus regulatory accounting to appear to have the capital necessary to grow. In this case, CenTrust had to appear to have the capital necessary to grow from $2 billion to $10 billion in order to try to outrun $525 million of goodwill that resulted from writing the assets down to market at the time David Paul acquired it. Remember, CenTrust had goodwill of over 20 percent when Paul bought it, which means that CenTrust had that many more paying liabilities than earning assets—and at the 10 percent level an S&L is doomed to lose money *forever*. Therefore, Paul had to skim the profits and he had to grow, or he had no chance. In addition, he bought junk bonds, traded mortgage-backed securities feverishly, issued his own junk bonds to raise the only kind of capital he could, made risky real estate and commercial loans, built the CenTrust Tower, and so forth. We know the litany by now.

Did David Paul know what he was doing when he bought the old, dead Dade County S&L and turned it into CenTrust? I don't think so. As a real estate entrepreneur, he probably saw a great opportunity with great leverage in that great South Florida market. He used illiquid land that he claimed was worth $36 million (and turned out to be worth $7 million) to buy an apparent $2 billion of assets, most of it liquid. In real estate, that's a good deal. Who knew from interest-paying liabilities vs. interest-earning assets? If you control assets, you can make money.

Paul almost pulled it off. He managed to report profits regularly. With help from Drexel Burnham, he convinced public stockholders and bondholders that he could do it, and thereby managed to raise capital. When he did a deal with Lincoln to park some securities, it was CenTrust that made the money and Lincoln that did the window dressing. Paul stayed away from Wall Street's worst inventions. He did develop a pretty good retail branch network. But he couldn't outrun that half a billion dollars of goodwill. Too many risks eventually caused losses, and when that happened, he had no sympathy from the regulators, whom he had mistreated. His personal excesses made him a marked man.

I don't know whether David Paul will be indicted or convicted of anything. If he is, most likely it will be for alleged kickbacks or the boat called "Bodacious"—or for the Rubens that may not even be genuine.

On the night before CenTrust was taken over, its Miami tower blazed white against the night sky. On the night after, the tower's lighting was red, white and blue—symbolizing the nationalization of a large part of the S&L industry. In retrospect, government sources suggest, the white may have been a signal of surrender.

12 The Junk Bond Connection

The role of junk bonds in S&L failures has been overstated. Only six S&Ls invested over 10 percent of their assets in junk bonds. These include four of the most expensive failures—Lincoln, CenTrust, Imperial, and Columbia—but junk bonds are the biggest part of the story only at Columbia. Only about 150 out of the country's 2,000-odd S&Ls invested in junk bonds at all.[1]

The term "junk bonds" sounds so awful that it gets in the way of understanding what they are, what their role has been, and what their risks and rewards can be. Junk bonds are loans with equity characteristics. Typically, they represent loans that are subordinated* to other loans. Therefore they will pay off only if the other loans are paid off first. That's why they have high yields and that's why they're called "junk," to distinguish them from investment grade bonds. Technically, junk bonds (or "high-yield" bonds, as those who sold them preferred to call them) are any debt securities that the rating agencies, such as Standard & Poor's or Moody's, rate below their five highest ratings.

There is nothing inherently wrong with subordinated debt. It is much riskier than a senior loan to the same company and therefore earns a higher interest rate. But the money borrowed from the subordinated lender may be used by the borrower for the same purposes—good or bad—as the money borrowed from the senior lender.

Junk bonds have been used mostly to fund takeovers and leveraged buyouts—indeed, most takeovers and LBOs of the 1980s would have been impossible without junk bonds, which were the key to the three-tiered structure of senior debt, subordinated debt, and equity. About 60 percent of the money was lent by major banks as senior lenders. These lenders took security interests in just about all of the borrower's tangible assets. Between 5 percent and 20 percent of the money came from common stock investors, who were the people that firms such as Kohlberg Kravis Roberts and Merrill Lynch put together to make the deals and who could make the most money if the deal worked well. They are the owners of the enterprise who are entitled to all of the profits after paying off the senior and subordinated lenders. The subordinated lenders—the junk bond owners, sometimes called the "mezzanine" lenders—were in between. They received a fixed rate of interest that often was accrued or "paid in kind"—that is, paid in more subordinated bonds rather than being paid in cash—until after the senior debt was paid off.

Timing was exceedingly important in putting takeover and LBO financings together because typically there was a bidding war for the target company and credible financing was crucial to having a bid accepted. In most bidding wars there wasn't time to put together public offerings of subordinated debt or extensive bank syndicates, so "bridge" loans were provided to the promoters (the people putting up the equity money) both for the senior debt and for the subordinated debt. The senior bridge loan usually was provided by a small group of major commercial banks, which also would provide the permanent senior financing. They would later syndicate that senior financing through loan participations to dozens of other banks.

The subordinated bridge loan almost always had to be made by the investment banking firm that was going to sell the subordinated debt to the public. The firm that made the subordinated bridge loan took an enormous risk—it could be stuck with all the subordinated debt if the public market didn't buy it—but it also had an opportunity for enormous rewards. It might get a few million dollars for providing advice, a few million more as a bridge loan fee, an interest rate like 6 percent over prime on the bridge loan, and typically an "underwriting spread" of about 4 percent on the sale of the junk bonds to the public. If the deal worked right, the bridge loan lasted only a few months, so the effective rate of interest on the loan could be fantastic.

Drexel Burnham's specialty was the subordinated bridge loan followed by the public sale of the subordinated debt. First Boston, Merrill Lynch, and Salomon Brothers played the same role in many deals late in the game. First Boston got caught holding a lot of paper it couldn't sell after the Campeau takeover of Federated Department Stores. Drexel lived by the sword and died by it.

The whole game wouldn't have been possible without the junk bond *buyers*. They were the key because the subordinated bridge lender had to *know* that there were buyers of junk bonds to refinance the bridge. That's what made Drexel Burnham and Michael Milken so powerful: Milken could practically guarantee that his customers would buy the bonds to take out the bridge loans his firm was making.

In particular, he knew that a few dozen institutions, prominently including three S&Ls, would buy what he told them to buy because he treated them right. I don't know the whole story, but apparently he entertained them exceedingly well, helped to make them famous, and made sure they got in on the best deals. He also made sure that *their* capital securities found buyers. For example, Drexel was able to sell CenTrust's subordinated debt to the public despite CenTrust's awful balance sheet. Drexel also sold capital securities for ACC (Lincoln's parent) and Columbia.

The junk bond market as described here was almost strictly a 1980s phenomenon. Of course there had been below-investment-grade debt before, but it had consisted mostly of "fallen angels," that is, debt that had originally been issued with an investment-grade rating that had been reduced by the rating agencies due to declines in the issuer's earnings or prospects. Most fallen angels were not subordinated bonds but senior debt of weak companies.

Because the junk bond market began only in the 1980s, the market hadn't existed through a full economic cycle, which made performance figures relatively meaningless. The statistics that one could look at in the mid–1980s, however, were very impressive. Junk bonds carried interest rates of 400 to 600 basis points over Treasuries but had default rates of only 1 or 2 percent. Studies by the GAO and Wharton Econometrics in 1988 showed that junk bonds were S&Ls' second most profitable investment, after consumer debt. The only problem with these statistics is that subordinated debt is *subordinated;* that is, when, due to economic conditions, a lot of it goes into default, the percentage of loss will be huge because the senior debt has to be paid off first.

If junk bonds really involve so much risk, how did S&Ls get authority to buy them when commercial banks don't have that authority? In 1983 the Pratt Bank Board ruled that bonds could be purchased under the commercial lending authority granted to federal S&Ls by Garn–St Germain (on the sound reasoning that a bond is a loan in security form) and ruled further that subordinated bonds were loans, too, which they are. Many state laws, including those of California, Texas, and Florida, permitted investment in subordinated debt. In fact, the vast majority of junk bonds held by S&Ls were bought by state-chartered institutions, with California by itself accounting for over 50 percent of the total.

The legal authority to buy junk bonds does not, however, explain why S&Ls in fact bought them. S&Ls also had power to participate in the senior bank loans being made by commercial banks on the same deals. The senior loans were demonstrably — indeed, by definition — safer than the subordinated loans represented by junk bonds. Although they didn't pay interest rates as high as junk bonds, they still paid very good rates. Why should S&Ls have taken the big risks that commercial banks were unwilling to take?

There are several answers:

- S&Ls had no credit staffs. Therefore they couldn't evaluate the detailed information that commercial banks would send in connection with participations. They thought prospectuses were easier to look at.

- Most of the S&Ls that bought junk bonds in big quantities had low real capital and little real business, so they needed the extremely high rates to make money (moral hazard again).

- Junk bonds could be *sold* to people because the statistics looked excellent. The rates were high; the bonds usually paid off early; default rates looked low.

- Junk bonds were easy to diversify. Drexel would sell you a whole set.

- Junk bond salesmen have big expense accounts.

Columbia Savings and Loan, conveniently located in Beverly Hills near Michael Milken's office, held almost $5 billion of junk bonds, by far the most of any S&L. It prided itself on being a junk bond specialist, with the best analysts of the market and the most diversified portfolio. Columbia was among the top ten S&L performers in 1986, 1987, and 1988, and its portfolio performed extremely well until 1989. Imperial Savings—also Los Angeles-based—and Lincoln each held over $1 billion of junk bonds in the late 1980s. These institutions accounted for about half of the top amount of $15 billion of junk bonds held by the industry. None of the buyers suffered losses until 1989, when FIRREA combined with market forces to destroy the market for high-yield bonds.

It is surprising that FIRREA's changes in S&Ls' ability to hold junk bonds played such a big role in the junk bond market's demise, since S&Ls owned only about 7 percent of outstanding junk bonds, as opposed to an estimated 30 percent for mutual funds, 30 percent for insurance companies, and 16 percent for pension funds. But when FIRREA, passed in August 1989, said that S&Ls could not hold junk bonds past 1994, that decree had a domino effect.

When Congress gave S&Ls five years to sell, GAAP required the S&Ls to mark most of their junk bonds to market because accounting theory says that you can carry a bond at cost only if you have an intention *to hold it to maturity*. Since the maturity of most of the junk held by S&Ls was later than 1994, they *couldn't* intend to hold it to maturity. They therefore had to mark it to market.

Once you have to mark a security to market in a thin* and volatile market, you have a big incentive to sell right away. These sales caused a panic in the junk bond market, and prices began to tumble. Insurance companies joined the sellers because they reasoned that if Congress was prohibiting S&Ls from owning junk, the state commissioners who regulated them wouldn't be far behind. They didn't want to get caught.

Then the public, which owned the shares of the high-yield mutual funds that accounted for almost a third of the market, decided they had better get out, too. So they began redeeming shares, which forced the funds to sell bonds held in their portfolios in order to raise cash.

Meanwhile, in that kind of market nobody could issue new junk bonds, so Drexel's greatest source of income dried up. Drexel's capital also went down significantly because brokers, unlike banks and S&Ls, have to mark everything to market every day, and a large part of Drexel's assets was its inventory of depreciating junk bonds. That, in turn, deprived Drexel of the borrowing power necessary for it to continue to make a liquid market in the bonds, which, since Drexel *was* the principal market maker for many issues, depressed the market further.

The junk bonds held by S&Ls lost over 50 percent of their value in less than a year without there having been an enormous number of defaults. The default rate had gone up, but not nearly as much as the market's decline would suggest. The government's loss on S&L junk bonds probably will be about $4 to $5 billion.

The domino effect hasn't stopped yet. Junk bonds propped up the stock market because they promoted takeovers whenever stocks were low. Without junk bonds, takeovers will be done at lower prices. Chalk up maybe 10 percent of the 1980s' increase in stock prices to junk bonds and those who sold them. But assign junk bonds only 2 percent to 3 percent of the S&L losses.

13 Fraud and Misconduct 101

Reports of fraud and misconduct by S&L owners and officers, more than the amount of money that taxpayers will pay, is what has made the American public angry about the FSLIC bailout. The large sums of money are not comprehensible. But the idea that the S&L managers who portrayed themselves as pillars of society made off with the loot excites people.

If we want to understand where fraud fits into the picture, we have to make distinctions between the different kinds of misconduct that afflicted failing S&Ls. The numbers that we read in the newspapers are misleading because our public servants, wanting to look like great crimebusters, lump together crimes of varying degrees, regulatory violations, mismanagement, and personal aggrandizement by S&L officers. A 1989 GAO report, for example, studied twenty-six institutions and found "insider abuse" in all of them. The RTC has reported that 60 percent of institutions in conservatorship have been "victimized by serious criminal activity." In all, over 2,000 criminal referrals have been made in S&L failure cases.[1]

In order to understand these broad statements better, let's examine 1987 testimony by a supervisory agent from the FHLB of San Francisco, Charles Deardorff.[2] He testified: "In a review of 35 failed or failing institutions since year-end 1984, insider misconduct was noted to some extent in 27 institutions, or 77% of the sample." This sounds like an enormously high percentage until we focus on his language. The term he used is "insider misconduct" — not a precise term or one that has a legal meaning — which was "noted [not proven] to some extent."

To his credit, Deardorff went on to explain in some detail what he meant, but the ten-second sound bite that the public would have come away with was "misconduct in 77% of failed S&Ls."

Deardorff explained that there were nine categories of "insider misconduct," which included payment of "exorbitant" personal expenses (which may have been legal), loan "concentrations" to affiliated companies of insiders (which may not have violated any law), inaccurate financial reports, and false information submitted by borrowers. These are not nice things, but the only one that is insider conduct and that historically sinks a bank or S&L is the loans to affiliates of insiders* — and even these may not violate regulations.

What kills banks — and what made S&Ls so deeply insolvent — is bad loans. Paying exorbitant personal expenses doesn't make banks insolvent. Filing false reports is done after insolvency and covers it up, which permits managers to roll the dice to try to become solvent. But the kinds of fraud or misconduct that we should care about most are the kinds that result in bad lending decisions. Other illegal conduct needs to be punished, but we have to understand that it didn't *cause* the S&Ls to fail. The interest sensitivity mismatch and imprudent lending decisions *caused* all but a relative few of the failures.

The kinds of misconduct that killed some of the S&Ls and cost the insurer lots of money are the following:

Type 1. An insider (an officer, director, or owner) gets a direct or indirect payoff in his or her personal capacity in exchange for the institution's making a loan or investment.

Type 2. A loan is made to an insider (or affiliate of an insider) without an independent credit judgment being made.

Type 3. An outsider — usually through misrepresentations in the loan applications process — induces the S&L to make a loan based on false premises about credit or security.

Type 1 misconduct is the only one that necessarily involves *illegal* conduct by an *insider*. Type 2 misconduct necessarily is mismanagement — but that, while it may be subject to a civil action for damages, is not illegal under the criminal law unless it violates a specific rule. Type 3 misconduct is illegal but the illegality is committed by an *outsider*, not necessarily with the complicity of an insider, although it usually is facilitated by lax management.

When we say that insider fraud caused a failure, we should be talking only about Type 1 misconduct. Types 2 and 3 may well cause failures — they caused some expensive ones — but usually they either aren't criminal misconduct or aren't perpetrated by insiders. Indeed, even some Type 1 misconduct may have not been illegal, given the relative laxity of the S&L conflict-of-interest regulations in force during most of the 1980s.

Regulators, prosecutors, and Congressmen tend to lump together Types 1, 2, and 3 fraud and misconduct with a host of other types of insider misconduct, such as keeping inaccurate records, filing incorrect reports, paying themselves too much, and spending too much corporate money entertaining themselves and their customers. These other types of insider misconduct, while they do evidence the kinds of attitudes that lead to laxness and mismanagement—and often accompany Type 1 and Type 2 misconduct—are even more frequently symptoms that there is no real capital at risk for the owners and directors to protect. Expense account liberties and high corporate living, while repugnant to low-paid regulators—and especially repugnant after an institution's failure—are almost never of a sufficient magnitude to cause insolvency. David Paul's excesses at CenTrust, including buying an art collection, a yacht, a sailboat, Limoges china, and Baccarat crystal, didn't lose more than $20 million (after selling them all at auction) against an insolvency of $2 billion—less than 1 percent. It sounds pretty sensational, but it is not the heart of the problem.

A different type of misconduct—which we can call Type 4—probably cost more than all the others put together, even though it didn't *cause* any failures. This type of misconduct involves covering up bad loans. Type 4 misconduct has two basic categories: (1) concealing loan defaults and (2) filing false reports. Phony transactions are used to conceal loan defaults. Those transactions are falsely reported to the regulators, often along with a variety of bogus or questionable accounting entries. These actions are designed to mislead the regulators and prevent them from exercising supervisory and enforcement powers. Often, during the period that the regulators are being misled, the management does most of the real looting. Although the S&L usually is insolvent before the Type 4 misconduct takes place, it can cause substantial losses if the regulators are lulled by it, as so often they were.

Many people in the business wondered what all those Texans thought they were accomplishing by trading bad mortgages around. We didn't know that "a rolling loan gathers no loss" because the regulators took years to figure out that the loans weren't really performing. We didn't know that the regulators didn't immediately catch on when loans were sold for nonrecourse notes. These are ancient scams. Who wouldn't see through them? But in many cases, these transactions bought S&L managers a year or more before they were kicked out or shut down.

Why was there so much fraud at Texas S&Ls? Substantially all of the banks there failed, too, yet there have been few allegations of fraud by bankers. Were the bankers better people? Or were there other reasons why fraud was prevalent in the S&Ls and not in the banks?

I believe that the way S&Ls traditionally have been run and supervised had a lot to do with bringing out the criminal tendencies in the particular owners and managers who ran the Texas S&Ls in the 1980s. The conflict-of-interest rules weren't very good. There was a tradition of minor self-dealing. It was a good ol' boys' bidness. Texas S&Ls weren't getting examined very often by the FHLBB. The S&L Commissioner was one of the good old boys who had gone to the S&L school in Indiana, and he came into politics through the S&L business. For these reasons, it looked to the S&L owners and managers like they just might get away with it. They just might stay one jump ahead. They just might be able to defend themselves because everybody was doing it.

I haven't seen any evidence that organized crime was involved in the big losses. Some of the smaller cases seem to have involved small-time operators with organized crime connections who defrauded all-too-willingly-dumb S&L managements. But organized crime itself would have done those jobs better. They wouldn't have been caught and convicted so easily.

BOARDS OF DIRECTORS

When all the bad loans were being made and insider deals were being cut, where were the boards of directors? Didn't they have a duty to make sure the institutions were run prudently? Didn't they see that management was gambling? Shouldn't they have put a stop to it?

Of course they should. But most board members didn't have the technical capacity to act independently, and in most S&Ls they didn't get all the information that would have been necessary to enable them to form their own judgments. How do you investigate a loan on an office building construction project if you are a doctor or a car dealer? Do you know what the rent per square foot will be in two years, when the building is completed? Do you know whether there will be a market for the space? Do you know whether it should cost $50 a square foot or $100 a square foot to build? A loan officer who touches all the bases will convince you almost every time, even if you're pretty sharp. So you rely on the appraisal. An S&L board was a sort of chowder and marching society.

Of course some boards weren't just fat, dumb, and happy. Some got treated right by the CEOs, with fancy perks, consulting contracts, or pieces of deals. A lot of that wasn't illegal the way the laws were structured; and the perks made it unlikely that the board members would rock the boat.

Nor are the standards for director conduct very clear. The law says that the director owes a "fiduciary" duty—but what's that, and to whom is it owed? We know that the duty is owed to stockholders and somehow to the corporate entity itself, but we don't know much about how conflicts between those two should be resolved. We don't have a law (yet) that says a director owes a special duty to the deposit insurer.

FSLIC and its successors now are bringing cases against directors to recoup money from them, on the ground that they violated their fiduciary duties by failing to supervise management properly. These cases are likely to establish new, more rigorous legal standards because the judges will feel political pressure to get some of the money back. In cases where directors got more than directors' fees and a trip to a convention, the judges will want to get back whatever the directors took.

The tough questions will be about directors' duties to investigate and understand the loans and other transactions that they approved. Most judges will know that they themselves also couldn't have distinguished a good loan from a bad one. But with hindsight you usually can see the seeds of a bad loan in the original proposal. My guess is that the judges won't make directors pay for ordinary mistakes—and they shouldn't—but that they will make directors pay if they were just rubber stamps who collected fees and perks. Many former directors are going to have a hard time showing that they did their homework but still made mistakes.

THE LAWYERS

Allegations abound that lawyers participated in or facilitated fraud and misconduct, and in a number of cases lawyers have been convicted of doing so or have made large civil law settlements to avoid trial. We have to be careful not to paint with too broad a brush, however, because when working on private transactions, a lawyer's public duties only arise in extreme cases. I have not done the research into enough specific cases to be able to offer an opinion on the performance of lawyers in general in the S&L context. Clearly, many lawyers represented clients zealously even though those clients were themselves committing wrongs, but it is hard to know whether to impute knowledge of those wrongs to the lawyers. We should remember that in our system a lawyer's job is to represent the client zealously unless by doing so the lawyer would assist the client in committing unlawful or fraudulent acts.

14 Wall Street Remakes the Mortgage Business

In the 1980s, the Wall Street investment banking firms made billions of dollars by catering to S&Ls. The S&Ls had mortgages to sell, they would buy vast amounts of securities, they needed to raise capital, and they were pretty unsophisticated. The Wall Street houses developed new departments of mortgage finance and dozens of new products to serve the S&Ls. The investment bankers:

- created a huge secondary market for mortgages and mortgage-based securities

- created collateralized mortgage obligations (CMOs) to chop up those mortgage-based securities into pieces of cash flow that different investors wanted

- sold mortgage-based securities and CMOs to the S&Ls

- sold "residual" CMO securities to the S&Ls

- sold IOs, POs, superfloaters, and other mortgage-based securities with unusual interest rate risk characteristics to S&Ls

- created a market for "mortgage servicing"

- developed complex asset–liability management techniques for S&Ls and sold them the products they needed to create the complex hedges that were part of those strategies

- underwrote and encouraged the conversion of S&Ls from mutual to stock form and the public offering of their stock.

Often the investment bankers sold these products before even they fully understood the products' characteristics, much less their implications. The S&L managers, impressed by the slick presentations with graphs, charts, and tables and the trappings of the great Wall Street firms, bought all kinds of securities, often without really understanding them. Some of the securities worked well; others didn't.

The investment bankers were the agents of economic changes that had been made possible by 1980s' computer and communications technologies. Like good football teams, they took what the defense gave them.

HOW THE SECONDARY MORTGAGE MARKET TRANSFORMED THE S&L BUSINESS

Wall Street's inventions *transformed* the traditional single-family lending part of the S&L business. At the same time that deregulation and excessive deposit competition were driving deposit rates up, the secondary market for mortgage loans was driving down the interest rates that S&Ls could earn on single-family mortgages. Spreads therefore contracted rapidly as the secondary market began to set the interest rates for mortgages. Whereas once an S&L manager only had to look either at the usury ceiling or at the interest rates that his or her few S&L competitors were charging, in the 1980s an S&L manager had to understand what Wall Street and the federal mortgage agencies — GNMA ("Ginnie Mae")*, FNMA ("Fannie Mae")* and FHLMC ("Freddie Mac")* — were paying for mortgages. If an S&L charged a rate of interest that was higher than the rate at which the agencies would buy mortgages, independent mortgage bankers would come into the market and undercut the S&Ls' rates and steal their business. If the S&Ls charged lower rates, they reduced an already thin spread. In effect, the new mechanisms provided a global supply of money for American home financing, but it destroyed many S&Ls' ability to make profits.

Although the Wall Street firms created the secondary market for mortgage-based securities and created and sold various derivatives, the basic pressure that drove mortgage interest rates down relative to Treasury rates came from the federal mortgage agencies, which have low operating costs and can raise long-term money at a few basis points over government bond rates because their bonds are backed by an actual or implied federal guarantee. They therefore are willing to buy mortgages at narrow spreads over Treasury rates. S&Ls can't compete profitably at these rates because they have the built-in expenses of retail branch networks and can't raise long-term money at such low cost. Thus, while the federal mortgage agencies help the American homeowner by lowering mortgage interest rates a little and help efficient S&Ls by buying mortgages that they originate, many economists argue persuasively that they have helped to destroy the S&Ls.

CMOs

The secondary market grew almost exponentially in the early 1980s. At first, Ginnie Mae securities—securitized fixed-rate mortgages with a government guarantee—accounted for most of the market. It was a big market, but eventually its growth was limited by the financial world's appetite for investments that had a thirty-year stated maturity but that everyone knew would, on average, pay off in eight to twelve years as people sold or refinanced their homes. Both the long term of the mortgages and the uncertain nature of prepayments by borrowers limited the number of potential buyers because the buyers couldn't know exactly what their cash flows from the investments would be.

Then, to create more certain cash flows for investors, Wall Street invented the multi-tranche collateralized mortgage obligation. The CMO is a very complex instrument but, boiled down to its essentials, it is understandable by taking an example. An S&L takes a group of mortgages—maybe $150 million worth—and puts them into a subsidiary to separate them from the rest of the institution. The investment banker then sells to investors a series of different interests in the pool of mortgages in the subsidiary. The first series gets *all* cash flow from *all* of the mortgages until it has been repaid at a specified interest rate. That may be projected to take two years. The second series gets only a stated rate of interest until the first has been repaid, but then it gets all of the next cash flow until *it* is repaid. That might take five years. The third series gets no cash flow except interest until the first two have been repaid, but then it gets all cash flow until it is repaid, which might take twenty years. The three series are known, naturally enough, as the short, medium, and long tranches.

This mechanism expands the market of buyers so that someone who wants a two-year investment, someone who wants a five-year investment, or someone who wants a twenty-year investment can be happy buying one of the series. The investment banker can divide the cash flows into whatever lengths of series it needs in order to satisfy customers' needs.

There also is cash flow left after all of the fixed series have been paid because the subsidiary will sell only maybe $100 million of interests in the series against the $150 million face amount of mortgages. There has to be a cushion in the event that the mortgagors—that is, the people who borrowed the money to finance their homes—take longer to pay than expected. If they do take longer, then each series will take longer to be paid off and there will be less left over at the end. The right to the residual cash flow, after the three fixed series are paid off, is called a "CMO residual"—or in some cases a "STREMIC"—a very speculative security that fooled a lot of S&Ls. Silverado, you may recall, was the champion STREMIC buyer.

Many S&Ls thought that these CMO residuals were like mortgages. Instead, they are like sitting at the end of a long dining table in a boarding house. If cash flow to the fixed series is slower than expected, there won't be any left for the CMO residual, which will be wiped out. You don't have to invest in Texas real estate to lose money in the mortgage business. Variations in prepayment speeds on single-family mortgage loans can get you, too.

Uncertainty of Prepayments, Negative Convexity, and All That

Whereas in 1980 S&Ls held only 3 percent of their assets in mortgage-based securities, by 1987 such securities represented 16 percent of S&Ls' portfolios. The characteristics of these securities therefore became extremely important to a majority of S&Ls.

Mortgage-based securities earn rates of interest that are higher than U.S. Treasury security rates because, even if they have government guarantees, nobody can predict when mortgagors will prepay. If you buy a mortgage-based security on the assumption that the underlying mortgages will be prepaid, on average, in ten years, you take the risk that interest rates will go up and cause mortgagors to prepay *less* quickly at precisely the time you want them to prepay *more* quickly so you can reinvest the money at the higher rates. Conversely, you also take the risk that when interest rates go down, the mortgagors will refinance their homes and prepay *more* quickly, just when you hoped you could keep earning the higher rate on the mortgages. The mortgagors have an "option" whether to prepay and, on average, they will exercise that option when it is in *their* best interests to do so, which is when the owner of the mortgage wants it least. This perverse quality of mortgages and mortgage-based securities is known as "negative convexity." The concept applies to both variable-rate and fixed-rate mortgages, as well as to securities based on their cash flows.

Both the Wall Street firms and the S&Ls lost hundreds of millions because at the beginning of the secondary market boom they didn't understand negative convexity. They took historical rates of prepayment, projected them into the future, and based the prices of mortgage-based securities on those assumptions. When the assumptions turned out to be incorrect, the securities declined in value and the market demanded a higher premium over Treasury securities.

Still, S&Ls held over $400 billion of mortgage-based securities at the end of 1989 and took the attendant risks of changes in prepayment rates. Most of them still don't recognize that prepayment rates depend on psychology, mobility, general economic conditions, and so on, as well as on interest rates. People will sell or refinance for reasons that not only are not knowable at present but also are bound to change. Does the spread over Treasuries fully reflect that uncertainty? Who knows?

Unbundling the Single-Family Mortgage

The growth of the secondary market led to an "unbundling" of three parts of the single-family mortgage business: It became possible to separate originating a mortgage from owning a mortgage and from servicing a mortgage. The originator is the S&L or mortgage banker that makes the loan; the owner or holder is the entity that decides to hold it and receive the stream of interest and principal payments from the borrower; and the "servicer" is the institution whose functions are to collect from the borrower and to foreclose on the property if the borrower stops paying. The servicer passes on the borrower's payments, net of the servicing fee, to the owner.

The secondary market makes this unbundling possible by allowing individuals or institutions that don't have origination or servicing capabilities to own mortgages. In addition, through guarantees by Ginnie, Fannie, or Freddie with implicit government backing, or by a private mortgage insurance company, the owner or holder gets not only the right to the cash flow from the mortgage but also a "credit enhancement" that removes any credit risk from the mortgage, so that the buyer has to consider only the cash flow characteristics. Eliminating the credit risk opens the mortgage ownership market to almost any type of investor.

Unbundling also caused reevaluation of the servicing side of the business. Traditionally, servicing was a forgotten back office function that was a necessary nuisance—a cost center, not a profit center. All of a sudden, servicing had value. You could sell the servicing for a profit, regardless of whether you sold the mortgage to someone else or held the mortgage yourself. When an S&L management analyzed the situation, it had to ask whether it could service mortgages as efficiently as someone else. If the market would pay 30 basis points a year for servicing, did the S&L make money by performing servicing at a cost less than that? If not, then the S&L should sell its servicing to someone more efficient. Thus a secondary market in servicing developed and, because economies of scale are significant in servicing, major companies like GMAC (a subsidiary of General Motors) and Citicorp, rather than the S&Ls, took over the largest share of the mortgage servicing business.

The S&Ls got some temporary benefits by selling the servicing on many of their old mortgages and taking profits on those sales. But those profits were made by selling the family jewels. They could do it only once.

The larger effects of the secondary market and the unbundling of mortgage components have made it very hard to make money by taking in deposits and originating, holding, and servicing mortgages in the traditional way. The S&Ls that abandoned or gave less emphasis to single-family mortgage lending weren't all speculators throwing the dice. Economics had forced them to try to find a new business. They simply were unsuccessful in finding less competitive businesses because money is fungible and we already had 14,000 banks in the United States competing for corporate and individual customers.

HEDGING INTEREST RATE RISK

Bankers debate endlessly about how to deal with interest rate risk. They debate about the fine points of whether there is a "liquidity premium" at the short end of the interest rate curve and whether various measurement systems properly reflect the actual amount of interest rate risk that a bank is taking. But basically, bankers agree that interest rate risk should be managed closely and should never be so big that it could wipe out a large part of profits for the year if it turns out that you made the wrong interest rate bet.

S&Ls, as we know, historically didn't manage their interest rate risk. They relied on government regulation of interest rates. But after 1982 most S&Ls tried to learn to manage their interest rate risks.

The easiest way to protect yourself from rate changes is to create "natural matches" between your assets and your liabilities. For example, you sell a six-month CD and use the proceeds to buy a six-month T-bill. You know that the asset and the liability will fall due on the same date. You know that the government isn't allowed to prepay you. You know that the CD owner doesn't have an option to require you to prepay him or her (if you haven't foolishly given that option). This is a perfect match that has no interest rate risk. But it also isn't likely to have any profit, because no one is likely to buy your CD if it pays very much less interest than a T-bill.

So in order to make a profit on the money you get from selling the six-month CD, you may decide to invest in something else that doesn't have too much credit risk. For example, you make a thirty-year fixed-rate, single-family mortgage at a 75 percent LTV. This is a safe investment that will produce a nice spread against the money you got from selling the CD. Maybe the spread will be as much as 300 basis points if the yield curve is going your way.

The problem you now have is that you will have to repay the CD in six months but the homeowner won't have to repay you for thirty years. If rates go up in six months, you will have to pay the new market rate for money when the CD comes due. And if you finance thirty-year mortgages with six-month CDs, you will be at risk every six months for the whole thirty years unless the mortgage is prepaid. Of course you could go out and borrow for thirty years to match the thirty-year mortgage. You might have trouble getting anyone to lend your S&L money for thirty years, but if you could get it, you still would have two problems: (1) the cost would eat up most, if not all, of your 300 basis point spread; (2) the institution that lent you the money wouldn't give you the option to prepay if the mortgagor to whom you lent the money prepaid you. You would still have to pay the fixed rate for thirty years. So you wouldn't have much, if any, profit and you would still have interest rate risk.

For these reasons you would be unlikely to try to hedge your long-term mortgages by making long-term borrowings. Instead, you most likely would buy a "synthetic" hedge, meaning a security that has the opposite characteristics of the ones that your thirty-year mortgages have when interest rates go up.

You might try a variety of synthetics, such as "swaps," "IOs," and "POs." When you buy an IO, you buy the right to all of the interest from a mortgage-based security. When you buy the PO, you buy the right to all of the repayments of principal. These securities, standing on their own, obviously are highly speculative. The IO will continue paying as long as the mortgagors don't prepay. But it will stop paying entirely when they do. The PO will always pay back your principal, but it may do so at the wrong time. The IO, at least in theory, will give you more income when interest rates go up, so it will hedge your problem with the fixed-rate mortgage in that circumstance. The PO would repay you faster when interest rates went down.

But after investigating all these hedges, you would find that none of them really match the uncertain cash flows that you were going to get from the mortgage, and most of them would reduce your spread to nil.

The point of all this hedging discussion is not to make the readers of this book experts on hedging but to illustrate how complex it is to reduce the interest rate risk that is inherent in seemingly simple single-family mortgages and securities based on them. We have used fixed-rate mortgages in our example, but variable-rate mortgages—trumpeted as a panacea by many in the early 1980s—while easier to match in some respects, give even more complex hidden options to the borrower than fixed-rate mortgages do. For example, all variable-rate mortgages now have periodic and lifetime caps. That is, the rate usually can't go up more than 200 basis points in a year or 500 basis points over the life of the mortgage. The holder of the mortgage takes the risk of wider interest rate swings.

Any holder of mortgages or mortgage-based securities that uses borrowed money (such as deposits) to hold them will have difficulty in matching the cash flows. More and more complex hedges are what the investment bankers will advise in order to protect the holder against the cash flow uncertainties.

THE WIZARD OF OTTAWA, KANSAS

Ernest Fleischer—former whiz kid from St. Louis, CPA, Harvard Law School graduate magna cum laude, and tax lawyer—had an investment in a little S&L in Ottawa, Kansas (just outside Kansas City), called Franklin. He'd had the investment since 1972, and he looked on it as part of his retirement planning. So, like everyone else who had an investment in an S&L in 1980, he was deeply distressed when Franklin started losing money as interest rates went up. Unlike a lot of other investors, however, Fleischer decided to do something about it.[1]

He took control of Franklin in 1981 and set out to minimize the interest rate risk that seemed to be inherent in the S&L business. He consulted professors and Wall Street hedging gurus. He learned that no hedge is perfect, but that you can still make money without a lot of interest rate risk if you are very efficient and control your costs.

By 1985, little Franklin had grown to $2 billion, up from $200 million in 1981. By 1989, it had $11 billion in assets and was not only the biggest S&L in Kansas but the biggest S&L in the Midwest.

But Franklin wasn't a typical S&L. It didn't originate a lot of home loans. It didn't make a lot of construction loans or permanent loans on commercial real estate. It didn't make a lot of consumer loans. Its 1989 balance sheet showed only $200 million of loans out of $11 billion of assets. Mostly, Franklin bought mortgage-based securities, many with government guarantees. When those securities went up, Franklin took profits. In the meantime, Franklin engaged in complex hedges to maintain a spread over cost of funds through a variety of interest rate environments. (We should note that Franklin wasn't risk free. Fleischer didn't like interest rate risk, but he bought over $250 million of junk bonds, guaranteed a similar amount of industrial revenue bonds, and bought the remains of the brokerage firm L. F. Rothschild. Franklin lost money on all of these adventures, but it was the hedges that finally got Fleischer in trouble.)

Franklin didn't look normal on the liability side of the balance sheet, either. By 1989, out of $11 billion of liabilities, less than $4 billion were deposits and over half of those were brokered. The rest of the liabilities were repos, FHLB borrowings, CMO issues, and other kinds of borrowings, many of them structured to match the cash flow characteristics of the mortgage-based securities.

Franklin was able to grow from $200 million to $11 billion in eight years without violating regulatory capital requirements because in the mid–1980s it took big profits on sales of mortgage-based securities and sold capital securities to the public through Wall Street. In those respects, it looked a lot like Cen-Trust, skimming the profits from the securities portfolio to be able to grow.

Without the securities sales, Franklin didn't make much money from operations. Franklin was different from CenTrust, however, because it wasn't just selling the best from its portfolio so that the remainder was under water. In fact, in 1989 Franklin was able to designate substantially its whole securities portfolio—$9.5 billion worth—as held for sale and to carry it at the lower of cost or market with almost no resulting write-down.

Sounds wonderful, but the OTS (the Bank Board's successor under FIRREA) didn't think so. It didn't think that Franklin was accounting properly for its hedges under GAAP. It said that $330 million of hedge losses that Franklin, with the approval of its auditors, Touche, Ross, had deferred (not recognized) had to be taken as current period losses under GAAP. That would put Franklin under its capital requirements.

Both the OTS and Touche, Ross were using GAAP accounting. How could Touche, Ross and the OTS have a $330 million disagreement about how to apply generally accepted accounting principles? Either the method that Franklin was using was generally accepted or it wasn't, no?

No. As we have seen, GAAP evolves. And it evolves in arrears, trying to catch up with technology. GAAP has a pretty simple rough concept about hedges. It says that if there is a "high correlation" between the downward valuation of the hedge and the upward valuation of the hedged asset (or liability), you don't have to recognize the hedge's loss of value until you sell the asset. If you don't sell it, you amortize the loss against interest income over the life of the asset.

The OTS and Touche, Ross agreed that the theory of "high correlation" was GAAP. They disagreed, however, about how to measure it. The way OTS measured it, the correlation wasn't high. The way Touche, Ross measured it, the correlation was high. The consequences of the OTS position were enormous. If there wasn't a high correlation, then the hedging losses had to be recognized. That would take Franklin below capital requirements. If Franklin reported that it was below capital requirements, that would have further consequences under various agreements under which Franklin had borrowed money. Eventually, insolvency would become almost inevitable.

As one of his last official acts, Danny Wall took over Franklin Savings on February 16, 1990. The takeover was based primarily on the asserted hedging losses. Franklin sued the OTS, alleging that the takeover was illegal. We'll examine the outcome in a later chapter. For now, let's observe that mortgages and mortgage-based securities have built-in interest rate risks that are hard to hedge. When somebody (Franklin) did try to hedge those risks by using all the available complex computer models and mortgage derivative securities, the regulator claimed that the hedge didn't work, with drastic consequences.

There are over $1 trillion of mortgage-based securities (broadly defined) being traded in the American financial markets. Does anybody know what their consequences are? Remember: Even Ernie Fleischer, when he testified that the OTS had taken over Franklin illegally, admitted that he *didn't understand* all of the hedges that Franklin had. Only his specialists, he testified, whom he had hired from Wall Street and academia, understood just how the securities and computer models worked. And maybe they didn't understand so well, either. As evidence comes out, it looks like some of the hedges didn't end up working very well.

WHATCHA GONNA DO?

If you were an S&L manager in, say, 1986, faced with declining spreads, recommended hedges that were impossible to understand, negative convexity, and special insurance assessments, what would you have done? Even Ed Gray, who was in the midst of decrying fast growth, used self-funded mortgage-backed securities deals to inflate FCA's balance sheet in an effort to save it. It's no wonder so few S&Ls made money.

MUTUALS SELL STOCK TO THE PUBLIC

Some commentators have asserted that the investment-banker-promoted conversions of mutual S&Ls to stock form that began right after Garn–St Germain was passed caused a lot of the S&L losses. They base this assertion on two facts. First, whereas in 1979, 80 percent of S&L assets were held by mutual institutions and only 20 percent were held by stock institutions, ten years later the numbers were almost reversed. Second, stock institutions incurred over 80 percent of the losses suffered in S&L failures. These facts are correct, but the conclusion isn't.

To analyze what happened, we need to break the transfer of assets from mutual to stock institutions into two parts: the growth of small stock institutions, on the one hand, and the conversion of mutuals, on the other. A larger part of the transfer of assets came from the superfast growth of small stock institutions such as Vernon, Sunbelt, Independent American, Silverado, and Lincoln, which grew much faster than the mutual institutions did. These little, closely held S&Ls caused a disproportionate share of the growth of stock institutions and a disproportionate share of the losses. The states where the biggest losses occurred—Texas, California, Florida, Arizona, and Colorado—already had stock S&Ls, many of which were privately owned, before Garn–St Germain.

The wave of conversions and public offerings of stock that followed Garn–St Germain accounted for about 300 institutions and raised about $5 billion of new capital, mostly for S&Ls whose net worth had been badly damaged by the interest rate ravages. Big California S&Ls like Home Federal and California Federal, the two largest mutuals in California, converted in 1983, raising over $700 million of new capital. Other big S&Ls, some of which have failed, such as Sooner Federal in Oklahoma and City Federal in New Jersey, got new life by raising capital from the public. Even some insolvent S&Ls, such as First Federal of Arkansas, managed to go public. Today First Federal of Arkansas is insolvent again.

A last wave of conversions of S&Ls desperate for capital took place in 1986–87, prominently featuring two former New York savings banks, Anchor and Empire of America, which had converted to FSLIC insurance in order to acquire failing S&Ls in 1982 and had loaded up on goodwill as a result. Both Anchor and Empire of America were insolvent measured on a tangible basis when they went public, and nobody should have bought their securities. In fact, almost nobody did buy the Empire securities, as the investment bankers kept on having to downsize the Empire offering and eventually sold the whole $11 billion institution for $75 million to people who wanted to take a long shot on a sick interstate franchise. Anchor sold more easily, as depositors and the public identified with Don Thomas, Anchor's chairman, and his wife, Barbara, who had done "Anchor Banker" ads on radio and TV for years. Don and Barbara raised $176 million for Anchor on the strength of their late-middle-aged Midwestern voices and homespun humor.

Empire of America was taken over by OTS and chopped up and sold by the RTC in 1990. Anchor is still hanging on, selling everything that has any value in an effort to survive.

By and large, the institutions that failed after converting in public offerings were very weak when they went public. The new capital tended to shore them up. In some cases, however, it wasn't enough to overcome all the goodwill and low-yielding loans. (The New England savings bank conversions had different consequences, but they are not part of our story.)

The investment bankers, lawyers, printers, and accountants loved conversions. We all (but especially the investment bankers, who got a 6 percent to 7 percent underwriting spread) made a lot of money advising managements who, almost by definition, had no experience with the relatively mysterious conversion process and therefore wanted their collective hands held every step of the way. Conversions were fun for everybody involved because there were no losers. Depositors were happy to buy stock, managements were happy to get stock options, boards of directors were happy to get more capital, and the rest of us were happy to get paid. The closing dinners were fun, too, although some of the fun seemed a little hollow a few years later.

15 Politics as Usual – Everybody Fiddles While the FSLIC Burns

By 1982, if FSLIC had been a private company, its creditors (the depositors) would have forced it into bankruptcy because it didn't have enough money to pay them by liquidating S&Ls as they became insolvent. Instead of having to declare bankruptcy, however, the FSLIC did what only a government agency could do: It changed the rules under which its obligations were measured. The Bank Board changed S&L net worth rules, adopted liberal purchase accounting and deferred loss rules, and generally permitted S&Ls to report inflated earnings. If the S&Ls didn't report themselves as insolvent, then the FSLIC didn't have to take them over and liquidate them with the money it didn't have.

The FSLIC's financial statements looked fine even as late as 1985, when they showed "reserves" (the equivalent of net worth) of over $4 billion. FSLIC's people managed this by not making provision for contingencies that were not "estimable" in amount, which GAAP seemed to permit them to do. They didn't accrue for spread guarantees to acquirers, and they carried net worth certificates and income capital certificates issued to insolvent institutions on their books with an obviously inadequate collectibility reserve. They recorded no contingency reserve for the many insolvent S&Ls that they left open but had to know would cost billions to resolve eventually.[1] To Ed Gray, FSLIC accounting was just an "esoteric exercise."

The rose-colored FSLIC accounting fooled everybody. The public, the Congress, even the Bank Board itself saw the $6 billion, $5 billion, $4 billion reserve balance and believed it. The balance was declining from 1982 through

1985 and the total of insured deposits was rising, which was cause for concern, but the alarm bells weren't going off, the red meltdown lights weren't flashing. Until they are, Congress won't pay attention to legislation that doesn't bring votes.

Even the General Accounting Office (GAO), which audits government agency financial statements for the Congress, doesn't seem to have noticed that anything was wrong until 1986, when it was auditing the FSLIC's 1985 statements. At that time the GAO told the FSLIC that it had to set up some kind of reserve for all the insolvent but open S&Ls. And when the FSLIC set up an obviously inadequate $1.5 billion (obviously inadequate because it was telling Congress it would cost $10 to $15 billion to solve known problems), the GAO merely said in its letter to Congress that it thought the number was too small—a proper accounting response but too subtle for the Congress.

Only in 1987 did the GAO convince the FSLIC that the 1986 financial statements should contain a big enough contingency reserve ($11 billion) to make it insolvent (by $6 billion). The FSLIC never established reserves for all of its obligations to acquirers of failed institutions until 1989, when it didn't really matter anymore.

The cover-up shouldn't surprise anyone. The public's confidence in the fund's ability to make good on its promises to depositors was thought to depend upon an appearance of financial health. Everyone—including the Congress, the regulators, the U.S. League and the administration—worried that runs on S&Ls could be triggered by the wrong news. Ironically, in 1987 the reports of FSLIC's insolvency caused hardly a ripple among depositors—a few basis points' increase in S&Ls' cost of deposits.

THE NUMBERS GAME

Although it hadn't yet admitted that the FSLIC was insolvent, the Bank Board began working on an FSLIC "recapitalization" plan early in 1985. The Board floundered around for about a year, asking *somebody* to do *something*. Finally, in the spring of 1986 the Treasury proposed a plan. But the Treasury plan wasn't enacted by Congress in 1986, even though both houses passed it. Then in 1987 Congress passed an inadequate plan that allowed it to say it had done something. Who was to blame? The U.S. League, Speaker Jim Wright, maybe Rep. Henry Gonzalez, Freddie St Germain, Ed Gray, or Charles Keating—and certainly the usual politics of banking legislation—combined to create too little, too late.

Throughout the two-year debate that temporarily ended in the passage of the Competitive Equality Banking Act of 1987 (CEBA), the leading players never agreed on what it would cost FSLIC to deal with all of the known and currently foreseeable insolvencies. The Bank Board would come out with a number; the GAO would say it was too small; the U.S. League would say it was an exaggeration—"scare tactics." Traditions of secrecy about failing banks and S&Ls prevented public access to the underlying numbers. All an observer could know for sure was that no official ever said that the amount needed was larger than $25 billion.

In March 1986, when everybody made an estimate, the Bank Board said the FSLIC needed to spend $16 billion over the next five years and had only $6 billion.[2] The Treasury said the FSLIC needed between $5 and $25 billion.[3] The U.S. League said the FSLIC needed between $8 billion and $15 billion, against its $6 billion in reserves.[4] The GAO said the number was hard to evaluate.[5] At the same time, some analysts were privately advising their clients that the problem could be as big as $100 billion. Maybe the Bank Board didn't really want to know. Nobody wanted the problem to be bigger than the S&Ls could handle themselves.

The Bank Board and the U.S. League had fairly specific agendas that they wanted their numbers to justify. The Bank Board wanted to be able to deal with its worst problems promptly and gradually to dig itself out of the hole it was in, but it didn't want to make the problem so big that it (the Board) would look bad—the same people had run the Board since 1983—or so big that the Congress would get angry and do away with what Ed Gray referred to as the "Federal Home Loan Bank System," meaning the Bank Board, FSLIC, the FHLBs, and the whole system that subsidized housing finance. The U.S. League's agenda turned out to be more complex.

THE U.S. LEAGUE'S POLICY AND PERSPECTIVE

The U.S. League not only wanted to protect the FHLB system; it also wanted to preserve its individual members and to minimize the cost of any solution to its healthy and most powerful members. The U.S. League's policy dynamics, political power, and misguided campaign against the Bank Board in Congress reveal how American trade association politics can mold political results. The League's influence set a new standard for politics as usual.

In the mid–1980s, the U.S. League had two powerful constituencies: the healthy S&Ls, led by the Californians, and the troubled institutions of the Southwest. The healthy institutions were as angry about the size of the problem as the public later became. They already were paying for the asset problems through the special insurance assessment imposed by the FSLIC in 1985, and they foresaw that they logically could be stuck with a lot more of the bill. Their goal was to pay as little as they could to bail out the FSLIC.

The people who ran the strong, traditional institutions didn't much like the oil patch good old boys, but they knew that to influence Congress would require a unified effort from all parts of the country. Therefore the healthy institutions made common cause with the sick and the weak from the Southwest. The U.S. League staff encouraged the alliance because they didn't want to lose members and because they didn't want a fight within their ranks. "Never choose sides among the members" is the first rule of trade association management. A trade association by its nature cannot resist trying to find common ground among its members and to formulate a policy on that basis. The policy then takes on a life of its own.

The policy objectives that the healthy members and the sick ones could agree on were (1) get FSLIC to spend less money, (2) in order to spend less money, keep the failing S&Ls open as long as possible, and (3) get the money from anywhere except more insurance assessments. These objectives led the League to advocate

> that the problem wasn't as big as the Bank Board said it was
>
> that the FSLIC couldn't efficiently spend more than about $3 billion in a year, no matter what the size of the problem was, and
>
> that the problems resulted mostly from regional economic problems for which individual members shouldn't be punished.

These positions naturally led to demanding

> "forbearances" for low-net-worth institutions that the League said could recover as the regional economy came back,
>
> a go-slow approach on requiring reserves for underwater loans (the banking regulators had recently gone easy on requiring reserves for farm loans and international loans), and
>
> a reduced amount of funding for the FSLIC.[6]

As we know now—and the League should have known then—these policies were seriously mistaken because (1) the problem was bigger than the FHLBB claimed it was; (2) you can clean up a lot of S&L problems in a fairly short period of time (but you have to spend a whole lot of money to do it); and (3) most important, a broke S&L will continue to lose money forever. The local economy may come back, but it will come back too late to help broke institutions, and when the problem is overbuilding (as it was), the economy will take years to absorb all the surplus buildings at reduced prices.

With the help of southwestern real estate developers, who also were in trouble, the League and its members were totally effective in convincing the Congress to spend less, provide forbearances, and slow down the asset revaluation process. Their effectiveness was the culmination of many years of hard work and carefully targeted contributions. The League and its members — remember, the League had members in every Congressional district and members held the mortgages on an awful lot of Representatives' and Senators' homes — had been working the Congress for years.

CAMPAIGN CONTRIBUTIONS AND OTHER POLITICAL RELATIONSHIP BUILDING

To have influence with a legislator, you need to convince him or her (1) that you gave campaign money, (2) that there's more where that came from, and (3) that your cause has some merit. Items (1) and (2) set the stage for item (3). They get you an audience in a busy schedule and they get you the benefit of the doubt. Relationships formed at dinners and golf outings also help to get you taken seriously. A guy with a 5 handicap who understands the political process deserves respect.

Almost every banking committee member got contributions from banks and S&Ls without trying very hard. The national trade groups each had a PAC, each state trade group had a PAC, many individual institutions had PACs, and bank and S&L executives understood they had an obligation, as part of getting their salaries, to contribute to the PACs for state or national matters and to local Congressional candidates on their own.

Members of Congress are always having fund-raising dinners and cocktail parties. They hold some of them in the home district, but some are held unabashedly in Washington so that the lobbyists can attend. At any Banking Committee member's function, whether at home or away, you would think you were at a joint meeting of the U.S. League, the American Bankers Association, the Independent Bankers Association of America, and the Securities Industry Association. They all paid their thousand dollars or so to attend.

Back home, S&L executives would organize dinners for key Senators and Representatives, and cajole or threaten all of the S&L's suppliers and borrowers to attend for $500 or $1,000 apiece. Lawyers and accountants who valued their clients, financial printers, computer paper salesmen, ATM vendors, appraisers, investment bankers — everyone who wanted to do business with the S&L — would pony up to stay on the boss's good side. Some S&L CEOs could raise hundreds of thousands of dollars in a single evening. From the campaign contribution reports, it looked like the money came from a few hundred different sources unrelated to the thrift industry.

In addition, campaign contributions don't include speaking fees, euphemistically known as "honoraria." S&Ls used to pay honoraria to dozens of Congressmen every year. Apparently, S&L executives loved to hear Congressmen speak.

Some of the Texas S&L owners weren't so subtle. Don Dixon, for example, bought the yacht *High Spirits* and anchored it on the Potomac, where it could be used for fund-raising parties by complaisant politicians. Sometimes Vernon, his S&L, even picked up the tab for the party.

Tom Gaubert was national finance chairman of the Democratic Congressional Campaign Committee. Dozens of other S&L owners and executives were active in lesser capacities.

THE LEAGUE AND THE BANK BOARD JOCKEY FOR POSITION

In 1985, Ed Gray told the Congress over and over that FSLIC needed help. His position was clear: "A legislated solution . . . which emphasizes long-term replenishment and maintenance of adequate reserve levels . . . is absolutely essential."[7] But he kept on giving the Congress too many alternatives, and the U.S. League never supported any of them. (One wag described Gray's approach as "the Chicken Little school of bank regulation.") Freddie St Germain complained that if there was such a big problem, where was the administration? Didn't it have a proposal?

Meanwhile, the FSLIC wasn't liquidating failed S&Ls because it didn't have enough money. When FSLIC Director Peter Stearns, whom they regarded as a loose cannon around the Bank Board, was forced out in November 1985, he fired some parting shots.[8] First, he said that the FSLIC was overestimating the value of its assets. The fund's real assets, he said, were lower than reported.

Next, Stearns refuted optimistic statements that recently had been made by Director Don Hovde. Hovde had just told the U.S. League's convention that there had been a

> host of misinformation on the Bank Board's ability to deal with problem institutions and preserve the FSLIC Fund. . . . What I want to tell you is that our insolvency caseload is manageable. I want to tell you that we have the case resources to spread over time to deal with the case resolutions for each and every insolvent thrift.[9]

"I disagree," said Stearns. "I think these management cases are getting worse, not better, the longer they are not resolved. But the solutions are incredibly expensive." When asked whether there was any chance that the 434 GAAP-insolvent S&Ls that had been identified in a recent GAO study could return to profitability, Stearns replied, "Maybe. Five percent to 10 percent of them will work their way out of their problems." By contrast, the Board was only talking about having 250 problem cases over the next two years.

"What is being built up," Stearns concluded, "is a potential keg of dynamite, which sooner or later is going to explode."

The U.S. League still would have none of it. The industry, it pointed out, was achieving record profits in 1985 and could project still greater profits in 1986. Reported net worth of savings institutions was higher than at any time since the dark days of 1982, it said. Interest rates were trending downward, and even S&Ls' fixed-rate loan portfolios were more than $100 billion closer to par on a market value basis than in 1982, so that *real* net worth would exist for the first time since the 1970s. Yes, there were bad apples; yes, there were institutions that had to be dealt with. But the MCP was working, and the hateful special assessment was providing cash to the FSLIC. The FSLIC could borrow from the FHLBs if it needed money. Over time, things could be worked out. In testimony before Congress, Jay Janis, Chairman of Gibraltar Savings in Los Angeles and a former Chairman of the Bank Board, summarized the League's position: "I think it is important," he said, "that we avoid being panicked by faulty press reports and confusing studies. I believe . . . the greatest danger is coming up with the wrong solution. This is one case, simply put, where no solution is better than the wrong solution."[10] At the League's convention, its director of research declared that "claims that the savings institutions business faces a crisis have no substance in fact."[11]

THE LEAGUE'S RECAP PROPOSAL

The League finally made a recap proposal in the spring of 1986, after a year of committee work and infighting. The proposal proceeded from the premises that the FSLIC had $6 billion in reserves and had problems that would cost $8 billion to $15 billion to resolve. The proposal would resolve these problems over a ten-year period and provide $23 billion of funds over that period. That money would come from an infusion to the FSLIC from the FHLBs, continuation of the special assessment for three years, and regular insurance premiums thereafter. The proposal further envisioned the FSLIC accelerating its case resolutions by changing its accounting so that it wouldn't report the present value of future obligations under assistance agreements as obligations on its balance sheet. "The problem is," the League said, "that current accounting rules for the FSLIC require it to create loss reserves for future expenditures [under long-term assistance agreements]. On the other hand, the FSLIC is given no credit for its future income stream. What our business needs is to stretch out the costs facing the FSLIC over a number of years." The League called this FSLIC's "timing of expenses" problem. It said FSLIC didn't have a "lack of money" problem.[12]

THE TREASURY PLAN

The administration finally broke its silence in the spring of 1986 and, through the Treasury Department, announced its plan to recapitalize the FSLIC through $15 billion of borrowings that the Treasury sought to keep off-budget and therefore not part of the federal deficit. The Gramm-Rudman Law, requiring annual decreases in the deficit, had just been passed, and the administration didn't want the FSLIC problem added to its existing budget problems.

These budgetary concerns led to a complex structure for borrowing the money, which the Congressional Budget Office (CBO) promptly said didn't work. It said the borrowing had to be on-budget. Six weeks of wrangling ensued, during which the Congress, ready to take up an off-budget plan, postponed action. Eventually, in July, the Treasury and the CBO reached an agreement that the recap could be off-budget if the borrowing corporation (called FICO) got its interest money directly from insurance assessments on insured S&Ls rather than through the FSLIC. The legislation therefore contained provisions that now would allow two entities—one owned by the government (FSLIC) and one owned by the FHLBs (FICO)—to make insurance assessments on S&Ls. Nothing, as usual, could be straightforward.

NONBANK BANK COMPLICATIONS

The House and Senate Banking Committees had been waiting for the Treasury–CBO compromise. Everyone said they were ready to approve an off-budget Treasury Plan.

But a new delay arose. The nonbank bank loophole in the Bank Holding Company Act, which had permitted interstate banking without explicit Congressional permission, was a bête noire to Congressman St Germain and Senator Proxmire. American Express, the owner of the largest nonbank bank, and the major commercial banks had been able to bottle up St Germain's loophole closer bill, so he announced that he wouldn't move on any other banking legislation until that bill was passed. Proxmire, the ranking minority member on the Senate Banking Committee, took the same view.[13] The Bank Board was caught in a bind because it supported the loophole closer on the ground that commercial banks' ability to operate interstate through the nonbank banks was depriving them of being able to offer incentives to buy failing S&Ls and take them off FSLIC's hands. (This was a silly position. Nonbank banks had nothing to do with selling failing S&Ls.)

The nonbank bank loophole may seem pretty esoteric, but these were esoteric days. Lawyers were finding loopholes and ways around statutory restrictions on banks every day. Congress wasn't making legislation that kept up with technological and market changes, so the regulators were listening to the inventive theories. The nonbank bank theory had been blessed by the Office of the Comptroller of the Currency (OCC)* in 1980 and had been used, litigated, and lobbied about ever since then. Congress had done nothing about it because it is harder to pass statutes than to stop them from passing.

ED GRAY IS INVESTIGATED

While Congress was playing its games, the *Wall Street Journal* published a story on July 16, 1986, that questioned the propriety of the U.S. League's having paid Ed Gray's expenses at conventions. Gray's $47,000 office renovation already had been investigated by the FBI. More charges of personal improprieties he didn't need.

The Bank Board referred the question to the Office of Government Ethics, which later expanded the investigation to include Gray's expenses that had been paid by the FHLBs (all those West Coast trips). The FHLBs, remember, were owned by the S&Ls, not by the government. In the end—in December—Ed Gray paid $26,000 of his own money as a reimbursement for expenses that had been borne by the FHLBs and the U.S. League. The Office of Government Ethics cleared him. In the meantime, however, lobbyists readily suggested that the Congress shouldn't trust Ed Gray with billions of additional dollars.[14]

THE BILL STARTS TO MOVE

In September, St Germain relented. He agreed to take up the FSLIC recap bill even though his loophole-closing bill hadn't been passed. Ed Gray brought him up to date on the state of the FSLIC in a confidential letter dated September 17. "As of today," Gray wrote, "there are 252 significant supervisory thrift institution problem cases which we project will require FSLIC assistance to resolve. Those institutions are reporting close to $95 billion in assets." He then explained that these cases could be broken down into two components: 130 "severely troubled" institutions with $47.6 billion of assets, and another 122 with $47.3 billion of assets that he expected to be added to the caseload in the next year. "The cost of resolving the 130 cases now in the FSLIC caseload is expected to range from $7 to $10 billion," he wrote. He then put the case for quick enactment of a recap bill:

> Any delay in the enactment of the legislation to recapitalize the FSLIC will further exacerbate the cost of resolution of severely troubled FSLIC-insured institutions because most all of these very weak thrifts are paying excessively high rates to attract deposits to maintain liquidity. They are paying such rates because of their weakened condition and the public perception of a weakened FSLIC fund which insures deposits. . . .
>
> The extremely weak institutions which have been placed in the Management Consignment Program are among the very highest rate payers for funds in order to maintain their deposit bases. . . .
>
> The longer action on such cases is deferred by the FSLIC—because of inadequate resources to resolve them—costs to the insurance fund will continue to mount, thus increasing the impact on the resources contemplated by the FSLIC recapitalization program.
>
> The Bank Board estimates, made and relayed to Congress some five months ago, that the cost of resolving severely troubled thrift cases over five years would approximate $16 billion, will continue to grow to the extent any final action by the Congress is delayed. . . .

So Gray was sticking by $16 billion over five years, despite the oil shock and its logical consequences, but he was warning Congress that the institutions he euphemistically styled "extremely weak" would continue to lose money and raise the eventual cost.

The House Banking Committee went forward with the recap bill, rebuffing its chairman, St Germain, when he tried to attach his loophole closer. The Senate Banking Committee went forward as well, Proxmire also having relented on the nonbank bank issue. Both approved up to $15 billion of borrowing, as requested by Treasury.

The bill—attached to a big housing bill—was then set to move in the House at the end of September.

ENTER JIM WRIGHT

Jim Wright, then Majority Leader of the House, later Speaker, and longtime Representative from Fort Worth, pulled the FSLIC recap bill off the calendar.[15]

Wright had been lobbied by the Texas S&Ls—including prominent high fliers like Dixon and Gaubert—to stop the recap bill because the FSLIC wasn't going to give them a chance to recover from the regional problems they were experiencing as a result of the oil price break. He also had been lobbied by Dallas developer/syndicator Craig Hall, who had troubled properties scattered all over the Southwest. Hall feared that if FSLIC got hold of his loans, it would put him under. He had a better chance if he could deal with the good old boys who made the loans.

There are many stories about the S&L people and the real estate crowd making large campaign contributions to Wright. These stories insist there was a quid pro quo. But, of course, politics as usual doesn't require a stated quid pro quo. Everybody knows the game, especially in Texas.

The S&L people also complained to Wright that the FHLB of Dallas was using "Gestapo" tactics in supervising them. H. Joe Selby, who had spent thirty-two years at the OCC and had been Acting Comptroller at one time, had retired (or been pushed out). Ed Gray had hired Selby to head supervision for the Dallas FHLB in May 1986. Selby, a good, tough regulator never known for being tactful, had come down to Texas—his home state—swinging. He knew that two years after the problems had surfaced, the situation was still out of control. There were still S&Ls that hadn't been examined in two years. There were 2,000 enforcement actions in various stages of preparation. (Working with the enforcement lawyers was "like walking through molasses," he says.) The examiners were trying to implement the new loan classification system, which they didn't understand. Joe Selby was determined to get control of the whole mess, fast.

Selby quickly identified the high fliers as problems and began the process of forcing them out of business. He wasn't gentle. Don Dixon referred to Selby as "Himmler."

When Selby took over Western Savings in September 1986, the other members of the daisy chain group could see the handwriting on the wall. If the FSLIC got money, they would be out of business unless they could get something special in the legislation to protect them. Even many of the non-fraudulent S&L managers in Texas could see that they wouldn't survive without help because the real estate situation was so bad.

After meeting with the Texas S&L people, Jim Wright decided that he had enough evidence to pull the recap bill off the calendar. He met with Ed Gray and sought assurances about the Gestapo tactics and about forbearances for "honest operators" who were down because of regional economic problems. It appears that Gray gave him some assurances and changed the conservator* at Westwood Savings in California who was giving Craig Hall a hard time. The recap bill was back on the House calendar in a week, about ten days before adjournment.

THE RECAP BILL IS PASSED

The House passed the $15-billion-borrowing recap bill, attached to a big housing bill, and waited for the Senate.

The Senate hadn't yet taken up the recap bill because first Proxmire blocked it while insisting on the nonbank bank loophole closer, then Jake Garn was in the hospital giving a kidney to his daughter, who needed it to survive. When Garn came back a few days before the end of the session, looking frail and pale, the Senate took up the bill and passed a $15 billion version much like the one that had been passed by the House.

THINGS ARE SELDOM WHAT THEY SEEM

Essentially the same bill had passed both houses, but one was attached to a housing bill and the other wasn't. A conference therefore was in order to try for a quick resolution of the differences before the end of the session. Garn selected the Senate's conferees, but St Germain refused to go to conference because he said it would be academic unless the Senate would include the housing bill. Representative Henry Gonzalez (D, Texas), the sponsor of the housing bill and the senior member of the House Banking Committee, St Germain explained, wouldn't let the recap bill through conference unless it included his housing bill. The Senate wouldn't contemplate the housing bill as part of a conference, so no conference was called.

Garn and Proxmire tried a last-minute compromise late on the night of October 17, as the session was about to adjourn, proposing authorization of only $3 billion of borrowing for one year under the Treasury structure. But St Germain and Gonzalez held firm, and Congress adjourned for the year on October 18.[16]

Everybody was clean. Garn and Proxmire had tried. St Germain's hands were tied, Gonzalez hadn't opposed the bill, and Jim Wright hadn't stood in the way after he got his reassurances. This bill wasn't passed even though everyone was for it.

Or were they? Was it a coincidence that Wright and Gonzalez were from the same state and party? St Germain was rumored to be in trouble in Rhode Island. Gonzalez wanted to succeed him as head of the Banking Committee. Wright, who would be the next Speaker of the House, would be key to that. Did that have anything to do with it? St Germain and Proxmire were disappointed that they hadn't been able to attach the nonbank bank loophole closer. Were they lukewarm? Many S&Ls didn't want the legislation. Had they been able to influence the process behind the scenes? Charles Keating had his lobbyists there at the Capitol that evening in case the bill started to move and contained anything on direct investments. Ed Gray was still lobbying for that. Did that have anything to do with it? We can all have our guesses. I can't give you a definitive answer.

In the aftermath, St Germain complained to the U.S. League that it had a "divided house." League members who publicly supported the recap bill were privately saying "Don't give any more money to Ed Gray." Get your act together if you want legislation, St Germain told the U.S. League. But did the League want recap legislation? It didn't look like it.

THE TAX REFORM ACT

In the summer of 1986 many S&Ls had been as concerned about the Tax Reform Act (TRA) as about the FSLIC recap bill. Certainly the Congress and the rest of the country had been far more concerned about the Tax Reform Act, which did away with a lot of deductions, had threatened to do away with a lot of others, and had lowered rates for individuals drastically. What's a FSLIC recap compared with a top tax rate of 28 percent instead of 50 percent?

Savings institutions had been unusually successful in keeping their tax privileges under the TRA. They even expanded some of them.

In 1986 the savings institutions weren't yet the bad guys. They were still recovering from 1979–82, and they convinced Congress that they still needed tax help. Initially, their special bad debt deduction was threatened, and they were threatened with having to "recapture" their previous bad debt deductions. In addition, without further action, the exemption of FSLIC assistance payments from taxation would sunset at the end of the year, and net operating loss carryforwards (NOLs)* arising from 1982 losses would soon expire if they weren't extended and permitted to be transferred in sales of failed institutions. These items would become crucial in the 1988 deals to sell the failed Texas S&Ls.

The S&Ls did well on all points. In the Tax Reform Act passed in September 1986, they got a compromise on the bad debt deduction so that, with the new tax rate, the bad debt deduction stayed effectively the same. They got no recapture of previous bad debt deductions unless they stopped holding 60 percent of their assets in "qualifying" assets. They got their NOLs extended for three years. And they got FSLIC assistance treated as nontaxable through 1988—a big point, because if FSLIC assistance wasn't taxable, then FSLIC could offer less of it.

The S&Ls were not unaware of what the Tax Reform Act was going to do to real estate values. They saw what was going on and told Congress that changing the rules to reduce deductions and passive losses would damage real estate values. But they had major issues that affected them directly, so they didn't lobby hard on the real estate issues. Real estate looked like somebody else's ox.

Maybe the depreciation and passive loss provisions caused $10 or $20 billion of damage to the FSLIC.

RECESS APPOINTMENTS

In the meantime, President Reagan hadn't filled Mary Grigsby's Democratic seat on the Bank Board even though she had left in April. Professor George Benston had been the leading candidate, but the U.S. League put the kibosh on his appointment. Then the President didn't fill Don Hovde's seat for six weeks even though with only Ed Gray in office the Bank Board couldn't act formally because one member doesn't constitute a quorum. (Or was that intentional?) Finally, after the 99th Congress had recessed in October, Reagan made two recess appointments. Under the rules, a recess appointment can serve for up to a year without being confirmed by the Senate.

Larry White, a New York University Business School professor, came to the Bank Board as the Democratic member (the law required that there be one), well prepared to understand the economic, legal, and accounting issues but perhaps a little naive. First of all, nobody had prepared him for the magnitude of the problem. After about two weeks he began to understand. His reaction was an understandable "Holy shit!" A second kind of naivete doesn't wear off quite so fast. Professors usually believe more of what businesspeople, lawyers, and politicians say than they should, and early on, White suffered a little from this occupational disability. Nevertheless, he wasn't fooled by Charles Keating, and he played an important role in making some rational policy in his two years on the Bank Board.

The other appointee, Lee Henkel, an Atlanta tax lawyer, quickly got himself into hot water and resigned rather than try to get through the confirmation process.

The interim appointees had to deal with some ticklish issues almost immediately. Only a month after their appointment, the Bank Board had to vote on extending the direct investment regulation, which would sunset at the end of 1987 if not renewed. Henkel proposed that the rule be watered down (in Lincoln's interests, by "grandfathering" its violations of the rule) as well as extended. Gray had a fit. White tried to mediate, eventually proposing and gaining acceptance of a two-month extension of the existing provision during which he could get a better understanding of the issues.

Charles Keating was in his heyday as a political operator. He had lobbyists

and lawyers everywhere, and he clearly was the instigator in the direct investment fight. Funny thing: It turned out that Lee Henkel had a connection with
Keating (he had millions of dollars of loans from Lincoln). It also turned out
that Keating had been instrumental in his appointment.[17] Henkel denied
wrongdoing but didn't give his cause much credence by resigning. Eventually
he was replaced by Roger Martin, a mortgage banker who became the board
member in charge of the Southwest Plan.

So again Mr. Keating had tried to pervert the system and had failed. Despite
his enormous contributions and batteries of lawyers, he always ultimately
failed. But along the way he caused an awful lot of damage.

BACK TO THE DRAWING BOARD

When the 100th Congress convened in January 1987, the leaders of the
Banking Committees made it quite clear that they had a new slate to write on.
The Republicans had lost control of the Senate in November, and Proxmire
consequently had replaced Garn as head of the Banking Committee. He
wanted a bill that would close the nonbank bank loophole. So did St Germain, who had been reelected for the last time. Things were getting worse and
worse for Wright's friends in Texas, so they kept giving him more and more to
get his help, which they expected to be considerable, since he had just become
Speaker of the House.

The U.S. League saw the new Congress as a new opportunity to gain control of the process. A $15 billion debt for the industry to repay would be
enormous. The League set out to reduce it to $5 billion and stretch out the
resolution process. "Our members question the need to 'mortgage their future'
by taking on the debt service of $10 to $15 billion flotations for up to 30
years," League spokesman Gerald Levy testified.[18] He called the League's new
plan a "self help plan" that would include only $5 billion of borrowing—no
more than $2.5 billion per year—and "forbearances" for "well-managed institu-
tions" in "economically depressed areas," meaning no takeovers of these institutions, regardless of their financial condition.

The administration came back with the same Treasury plan that had failed
to pass the 99th Congress.

Five big battles surrounding the FSLIC recap bill began to take shape:

- The amount of borrowing
- How much would FSLIC be allowed to spend per year
- What kind of forbearances for "well-managed" institutions the legisla-
  tion would contain

- What standard would the Bank Board be allowed to use in evaluating real estate loans—its appraisal standard or the GAAP standard

- Under what conditions, if any, would an S&L be allowed to leave FSLIC and become insured by FDIC.

The U.S. League effectively lobbied the Congress on these issues—and won at least partial victories on all of them.

Again the League put the black hat on the Bank Board. The banking agencies had provided "forbearances" for banks that had low capital due to regional economic woes, such as those in farming or oil. Under those forbearance plans, the banking agencies said they wouldn't take over any bank in a depressed area that was solvent and well managed, so long as its low capital resulted purely from regional economic factors. The banking agencies made it clear that they would closely monitor these low-capital banks, but they wouldn't put them out of business. The Bank Board hadn't adopted any similar plan, although it was abundantly clear that in practice it was following the same plan—and going even further. The Bank Board simply never took any S&L over if it was solvent. In reality, it didn't need a plan.

Nevertheless, the Board's failure to adopt a nice-sounding forbearance policy was an easy mark for populist Congressmen like Rep. Frank Annunzio of Illinois, who proclaimed, for example:

What rationale allows a commercial bank in a depressed area to be considered as solvent and operating when it is allowed forbearance and traditional accounting standards, while a savings institution across the street with some problems is a potential liquidation case solely because it was not given financial oxygen by the Federal Home Loan Bank Board?[19]

After a few months of Congressional pressure, the Board responded by adopting a forbearance plan. But it was too late. Congress didn't trust the Board, and the forbearance provisions and GAAP accounting standards went into the bill.

The Board fared better on the exit fee issue. It got a one-year moratorium on anyone leaving the FSLIC, plus an exit fee. But the U.S. League didn't oppose that point because only a few S&Ls thought they could get out.

The biggest issues remained how much money and how much per year. The Senate Banking Committee under Proxmire was going in the direction of $7.5 billion over two years. The House Banking Committee under St Germain was going for the League's $5 billion, two-year program.

WHAT WAS THE RIGHT NUMBER?

In the spring of 1987, as the committees worked on including the recap bill as part of a Christmas tree package of banking legislation, word leaked out that the GAO was about to report that the FSLIC was insolvent. "Reports that the FSLIC is insolvent are outrageous," the U.S. League's chairman said publicly. "It would appear to some that the GAO is manufacturing a book-keeping crisis to pressure Congress into passing an excessively large FSLIC funding program."[20]

As we know, the GAO was about to say that the FSLIC was $6 billion underwater. But that didn't answer the numbers question. The Bank Board and the Treasury were still saying the FSLIC needed to borrow $15 billion, which together with premiums would provide $25 billion to it over ten years. They were saying that this amount was adequate, and the Bank Board was sticking by its $16 billion number for losses from known problems.

While the U.S. League was decrying the Bank Board's and the GAO's "scare tactics," others were beginning to say that $15 billion would be totally inade-quate to deal with the problem. Bert Ely, a feisty Washington-based consul-tant, injected himself into the process by predicting the highest cost numbers for solving the FSLIC problem. In July 1986, after Treasury had just made its proposal of $15 billion over four years, Ely wrote that the Treasury plan would fall at least $17 billion short. "The Plan," he said, "is nothing more than a 30-month punt of the FSLIC mess into the next administration." Over a thousand thrifts must be dealt with, he said. Few listened.[21]

By the spring of 1987 Ely had revised his estimate. The Tax Reform Act had made the problem far worse, he said. As a result of it, he asserted, values can never come back, and more thrifts will fail. The FSLIC needs $50 billion, he said, as opposed to the smaller amounts being discussed.[22]

This time more people started to listen. Representative Stan Parris of Vir-ginia took up the cudgels on the floor of the House and warned:

> Reality is that the taxpayers of this nation will ultimately have to provide money to solve the problem. To think otherwise is pure fantasy. To wait for the problem to become worse adds billions annually to the cost of the solution of this situation.[23]

Practically no one in Congress could conceive of tax dollars being used to pay for this problem. They got angry if you suggested the possibility.

Warnings like Ely's and Parris's were just background noise. The U.S. League had a good handle on the situation. Speaker Wright and powerful members of the Banking Committees were saying $5 billion or so was plenty.[24] Don't give the FSLIC more, the Bank Board's opponents said, or it will just do damage by putting a lot of good folks out of business.

SOME BEAUTIFUL POLITICS

At the same time that Parris was warning that $15 billion wasn't enough, the House Banking Committee was considering the "5 or 15" billion dollar question. A subcommittee approved $15 billion by a 23–20 vote; then it was reversed by the full committee in a 25–24 vote, with Chairman St Germain casting the deciding vote for $5 billion.

The U.S. League stuck to its guns:

Five billion dollars of borrowing when added to $5 billion from FSLIC's premium, special assessment and investment income will provide the FSLIC $10 billion. This is all the money they can use for the next two years, according to the U.S. Treasury. To agree to a larger borrowing authority would be to invite wasteful uses of the money collected by FSLIC.[25]

The administration also didn't flag in its lobbying efforts. The Treasury and the Bank Board went to the mat with Wright and St Germain, arguing that the $5 billion wasn't enough and that the forbearance provisions would protect the legitimate interests of Wright's constituents. (Meanwhile, Wright's biggest S&L patron, Don Dixon, finally lost his S&L when it was taken over by FSLIC and Dixon was accused of wrongdoing. Wright no longer wanted to be associated with Dixon.)

The administration's strong lobbying effort prevailed; Wright and St Germain relented. They said they would propose a $15 billion amendment when the bill came before the House. "We are hopeful," they said in a joint statement, "that the adoption of an amendment providing for this additional funding will speed consideration, reduce controversy, and send a signal that there is broad bipartisan support in the Congress for dealing with the FSLIC problem."[26]

On the evening of June 12, 1987, the bill came before the House and St Germain actually did move to amend his own bill. He had preserved the $5 billion number against all attacks for months, but "I've been convinced by the GAO that we need $15 billion," he told his colleagues. He would support the Treasury's bill. Wright told the House he was satisfied that the bill with $15 billion of borrowing authority wouldn't "give an 'open sesame' to overzealous regulators."[27]

More junior members, primed by the U.S. League, responded with high rhetoric on the other side:

> Rep. Dymally of California: [The bill should] not allow the FSLIC to snuff out the smaller, weaker institutions that serve important functions in our communities despite their modest means. . . . The FSLIC must be given a $5 billion license to heal. It must not be given a $15 billion license to kill.
>
> Rep. Vento of Minnesota: There is a world of difference between giving the patient a shot of penicillin and bleeding the patient to death, and that is what this $15 billion amendment . . . tends to do, is to bleed the patient to death.
>
> Rep. Coelho, the Majority Whip from California with the well-stocked campaign coffers: It is no secret that the FSLIC is an agency with severe managerial problems. . . .
>
> Rep. Inhofe of Oklahoma: When they pay back this debt, those dollars are not available for home lending.[28]

Some say it was the night the U.S. League beat the leadership. Certainly it was the high-water mark of the League's political power. And certainly it was the night that everyone in Congress resented most when it turned out that the League had hornswoggled them.

The vote was 258–153 against St Germain's $15 billion amendment. But it looks to me like he and Wright weren't even trying. They were both very good at counting, and they knew before they brought the bill to the floor that they didn't have the votes for $15 billion. They were just going through the motions. The U.S. League duped the House and beat the administration, but no way do I believe that they beat the leadership. The $5 billion recap passed almost without dissent.

But the story wasn't over.

The Senate had already passed a two-year, $7.5 billion borrowing package, with a nonbank bank loophole closer and a bunch of other banking provisions hanging from it like ripe bananas. The two bills would go to conference, with the White House threatening a veto if the bill closed the loophole and didn't contain enough money for FSLIC.

Meanwhile, someone leaked a Booz Allen study done for the Bank Board which had indicated that the FSLIC was poorly organized and mismanaged. Again, Ed Gray had to go before a House committee and explain. FSLIC, he said, was just understaffed and underfunded.[29] But it was amazing that anyone was providing FSLIC *any* money in these circumstances.

THE CONFERENCE

The House-Senate conference on the recap bill began at the end of June 1987. Although the two numbers on the table were $5 billion and $7.5 billion, the chairmen of the conference, Proxmire and St Germain, had voted for $10 billion and $15 billion, respectively, and a majority of the House delegation also had voted for $15 billion. So the conference came out with $8.5 billion as a compromise between $5 billion and $7.5 billion. It also adopted the nonbank bank loophole closer, mandatory forbearances for well-managed institutions, GAAP accounting for troubled loans, a one-year moratorium on leaving FSLIC, a moratorium on regulators' giving banks new securities powers, and a "qualified thrift lender" test that would take away the right to borrow from the FHLBs if an S&L didn't invest at least 60 percent of its assets in home loans and other specified assets.

The President threatened to veto the bill.

After a month of struggle, at the end of July, the conference reopened its report and raised the borrowing limit to $10.8 billion with an annual cap of $3.75 billion. It also compromised on some of the other issues that the White House objected to.

So in August 1987, Ed Gray finally had his FSLIC recap. But his term had been up on June 30 and he already had been replaced by Danny Wall.

When he signed the bill, President Reagan said:

> From the outset, our guiding principle in working with the Congress on this bill has been to avoid a taxpayer bailout . . . for an industry that has the wherewithal to help itself. This legislation vindicates that principle. The Congress is clearly on notice that industry resources are to be relied upon to finance the FSLIC operations, now and in the future.[30]

At the signing ceremony, a naive Danny Wall declared that he had been provided "with the tools—people, money and expanded authority—I need to do the job."[31]

The cover of the 1986 FHLBB Annual Report shows a granite stone with the words "PUBLIC CONFIDENCE" carved into it in Roman letters. R.I.P.

WHERE DID THE RECAP LEAVE US?

Now we see how it took over two years to enact the recap after the Bank Board saw that it was necessary. We also can see that the $10.8 billion, with a one-year cap of $3.75 billion wasn't nearly enough. The big questions we have to ask, whomever we blame for the delays and the shortfall, are:

- What did the delay cost?

- What would have been saved if a much larger amount, say $30 billion, of taxpayer funding had been approved for immediate use in addition to the $10.8 billion of borrowing?

The delay cost a whole lot.

Some of the costs of delay resulted from just plain bad luck. Oil prices went down and damaged oil state economies. The Tax Reform Act depreciated real estate. Interest rates went down until mid–1986 and then went back up through 1989, thereby depreciating fixed-rate mortgages. The yield curve inverted in 1988 and stayed inverted until the end of 1989, which depreciated mortgage-based securities in relation to their fundings. All these things easily could have gone the other way but didn't. So we shouldn't blame those costs on the delay.

However, the costs of keeping zombie S&Ls open, the costs to other institutions of the competition from those S&Ls paying excessive rates, and the absence of discipline in the system that came from the FSLIC's inability to shut down insolvent institutions didn't depend on bad luck. They were natural consequences of the delay, and we should count them.

The costs of extra time are hard to quantify without exaggerating, but let's take some guesses. Let's assume that there were 100 institutions with $40 billion of liabilities that stayed open for two years longer than they would have. (That's a very conservative estimate.) If the institutions had been liquidated, we would have funded their assets with government money at government borrowing rates, which would have been about 3 percent lower than the rates the sick institutions were paying. In addition, although we would have had to spend about as much as the S&Ls did for managing their assets, we could have saved at least 1 percent by no longer needing the branches (they would have been sold or closed). So our savings would have been about 3 percent plus 1 percent times 2 (years) times $40 billion: about $3.2 billion is what theory says the number should be. That's not a lot compared with $150 billion, but what would you have thought about that number in 1986? And in practice the amount of loss due to delay seems to have been even greater than theory suggests.

The sick S&Ls paying excessive rates drove up the cost of other S&Ls' deposits from 1985 through 1989. For this purpose, we'll measure just two years and assume that rates were up by fifty basis points. The healthy S&Ls had about $750 billion of deposits at this time, so the cost to them may have been 1 percent of $750 billion, or $7.5 billion. Of course, that's not a direct taxpayer cost today, but if a third of what was left of the industry in 1985 fails, then you have a $2.5 billion cost plus the domino effect on the institutions that failed marginally—that is, marking all of their assets to market. That might be another billion or so, but it could be another $5 billion; it's a number we probably never could get a good handle on.

The cost of having no discipline in the system is even harder to guess. But certainly risk-takers would have been closed down earlier and others would have been dissuaded from taking risks by seeing the closure system operating properly. If a system doesn't operate, most businessmen will assume that it never will. My guess is that this cost another $3–$5 billion.

So the bottom line on the two-year delay is probably about $10 billion. Maybe more.

The shortfall in the amount of money that FSLIC really needed had even wider consequences because it set off a chain reaction that hasn't stopped yet. Here are a few of the consequences:

- The Wall Bank Board had to use expensive agreements, guarantees, and tax benefits rather than straight money to dispose of the 200-odd S&Ls that it dealt with in 1988.

- We experienced a full additional year of delay in 1989 while Congress deliberated and RTC got organized. Almost nothing was liquidated in 1989.

- Congress was so frustrated and angry when it got around to FIRREA in 1989 that it botched the job and put a lot of marginal S&Ls in the tank by changing the rules precipitously.

Maybe we should attribute $20 billion of cost to not doing the job right the first time in 1987.

You now know the story of how it took two years and how it didn't get done right. You now can see that almost no one was in favor of doing it right—which always would have required taxpayer money. Now *you* can judge who was responsible for this part of the losses.

16 Danny Wall and the 1988 Deals

M. Danny Wall is a good-guy. A conservative who spent ten years doing urban renewal in his native South Dakota. A man who goes to church but doesn't talk about his piety. A man who served in a top Senate staff position as aide to Senator Garn and chief of staff of the Banking Committee but got along with everyone and was never accused of being on the take. A man who drives his car for over 100,000 miles — until it falls apart — and whose wife, a former schoolteacher, is Senator Garn's secretary. His real name *is* Danny — at least his middle name is — but he calls himself "Dan." He is fit and trim and straightforward, and unless you have a *terrible* problem with beards, you have *got* to like him.

Danny Wall did some very good things. In particular, he pressed on with the job of dealing with failed S&Ls under conditions that would have deterred less determined people. When the losses were growing daily, his policy of getting deals done stopped some of the rot.

Nevertheless, Danny Wall blew it. Sad to say, he couldn't get his act together to explain the magnitude of the problem to Congress. He tried so hard to keep things peaceful that he did absolutely the wrong thing on Lincoln; he got taken in on Silverado; he started with a false premise in the Southwest Plan; he let himself be put into the FIRREA legislation as a sacred cow, which made him first a sitting duck, then a lame duck, and, in the end, inevitably, a dead duck.

WHAT DANNY WALL NEEDED TO DO

Danny Wall had a clean slate in the summer of 1987. He had new legislation to recapitalize the FSLIC, he had a new Board that didn't have emotional ties to the prior Bank Board administration, and he had the confidence and goodwill of the Congress. But he wasn't a numbers man, and he didn't have any real administrative or business experience—or enough money. His political deal-making experience eventually would contribute to his mistakes.

The Southwest Plan

The biggest and most urgent job the Bank Board had was getting rid of all the zombies in the MCP in Texas. Fully half of the Texas thrifts were insolvent but still open and operating. They were continuing to lose millions and millions every day, and they were continuing to drive up the costs of funds for thrifts and banks not only in Texas but across the country. People connected with the business couldn't believe that so many zombies were open and operating at such an obvious ongoing cost.

Danny Wall, being a positive thinker—he had promised the Senate at his confirmation hearing that he would "accentuate the positive"—didn't want to liquidate the Texas S&Ls or sell them to commercial banks and do away with the S&L industry in Texas. He wanted a creative program that would establish a strong new S&L industry from the ashes of the zombies.

The FHLB of Dallas had a theory that some of the healthy S&Ls could act as "mother ships" to acquire and consolidate the zombies. That had a familiar ring to Stuart Root, the new head of FSLIC, who had been a Wall Street lawyer and President of The Bowery Savings Bank, at one time New York's largest. Stuart Root remembered that his chairman at the Bowery, Bud Gravette, had advocated putting several failing New York savings banks together in 1984 to achieve economies. Gravette had drawn up an elaborate plan, which he presented to New York Superintendent of Banks Siebert and FDIC Chairman Isaac. Isaac had vetoed the plan, but Root thought that a similar plan could be devised for Texas based on the mother ship idea. Therefore the FSLIC hired Bud Gravette as a special consultant to evaluate whether such a plan would work in Texas and whether the Texas S&L managements were strong enough to take it on.

Not surprisingly, Gravette reported to FSLIC that great economies could be achieved by smashing several insolvent institutions together with a well-managed, solvent one, and that there were enough good managers in Texas to handle the job. Gravette also convinced the Bank Board that the best way to decide which institutions to merge together was to use a computer model that would delineate the optimal branch systems. Potential acquirers then would be asked to bid on and eventually negotiate deals for the packages that FSLIC assembled.

The idea was attractive. The Texas S&Ls very clearly had grown out of all proportion to the needs of Texas consumers for S&L services. Consolidations and branch closings therefore had to be effected before institutions could be profitable. The Southwest Plan would guarantee that the new efficiencies would be effected and that a strong thrift industry would emerge.

"Supporters of the plan [including the Texas League and the U.S. League] are baffled by the opposition and criticism," the weekly *Savings and Loan Reporter* advised.

> To them, it's the "most creative" recovery effort ever devised by the Bank Board.
>
> Not only does the program offer potential for saving and rehabilitating ailing savings and loan associations in Texas and other parts of the Southwest, they say, but it should give FSLIC a potential equity interest in the merged institutions and a share of the profits from their real-estate owned sales.[1]

The plan's many detractors weren't impressed. Smoke and mirrors, they said. You can't take a bunch of dead institutions and stick them together and expect to create a profitable one, they said. You need to attract capital, they said. And private parties, not the government, should be deciding the future pattern of the industry. Don't you believe in private enterprise anymore? You guys [the Bank Board] are supposed to be conservative Republicans, and here you go micromanaging like a bunch of socialists.

Speaker Wright was said to have a veto over any combinations that he didn't like. Rep. Gonzalez argued against creating a "handful of giant, local monopolies enjoying regulatory favors, subsidies and guarantees."[2]

But reality was that you had to have *some* plan, and any plan was better than no plan. By February 1988 the trade newspaper *National Thrift News* editorialized:

> [I]n recent weeks, what we've heard increasingly is a desire of the Federal Home Loan Bank Board to start using its new structure and its hard-won recapitalization in getting rid of the "body bags" that are acting as a drag on the entire thrift industry.
>
> From managers in big and small institutions; from former regulators; from investment bankers and consultants working with thrifts, the refrain is the same: it's time to act! The new board (dating from chairman M. Danny Wall's

July 1 arrival) started with a significant reservoir of goodwill (in this case a real asset).

But seven-and-a-half months into the process, there has been a great deal of study, reorganization and rhetoric, our readers are saying now, and not a lot of substance. . . . The Bank Board has built up the Southwest Plan for months, and appears ready to act. The industry is anxious to see progress. . . .

If it [the Board] is to enjoy the full confidence of the industry, it's time for action.[3]

But the Bank Board had difficulty attracting strong bidders who were willing to commit large amounts of capital. Marginal Texas S&Ls were ready to bid; they could see that their chances of survival would be significantly enhanced by being anointed as acquirers. Attracting outside capital was more problematical because:

- Not everyone wanted to bid on a package of branches put together by a computer.

- The FSLIC didn't have enough cash.

- Under a Bank Board rule, the acquirer of an S&L had to guarantee to keep the S&L's capital up to regulatory requirements, which meant that almost no one who had very much money wanted to buy an S&L.

- There was so much mystery surrounding the Plan and the process that a lot of potential acquirers just didn't want to waste their time playing around in the dark. "They don't purposely try to confuse you, but often the left hand doesn't know what the right hand is doing," a well-placed lawyer told a conference for potential bidders.[4]

The first deals that the Bank Board managed to do under the Southwest Plan weren't exactly winners. They were deals that required a lot of FSLIC assistance but brought in no new capital. For example, several "dead horses" were merged into Southwest Savings in Dallas, which was owned by Caroline Hunt, who put up no new money. Two years later, just as many observers had predicted when the deal was done, Southwest Savings failed.

Commenting on one of the early Southwest Plan deals, Rep. Gonzalez said, "It seems to me the FSLIC has stitched together six or seven corpses. They're still dead; the corpse is just bigger and it stinks more."[5]

The FSLIC was learning, however, that it had to attract new capital. The Bank Board began to understand that in fact there weren't any strong acquirers left in Texas, so it stopped trying to do deals like Southwest and devoted its energies to selling packages of failed S&Ls to new owners.

People with capital, however, didn't want to take on more liabilities than assets, and the depth of the insolvencies in Texas was too great for FSLIC to be able to fill the "hole" (the shortfall of assets vs. liabilities) with cash in order to attract buyers. The $10.8 billion of authorized borrowings under the recap legislation would disappear into the deep crater that the Texas S&Ls had become, which made even the most optimistic observers recognize, just a few months after CEBA was passed, that FSLIC still didn't have enough money to do the job. Either it had to give up in despair or it had to issue its own notes—corporate IOUs of the FSLIC—instead of cash to bring the assets up to the level of the liabilities being acquired.

In addition, potential acquirers (quite properly) weren't willing to take the risks inherent in the Texas real estate loans that comprised the supposed assets of the dead institutions. As a consequence, the FSLIC had to guarantee collectibility of billions of dollars of loans that everyone knew would never be worth a hundred cents on the dollar.

And in addition to that, these loans were nonperforming (not paying any interest), so in order to get acquirers to put up capital, FSLIC had to guarantee that the loans would earn a rate of interest until they were paid off. No one, of course, would acquire an S&L with assets that don't pay interest. So FSLIC had to offer spread maintenance on top of IOUs and collectibility guarantees.

But acquirers weren't sure they could trust these FSLIC obligations. FSLIC's ability to perform on the notes, guarantees, and spread maintenance* was subject to doubt because FSLIC was formally insolvent, and the U.S. government hadn't issued any binding guarantee of its obligations. Accountants questioned whether the Federal Home Loan Banks could carry FSLIC notes on their books at par.[6] Publicly held corporations (including the major banks that otherwise might have been bidders) were afraid to bid for S&Ls and have to take FSLIC notes because they feared that *their* auditors wouldn't let them record the FSLIC notes at full value. Even privately owned companies or individuals insisted on premium interest rates or FSLIC notes.

It would have been far better and cheaper to use cash to make up the shortfall between the dead S&Ls' assets and liabilities. It probably would have been significantly better to liquidate the dead S&Ls by selling their branches and then liquidating the assets, but that would have taken even more cash. But, whatever their merits would have been, FSLIC didn't have enough money to implement these alternatives.

About the only thing the FSLIC had going for it was the ability to offer tax incentives to acquirers. In theory, FSLIC would be able to offer less assistance because the tax incentives would entice investors to accept smaller returns.

The tax incentives derived from the federal tax exemption for all FSLIC assistance that applied to deals done by December 31, 1988, and from the ability of an acquirer of a failed S&L to carry forward the S&L's tax losses.

With the tax loss carryforward, if an acquiring corporation had income, it could shelter that income with the losses that had been incurred by the S&L before it was sold. If those losses were $1 billion, then the acquirer could get deductions of up to $1 billion on its tax return, which, at a 40 percent tax rate, could be worth $400 million. Not many corporations could use losses on this scale, but for those which could, the value was obvious.

The tax exemption for FSLIC assistance operated more subtly to provide significant incentives to a wider variety of acquirers. In effect, this provision could exempt *all* of an acquired S&L's earnings from federal tax because an S&L's *net* is such a small fraction of its gross earnings. Indeed, because of assistance being exempt from tax, an acquired S&L receiving a lot of margin maintenance or other guaranteed interest could be accumulating tax-loss carryforwards for the future while it was realizing cash profits and paying large dividends.

The FSLIC had significant incentives to use tax benefits as much as it could to diminish the amount of assistance that it would have to provide. Even though we might say today that a dollar of tax saved by an acquirer (and therefore not paid to the government) is equivalent to a dollar spent by FSLIC, a lot of the Bank Board people didn't think that way in 1988 because the Bank Board hadn't admitted that taxpayer money was going to be necessary to bail out the FSLIC. Danny Wall was still trying to prevent taxpayer funds from becoming necessary.

We don't yet know what the total cost of this tax policy will be. Even though in most cases FSLIC negotiated a sharing of tax-loss-carryforward benefits and in many cases got a piece of the new institution created after the merger, we can't estimate the cost because it depends upon future profits and the future performance of the bad real estate loans acquired. Recent estimates reported to Congress suggest a cost of $4–10 billion.

We shouldn't blame the Bank Board for using the tools that Congress gave it. Congress passed the key tax provisions in 1981 and renewed them in the TRA in 1986, when it could have foreseen how they might be used. Congress may not have known what a tax exemption for assistance meant. Not very many people did know. But Congress passed the law even though there wasn't any comparable exemption for FDIC assistance. The regulator shouldn't be blamed for using it. (Of course the regulator *can* be blamed for using it without getting comparable benefits for the FSLIC in the form of reduced assistance.)

The Bank Board had no good alternatives in 1988. Either it could announce that it had insufficient resources and go back to Congress for more money, which would unleash unknown forces that surely would kill the S&L business; or it could try to do deals with the tools that it had. Given the enormous amounts of money that every day of delay cost and the fresh memory of the two years it had taken Congress to pass a recap bill, getting on with the job had to look like the right course.

Southwest Plan Deals

In 1988 the FSLIC dealt with 109 institutions under the Southwest Plan, closing the bulk of the transactions in the last days of December under the threat that months and months of negotiations could go for naught if the deals weren't done before the tax benefits expired at the end of the year. When the clock struck at midnight, all the S&Ls' beautiful tax-exempt clothes would turn back into rags. Where would an insolvent FSLIC find new glass slippers, with a hostile Congress and deteriorating business conditions?

Selling 109 Texas S&Ls in one year would create a buyer's market in any circumstances. Negotiating against the clock when you *have* to do a deal and the other side doesn't, isn't recommended to achieve the best results, either, especially when the players on the other side include some of the sharpest negotiators in the country. Fail, Perelman, Bass, Utley, Ford, Simon, Parsky, Trammel Crow, Pritzker, Dworman, and Ranieri didn't show up by accident. They were there precisely because they believed that FSLIC would have to cut good deals for them when no one else was left at the table. They had the best lawyers and the best accountants to help them. The more complicated the deals got, the better off they were.

The press and members of Congress now vie to prove who got the best Southwest Plan deal. I don't know who did. It looks like they all got good deals. The position FSLIC was in guaranteed it. But the deals did create viable and vigorously competitive institutions for the future.

First Texas / Gibraltar

The deal that created the biggest Texas S&L included First Texas Savings and Gibraltar Savings, as well as the remains of Vernon. The combination provided strong branch systems in the Houston and Dallas markets. FSLIC estimated the cost of getting rid of the total $12 billion of deposits at $5 billion in assistance, net of FSLIC's share of future tax benefits and the profits it expected to get from its 20 percent ownership of the new entity. FSLIC estimated that a straight liquidation would have cost it $6.8 billion. (Some later estimates of the cost of the deal are much higher.) Larry Fink of the Blackstone Group, a respected new Wall Street firm, who had been hired as special adviser to FSLIC to provide independent review of the Southwest Plan deals, opined that the Ford/Utley/Perelman deal was the best on the table financially, both pretax and after tax, although there were a number of "close bids" with "different nuances."[7]

The First Texas/Gibraltar bidding and negotiation had gone right down to the wire at the end of the year, after the trade papers had speculated in early November that Columbia Savings of Beverly Hills, Golden West Financial, an S&L holding company from Oakland, Ranieri, Wilson & Co., and Ford Motor Company were the leading bidders.

Against this competition, Gerald Ford, a Texas banker, and Bob Utley, a Texas real estate developer-turned-financier—eventually with money from Ron Perelman, who had made his mark as an acquisitor by landing Revlon after a protracted hostile bidding war—outmaneuvered everyone. Ford and Utley hadn't intended to go after such a big fish. Ford ran a successful string of small banks in medium-sized towns of Texas. He ran them as traditional country banks, and they had come through the oil holocaust far better than the money center banks of Houston and Dallas. He and Utley had contacted Tom Lykos, who ran the Southwest Plan for FSLIC, to poke around and see whether they might pick up some S&Ls that would be compatible with Ford's growing country bank operations.

Lykos had to work hard to sell the big dead fish. The little ones he could get rid of more easily by attaching them to other deals. How would you like to "play in the big casino"? he asked. Lykos meant bid for First Texas/Gibraltar. Utley said no. Ford said yes. They decided to play.

Under the rules of the game, in order to play in the big casino, Ford and Utley had to qualify as bidders, which involved both background checks and a demonstration of financial ability to do the deal. The backgrounds checked out, but Ford and Utley didn't have the $200 million or $300 million that they'd need to do the deal. Moreover, they couldn't raise the money before they negotiated the basics—and they wouldn't have wanted to, because the earlier the money comes in, the less of the pie the dealmakers get. Ford and Utley instead turned to their investment bankers, Bear, Stearns and Lazard Frères, who provided "highly confident letters"—letters which said that, subject to various conditions, the two firms were "highly confident" (the standard language of Wall Street for pie-in-sky-but-this-isn't-crazy-and-we-know-these-people) that they could raise the money for the acquisition.

Bob Utley is a great dealmaker (I know; I have negotiated against him). At forty-three he didn't look like a man who had gone to college on a football scholarship before he tore up his knee. A bit overweight, wearing somewhat eccentric-looking little glasses perched under a practically hairless dome, the always impeccably groomed Utley, in his Hermès ties and Turnbull & Asser shirts, would work twenty-hour days, carrying on business over every meal in the best restaurants of Dallas, New York, and Washington. Never in a hurry, he would probe every point and evaluate every angle. And he knew how to use his accountants and lawyers, who were among the best. (My former partners, whom I haven't talked to about First Texas/Gibraltar, were his lawyers.) A model Texas dealmaker, Utley was active in Democratic fund-raising, was a member of the Texas Securities Board, and knew everybody who counted in the state.

Ford, Utley, and their team negotiated with Lykos and his group for months. They argued about everything, from the value of the FSLIC notes to how the guarantees should be written to whether there could be different agreements for different parts of the deal to whether they would take all the components. Lykos advised them that they were the leading bidder.

In November, Larry Fink changed the tempo of the deal; he told Ford and Utley that the highly confident letters weren't good enough. To negotiate the deal to conclusion, they would need a commitment, not pie in the sky. They knew that a commitment before a deal was really in place would reduce what they would get, but they had no choice.

New York, where the money is, had to be the next stop. Bob Utley had been through the drill before when he raised money to buy the Seamen's Bank in New York in 1985 (of which he was still vice chairman). But then he raised $75 million. Now he needed $300 million, and he didn't have time to make a private offering to numerous institutions, as he had in 1985.

Bear, Stearns and Lazard Frères introduced him to the likely candidates. He negotiated with Dreyfus Management and almost had a deal. He negotiated with GE Capital, but GE Chairman Jack Welch said no. He called Ron Perelman, who had taken over Revlon by using one of Drexel's biggest junk financings, and in twenty minutes he had $300 million. He didn't have as much of First Gibraltar (as it came to be called) stock as he hoped, but he had a deal that he could complete. He and Ford already had spent a lot of money on legal, accounting, and travel expenses. They needed the deal to work.

In the final days, as so often happens when you do deals under a deadline, they negotiated around the clock. The FSLIC lawyers, who were trying simultaneously to put together several deals before the witching hour, were exhausted. The deal was called off several times, as the parties argued over structure, language, everything. The buyers of First Gibraltar ended up with a deal that is guaranteed to make money. The only question is how much.

First Gibraltar is already acquiring additional failed S&Ls to enlarge its southwestern franchise. It will be a vigorous competitor.

Bluebonnet

In July 1990, Senator Howard Metzenbaum of Ohio, Chairman of the Senate Judiciary Committee's Antitrust, Monopolies and Business Rights Subcommittee, began holding hearings about an obscure Southwest Plan deal called Bluebonnet. Nobody outside Texas had heard of Bluebonnet, but Metzenbaum saw political hay in the FSLIC's approval of a man with criminal implications in his past to acquire an S&L with federal assistance. According to the *New York Times*, Metzenbaum called it an "abomination, the worst case" to emerge from the savings and loan scandal.[8]

Now, let's back up. At the end of December 1988, Jim Fail, an oversized good old boy now based in Phoenix, bought a group of miscellaneous failed S&Ls (fifteen of them) in a Southwest Plan deal. The fifteen S&Ls, with about $3 billion of liabilities, cost FSLIC what it estimated as $1.85 billion in assistance. (Again, recent estimates are higher.) Fail and his insurance company group—small insurance companies all over the country that he controls—put up $70 million and he is obligated to put in another $50 million of capital. Bluebonnet earned about $35 million in 1989, so the deal looks good for Mr. Fail so far. (The spread maintenance declines as time goes on, however, so the assistance guarantees less profit in future years.)

The "abomination" decried by Senator Metzenbaum is that after being represented by a lobbyist who used to work for George Bush, Mr. Fail was approved as an acquirer despite one of his insurance companies having pleaded guilty to a felony charge in Alabama in 1976. Mr. Fail himself had been indicted for the crime (securities fraud), but the charges against him were dropped when the insurance company—which already was in bankruptcy—pleaded guilty. Mr. Fail is still barred from the insurance business in Alabama. (Most of what Metzenbaum's subcommittee found out—at who knows what cost to taxpayers—had been published in the *National Thrift News* a year earlier.)[9]

Under the Bank Board rules for acquirers, there are certain past deeds that "presumptively disqualify" a bidder. These presumptive disqualifiers include having been indicted for securities fraud and having the company take the rap. Under its rules, the FHLBB could override a presumptive disqualifier if it found that the person or corporation had reformed itself and demonstrated that it would manage the acquired institution prudently.

To the date of this writing, the record isn't clear as to how the Bank Board concluded that Mr. Fail qualified as an acquirer. The process doesn't seem to have been very orderly or deliberate, and it doesn't seem that the Bank Board people knew much about what had happened in Alabama a dozen years earlier, but the Board could have concluded that Mr. Fail had outgrown whatever tendency the Alabama charges had exposed. We should note also, however, that in 1987 Fail had acquired a failed bank in Oklahoma and had been approved for that purchase by the FDIC, which has similar rules about acquirers. Apparently, Mr. Fail slipped through the FDIC process without incurring scrutiny of his run-in with the Alabama criminal authorities.[10]

In the Bank Board process, it seems that first Fail gave disingenuous answers, then he got through because at a late date it's hard to turn around and start negotiating with another bidder. If you are there at the end, chances are you will get the deal. Besides, the FDIC had approved him; why shouldn't the Bank Board?

President Bush's former aide, Robert Thompson, made introductions and helped the process along, but assuming that he complied with the various federal laws that apply to former government employees, what he did was business and politics as usual. Nothing mysterious here.

The FSLIC's rules that presumptively disqualified Mr. Fail weren't designed to make sure that acquirers could qualify for the Nobel Peace Prize or admission to the Knights of Malta. The idea wasn't to bestow these federal bounties on good people but to try to make sure that the people who ended up owning the recapitalized S&Ls wouldn't loot them or mismanage them all over again. (Conceptually, the person buying the failed institution isn't the beneficiary of the federal assistance. That's provided to the dead institution to induce somebody to assume the deposits that the insurer has guaranteed.) From what I've seen, you might not admire Jim Fail's business morals and you might, as a taxpayer, not trust him to run an S&L with federal deposit insurance; but so far, since he has owned Bluebonnet, reports don't suggest that he has done anything wrong.

Given the depth of public scrutiny of Mr. Fail to date and the consequent likely depth of future examinations of Bluebonnet, there's little likelihood that Mr. Fail can or will loot Bluebonnet. As long as he doesn't loot Bluebonnet, his ability to slip through the system hasn't cost anything. If he made the highest bid (which we have to assume until the contrary is proven), he helped the public. If he manages the S&L well, he also will benefit the public.

Mr. Fail's source of his $70 million contribution to Bluebonnet may be more dangerous than his Alabama past. He got most of the money from insurance companies. The state insurance regulators now are questioning the propriety of these insurance companies making these investments. It appears that these problems will force Mr. Fail to sell Bluebonnet promptly.

We can very easily say that the FHLBB wasn't very careful about the Bluebonnet deal. But bear the circumstances in mind. The Bank Board people *had* to do these deals before year-end or start over. They also knew that the new administration and Congress weren't going to let them start over. Their course was charted. They couldn't stop at a quarter to twelve and let the buyers turn into pumpkins.

Sunbelt

The Southwest Plan computer model called for selling three of the deadest and most costly S&Ls—Sunbelt, Western, and Independent American—as a unit, along with five smaller S&Ls. After months of trying to attract bidders, in August the Bank Board formed a new "phoenix" institution that would have $6.9 billion of liabilities but could get up to that level of assets only with what they estimated to be about $5.5 billion of FSLIC assistance. The Bank Board said it planned to shrink the institution by closing branches and creating efficiencies over a six-month period and then sell the new, spruced-up Sunbelt to investors.[11]

At this writing there have been no takers and the assistance cost is skyrocketing. Clearly it would have been better to pay off the depositors and liquidate. But depositors won't take FSLIC notes—and FSLIC didn't have the cash for a $6.9 billion payout and couldn't borrow it. As a consequence, the assistance might cost $10 billion! This is the tab for S&Ls whose aggregate size at the end of 1984—when the problems could have been identified and stopped—was still around $2 billion.

Naiveté Along the Potomac

When he announced the Southwest Plan, Danny Wall estimated that it would cost the FSLIC $6 to $7 billion, a number that he should have known was wildly low.[12] By the time the Southwest Plan deals were finished, the Bank Board was estimating that they had cost $35 billion. And when the GAO evaluated their cost in 1989, it found that they had cost $48 billion.[13] Recent reports suggest that the tab will be over $50 billion, maybe even $70 billion.

Did Wall give a lowball estimate to start with so that Congress wouldn't get too excited? Or were his people so unrealistic that they believed they could do the job for $6 or $7 billion? In Congress, people change positions every day. Did Wall think he could do that as head of the Bank Board and nobody would remember? I haven't discovered the answer. But whatever it is, it won't reflect well on Wall and his team.

Bass Buys American

Despite having been under practical government control since 1984, American Savings (Charlie Knapp's former shop) was still in business in 1988. It hadn't gotten any stronger under government guidance, but probably it hadn't gotten very much worse, either.

Selling American, the FSLIC's number-two 1988 priority after the Southwest Plan, effectively took all year. Beginning in 1987, Ford Motor Company's First Nationwide subsidiary was the leading contender to acquire American. The FSLIC gave Ford an exclusive right to negotiate and sought to come to terms. But Ford walked away from the proposed deal in January 1988. The FSLIC, left with egg on its face after the extensive publicity that the Ford deal had received, went looking for another buyer. Not very many people or companies could acquire an S&L with $30 billion of deposits, and the FSLIC certainly couldn't afford to liquidate it.

Robert Bass, a member of the Texas Bass family, became interested in buying American. Like so many of the other 1988 acquirers, Bass has a reputation for buying well. He would drive a hard bargain, but the FSLIC hadn't any choice.

Part of Bass's hard bargain was to demand exclusive negotiating rights on American. Granting these exclusive negotiating rights has become a subject of criticism by academics and others who review the 1988 deals, because exclusive negotiating rights give the buyer an option for a period of time. During this period of time, the critics point out, the potential buyer can negotiate the best deal and then decide whether to take it or leave it.

This is true, of course. The FSLIC people understood that perfectly well. I can only assume that the critics have never tried to dispose of a very large, complex troubled property in a deal that isn't going to be all cash. In those kinds of situations, buyers simply won't spend the time and money to negotiate past a certain point without an assurance that if you arrive at a deal within a specified period of time, they get to do it and somebody else won't be permitted to top it by a dollar. Yes, granting exclusivity naturally leads to a better deal for the buyer. But would there have been a buyer without it? I have to give the FSLIC people the benefit of the doubt.

Robert Bass and his group did negotiate an excellent deal for themselves. The basic deal on American almost can't fail. On top of that, they got tax benefits that FSLIC didn't fully count as a cost, and therefore more or less threw in to get the deal done.

The deal is variously estimated to cost between $2 billion and $5 billion, including tax benefits—which probably is not cheaper than a liquidation would have been. But at least American looks like it will be a strong, well-run competitor. Bass hired the President of Home Savings, Mario Antoce, to run American. Antoce, an experienced traditional S&L executive, is building American's net worth and its home lending capacity. It looks like Bass will make a lot of money on the deal.

The Ford Motor Deals

After playing in the high-stakes American Savings game and crapping out, and playing in the First Gibraltar big casino and hitting double zero, Ford Motor Company's First Nationwide finally came away with consolation prizes in the year-end scurry. Its consolidation prizes were Silverado, Cardinal (in Ohio), Pathway (in Illinois), and Columbia of Colorado, which expanded the First Nationwide franchise into three more states and garnered about half a billion dollars of tax benefits for Ford. Again, with the tax benefits fully counted, the deal looks expensive for the government. But at least the acquirer looks like a long-term useful institution. And three large failed S&Ls that were draining the FSLIC every day were moved down the road at a more fixed cost.

Beverly Hills Again

The FSLIC finally got rid of Beverly Hills—the first MCP thrift—at the end of 1988, selling it to Michigan National Bank at an estimated cost to FSLIC well over $1 billion. While the government ran it, from 1985 to 1988, Beverly Hills was the pluperfect example of the broke S&L that will lose money forever. It ran up staggering losses every year. Failing to liquidate Beverly Hills promptly in 1985 may have cost close to $1 billion.

TOO LITTLE CAPITAL?

When the first 1988 deals to sell S&Ls to private investors were done, members of Congress and industry observers questioned whether the amounts of capital that the private investors contributed—usually 2 percent–3 percent of assets acquired—were sufficient. Wasn't the FSLIC making the same mistakes all over again? With capital levels that low, wasn't FSLIC running the risk that investors would repeat the risky conduct of their predecessors and have little capital cushion when loans went bad?

FSLIC answered these charges by pointing out that although the capital levels were low in relation to the total assets acquired, they were not low in relation to the "risk assets" acquired—that is, the assets that weren't guaranteed by FSLIC. The capital coverage of the risk assets, FSLIC pointed out, usually was between 5 percent and 6 percent. And the capital "forbearances" granted with the deals would, they said, phase out as the FSLIC guarantees on assets "burned off."

Acquirers with higher leverage would have lower spread targets, FSLIC's defenders pointed out, to make the same return on their investments. Therefore FSLIC could attract investors with less yield maintenance than they would have had to provide to fully capitalized investors.

Only time will tell whether the FSLIC strategy will work. FIRREA has wiped out a lot of the forbearances, as a result of which many of the recapitalized S&Ls will have to shrink or raise more capital soon. But the lawsuits will be enormous if FSLIC's successor takes over a solvent but undercapitalized S&L that was created in a 1988 deal.

The FSLIC people's contention about cost is at least theoretically correct: The costs would have been higher if they had required more capital. Indeed, it may be that many of the acquirers would not have bid at all if they had been told that a condition of making an acquisition was immediate 6 percent capital. Leverage was still the main attraction in 1988.

ASSET MANAGEMENT

One of the goals of the FSLIC in the 1988 deals—which those deals did fulfill—was to get the acquirers to manage the bad assets that formed so big a part of each of the zombies.

Managing troubled real estate loans—that is, getting possession of collateral, fighting off other creditors in bankruptcy proceedings, running the legal maze of lender liability, usury claims, and environmental hazards while keeping the property from deteriorating, and eventually selling the asset—is a very demanding process that FSLIC turned out not to have the personnel or structure for. Ed Gray and his staff had understood this back in 1985 when the FSLIC first started acquiring large amounts of bad loans through receiverships. To create the necessary staff, they formed the Federal Asset Disposition Association (FADA). Whether you pronounced it FAY-DUH or FAH-DUH, FADA never worked. Formed as a mutual S&L so that it would be separate from FSLIC and therefore not subject to federal budgetary constraints, FADA was supposed to finance itself in the capital markets and to buy bad assets from the FSLIC and work them out. That idea was quickly discarded, however, when it became apparent that the financing was impossible. So FADA just managed properties and their sale under contract with FSLIC.

FADA quickly became a political football. Congress didn't like the fact that it avoided the budgetary process so blatantly. FADA's organizers didn't hire the right people at double or triple government salaries. By 1988 FADA could be described as scandal-ridden and ineffective. But FSLIC had no alternative sources of personnel to manage and dispose of the assets, so its only sensible recourse was to try not to acquire the assets in the first place.

Substantially all of the 1988 deals passed the bad assets to the acquirers along with the good, creating a sharing arrangement whereby FSLIC and the acquirers would divide the benefits of recoveries between them in exchange for the acquirers' managing the assets. Some study years from now will try to evaluate whether this strategy was better than alternative strategies. That study will see the substantial profits the acquirers made for managing the assets and will ask whether they could have been managed at less cost for the same results. Congress meanwhile will be up in arms at the profits made by the acquirers while the federal government took the losses. I hope that the essential point will not be lost. Danny Wall and the FSLIC staff had no reasonable alternative to inducing the acquirers to manage the assets. FADA had been ineffective (and FAY-DUHed away in 1989); FSLIC didn't have the staff; the loan records were where the S&L was; and local people work out real estate assets better than strangers to the situation.

HOW DANNY WALL SCREWED UP THE NUMBERS AND GOT EVERYBODY MAD

In the fall of 1987, a few months after he had taken over at the Bank Board, when Danny Wall was testifying before St Germain's Banking subcommittee, St Germain pressed him for an estimate of what it would cost to resolve all the FSLIC problem cases. Wall resisted answering because he really didn't have any idea, but St Germain was insistent. Finally, Wall spit out the number $15 billion, which was close to Ed Gray's last number. From that day until he left office in February 1990, Danny Wall was haunted by the numbers that kept escalating. He says that after the initial $15 billion number, he always used numbers that were the best estimates the Bank Board could make at the time—and I believe him. But after a few months he should have known that the estimates were way off the mark.

In May 1988 Wall testified that the number was between $22 and $30 billion; by July he was up to $30 to $42 billion;[14] and by October he was up to $45 to $50 billion and was saying that the numbers were still subject to revision.[15] St Germain started wondering whether Bert Ely's huge numbers weren't right. Rep. Charles Schumer's staff estimated $50 to $75 billion.[16] It seemed like a scene from a Marx Brothers movie, as everyone wondered what the next estimate would be.[17]

Maybe it didn't matter that nobody knew what the real number was. Maybe it just wasn't knowable, so the important point was to get on with the mergers and liquidations to get it solved, no matter what it cost. FSLIC already had incurred the obligation to depositors and had to make good on it, no matter what Congress said. But Congress wouldn't have agreed with that perspective. As one commentator put it, "Realistic projections are essential to the House and Senate Banking Committees, since they could determine whether the Congress should let the Bank Board proceed with its present program or intervene with some type of additional assistance loan or a merger of FSLIC and the FDIC."[18]

POLITICS, POLITICS, ALL IS POLITICS

The escalating numbers made Congress, the administration, the thrift industry, the Bank Board, and even the commercial banks uncomfortable. Congress had been snookered when it passed the recap in 1987. The leaders—especially on the Democratic side of the aisle—were getting angrier and angrier as 1988 wore on. St Germain kept calling Under Secretary of the Treasury George Gould back to Capitol Hill to defend the administration's recap. Gould kept insisting that a taxpayer bailout of FSLIC wasn't warranted. "We now hear cries from some quarters of the industry for a taxpayer bailout of massive, unprecedented proportions," he testified. "These bleatings are predicated on the dubious assertion that the Government caused the thrifts' problems and, therefore, it is time for the Government to ante up to solve the problem." He urged "in the strongest possible terms to resist mounting pleas for an unnecessary, budget-busting bailout of FSLIC."[19]

Danny Wall also kept telling Congress that FSLIC and the industry could handle the problem. As the cost numbers went up, he matched the increase by increasing FSLIC's projected cash flow, which he accomplished by lengthening it more and more years into the future and by deferring the projected date when the special assessment could be rescinded. The 1987 legislation had said that the special assessment would end in 1991. In March 1988, Wall announced that it would have to go on until 1995. In July, he said 1998.[20] Finally, in October he told Congress and the industry that the special assessment would have to last for thirty years.[21] Danny Wall, the good Republican soldier, was playing on the administration's team, keeping the 1987 punt of the problem into 1989 from coming to rest in the middle of the 1988 presidential campaign.

As the projected cost rose, the thrift industry's unity started to come apart at the seams. *Sauve qui peut* replaced the former unified approach to the recap. Great Western and Home Federal tried to position themselves to get out of FSLIC and into the FDIC. The U.S. League at the same time pooh-poohed the escalating numbers and prepared the groundwork for announcing that the financial burden of making good on FSLIC's promises was too big for the industry to handle. "This mess is beyond our power to resolve," the League's chairman said in August.[22]

Commercial bankers began to worry in earnest that the FDIC fund would be tapped and their premiums would be increased. Talk about using the Federal Reserve Banks' annual earnings worried them, too. Whatever happened, by mid–1988 bankers could see that the FSLIC's bankruptcy would change the world for all depository institutions in the United States.

The Congress wanted control of the problem. It (you rarely can talk about Congress as a unified "it," but on this point there was virtual unanimity) wanted control of what FSLIC was spending and what FSLIC was spending it on. Congress had just gone through an agonizing process over two years to authorize $10.8 billion of borrowing for FSLIC. Almost immediately afterward, here was Danny Wall not only borrowing the authorized amount and spending it, but on top of it borrowing more by issuing FSLIC notes in the Southwest Plan deals.

The Bank Board had begun issuing notes to acquirers to "fill the hole" between failed institutions' liabilities and the book value of their assets almost as soon as the ink was dry on the recap legislation, and by early 1988 critics had begun to badger the Board about spending more than Congress had authorized. By April, FSLIC had issued billions of dollars of notes, and the GAO began urging Congress to set a limit on the dollar amount of notes the FSLIC could issue.[23]

Board member Larry White worried about precipitating a constitutional crisis. He wrestled with whether FSLIC really had authority to issue the notes, after CEBA had provided specific borrowing powers. Ultimately, he became convinced that by issuing the notes FSLIC wasn't borrowing; it was just substituting one obligation for another.

Not everyone saw it that way. Representative Gonzalez, for one, was apoplectic. After fulminating about the Congressional budget process, he came to the point. "Yet, the FHLBB—without these specific authorizations—can go behind closed doors, enter into deals with individuals and corporations, give away tax benefits and commit the federal government to guarantees reaching long into the future."[24]

Danny Wall reassured Congress that the FSLIC wouldn't issue more notes than its projected cash flow could repay. But he kept enlarging the cash flow by extending the special assessment and adding years to the repayment period. As the number of years grew larger and larger, the process grew sillier and sillier.

The GAO urged Congress to give the FSLIC notes full faith and credit to reduce their interest rates, and also to set a limit on the amount of notes FSLIC could issue. Congress should reassert control of the process, the GAO contended.

By the middle of the year, the Southwest Plan seemed stuck in second gear, Danny Wall's numbers kept changing, the amount of notes FSLIC was issuing kept creeping up, and Congress was getting *very* edgy. The dollars were on-budget, but the Congress had no control over them.

In August, the Senate passed a bill to give full faith and credit for FSLIC notes up to $11 billion. The bill also would have capped FSLIC's authority to issue notes at that figure, which in very few months would have brought the resolution process to a halt.

St Germain refused to take up the Senate bill, asserting, "We should not provide such explicit approval of this agency's actions until Congress is satisfied that we understand the depth of the situation."[25] (Freddie, do you remember that old song, "How Deep Is the Ocean?")

Danny Wall kept his head down and forged ahead. He gave Congress whatever numbers his people gave him. He persevered with the Southwest Plan. He kept issuing notes. He was determined to clean up Texas and American Savings and to do 200 resolutions in 1988.

The Reagan administration was over. It had successfully avoided dealing with another unpleasant issue. Whoever won the election would have to figure out how to pay for FSLIC's bankruptcy.

The S&L problem should have been a big issue in the 1988 Presidential election. Everyone who had focused on the problem knew by September or October that there would be at least a $50 billion tax bill to pay for the fiasco. But the American people didn't understand the issue. It was too complicated. Too many officials from both parties had their fingerprints all over it. In the end, neither George Bush nor Michael Dukakis could figure out how to use it, although the Democrats should have used it simply by saying it had all happened under Reagan, while George Bush was head of the administration's task force on financial institutions.

The Democrats would have had a more easily identifiable issue if the FSLIC had taken over Silverado before the 1988 Presidential election. Although Neil Bush resigned from the Silverado board of directors in August, ostensibly so he could work on his father's campaign, if Silverado had been seized and its operations laid open to view at that time, Vice President Bush might not have become President Bush. Maybe Michael Dukakis could never have seized any issue to beat Bush, but the Neil Bush connection with a failed high flier would have been irresistible to almost anybody—especially in that malodorous campaign.

Silverado reported itself to be insolvent in August, shortly after Neil Bush resigned. Instead of taking it over, the Bank Board gave management a convenient deadline of November for raising new capital. So Silverado didn't get taken over until December, after the election.[26] Probably just as well; the issue would have been one more red herring in a campaign that was filled with them.

Meanwhile, Danny Wall had saved his party by throwing himself in front of the onrushing train. For his efforts, the Congress—particularly the members of the House Banking Committee—pilloried Danny Wall. When the 101st

Congress convened in January 1989, the House Banking Committee had a new chairman, Danny Wall's old friend Henry Gonzalez of Texas, who may have thwarted the recap bill in 1986 but now had that good ol' time religion and its fervor. The issuance of notes by FSLIC had particularly incensed Gonzalez (maybe he didn't understand the "spread maintenance" and "guarantees," but "notes" he could understand). "You don't have this power, to put it bluntly," Gonzalez lectured Wall. Representative Jim Leach (R., Iowa) charged that the 1988 acquirers "robbed you blind." It went on and on. Wall tried in vain to defend himself: "We are dealing with the laws, we are not dealing with what people would like to see happen," he argued, "or what I would like to happen if we had other resources or opportunities."[27]

Danny Wall probably dreamed of saying, but didn't:

> You two-faced baboons! You appropriated $10.8 billion to fix a $100 billion problem and then went on vacation, while I had to clean up the mess. I couldn't liquidate; I couldn't get people to buy without notes; the notes were more expensive because you wouldn't give full faith and credit when I pleaded for it. My choice was to do the job with the tools you gave me or not to do it and let it get worse. If we had spent $15 billion in 1985, we would have saved $25 billion. Instead, you took fat campaign contributions from S&Ls and real estate developers and voted their way. First you voted for nothing, then for too little.

You don't talk that way to Congress. You try to answer the questions and criticisms, and bear the slings and arrows stoically.

Congress had found its patsy in Danny Wall. He was going to be a scapegoat.

EVALUATING THE 1988 DEALS

How bad were the 1988 deals? That can't be evaluated today. It may never be evaluated very well, because evaluation would entail an examination of what eventually is realized from the assets of the failed S&Ls compared with what might have been realized if they had been dealt with by a different mechanism. As a consequence, any evaluation of the 1988 deals will be strictly hypothetical.

Today's comments on the 1988 deals must involve a lot of guesswork. My guess—and it is a pure guess—is that the FSLIC spent between $10 and $15 billion more than it would have had to spend if it had had the cash to do the job right. That would mean that the cost was 20 percent or 25 percent more than it might have been.

What makes it certain that the deals were very good for acquirers is that the commercial banks didn't bid. They can achieve greater economies, and therefore they theoretically will make the best bids—as they have done routinely since FIRREA, when the deals have been done for cash. The lack of cash kept them away from the table.

The government can still save a part of the $10 to $15 billion that I have guessed is excess cost. The FIRREA legislation called for the RTC to evaluate whether the 1988 deals could be renegotiated or repudiated. Consequently, several studies have looked at the question.[28] They conclude, not surprisingly, that repudiating the deals—unless the acquirers committed fraud—would not succeed and would lead to large (possibly successful) damage claims. The studies also concluded, however, that the government could reduce the cost by paying off the notes and buying back the bad assets at book value. The cost of government borrowing will be less than the cost of the notes and less than the cost of spread maintenance on the bad assets.

Larry White estimated that paying off the notes alone would save $800 million a year for eight years—that being his estimated difference between borrowing at government bond rates and at the rates stated in the FSLIC notes.[29] The present value of this approximately $6.4 billion of savings would be about $4.5 billion. The RTC suggested that a similar amount could be saved if Congress appropriated about $20 billion of on-budget dollars to pay off the notes in order to effect the savings. This was disappointing news to a Congress whose leadership had led it to believe that big savings could be achieved. Nevertheless, Congress finally saw that it would be irresponsible not to spend the $20 billion now to get $25 billion plus interest later, even though it is hard for Congress to understand how the time value of money works because the government accounts on a cash basis.

We, too, shouldn't neglect the time value of money when we criticize the Bank Board people for their imperfect handling of the 1988 deals. They had the biggest cleanup job in financial history. They had little infrastructure and less money to work with. They saw the cost going up by billions—who knew how many billions?—each year. They saw that it had taken two years to get $10.8 billion without a government bailout of FSLIC and with the administration behind the project. It is very easy to criticize how they proceeded. It is very easy to show that better deals might have been done by other methods. But right now it is hard to say that if the Wall Bank Board hadn't tried to do its job, we would be better off.

THE MISHANDLING OF LINCOLN

Even if history eventually judges that the FSLIC got fair value in the 1988 deals, Danny Wall's historical reputation will be ruined by his mistakes in handling Lincoln. Here's a short version of the story.

The folks at the FHLB of San Francisco who examined Lincoln weren't swift enough to catch up with Charles Keating's machinations. By 1986 they knew something was very wrong, but they didn't know what it was. They examined and examined—for a whole year. Finally they recommended that Lincoln be taken over as being operated in an unsafe and unsound manner. But according to Judge Sporkin, "The case for receivership that FHLB of San Francisco had built was essentially a technical case consisting of allegations that Lincoln's record keeping was deficient. The FHLB of San Francisco did not investigate to any great extent any specific substantive transactions."

This description doesn't do justice to the FHLB of San Francisco's recommendations, but the judge's impression illustrates why the FSLIC lawyers and Danny Wall were afraid to proceed on the basis of the FHLB of San Francisco's recommendation. They knew that Keating would sue; they knew that they hadn't used the "unsafe and unsound" takeover ground very often and could, therefore, be vulnerable in the courts; they knew that Keating had had a running feud with the FHLB of San Francisco; and they feared that his charges of vendetta had substance.

Nevertheless, my judgment is that the FHLB of San Francisco's 285-page recommendation dated May 1, 1987, has enough in it to justify appointing a conservator for Lincoln. Although, as Judge Sporkin's impression would suggest, the recommendation does devote too much space to minor rules violations, it also discloses that Principal Supervisory Agent Jim Cirona's description of Lincoln as a "ticking time bomb" was based on substance. If you read the recommendation today, you will see that it says:

- Lincoln never made a profit except by trading loans and securities.
- $50 million of Lincoln's reported profits came from the Gulf Broadcasting transaction.
- The trading profits were bleeding Lincoln's future ability to make money.
- Lincoln had a negative net interest margin and a minute net interest spread.
- 62 percent of Lincoln's assets were risky investments in vacant land, hotels, ADC loans, junk bonds, and equity securities.
- Lincoln had enormous interest rate risk as well as credit risk.
- Lincoln was making loans that were vastly too large for its size and capital position.
- Lincoln's RAP capital was actually about 1 percent, not 5 percent, as Lincoln claimed. Its tangible capital was several percent negative.

- Lincoln had violated the direct investment regulation by at least $599 million and was still at it.

- Lincoln's management had violated representation after representation to the Bank Board and therefore couldn't be trusted.

- Lincoln's filed reports consistently overstated its income.

Unfortunately, these facts were relatively buried in the mass of bureaucratic citations. Jim Cirona's people had the goods on Mr. Keating, but apparently nobody told them to put the ripe strawberries at the top of the basket, where they couldn't be overlooked in Washington.

The recommendation also discloses that the California Commissioner of Savings and Loans was prepared to take Lincoln under state law and then hand it over to the FSLIC for conservatorship, which would make the legal position much easier than it would be if the FSLIC were going in alone.

A copy of San Francisco's recommendation went to Ed Gray, who didn't act on it before his term was up, presumably because the Division of Supervision wasn't ready to formally pass the recommendation along.

About a month after he took over at the Board, Danny Wall got the FHLB of San Francisco's recommendation—with the Division of Supervision's concurrence that "The only way to stop the association [Lincoln] from speculating with the FSLIC's funds is through a receivership, a receivership based on unsafe and unsound practices and dissipation of assets."[30]

All kinds of things were going on in Danny Wall's new world. CEBA was getting passed; Wall was reorganizing the staff; he was trying to get geared up to deal with the zombies; he was getting a handle on the job. He had observed how acrimony had damaged Ed Gray's efforts, and he was determined to run an orderly and peaceful agency.

Keating wasn't yet a household name. Ed Gray hadn't yet publicized his April 1987 interviews with the "Keating Five." The FHLB of San Francisco's recommendation worried the lawyers. Keating came in and made the right noises. He said he would raise more capital. He was, he said, doing wonderful things for California and Arizona. The zealots at the FHLB of San Francisco, he said, were just out to get him because he had fought for direct investment powers. He was already in litigation with the Bank Board; they knew he wouldn't hesitate to sue everyone in sight.

Wall delayed any action on Lincoln for months, apparently transfixed by the problem. The Southwest Plan became all-consuming and wasn't getting off the ground. Congress constantly wanted answers to questions that nobody could answer. Wall didn't need another big blowup from a man who had good Congressional connections. (Remember, Danny had lived most of his professional life in the Senate; the Senators didn't have to meet with him to have an impact on his decision-making process.) His staff in Washington had professional rivalries with the people in San Francisco, which made it hard to get straight answers. The San Francisco recommendation depended on so many technical issues. How could you take over an apparently legitimate business that was reporting 5.8 percent capital when 300 zombies with negative net worth were still doing business?

So Danny Wall made the worst political decision of his life—and one that cost the FSLIC several hundred million dollars. He made a settlement agreement with Lincoln. On May 20, 1988, after almost ten months of delaying, he entered into a "memorandum of understanding" with Lincoln. This memorandum of understanding (MOU for short) terminated Lincoln's action against the Bank Board, removed Lincoln from the FHLB of San Francisco's jurisdiction, provided for a new examination to be performed by Washington personnel, required that ACC put $10 million of new capital into Lincoln, required Lincoln to improve its underwriting and record keeping, and restricted several categories of investments.[31] At bottom, however, the Lincoln MOU was a cave-in by the Bank Board.

Danny Wall had made a bush-league political mistake. If you are a regulator, you don't take jurisdiction away from your people in the field. If you find them incompetent, you can replace them, but you can't give effective preferential treatment to an institution by saying that it doesn't have to be regulated by the people designated under the rules. The system will get you for it even if you are right about the substance. The fact that Danny Wall ended up being wrong only made matters worse.

The examination performed by Washington eventually turned up the facts on which Judge Sporkin based his opinion.

We can't know whether Keating would have prevailed in his lawsuit if the Bank Board had taken over Lincoln in 1987. The climate then was different. It would have been more hospitable to his position. The Bank Board's case would have been weaker.

But Danny Wall chose the wrong risks. The system got him (and his Director of Supervision) for the jurisdictional move. And Lincoln went on a speculative tear to try to recoup its prior losses, while Keating siphoned money out the side door through the tax-sharing agreement. Lincoln grew by over $800 million between June 30, 1987, and April 1989, when it was seized. And most of that $800 million now consists of Arizona desert.

These are harsh judgments that I am making about close questions, but if you don't have the instincts, you have to get out of the deposit insurance business—as FSLIC now has.

17 FIRREA

President George Bush tackled the S&L problem in his first month as president. He knew he had narrowly escaped its becoming a major issue in the campaign, and he knew it would get worse, not better, if he didn't deal with it. Here is some of what he said when he introduced the FSLIC bailout bill:

> For more than a half century, the United States has operated a deposit insurance program that provides direct government protection to the savings of our citizens.
>
> This program has enabled tens of millions of Americans to save with confidence.
>
> For the last twenty years, conditions in our financial markets have grown steadily more complex, and a portion of the savings and loan industry has encountered steadily growing problems.
>
> These financial difficulties have led to a continuous erosion of the strength of the [FSLIC].
>
> Economic conditions have played a major role in this situation.
>
> However, unconscionable risk-taking, fraud and outright criminality have also been factors.
>
> Congress, previous Administrations, the regulators and the industry were not prepared to be tough on those who risked the public's money or abused the system.
>
> Because of the accumulation of losses at hundreds of thrift institutions, additional resources must be devoted to cleaning up this problem. We intend to restore our entire deposit insurance system to complete health.

> We will see that the guarantee to depositors is forever honored, and we will
> see to it that the system is reformed comprehensively so that this situation is not
> repeated ever again.[1]

The bill that President Bush put forward would commit $50 billion on top of the approximately $40 billion that FSLIC had already committed (which the GAO said exceeded its resources by $26 billion). It would provide this $50 billion off-budget and would hand over administration of the cleanup to a new agency called the Resolution Trust Corporation (RTC). The bill also proposed to integrate the FSLIC administratively with the FDIC, while keeping the two funds separate, and proposed to place most of the FHLBB's functions under the Treasury Department with the OCC, with Danny Wall being specifically named to continue as head of the new Office of Thrift Supervision (OTS). The bill proposed higher deposit insurance premiums for both banks and S&Ls. It proposed to limit S&Ls' investments to those which were lawful for national banks (thus overriding the historical regulatory powers of the states in the dual banking system) and to require that S&Ls meet national bank capital standards by 1991. It also imposed national bank loan-to-one-borrower standards on S&Ls, made penalties for crimes against S&Ls and banks harsher, and set new standards—with the same harsh penalties—for lawyers, accountants, and consultants who work with S&Ls and banks. And, finally, it provided more money—$50 million—for pursuing S&L criminals.

The President's plan also called on FSLIC to stop issuing notes immediately (FSLIC was by then up to $18 billion in notes issued) and called for the FDIC to act jointly with FSLIC as receiver of any insolvent S&Ls that FSLIC took over. As a result of the President's directive, within a week FDIC personnel basically put FSLIC out of the business of running failed S&Ls, and no failed S&Ls were dealt with from the date of the President's speech until the RTC was organized almost a year later. In the meantime, the backlog grew again; and again it grew at great cost.

The plan had some obvious flaws: (1) It didn't provide enough money; (2) the RTC would have an impossible start-up and couldn't possibly handle all of the real estate it would end up with; (3) many more S&Ls would fail because they wouldn't be able to meet the bill's 1991 capital requirements; (4) putting $50 billion off-budget was more "mickey mouse" accounting. But it was a plan, and under the circumstances we needed quick enactment of *something* in order to stop the bleeding, which some commentators estimated at $1 billion per month. (I think it was more like half a billion a month, which we used to think was a lot of money.)

The Bush plan won wide support from both Republicans and Democrats in

Congress. Donald Riegle (D., Mich.), Chairman of the Senate Banking Committee after Proxmire's retirement, said, "The President deserves to be commended for moving quickly with his proposal to deal with the savings and loan problem." Senator Garn said, "I believe the plan is generally workable."[2] But everybody had a qualifier. Everybody had another aspect of the bill that he wanted to tinker with. "This time we have to fix the problem, not just fund it," said Rep. Chalmers Wylie (R., Ohio), the ranking Republican on the Banking Committee.[3]

Controversy about on-budget versus off-budget, S&L capital issues, issues about switching from one insurance fund to the other, issues about RTC's governance and the extent to which the FHLBs could fund part of the problem all contributed to delaying enactment of FIRREA until August. Maybe that was fast action for Congress, but it still was another costly delay.

NEW CAPITAL REQUIREMENTS

The debate on the capital provisions showed how angry Congress was. People like Lew Ranieri warned that the proposed standards (particularly the tangible capital standard) would "bankrupt more institutions than it needs to." If the proposed standards went forward, he predicted, the plan would be "short $100 billion or so."[4] But the Congress—particularly Democrats, and especially House Democrats—didn't seem to care. They wanted blood—and they got it.

Larry White pleaded that the Congress make it clear that whatever costs they imposed on the industry would be the last. Above all else, he said, capital "will avoid uncertainty." He meant that investors won't risk Congress's doing something even worse to them next time. But Congress didn't listen to him, either, so practically no new capital has come into the thrift industry since FIRREA.[5]

The prevailing view in Congress was that lax capital standards had been a part of the problem and that lax capital requirements should end. Richard Breeden, the President's point man on the legislation, had long held the view that the only solution was to impose banklike capital requirements and take over whatever S&Ls couldn't meet them.

But open and operating S&Ls' capital fell some $20 billion short of the new requirements (that's four times the total amount of capital that S&Ls had raised in the whole of the 1980s). Everyone knew that the S&Ls couldn't raise $20 billion of capital.

Dozens of S&Ls failed immediately after FIRREA was passed because they couldn't meet the new capital requirements. Many of those had low capital because they had acquired failing institutions in 1982, 1983, and 1984, accumulating enormous goodwill in the process. Some of them couldn't be long-term survivors in a low-spread world, but a law that put them in the tank immediately was not smart. The system couldn't deal with so many failures at once; the sheer magnitude had to increase the cost.

THE LOGO FIGHT

The S&Ls didn't mind giving up their insurance fund. FSLIC had become a dirty word; they wanted FDIC insurance. The commercial banks didn't want the S&Ls to be able to say they were insured by FDIC—a petty position if there ever was one. Unbelievably, the question of what the logo on S&Ls' doors could say became a major topic of lobbying for two months, until it was resolved by changing both the bank and the S&L insurance logos.

DANNY WALL

Danny Wall stayed in the legislation as chairman of OTS without further confirmation by the Senate despite his coming under constant attack during the six months it took to pass the bill. Although he says he didn't want to be in the bill, the appearance was that in exchange for his services to the administration and Jake Garn, Wall was being protected. That only made Congressional Democrats go after him more vigorously, with the result that he had to resign less than six months after the bill was passed.

AND THE WINNAH IS . . .

When the turf battle was settled, the FDIC was the big winner. The FHLBB was gone. Its chartering and examination powers had been given to OTS, which was under the Treasury. The FSLIC was gone. Its insurance fund and insurance powers had been given to FDIC, which ended up with two funds, one called the Bank Insurance Fund (BIF, for banks, naturally enough) and one called the Savings Association Insurance Fund (SAIF for S&Ls). (It costs an exit fee from SAIF and an entrance fee to BIF to switch funds.) The FDIC Chairman automatically became Chairman of the RTC as well, and therefore the FDIC effectively runs the RTC. Everybody says that FDIC Chairman Bill Seidman played the politics right and was the big winner. Maybe so. But the RTC has to be a big headache.

The new structure will be very temporary. Having two insurance funds run by one agency doesn't make sense. Treating S&Ls differently from banks after saying that they can't have greater powers than national banks also doesn't make any sense. The next round of legislation will take more steps toward homogenization.

SUPERVISORY GOODWILL

The most unjust provision of FIRREA was the Congressional decision not to count "supervisory goodwill"—that is, goodwill that resulted from mergers where healthy S&Ls acquired failing ones—as capital. FIRREA required 1.5 percent tangible capital and permitted OTS to take over an S&L if it didn't meet this standard. This was unfair because in many cases the FSLIC had agreed with acquiring S&Ls that—as an inducement to make the acquisitions, and in some cases as an inducement to their stockholders to put up more capital—the FSLIC would count the supervisory goodwill as an asset for capital purposes and would apply reduced capital standards to the acquiring institution. FIRREA wiped out these FSLIC agreements.

The action was unjust because private parties dealing with what they thought was the government agreed to do things for the government's benefit (taking over failed S&Ls with little or no assistance) in exchange for government promises. In FIRREA, Congress welshed on the deals.

That action raises constitutional issues as well as fairness issues. Does Congress have the power to abrogate contracts made by the FSLIC after people had relied on them? At this writing, some courts had said "no"—Congress couldn't have meant that (thus dodging the actual constitutional issue)—and other courts had said "yes," that is within the power of Congress, whether fair or not. The Supreme Court probably will decide the issue. I predict that it will decide in favor of private contractual rights.

The cases are not so easy, however, and many of them will go against the S&Ls even if they win on the constitutional issue because many of the S&Ls aren't economically viable. If an S&L has 14 percent more liabilities than assets, for example—a real case—then even if the law allows it to say that it has adequate capital, it will be economically dead. Doomed to lose money forever, it might as well be taken over and liquidated promptly.

Nevertheless, the government (in this case our self-righteous representatives in Congress) reneging on deals is pretty ugly. And in some cases it also raises the cost to the government.

CONSERVATORSHIPS

Next to bad loans, nothing kills the value of a bank more certainly than a "conservatorship." Almost as soon as a bank goes into federal hands, its value declines; it is impossible to "conserve" it. For this reason, since its early years the FDIC had adhered to a policy of arranging to sell or liquidate banks before taking them over so that the full going concern value can be realized. The FHLBB began violating this policy wholesale in 1985 with the establishment of the MCP, and FIRREA enshrined the uneconomic credo by encouraging OTS to declare conservatorships and receiverships before the RTC was ready to dispose of the failed S&Ls. As a result, many marginally failed S&Ls have withered on the undernourishing vine of federal conservatorship for periods sometimes exceeding a year. The costs will be incalculable but in the billions — more money than people stole from the S&Ls in the whole 1980s.

I can only ascribe this counterproductive policy to Congressional and regulatory paranoia about the people managing S&Ls. Apparently, they are all presumed to be Charles Keatings until proven innocent. Paranoia, we should not find it surprising, leads to compounding the losses incurred in our earlier period of naiveté.

FEWER THRIFTS

The FIRREA structure made it almost inevitable that the hundreds of S&Ls sold after its enactment would be sold to commercial banks. The RTC had to do "clean bank" deals in which it sold deposits and good assets to acquirers and gave cash for the difference between those two. These are deals that banks can do. They don't want to take on the messy troubled assets that will skew their operating data and increase their risks. And bankers will do the deals they want to do at lower projected rates of return than entrepreneurs. Banks will look for 15 percent to 20 percent rates of return, and may accept less to enter a new market that they like. Entrepreneurs, including money managers for pension funds, will look for returns of 25 percent to 35 percent if they are taking equity risk in a highly leveraged business. Therefore the banks, in theory, should win all the bids—and they have.

The banks may have to run some of the acquired institutions as S&Ls for a time in order not to pay the SAIF exit fee and the BIF entrance fee. But the banks want to run the S&Ls as banks—and eventually they will, which will make less difference than anyone would have thought back in 1966 or so when all this started.

FIRREA capped the demise of the S&Ls. From a population of about 4,000 in 1980, they will be reduced by failures and forced mergers to fewer than 2,000. By the mid–1990s, it looks like not more than 1,000 will be left. The business that they were in as recently as the 1970s is obsolete, except for mutuals, which can be satisfied with small returns on capital.

Many in the government don't seem to care whether the remaining S&Ls

survive. But they should. Human institutions are worth preserving, since they are hard to replicate. Even though the old S&L is obsolete, the institutions have social value that we should preserve if they don't pose risks. The next round of technology may make them efficient again. Changes in the secondary market may make holding mortgages and funding them with deposits profitable again. Until those things happen, managements that need to adjust should be encouraged, not treated like criminals.

HOSTAGES

FIRREA essentially holds hostage all S&Ls that don't fail. FIRREA increased the percentage of qualifying assets that S&Ls have to hold in housing and government assets to 70 percent, thereby forcing them to rely on housing loans to generate spread and condemning them to take the interest rate risks inherent in mortgages. It made the survivors continue to hold Federal Home Loan Bank stock, even though the value of that stock has to decline. And it imposed an exit fee from SAIF and an entrance fee to BIF that confiscates about 1.5 percent of capital as a tax for an S&L to become a commercial bank. There is no 14th Amendment for S&Ls, which automatically are discriminated against by reason of a previous condition of servitude. That's the price for the U.S. League having prevailed in 1987.

As the FIRREA wound its way through the legislative process, House Banking Committee Chairman Gonzalez said:

> This entire exercise is a sham unless we change the way savings and loans operate. To leave these institutions undercapitalized would break the faith with the American public. I urge a strong bipartisan vote that signals a clean break with the past and business as usual.

He got that vote, and the clean break with the past has sent more and more S&Ls into receivership and oblivion because it required increased capital to be raised based on a reduced ability to earn. These are mutually destructive concepts.[6]

18 What Caused How Much of the Losses?

We need to know what factors caused what parts of the S&L losses because that knowledge can help us focus on what needs to be fixed, as well as on what we should be angry about.

The task of ascribing magnitudes isn't simple. As I have already suggested, it requires a lot of guesswork as well as compilation and analysis. But it is more than a parlor game and deserves our keen attention.

I and my assistant, Maryann Schembri, have identified 177 failed S&Ls that probably cost the most money. They are all S&Ls that failed from 1984 to June 1990 and had over $500 million of liabilities or, if smaller, had estimated losses of over $100 million. To create an analytical database, we have gathered earnings, balance sheet, and other key data about those S&Ls for the years 1981–87. We believe that these 177 S&Ls account for over 75 percent of the losses incurred through June 1990.

Some of the analytical complexity arises because a single dollar of loss can have several overlapping causes. To illustrate, let's take a typical Texas example, Empire of Mesquite. It started with low net worth. It was allowed to grow fast by five-year averaging, no cap on brokered deposits, and loan fee recognition; it was encouraged to make risky loans by loan fee accounting and no loan loss reserves; it was victimized by vast outsider fraud, abetted by a little insider fraud; the regulators saw it going on but didn't act promptly; and eventually the oil bust and other Texas real estate factors compounded the losses. We can only estimate what caused how much of Empire's $200 million estimated loss.

Another complication: All of the loss estimates will have to be "present value." That means interest payments don't count, but the effects of inflation between the date of payment and the present time do count. That is, we are always talking about today's dollars (call the date 12/31/90). A dollar spent in 1982 was worth almost 40 percent more than a dollar spent in 1990. Therefore, to get the 1990 present value, we will have to inflate earlier expenditures. By the same token, we will have to deflate dollars expected to be spent in the future. We will not count interest costs that result from budgetary decisions to borrow the money and pay it back later rather than paying taxes today. But we will have to count interest costs on "working capital" that — because it gets repaid from proceeds of asset sales — isn't counted as a cost at all except for the interest paid.

That's the theory. In practice, it is hard to apply.

The vast majority of our 177 institutions turn out to be either interest rate failures left over from 1982 or "nasty little fast growers" like Empire of Mesquite, Vernon, Independent American, and Western that started small in 1982 and grew extremely fast for between two and five years, speculating all the while. We have ninety-five interest rate failures and forty-three nasty little fast growers. Thirty-nine institutions didn't fit into either category; that is, they had a relatively healthy net worth at the end of 1982, didn't go off on a major speculative tear, but still failed. We call them the "eventual losers." Almost all of the thirty-nine eventual losers did, however, grow fast (that is, by more than 25 percent) in at least one year between 1983 and 1985, and the vast majority of them significantly increased their risk profile between 1983 and 1986.

Over fifty of the interest rate failures and eventual losers acquired other failing S&Ls during the 1980s. Their losses thus include the losses of many other interest rate failures whose losses were buried in the goodwill numbers for a while.

Our sample has sixty-three Texas institutions, which in the aggregate kept growing and taking big lending risks well after 1984. They grew from $24.7 billion in size at the end of 1982 to $51 billion at the end of 1984 (106 percent growth in two years) to $79.9 billion at the end of 1987. In 1987 alone, the group grew by $13 billion (20 percent), demonstrating how futile the Bank Board's regulatory efforts were.

We have investigated the source of each S&L's earnings, including the level of loan fees taken into income; the changes in its mix of assets; the amounts and timing of goodwill and deferred losses incurred; and RAP, GAAP, and TAP (tangible) capital ratios. The numbers are all suspect because S&L reporting was so bad, but we have tried to use the numbers in ways that depend less on their accuracy than on their trends, although sometimes even the trends are suspect. This is an art form, not a science.

THE NASTY LITTLE FAST GROWERS

By definition, the forty-three nasty little fast growers (NLFGs) all grew fast—over 50 percent in more than one year, almost always in the key years 1983 and 1984. A few of them were still growing fast in 1985 and 1986. Also by definition, they all engaged in risky lending and investment practices that resulted in large losses (as a percentage of their assets). Forty-two of them were stock institutions, all of which were privately owned and therefore not subject to securities laws disclosures. Only one was a mutual. Most of them had changes in control between 1981 and 1984.

The loan fees (and the high rates of interest that they charged) made the NLFGs look very profitable as they speculated. The NLFGs were very good at manufacturing earnings, but even with all their manufactured earnings, in each of the key years about a quarter of them had under 3 percent RAP capital yet continued to grow.

Loan fees accounted for all of the earnings at over half of the NLFGs in the key years 1983 and 1984. In the aggregate, the NLFGs reported more loan fees than they did net income in the crucial growth years of 1983 and 1984.

Permitting goodwill, appraised equity capital, and deferred losses to be counted as capital doesn't appear to have played a big role in the NLFG phenomenon.

The NLFGs used a variety of funding sources. Few of them relied exclusively on brokered deposits. Most of them relied heavily on jumbo deposits and other large liabilities to grow and fund their speculations.

What should have alarmed the regulators early in almost all of these cases was the abnormally high interest rates and fees they were charging on loans. When a bank or S&L is charging 18 percent in a 12 percent market—which is what most the NLFGs were doing in 1983—you *know* they are taking huge risks. Otherwise nobody would pay those rates. The regulators should have insisted on big reserves for those loans, but they didn't.

The NLFGs caused a disproportionate share of the total losses. Almost all of them were more than 50 percent underwater by the time they were dealt with. On average, they were underwater by 67 percent, by more if you believe the high-end estimates. A large part of those losses, however, was due to the fact that NLFGs weren't liquidated promptly. In fact, the average NLFG was run by the government for between three and four years after its failure had been identified, during which time it continued to lose money at an ever-increasing rate, the way a typical broke S&L is bound to do. We estimate that, against the rate of inflation, there was about an 8 percent per annum loss on all of the liabilities of each institution: a total loss due to delay of about 30 percent of total liabilities. We estimate these losses at $10 billion or more just for running the dead NLFGs until 1988 instead of liquidating them.

We also should observe that if the growth of the NLFGs had been stopped at the end of 1983, their total assets would have been $14.7 billion. They grew 79 percent in 1984 and eventually had a top size of about $30 billion. Some of them continued to grow after the Bank Board thought it had cracked down. Seventeen grew over 20 percent in 1985, four grew over that amount in 1986, and five did so in 1987, all the while making risky loans and increasing the size of the losses.

Total losses at NLFGs are estimated at $25 billion, of which between $10 billion and $15 billion was caused by the government's inability to close and liquidate or sell the institutions after their insolvency was apparent.

Allocating responsibility and causes for the remaining $10 billion is difficult. We can say that substantially all of it was caused by bad loans and investments which were the product of mismanagement, but that doesn't tell us much. We also know that the Texas crash and the Tax Reform Act of 1986 made matters worse. We also can say that twelve of the NLFGs invested over a third of their assets in land; but again, that no longer surprises us. What laws encouraged and permitted these excesses? What regulators failed in their oversight? What professionals aided and abetted the excesses?

The NLFG phenomenon was regional. Of the forty-three NLFGs identified, twenty-three were in Texas, four were elsewhere in the Southwest, nine were in California, and one was in Colorado (Silverado, which was a marginal addition to the group because it didn't crash as fast as the others). Only six were located elsewhere in the country, and some of these are marginal additions to the group. This sort of regional distribution, despite failed institutions in our sample from all over the country, suggests that national policies, while they may have been necessary conditions for the NLFG phenomenon, were not sufficient.

We also can observe that thirty-eight of the NLFGs were state chartered and five were federally chartered, although about 50 percent of all associations were federally chartered at the time. This again suggests that laws governing federally chartered associations, including the 1980 Act and Garn–St Germain changes in asset powers, weren't significantly involved.

We then are tempted to blame the state laws and regulatory authorities in Texas and California, with particular emphasis on the Nolan Act in California. But here we need to observe that half of the California NLFGs grew by over 50 percent in 1982, before the Nolan Act was passed. The Nolan Act certainly contributed to the problem, but the problem was emerging before the act was passed.

Our assessment is that lax regional regulators combined with an optimism about local economies and a frontier mentality to spawn a whole school of look-alike disasters in Texas and California.

The accounting fraternity needs to bear some significant responsibility for the NLFGs, as do many respectable thrift managers across the country. Recognition of loan fees (a RAP-accounting-generated phenomenon) and a dearth of loan loss reserves for obviously risky loans permitted the process to burgeon. Some lax auditing appears to have permitted the cover-ups to succeed for a while. The accountants should have known better (so should the regulators), but they were under heavy pressure from the S&L industry, including its most responsible elements, to make profits easy so that net worths, depleted by the interest rate ravages, could be rebuilt. Good accounting, the reasoning went, could come after survival. Quite simply, the more responsible elements of the business couldn't conceive of—literally couldn't conceive of, much less foresee—the excesses that occurred in Texas and California.

Those excesses, of course, were made worse by outright fraud. There were hundreds of frauds committed at the NLFGs. We don't *know* what they cost. Primary fraud by insiders (Type 1 misconduct) caused, we guess, about $2 billion of the NLFG damage. Cover-up fraud (Type 4 misconduct) certainly inflated the amount, since many of the NLFGs continued to grow and gamble to try to recoup their losses while under the cover of the cover-up fraud. We think that about $5 billion of the NLFG losses on bad loans might have been prevented had the cover-up fraud not been effective to keep gambling institutions in business. Our conclusions are, however, that the NLFG phenomenon did not depend upon fraud—the game would have worked for a time without it—and that the NLFGs all would have failed without fraud because they made loans indiscriminately.

THE INTEREST RATE FAILURES

The ninety-five interest rate failures (IRFs) will cost about $41 billion—almost twice as much as the forty-three NLFGs. This cost compares unfavorably with the $27 billion we think it would have cost to liquidate the IRFs in 1983 (15 percent of their then total asset size of $131 billion, brought to present value). The interest rate failures didn't grow as fast as the NLFGs, but by 1987 even they had grown 67 percent, to $214 billion.

The 95 interest rate failures have been categorized as interest rate failures because they emerged from 1982 so weakened that they could not have achieved profitability and normal capital levels without either growing very fast or taking above-average lending risks and getting lucky, or both. About half of them were insolvent on a tangible basis in 1983; the rest had very low capital on any basis. Most of the IRFs, encouraged by the prospect of loan fees and a positive spread, both grew rapidly in at least one year after 1982 and engaged in riskier types of lending to try to survive. Sixty-five IRFs grew at least 25 percent in at least one year despite low capital and scant earnings. In 1984, the group as a whole grew by 27 percent. Most of this rapid growth was accomplished by bidding for jumbo CDs and brokered deposits.

Three-quarters of the IRFs significantly increased the riskiness of their loan portfolios after 1982. The more prudent few stumbled along toward failure without any real chance to survive in a world of reduced spreads. Those who took their risks early (1983–84), however, lost less than those who started to gamble for salvation in 1985 and later. On average, the late gambling group lost 1½ times the percentage of their assets as the early gambling group, and more than twice as much as the ones that didn't gamble appreciably.

Generally, loan fee income and other forms of nonrecurring income, such as skimming loan and securities portfolios, skimming goodwill, and selling mortgage servicing, gave the IRFs an appearance of making progress in the mid–1980s when in fact they were going backward.

The IRFs couldn't recover because they couldn't generate enough spread to make money in the banking business without accounting gimmicks. Sixty-eight of the ninety-five IRFs never (after 1980) had a net interest margin (spread adjusted for the ratio of earning assets to paying liabilities) of over 200 basis points. Most of these never had a net interest margin of over 150 basis points, and many of them never even got over 100 basis points. Since average S&L operating costs during the period were over 200 basis points, these low-margin institutions began each year knowing that if they didn't pull rabbits out of hats, they would lose money.

Some of the IRFs were in particularly bad positions because they had acquired failing institutions in transactions that had created goodwill exceeding their capital. That is, their capital was negative tangible as a result of taking on weak institutions. Of the ninety-five IRFs, forty-two took on (and were encouraged by the regulators to take on) other institutions that were in even worse shape than they were. In effect, each of these forty-two big S&Ls became a phoenix without being called one. After assuming this level of goodwill, it turned out that they were themselves weak institutions which couldn't survive. In many cases they compounded their problems by trying to.

About 90 percent of the IRFs utilized deferred losses to some degree, but we can't tell how much those deferred losses contributed to their inability to recover. The incidence of deferred losses among the IRFs certainly is higher than in the S&L population generally, but we don't know whether these institutions were worse off to begin with or whether weak managements self-selected. We suspect that, although deferred loss accounting probably increased the size of losses somewhat, it did not cause failures that otherwise wouldn't have occurred.

The IRFs were victimized by relatively little insider fraud. However, because desperate bankers make desperate loans, several of the IRFs that would have failed anyway were victimized by borrower frauds.

THE EVENTUAL LOSERS

Our third category of failed S&Ls consists of thirty-nine institutions (with $53.6 billion of assets and $17 billion of projected losses) that on paper looked like they could survive at the end of 1982 but instead slid into insolvency along the way to the 1990s. Despite better capital ratios than the IRFs, about a quarter of the eventual losers (ELs) never achieved a net interest margin sufficient to make money regularly, and many more achieved such a margin in only one or two years during which they were engaging in aggressive or risky lending that temporarily increased spreads before the loans started to go bad. Thus, about half of the ELs failed for fundamental banking business reasons.

About 40 percent of the ELs acquired other S&Ls and took on amounts of goodwill that wiped out their tangible capital. The goodwill made their financial statements look similar to the IRFs' and encouraged them to increase the riskiness of their loan portfolios the same way that the IRFs did. Most of the ELs also deferred some losses, although usually not a large amount. Combining the effects of goodwill and deferred losses, about half of the ELs had negative tangible capital by 1983.

The ELs grew a bit more than the IRFs. Thirty-four of them grew at least 25 percent in at least one year, and twenty-six of them did so in two years. As a group, the ELs grew 150 percent between year-end 1982 and year-end 1987, an average compound growth rate of over 20 percent.

The ELs significantly increased their risk profiles after 1982, with thirty-four out of thirty-nine doing so to a significant extent. Only two of the ELs didn't either increase their risk profiles or take on goodwill that wiped out their tangible capital. We believe that almost all of the ELs outside Texas could have survived (though they would have been weak earners) if they had neither taken on goodwill nor increased their risk profiles.

We now wish that we had control group data for surviving institutions that in 1982 looked the same as the ELs that failed. Control group analysis and comparison would have helped us to identify the causes of EL failures more precisely. For us, at least, the control group data will have to wait for another day.

We believe, however, that at least 50 percent of the ELs' $17 billion approximate cost should be attributed to pre-1983 interest rate problems—both their own and the ones they took on in acquisitions. The remaining 50 percent or so would have to be attributed to a variety of causes. In Texas (where there were nineteen ELs with $28.1 billion of assets) the "Texas premium" on deposits made adequate net interest margins impossible, and the economy's decline made loan losses inevitable. In addition, Texas institutions invested a far larger percentage of their assets than other S&Ls in inherently risky land loans, and the Texas ELs grew faster than ELs elsewhere, with thirteen of them growing at least 25 percent in at least two years. These Texas factors would have accounted for over $10 billion of the ELs' losses.

Fraud played a role in some of the ELs' losses, but usually, it appears, only at the end, after their failure was inevitable. Therefore, while it may have contributed to increasing the size of EL losses, fraud doesn't appear to have caused EL failures, almost all of which can easily be explained by interest rate problems and the real estate bust.

Even though most of the ELs were declared to have failed only after FIRREA was passed, their 1985 balance sheets and earning power would have suggested eventual failure unless managed extremely well. In most cases, that extremely good management wasn't there, as is evidenced by a generally high level of operating expenses among the group.

CONCLUSIONS

A box score of causes would overstate the certainty of our results. We believe, however, that our research demonstrates that a large percentage of the losses after 1984 resulted from unrecognized pre-1983 interest rate failures. It also demonstrates that the accounting rules which were intended to help S&Ls look better played a perverse role in permitting rapid growth without real capital and in encouraging risky lending practices. The single accounting practice that was most at fault was immediate loan fee recognition.

The NLFG phenomenon, as costly as it was, was largely unrelated to the underlying problems of thrift institutions. The basic problems were interest rate failures and the disappearance of profitable spreads in the traditional mortgage business. The NLFG phenomenon was not, in our opinion, caused by either of those problems. The NLFGs resulted from the acts of speculators who took advantage of lax regulation and regulatory rules to engage in once-in-a-lifetime flings. Prompt detection and preventive action could have reduced the NLFG losses to 10 percent or 20 percent of what they eventually became.

The IRF and EL losses were less preventable. The mismatch, followed by reduced spreads, followed by the Texas crash, followed by the 1986 Tax Reform Act, caused a majority of those losses. Gambling for salvation and real estate crashes in Arizona and the Northeast made these losses worse, as did FIRREA's overreactions, some less-than-optimal deals, and deferred resolutions.

Deferring resolutions clearly accounted for a large part of the losses in the worse cases. At Sunbelt, those losses are continuing to run.

We have tried to evaluate whether forbearance programs have increased or decreased the costs of dealing with institutions that might have been taken over but for the forbearance. What we find is that forbearance by changing the rules is very dangerous. It increases the costs dramatically. However, forbearance by creating a program in which specially identified institutions can qualify for forbearance in exchange for submitting to increased oversight does not seem to increase costs. Our study showed that none of the NLFGs had received net worth certificate assistance and that the IRFs which got such assistance in 1983 didn't tend to gamble and significantly increase the cost of dealing with them. The FDIC's experience with net worth certificates tends to confirm these findings. It therefore appears that when the program is run right, the combination of self-selection and actual oversight can make a forbearance program work without greatly increasing the insurer's risks—at least until the insolvency reaches a depth that makes the institution doomed to lose money forever.

We still don't have confidence that we know what the whole debacle is going to cost. There are too many variables, too many unknowns, and too many other people who have damaged their reputations by guessing at the total cost. We can't differ with the conventional wisdom of the moment that says $150–200 billion, present value, January 1, 1991, dollars is a good guess. Beware of those $500 billion numbers, if you finance anything for long enough, the cost becomes infinite if you don't use the present value concept. At compound interest, the $24 that it cost to buy Manhattan Island in 1626 would amount to more than $4 quadrillion today.

19 High Rollers

In one way or another, almost everyone involved in this story got sucked into being a high roller:

- The S&Ls that survived the interest rate ravages of 1980–82 with low capital and anemic spreads almost *had* to gamble for salvation.

- The healthier institutions that took on failing ones in exchange for goodwill accounting thought the risks were prudent because their regulators encouraged the deals.

- The natural high rollers bought S&Ls because of the extreme leverage that the regulators allowed.

- Dick Pratt adopted goodwill accounting and other policies that made it hard to count and encouraged growth without adequate capital because FSLIC didn't have enough money.

- Danny Wall gambled his career on the 1988 deals because FSLIC didn't have enough money.

- Ed Gray gambled with the costly MCP, FADA, FCA's growth, and policies of deferral that sought to preserve the industry, all because FSLIC didn't have enough money.

- The Reagan administration put a big bet on what it thought were free markets, but it forgot about deposit insurance; and it thought that FSLIC didn't need more money.

- Congress enacted the legislation that set the boundaries for everyone else's choices; Congress didn't give FSLIC any money until it was too late.

When everything goes wrong, as it did with the S&Ls, it looks like everyone took unconscionable risks. But economic decisions are, of necessity, decisions about which risks to take. Except for the NLFGs, all the players in the S&L game were measuring the risks they took against other risks they decided not to take. If they chose the wrong risks, it was because they didn't accurately foresee the consequences, not because their alternative was a riskless solution that they willfully chose to reject.

Part II
The Lessons of the Piece

The bad loans and the cover-up deals that ended up compelling the taxpayer bailout of FSLIC can be traced to public policies and business standards that denied reality.

We denied reality:

- When we imposed deposit ceilings in 1966

- When we bent the capital rules by instituting five-year averaging in 1972

- When we invented all the RAP accounting gimmicks to make S&Ls look better in 1981–82

- When we used purchase accounting as a substitute for money to induce acquisitions of failed S&Ls

- When we stopped liquidating insolvent institutions in 1983

- When we didn't show that FSLIC was insolvent from 1982 to 1987

- When we passed an inadequate recapitalization bill in 1987

- When we consistently underestimated the size of the problem, usually in order to preserve "the system"

- When we appointed regulators who didn't have the technical background and skill to understand the intricacies of the system

- When we pretended that market discipline by depositors inhibits excessive risk-taking by institutions that have deposit insurance

- When we allowed bank officers to be wined and dined by borrowers and Wall Street securities salesmen in the name of "relationships"

- When Congress thought that it controlled the purse strings, while in fact the government already owed the money as a consequence of the deposit insurance contract.

Congress still wants to pander, not to educate. Congress still isn't ready to transform its own relationship to deposit insurance. Congress doesn't like to admit that it, too, is subject to money's conceptual laws. As Professor Edward Kane of Ohio State observed in his book on the subject in 1989, "[C]ongressional procedures for budgeting and for overseeing the operations of the deposit-insurance bureaucracy made the regulatory strategy of cover-up and deferral practically irresistible."[1]

The Republicans want to blame it all on the Democrats. So they magnify the "Keating Five" incident and the role of Speaker Wright, etc. The Democrats want to blame the Republicans, so they pillory President Bush's son, which has nothing to do with the case. But this shouldn't be a partisan issue. Both Democrats and Republicans are responsible — Presidents, Senators, Representatives, regulators from both parties, fund-raisers, businesspeople, and even voters. I hold Presidents Johnson and Reagan most responsible. Johnson set the process in motion by consistently denying reality. Reagan not only presided (or failed to preside) during most of the worse of the problem, he also set up the climate that unleashed the excessive credit that fueled the boom. It is the boom, not the bust, that causes the damage. The bust is a logical consequence of the overbuilding that results from the boom psychology. The operators and con men prey on the boom psychology.

SUPPLY SIDE RUN AMOK

The boom of the 1980s was fueled by loans on real estate and LBOs. As Brookings Institution Senior Fellow Anthony Downs observed in 1986, "A surplus of capital has generated massive overbuilding . . . because development has been driven by money availability, not by the demand for space nor the markets themselves."[2] Not only the S&Ls but also commercial banks, insurance companies, and pension funds made excessive loans. They are all paying for that now — and through the federal safety net, all Americans will pay for the S&Ls' share.

Perhaps there wasn't any boom at all. Perhaps we just borrowed the money from ourselves by creating an artificially large supply of money that had to chase risky deals. Those deals drove up stock market prices and real estate values. When those deals go bad, value declines and money effectively gets taken out of the system. That's where most of the money that the S&Ls lost went—up in a cloud of rising interest rates and declining southwestern property values.

THE ANALYSIS AHEAD

The following eight short chapters analyze:

- The impact of deregulation
- The role of numbers in formulating policy
- How complexity can prevent effective regulation
- Why fraud always threatens banks, and what we can do about it
- What regulation and enforcement can—and can't—accomplish
- How regulation can—and can't—deal with technology
- What kind of deposit insurance reform we should have
- Some implications of the FSLIC bailout for the American banking system of the future.

I hope that your ability to understand and cast a critical eye on these analyses will reward your patience in learning about the S&L business and how it was regulated.

20 Evaluating Deregulation

Free-market theory says "Don't interfere with the marketplace." Markets, left to their own devices, will produce "optimal" results. In general, that seems to be true, even though "optimal" isn't always good.

The trouble with stopping here is that we don't have free markets. We *can't* have free markets because the world is too complex and interdependent to let everyone run around doing whatever he or she wants to do. As a society, we have to regulate conduct when it interferes with other people's freedoms or when it threatens damage to other people's property. We also have to regulate conduct when it distorts rather than enhances the operation of free markets.

Because we need to have some kinds of regulations, we should operate with a "free market presumption" rather than with an absolute faith in free markets. This presumption has to be weakened even further, however, when government has interfered in a business by regulating it to achieve specified public goals. In the thrift industry, we are talking about the public goals of promoting housing and giving people safe places to save their money. We set up the FSLIC to insure savings and provided the FHLBs and tax incentives to encourage home lending. We went even further by setting up Ginnie Mae, Fannie Mae, and Freddie Mac to insure mortgages so they could be traded readily in a secondary market. As a result, we should have a very weak free market presumption about the savings institution business. It has several federal subsidies, so the federal government has a right—and a need—to protect itself from misuse of those subsidies.

Business in a subsidized industry can't be allowed to be as free as business in an industry with no subsidies. The Reagan administration violated this principle when it left the subsidies in place but tried to free management's conduct from regulation. (For those who would play partisan politics with this: The Carter administration was going in the same direction.)

The natural consequence of this kind of mistake is that people will enter the subsidized industry to take advantage of the subsidized opportunities. And in 1982–83 there *were* advantages to owning an S&L and using it as an investment vehicle.

INTEREST RATE DEREGULATION

The advantages were opened up by interest rate deregulation, which enabled S&Ls to buy as much money as they wanted. This new ability to buy money should have led the government to impose at least the same kinds of safety and soundness controls on S&Ls that it imposed on banks—that is, capital requirements, accounting requirements, loan-to-one-borrower limitations. Instead of imposing these requirements, the FHLBB left five-year averaging in place, didn't enforce any capital requirements because it couldn't afford the ultimate sanction (liquidation), created and then left RAP accounting gimmicks in place, and didn't apply loan-to-one-borrower limitations to real estate lending. The states went further and permitted S&Ls to make equity investments and equity participation (ADC) loans. This structure practically drove speculators into the S&L business.

But we shouldn't blame the problem on interest rate deregulation. The alternatives of federally funding the billions of dollars of deposits that were fleeing low-rate accounts in 1979–82 or forcing S&Ls to sell long-term mortgages at significant losses to fund the outflows were less attractive; either one would have cost the federal government many billions of dollars and would have left in place a system of regulation that events had proven not to work. The bottom line, in my opinion, is that the country needed interest rate deregulation. Unfortunately, so many things were changing at once that the regulatory system adjusted in the wrong ways by covering up the real losses that had taken place and encouraging fast growth without capital so that institutions could try to recoup.

THE $100,000 INSURANCE PROBLEM

The increase of deposit insurance coverage from $40,000 to $100,000 came in 1980, at about the same time as interest rate deregulation. Commentators such as former FDIC Chairman Sprague have asserted that this change was a principal cause of the problem because it permitted S&Ls to bid in the open market for insured deposits.[1] In 1980, interest rate controls still applied to most types of deposits but didn't apply to deposits of $100,000 or more, so when the insurance limit was raised to $100,000, S&Ls could, for the first time, bid whatever interest rate they chose for deposits that were fully insured.

Designating the change to $100,000 of insurance as a major cause of the S&L losses works only up to about the end of 1982. By that time the DIDC's rate deregulation was sufficiently far along that S&Ls could have competed openly for fully insured $40,000 deposits, if that had stayed the insurance limit. Since most of the explosive growth took place in 1983 and 1984, I do not assign a key role to the increase to $100,000 of insurance.

ASSET SIDE DEREGULATION

Commentators blame asset side deregulation for the losses even more often than they blame interest rate deregulation. The 1980 Act and the Garn–St Germain Act gave federal S&Ls new powers to make commercial and consumer loans, removed geographic limitations on commercial real estate loans, and removed LTV requirements. Many state laws went further than federal law.

Were these forms of asset side deregulation also responsible for part of the problem? I conclude that the psychological climate created by the Texas and California laws was instrumental in creating the anything-goes, nowhere-to-go-but-up attitudes that drew buccaneers into the S&L business. These laws, combined with the Reagan rhetoric and the lax supervision by the FHLBB, led these entrepreneurs to believe that "deregulation" meant "hands off." To them "deregulation" meant "no regulation." They were genuinely surprised when the regulatory system began to function again and closed them down. But the asset side of deregulation, in and of itself, didn't cause a lot of the problem. The FHLBB reacted reasonably promptly to curtail direct investments. The land and commercial real estate loans that caused most of the losses had been lawful for many S&Ls before deregulation (albeit with LTV restrictions), and most of them were made close to home, so the increased geographic diversity that Garn–St Germain permitted had relatively little impact on the size of the problem. (Some of the small S&Ls that failed because of Texas loan participations were exceptions to this generalization.) The new corporate and consumer lending powers didn't cause *any* of the failures.

Logic suggests that asset side deregulation to equalize the powers of thrifts with the powers of banks *had* to follow interest rate deregulation unless we were prepared to further subsidize the thrifts. The problem with asset side deregulation was that too many S&Ls rushed into the real estate development business at the same time that banks were expanding their investment in that business. Loan fee accounting drove S&L money into commercial real estate because that's where S&Ls could make easy money (or at least report that they had made it). At the same time, removing the LTV limitations did damage because, with so little capital at stake and the boom psychology, many S&L managements didn't exercise any self-restraint. The losses in Texas would have been significantly lower if LTV requirements had not been removed or had been promptly restored when the problem came to light. I don't believe in lending by appraisal, but Texas S&L managements certainly demonstrated that they needed the restraints imposed by LTV requirements.

Real estate markets are fueled by money and leverage, so the excess supply of money overheated the market. It happened in spades in Texas, but it also happened in almost every other market in the country.

DESTRUCTIVE COMPETITION

Banks always seem to want to expand too fast, to bring in too much money, to open too many offices. The 1980s overexpansion was not the first in American banking history; and deposit insurance exaggerates bankers' natural tendencies to grow too fast.

For a while after the 1930s, the regulators restricted branching and only very reluctantly granted new charters. Then, beginning in the late 1970s, in the spirit of private enterprise and deregulation, they said, "Boys will be boys, let them compete."

As a result, by 1989 our system of depository institutions had about one-third more deposits than it should have had, all chasing a declining pool of creditworthy loans. At a time when technological innovations such as ATMs and home video banking would have suggested that we should have had fewer bank branches, we had banks on more street corners than ever before. Bert Ely calls the phenomenon "overintermediation," meaning that the banks and S&Ls, as financial intermediaries, took in too much money compared with the natural amount that needed to be lent out.[2]

Classical free market economics teaches that there is no such thing as "destructive" or "excessive" competition. Competition, it insists, is the market's way of creating a balance. It has to be expected, in this view, that along the way some firms will fail. That doesn't make the competition destructive or excessive.

As I said above, I buy the free market hypothesis. But the psychology of money makes banking different from other businesses.

THE PSYCHOLOGY OF MONEY

Maybe banking naturally attracts excessive competition because money has a different psychological cachet than other goods. Its control seems to bring a greater sense of personal well-being than control, say, of socks or sweatshirts, even though socks and sweatshirts appear to provide more stable businesses.

Money also seems to give greater psychological satisfaction than socks or sweatshirts because people are grateful when they borrow money. The sweatshirt magnate very rarely gets a heartfelt thanks for permitting Sears or Penney to buy a hundred gross of extra-large heavyweight-all-cotton shirts suitable for silk screening with the latest pattern.

Money also is fungible. There can't be any difference between the money that this bank or that bank lends. The banker can't create a better dollar bill. To show prominence a banker has to have a *big* bank. Nobody asks how much a bank made last year. That would be gauche. Instead they ask, "What are your footings?" old man. Much more civilized. "How much money do you control?" Not "What do you do with it?"

Money attracts people who want to steal it. It attracts borrowers who want to borrow and not repay. It attracts bank owners who want to use the bank's money or the power of the bank's money for other projects. The banking business is trusting people to repay later, so the bank is the place to go if you want to commit fraud.

These psychological attributes of money and banking tell us that even honest bankers, being differently motivated, act differently from other businessmen. We shouldn't assume, therefore, that bankers always will act in ways that the free market hypothesis suggests. We need, unfortunately, to regulate and supervise the conduct of people who control pools of that magical substance, money.

The actual deregulation that the 1980 Act and the Garn–St Germain Act effected made necessary adjustments to a system that had gotten out of balance. That deregulation didn't cause the losses. But people respond to simple concepts. The word "deregulation" proved more powerful than the laws that implemented it.

21 Because Banks Are Where the Money Is

Fraud and theft have been causing banks to fail for more than a thousand years. Many, perhaps most, bank failures in the history of the United States have involved fraud or some other kind of theft. Much of that fraud would qualify for the category that we have called Type 1 misconduct—that is, fraudulent behavior designed to benefit an officer, director, or owner of the victimized institution, usually by providing money to such a person through an indirect lending transaction.

The huge number of S&L failures that involved Type 1 misconduct raises three compelling questions: Why were there so many at once? Why did the perpetrators think they could get away with it? What can we do to prevent it in the future?

Almost all of the Type 1 misconduct took place in Texas, Louisiana, and California. Almost all of it took place in small institutions that grew very fast in 1983 and 1984. Almost all of it was perpetrated by people (almost all of them men) who came into the S&L business in 1981, 1982, and 1983. Most of the perpetrators were youngish men who wanted to get rich quick. Most of them have filed for bankruptcy, been sentenced to jail (or at least indicted), or died a violent death. Some are both bankrupt and in jail.

Several books have contended that the frauds were the product of a conspiracy. Both *The Big Fix* by James Ring Adams and *Inside Job* by Stephen Pizzo, Mary Fricker, and Paul Muolo contain elaborate reporting of the connections between the owners and managers who perpetrated the insider frauds at the defrauded institutions. They point out that Mafia-related figures were involved in several cases and that organized crime's techniques were used. Their good investigative reporting makes it tempting to blame a conspiracy for the large number of relatively similar loan frauds.

Connections and similarities, however, do not a conspiracy make. People who do business similarly tend to know each other, especially when large sums of money are involved. Moreover, most insider frauds look roughly alike. No matter how many straw borrowers or dummy corporations you put between the bank and the perpetrator, the game is the same. Take money from the bank, lend it to somebody apparently unrelated, and have that borrower give some of it to an insider. These people who defrauded S&Ls didn't invent anything new. Indeed, with few exceptions (such as Mr. Keating), their methods were so amateurish and transparent that they lead inevitably to the question of how they thought they could get away with it. Any kind of master plan would have done it far better.

There is evidence, of course, that *some* of the people who came into the industry in Texas knew each other and financed or encouraged each other when they came into the business. The evidence to date, however, doesn't suggest that they came into the business with fraudulent intent. Greed was motive enough when Texas was booming and an S&L provided minor league talent with access to big league money. In 1983–84, when they were reporting big profits, I think that people like Dixon, Gaubert and McBirney *believed* they were making big profits. Their operations were sloppy and bound to fail, and probably borrowers were defrauding *them* left and right, but at the beginning they appear to have been outlandish, careless, and flamboyant rather than crooked. They were making so much money from dividends, salaries, and perks that they had no need to steal. No court has yet found otherwise, although we haven't come to the end of the investigations, revelations, and trials.

In many cases, of course, the perks were excessive. And in at least some cases, they weren't approved by boards of directors, as they needed to be under the law. But even if some of the perks, like Don Dixon's beach house in California, perhaps, were criminally obtained, they will not be the cause of the losses. If the reported profits had been real, the perks just would have put Dixon on "Lifestyles of the Rich and Famous."

In the big cases, the fraudulent stuff, it appears, began after the loans and the markets started to go bad. Then the Texas conspiracy *does* appear to have been formed because (1) the high fliers saw that the house of cards would fall eventually, so they had less to lose, and (2) conspiratorial trading became the only way to conceal the bad loans and make apparent profits to conceal worsening operations.

Outside Texas (and Lincoln), most of the insider frauds appear to have been more directly perpetrated by inexperienced small-time operators who somehow didn't understand the consequences. They didn't seem to know that when big loans go bad, investigations begin. Regulators come in. They get suspicious. They talk to prosecutors. The official world doesn't like money going out the side door. Somehow the perpetrators didn't know that the official world would be assiduous in pursuing them. Even Charles Keating was naive on this point. Could they have thought that deregulation had repealed *all* the laws?

Both types, however—those with original criminal intent and those who later turned to crime to cover up—were attracted to the S&L business in 1981, 1982, and 1983 out of greed. They could see the enormous leverage. They could see the cozy relationship between the S&Ls and their regulators. They heard the words of deregulation. They knew that you could make money in the stock market only if you had some to start with. They knew that a real estate developer could do no better than succeed project by project, and always had to convince a banker to lend the money. They also knew that owning an S&L was prestigious. It made everyone in town sit up and take notice. Everybody treats you well when you have the power to extend or withhold credit.

So how do we prevent banks from being defrauded in the future? The fraud caused a lot of losses, even if not as much as most people want to believe.

Fraud by outsiders generally can be prevented by good lending procedures and good record keeping. Every bank is defrauded now and then in some small way, but the big frauds happen only when procedures are lax. Good process and regulatory emphasis on good process stop most outsider fraud. (Maybe stiff penalties help. But the costs of long-term incarceration are so high that I wonder whether we need ten- and twenty-year sentences for people who steal $100,000 by trickery. The long sentence won't help us get the money back, and jail costs the taxpayers about $25,000 per year.)

Insider fraud is another story. Some of the insider fraud could have been prevented by more rigorous regulatory supervision. It was perpetrated after the institutions were economically dead and therefore should have been taken over.

Some of the fraud was simply endemic to business. Various kinds of triangular, quadrangular, and pentangular relationships are common in American business. They probably are common in business anywhere in the world. Payoffs also are a common part of business. Sometimes they're small and sometimes they're large, sometimes they're blatant and sometimes they're subtle. But they *are* omnipresent, and they do dull a businessperson's ability to distinguish right from wrong.

We mentioned in Chapter 5 that Congress had passed a law in 1984 that made it a federal crime to pay any employee of a federally insured bank or

S&L in connection with any business. Few laws in my twenty-five years connected with banks and S&Ls so upset the savings and loan community as this law, which was designed to protect them. This law, which would have made it illegal for a loan officer to accept football tickets from a borrower, seemed to them to threaten their way of life. But under that law, the bank or S&L could have made the transactions legal by paying for the tickets. Certainly, the borrower wouldn't have objected to that.

The U.S. League of Savings Institutions led a two-year fight against the Bribery Law that ended with an amendment to the statute in 1986 that made the conduct unlawful only if it was done with "corrupt intent."[1] Obviously, you can almost *never* prove corrupt intent. Apparently, the people who ran the U.S. League (and other banking trade groups that supported them) would rather have their institutions at risk for bad loans made by overly grateful loan officers than face the possibility of paying for their own golf games.

We have to grow up about this petty bribery. We all know when we're being bribed; we can feel it. But it's so pervasive that it's hard to turn down. If we could outlaw the petty bribery, we could change the climate that leads to insider fraud. Most people aren't very subtle about drawing lines between permissible and impermissible conduct. The lines therefore have to be very clear.

22 The Importance of Counting

Although knowing "reality" is our goal, we must understand that this abstract "reality" is different from the depictions we get of it, whether the images that we see come in the form of TV news, photos, newspaper descriptions, or, in the case of banks, financial statements. All these media are the shadows that we see on the walls of the cave that we, like the people Plato described in *The Republic,* inhabit. We can see the shadows, but we can't see the world outside the cave. We can only derive an idea of the reality of that world from the shadows cast into our cave.

In the financial world, numbers—in financial statements, statistics about loans, delinquencies, failures, costs, interest rates—are the shadows. How they are arranged determines how we see reality and what we believe is happening. Therefore the systems by which we arrange the numbers determine what we can see. The numbers exist only in relation to the system from which they derive; they are not an abstract reality.

In philosophy these are commonplace observations, but in business and politics they are not. The accountants "certify" the numbers, then everyone can act on them; that's the prevailing thought.

The accounting profession has encouraged us to think this way. It gives accountants power and importance—which the world otherwise doesn't accord them—and it leads to their methods not being questioned. It also leads accountants to be sued and badgered by Congress when things unexpectedly go wrong.

Most accountants know better. They understand the inherent limitations of a system they call GAAP; they understand the inherent limitations of an "audit." In order to convey these limitations without giving up too much of the profession's mystique, the accountants are forever tinkering with their "form of opinion." The accountants don't "certify" anything. They "opine," like lawyers. And they opine only that the annexed financial statements have been prepared in accordance with a set of rules, not that they are fair, are true, or present a realistic picture. A CPA is an accountant who has a certificate, not a person who certifies.

Accountants are trained to follow the systems laid down by the profession, which are embodied in GAAP and in the auditing principles that also are known as "generally accepted." The accountants who audit corporations aren't philosophers. Their job is to prepare the shadows that we are going to see on the wall of the cave.

THE SHORTCOMINGS OF GAAP

GAAP was the system that accountants used to prepare the shadows which described S&Ls in the 1970s. GAAP wasn't perfect, as we noted in Chapter 2. It didn't reflect market values, so it didn't really tell you what would happen if you sold assets to pay liabilities.

That's a serious shortcoming. The system didn't tell the user something that the user really wanted to know. Indeed, most economists would say that GAAP *prevented* the system from telling the user the *only* thing he or she really cared about: Was the institution solvent on a market value basis? Could the institution pay all its creditors by using its existing assets?

If GAAP hadn't had this inherent shortcoming, one can argue, the Congress wouldn't have imposed deposit interest rate ceilings in 1966, because the S&Ls' assets still would have been underwater and everyone would have seen that they were quickly becoming insolvent. The accounting would have shown that this type of market regulation couldn't work.

But wait a minute. That's not necessarily true. You're valuing the asset side of the balance sheet but not the liability side. Sure, the assets would have a lower value on the balance sheet, but so might the liabilities. If you're going to use market value accounting, you have to value both sides of the balance sheet. And if you put a ceiling on deposit rates, then the value of the deposit is higher to the S&L than its face value, which means that the deposits should be reflected on the balance sheet in a *lower* amount. How much lower depends upon how long you assume the regulations will stay in place and whether competing, unregulated investments will draw the deposits away.

So the matter of market value accounting isn't so simple. How are the accountants going to make the necessary assumptions to reach a true market value? Are they going to do it individually? By firm? All together? By regulation? Whichever method they use, will market value accounting be any more precise than GAAP? At least with GAAP we know what we're getting.

WHY NOT RAP?

The Bank Board people went through all this in the early 1980s. It's not new. They concluded basically that since market value accounting was difficult to achieve and GAAP was so flawed, they could fuzz up the numbers further. Hence goodwill accounting, deferred loss accounting, appraised equity capital, five-year averaging, 2 percent loan fee recognition, and some lesser deviations. In the aggregate, the deviations led to a totally misleading picture of the S&L industry. It allayed fears; it made it hard for regulators to act to protect the system; it made Congress incredulous when it was told about the problem. It obscured the most important fact of all: FSLIC wasn't doing its job, and *couldn't* do it because it didn't have enough money.

ACCOUNTING CAN'T KEEP UP WITH TECHNOLOGY

Even without RAP, accounting for S&Ls wouldn't have been easy in the 1980s. Things were changing too fast. There were too many new financial instruments, too many new hedging techniques. The FASB's Emerging Issues Task Force, created in 1984, spent over half of its time for its first four years dealing with S&L-related accounting problems. The ADC loan and loan fee issues discussed in Chapter 6 were the biggest issues, but almost every time Wall Street came out with a new mortgage derivative, it caused a new accounting problem. The accountants were caught time and again not knowing what to do with the uncertain cash flows. Present value? Deferral? Estimation? Impact of limited markets? Correlation? Interest method? Level yield method? How do you decide what kind of shadows to throw on the wall when borrowers' conduct keeps changing the cash flows? Where do you get reliable statistics? How do you make reliable assumptions?

The Franklin Savings case illustrates the problems. When we last saw its chairman, Ernie Fleischer, he was on the stand in a Kansas courtroom trying to get his S&L back. He had engaged in the most complex hedging operation ever. His accountants had approved his hedge accounting, saying there was a "high correlation" between the value movements of the hedge and the value movements of the hedged assets. The OTS had disagreed and had taken him over as a consequence.

Both sides called experts at the trial to show whether or not there was a high correlation. The judge heard all kinds of esoteric testimony about methods of measurement. What, the court wanted to know, was the proper treatment under GAAP? It wasn't cut and dried, because the whole area was too new. The types of instruments were changing too fast. The judge eventually ruled in Fleischer's favor—effectively making a decision that there was a "high correlation"—and ordered the OTS to give Franklin back to its stockholders.[1]

We can't let a judge's decision on accounting—right or wrong—determine whether an $11 billion publicly owned S&L lives or dies. The institution, the public, and the regulator need to know in advance what the rules are. Nor can we blame the accountants for not making clearer rules. The accountants had propounded a rule—called FAS 80—only a few years earlier that covered the subject and said clearly that a "high correlation" was necessary to defer losses. There just hadn't been time for practice, literature, and debate to clearly formulate more specific accounting rules for every type of hedge.

This situation poses a real problem for all depository institutions that invest in mortgages. If they don't hedge, they incur large interest rate risks. If they do hedge, they can be second-guessed when they use or invent new hedges. Reluctantly, the answer has to be that an insured institution can't defer losses on a hedge unless the insurer has approved the correlation of the hedge in advance. Then we won't have terrible surprises. The financial world will move more slowly and uninsured institutions will have a theoretical advantage over insured ones. But the public's interest in certainty has to take precedence.

MARKET VALUE ACCOUNTING

The need for certainty also will drive S&Ls and other financial institutions in the direction of market value accounting. We noted some of the practical problems with market value accounting earlier in this chapter. But nearly all commentators and regulators agree that market value accounting for banks and S&Ls is desirable in theory. Quite simply, market value accounting tells you whether the enterprise has more financial assets than it does liabilities and, on a periodic basis, the changes in that mix tell you whether the enterprise is making money. If we can know those things, the shadows we see will be more lifelike. In addition, if the deposit insurer is encouraged to close institutions a little short of market-value balance sheet insolvency, the insurer will lose money only when the assets or liabilities have been wrongly valued or markets change so fast that asset values decline between the time the institution is taken over and the time it is sold.

However, nobody knows whether this utopian talk about market value accounting can work in practice because several troublesome valuation problems interfere with having confidence that we can know market values.

Some assets and liabilities are easy to value because there are active markets that price them every day. Treasury securities, some corporate bonds, many types of mortgage-based securities, and even home mortgages fall into this category. Look at the screen every day and you know the market values.

A second category of assets poses "thin market" problems. That is, these assets have markets in which they are traded and you can get quotes, but so few trades occur that a meaningful market price often can't be found. This might be the case with junk bonds, participations in loans to major companies, Third World debt, or consumer loans. These assets have credit judgment components that make different buyers react differently. Although there is a market in these assets, we don't have a good theoretical framework that would allow us to mark them to market in a way which wouldn't be subject to volatile swings related to the valuation method rather than to the market. Work has to be done here before market value accounting is practical.

Marking ordinary commercial loans to market is even more difficult because they don't have an organized market. Construction loans, working capital loans, and inventory loans all depend upon the credit judgment made by the banker. The market won't give much credence to that credit judgment unless the banker provides a guarantee. Therefore you can't find a true market value for these loans. They may be worth more or less than face value.

GAAP has tried to deal with the credit judgment problem by means of loan loss reserves. They are supposed to reflect the likely losses in the loan portfolio. The only problem with that approach is that we *know* from experience that it doesn't work. Loan losses in excess of reserves keep on popping up and getting banks in trouble.

We could, of course, say flatly that no S&L—even no bank—can make a loan that doesn't have a secondary market and, therefore, a reasonably ascertainable market value. But that would take banks out of one of the two fundamental functions of the banking business: the business of intermediation. We still need banks to make loans to home builders and small and medium-sized businesses that don't have access to the capital markets through Wall Street. The Street will rate only credits that are big enough to pay their fees. The banks still seem to provide cheaper credit to small and medium-sized businesses than lenders who can't take deposits. (Individuals may no longer need banks for credit because uniform credit scoring practices determine what almost anyone will lend. Consumer lending may not be done well—and I suspect that it is priced wrong—but from a pure economics point of view, banks don't have to be able to do it.)

We can't embrace market value accounting as all it's cracked up to be theoretically until we can solve the loan loss reserves problem. But that isn't all. We will have even greater difficulty valuing the liability side of the balance sheet because many types of bank accounts provide options to the depositor. CDs are the easiest accounts to deal with. They come due on a known date and they stand either below or above the market rate. They may have some additional value as representing "customers," but that value probably is insignificant if CDs are the only relationship between the customer and the institution.

But how do you value passbook accounts, money market accounts, and checking accounts, all of which pay less interest than CDs, all of which the depositor can withdraw on demand, but all of which depositors tend to leave at "their" bank for long periods of time? These deposits could be sold to another bank (along with the branch, if it is efficient) for somewhere between 3 percent and 10 percent of their amount. That value should be included in the market value of the enterprise, but it is subject to wide fluctuation as markets and business fashions change. We need a methodology for valuing these deposits before we can have a good market value accounting system.

Market value accounting for financial institutions will come—and it will come fairly soon. But unless these practical problems are overcome, the shadows that market value accounting throws on the wall may be no more helpful than the shadows that GAAP throws. And some people in the cave will mistake the new shadows for reality.

ADVANCED COUNTING—SOME LIMITATIONS OF STATISTICAL STUDIES

Accountants and economists usually know that they are merely projecting shadows on the wall. Nevertheless, they cling to their numbers and use them as if they were real. They do this because they want to be engaged in scientific inquiry (which by definition is quantitative) rather than in making subjective judgments about shadows with hazy outlines. Numbers, we might observe, obscure ignorance. In the dialogue about S&Ls over the years, this methodology of using sophisticated computer programs to manipulate meaningless numbers has led to numerous nonsensical studies and conclusions.

Garbage in, garbage out, the cliché goes. And the data about S&Ls were no good at all. The only data that existed came from the FHLBB. Therefore income data included 2 percent loan fees, skimmed loan and securities portfolios, purchase accounting shenanigans, and inadequate loan loss reserves. Balance sheet data included the fruits of all this. You couldn't tell who was making money and who wasn't, or who was solvent and who wasn't. You couldn't even tell who had failed and who hadn't, because the Bank Board continued to run failed institutions.

Bank Board economists worked with this data, of course. But so did the GAO when Congress asked it questions about S&Ls. And the good people at the GAO took the data seriously for a long time and made estimates for Congress and drew conclusions that didn't work. They did note that they were starting with Bank Board data and that it had shortcomings. But Congress pays attention only to the conclusion — the ten-second sound bite. The conclusions looked concrete and numerical to Congress.

We need to learn when statistics are meaningful and when they aren't, which requires judgment, logic — and some guesswork. Several books on S&Ls contain elaborate statistical analyses based on quicksand. (I'm guilty, too. The GAAP numbers for insolvent S&Ls, which I *had* to use because they were the only numbers available, portrayed only what was known at the time. They are fuzzy shadows from which analysis was impossible.)

Sometimes, of course, statistics don't work at all. For example, in 1990 the *New York Times* reported on a study to the effect that the FSLIC bailout would result in a huge transfer of wealth from the Northeast to the Southwest. The study, done by Professor Edward W. Hill of Cleveland State University, found that the FSLIC bailout would cause about a $50 billion transfer from other states to Texas because depositors of failed Texas institutions would have received that much more than the Texas taxpayers would pay.[2]

The numbers from which Professor Hill derived his conclusions appear to be correct. The idea that there may be a wealth transfer among areas of the country is interesting and may have merit. But the reasoning — and therefore the conclusion — doesn't work. Here's why:

- The depositors got back only their money plus interest. They got a little extra interest for the "Texas premium," but that's relatively immaterial. They didn't get any wealth transfer by getting their money back.

- Nobody — including Texas residents — would have put money in those Texas S&Ls if they hadn't had federal deposit insurance in the first place.

- Many of the depositors weren't from Texas. The Texas institutions had over 50 percent brokered deposits from elsewhere in the country.

- The money didn't go to the depositors. It went to build all the buildings that nobody needed.

Nevertheless, the idea is intriguing. Texas does have all those buildings that it wouldn't otherwise have. It does have some residents who would have left if the building boom hadn't kept going beyond its time. Of course a lot of home values were destroyed. And a lot of people were laid off in the bust. The idea is worth exploring even though it may not amount to much. But don't jump to Professor Hill's conclusion that "the solution will have wide-ranging implications by shifting vast amounts of wealth between the states."

SUITS AGAINST ACCOUNTING FIRMS

Partly because the limitations of counting aren't well understood, accountants almost always are sued when their clients fail. With hindsight, it usually appears that the accountants who audited the failed firm's books knew or should have known of the problems that caused the failure long before the failure occurred. Various parties, who might have lost less money had the failure been discovered earlier, therefore sue the accountants because they and their insurance carriers remain solvent when no one else who may have responsibility can pay the bill.

Almost every major accounting firm in the United States has been sued in connection with S&L failures. Almost every firm has been sued by the FSLIC, RTC, FDIC, or some other federal regulator for failing to properly report on the financial statements of some S&L.

The wrongdoing that is alleged against accountants in these suits runs the gamut from intentional fraud (in a few cases) to underestimating loan loss reserves. We already know about the loan loss reserves problem. Nobody is very good at guessing what loan loss reserves should be.

The in-between kinds of allegations are the most interesting, that is, the allegations that accountants permitted S&Ls to recognize income from transactions that lacked substance. These allegations cause problems for the accounting profession because often accountants do have knowledge of facts that rightly lead them to suspect that transactions do not have the kind of substance which is required for them to be recognized as transactions that can generate income under GAAP. For example, an accountant may suspect that two transactions are linked, as Judge Sporkin found that transactions were linked in the Lincoln case.

Judge Sporkin described a transaction in which Lincoln sold 1,000 acres of land in Hidden Valley, Arizona, to a company called Wescon for $14 million. Wescon paid for the land with $3.5 million in cash and a nonrecourse note for $10.5 million. Lincoln's cost of the property had been $3 million, so it took an $11 million gain, which was appropriate under GAAP, since Wescon had made a 25 percent down payment in cash. At the same time, however, Lincoln was making a loan of $20 million to E. C. Garcia & Co. and Garcia was passing along $3.5 million of that to Wescon to make the down payment to Lincoln.[3] Those connections made Lincoln's recognition of the $11 million of profit distinctly improper under GAAP. That income recognition looks like fraud to me.

But did Lincoln's auditors know? They could have seen that the sale of land to Wescon and the loan to Garcia closed on the same day. Were there any other facts that should have led them to believe that the two were connected?

Judge Sporkin doesn't cite any. If there were no other grounds for suspicion, we can't, and shouldn't, expect that auditors will probe possible connections between all contemporaneous transactions. If there were additional grounds for suspicion, however, the accountant's responsibility would be to investigate the transactions until being satisfied that the linkage either existed or didn't exist. The auditors could do this by, for example, insisting upon seeing evidence of the source of Wescon's down payment.

On these kinds of issues, the accounting profession's role tends to break down at times of stress. The accounting *rules* require the accounting firm to be completely independent, while the imperatives of the accounting *business* require that the firm have clients in order to prosper. When the client assures the accountant that two transactions are unrelated but the accountant, after investigation, believes but can't prove that the two transactions *may be* related, the accounting firm's choice becomes very uncomfortable. It is a choice between (a) telling the client that he or she is a liar and (b) finding some basis for going along with the client's accounting treatment. Accountants who call their clients liars don't have those clients very long.

Many accountants did their jobs in auditing S&Ls and lost clients as a result. Lincoln changed auditors three times in the few years that Keating owned it. Many other S&Ls that turned to fraud to create income also changed accountants frequently. Sometimes the incoming accountants weren't suspicious enough. My guess is that, in many cases, S&L accountants went along with accounting treatments that weren't warranted by what they believed were the facts. But they couldn't prove what they believed, so they kept quiet. Our accounting theory says that in such cases the accountant has a duty to spell out the problem in the opinion on the financial statements, which of course the accountants didn't do in these cases. If the accountants really stop believing the client, they have a duty to resign and not opine at all. Too few firms were willing to take this course of action. Some of them will have big liabilities as a result.

Accountants can audit honest businesses well. But auditing doesn't catch insider fraud very well because to do that the auditor would have to investigate every transaction. The time spent doing that would cost so much that few honest businesses could still be profitable. That's one of the limitations of counting, but nobody has ever wanted to believe that.

23 Avoid Complexity That No One Can Understand

The American bank regulatory system, already burdened with state–federal duality, separate holding company and bank-level regulators, and separate regulators for banks and thrifts, became progressively more complex in the 1980s, as creative bankers and lawyers peeled back the Glass–Steagall Act barriers between banking and the securities business, and investment bankers and the government created active secondary markets for financial instruments such as mortgages, car loans, and credit card loans. The accountants, the regulators, and bank and S&L managements struggled to keep up with the pace of change and the new complexities. Even the best lawyers in Washington, New York, and Los Angeles didn't understand all of the legal intricacies. Nobody understood all of the risk and reward features inherent in the accounting, legal, and cash flow characteristics of the new instruments and businesses.

Bank and S&L managements could see their traditional spreads eroding in this world of new competition and complexity. Depositors demanded higher interest rates because open market competition offered high interest rates on mutual funds and government bonds. Many S&Ls drove rates up further by trying to grow out of their problems. The best corporate borrowers no longer needed to borrow from banks because Wall Street offered them the option of direct borrowing from the public without banking intermediation. To get their business, bankers had to offer to lend at lower rates. Bank managements could see that they had to do something different in order to make money in the new competitive climate. They could take old-fashioned interest rate risk, like the risks of short-funding fixed-rate mortgage loans that brought S&Ls

low in 1981–82. They could shade their credit standards a little bit to compete with other lenders. They could lend a little more on this property, up to a little higher leverage ratio to that business. They could try to get ahead of the markets by buying new instruments as soon as they were invented, while few buyers understood them and therefore the pricing was better for buyers. Or they could go into new businesses, such as selling securities, insurance, and travel services to consumers or, for the bigger players, competing with Wall Street by providing merger and acquisition advisory services, underwriting capabilities, and LBO financing.

Many thrifts, as we have seen, took the extra credit risks, either in the real estate markets or by buying LBO junk bonds. Others, like Franklin, played the complex Wall Street game. A few also played what became known as the political "rat ball" game. They became masters of the legal and regulatory complexities in order to fashion discontinuities in the law so that their activities would be less restricted than their competitors'.

Unless you were a lawyer who dedicated his or her life to understanding all the illogical complexities, you wouldn't know from day to day

Which kind of institution could engage in what kind of securities or insurance activities

Whose CMOs and repos would be treated as borrowings and whose as sales

Who had what capital requirements or even what some of the capital requirements meant

What the consequences of various kinds of loan participations would be if the lead lender went under.

Accountants, as we have seen, couldn't formulate new rules fast enough or with enough certainty to properly portray what was going on, especially in the face of regulators like the FHLBB constantly making rules to make S&Ls look better. Not surprisingly, Congress couldn't understand what was going on. It couldn't sort out the public interest; it could only understand that lobbyists on different sides were saying different things. Often even the various regulators couldn't agree on what public policy ought to be. Meanwhile, the Reagan administration basically plowed ahead with its free market theories.

I am not from the Flat Earth Society. You can't go back to some earlier, simpler time. But we do need to simplify the way our financial system works and how we regulate it. Every federal panel that has examined the question over the last quarter of a century has come to this conclusion despite active lobbying by all the interest groups that wanted to keep their fiefdoms. Simplification should be possible in the political climate following the S&L debacle. FIRREA grasped some of the nettles by creating a single deposit insurer, by moving the OTS under the Treasury, and by bringing S&L and bank capital requirements closer together. The Congress still needs to reexamine Glass–Steagall and the Bank and S&L Holding Company Acts, as well as to complete deposit insurance reform.

We shouldn't want to stamp out innovation, but banking works best when it sticks to traditional values, even though those values change over time. This is because spreads are inherently thin, and high leverage is the nature of the business, which magnifies the consequences of mistakes and turns them from problems into disasters. Banks weren't meant to take entrepreneurial risks.

You can't regulate what you can't understand. Ed Gray's experience proves that. The Franklin Savings brouhaha proves that. Since we need to regulate our banks and S&Ls, we need to keep their businesses understandable by the regulators and those Congressional leaders who really want to understand.

Wall Street whiz kids and their computers won't stop inventing new ways to chop up loans and sell them—we wouldn't want to stop that innovation—but we need to impose some restraints on banks and S&Ls using those new instruments until the regulators and accountants are ready to deal with them. Yes, that will give unregulated enterprises a theoretical advantage; but if the government provides the safety net, it has to have the ability, as well as the theoretical right, to regulate activities in the interest of safety and soundness.

At the same time, Congress and the regulators have to make the regulations more consistent. Many sound institutions failed and honest people got hurt by the ways the rules were changed over time. The best example is the combination of changing rules about goodwill and changing capital requirements. The FHLBB induced many of its soundest thrift institutions to become acquirers of failing institutions in the early 1980s on promises of goodwill treatment and, if necessary, capital forbearance. We can easily say today that managements should have known that their institutions were going to be weakened by taking on all the goodwill, but few saw it that way at the time. Their regulator was *asking* them to help out. Their regulator was telling them their good deeds wouldn't be forgotten. Their regulator was telling them they would *benefit* by expanding their franchise. Then FIRREA cut them off at the ankles. It said you couldn't count goodwill as an asset, even if it came onto your books as part of a transaction in which you saved the FSLIC money in dealing with a failed institution. It said you couldn't rely on any promises about capital that your regulator had made. It said if you had issued preferred stock to the public to beef up your capital, it no longer counted unless it was the right kind of preferred stock. And it said if you couldn't comply with the new capital requirements, you should be taken over. Yes, you would have a chance to propose a plan to the new OTS, but the climate didn't encourage the OTS to take any chances by approving many plans.

Those kinds of policy changes which ruin private institutions that people have worked hard to maintain shouldn't happen. These policy changes happened in an extreme time, when the Congress was angry because it had been duped, when it was angry because it had no choice but to pay a bill that, ostrich-like, it hadn't previously understood was the government's, when it wanted to bash S&Ls just to bash them. The next time around we should try for more regulatory stability. The inconsistency increased the cost, both in money and in the rips in the social fabric.

But to be more consistent, we will have to be simpler as well. Fewer regulators, fewer different kinds of regulated institutions, fewer different kinds of institutions protected by the federal safety net. We will need to put most of the innovation and complexity firmly outside the safety net. We will need to put it into a world where we rely on disclosure and informed decision making rather than on government control, even though we know that bad decisions still will be made and people and institutions will be hurt when the complexity doesn't work.

Will we still have a dual banking system? FIRREA already says that state-chartered S&Ls can't have powers that national banks don't have. Should that be extended to state-chartered commercial banks? At the moment, there's no compelling case one way or the other. But because state-chartered S&Ls caused a lot more of the damage than federally chartered S&Ls, and because the existence of the dual banking system adds considerable complexity, we should have a vigorous and focused debate on the subject, if such a thing is possible.

24 Supervision and Enforcement

Having represented regulators for much of my legal career, I am reluctant to criticize them too sharply for lax supervision in individual cases. The facts about a failing institution that later seem so simple and clear, in practice accumulate over a period of time and lie in a relatively unorganized mass until someone has the instinct to cause the process of compilation and organization to be done. The tugs of regulatory routines, politics, too many institutions to regulate, and the criticism that's heaped on regulators when institutions fail all contribute to the inertia that defers the hard analytical work.

In the mid-1980s, budgetary constraints on the FHLBB exacerbated these natural tendencies. There simply were too many troubled institutions to be supervised by too few relatively low-paid government employees.

Nevertheless, the FHLBB's supervisory performance has to be rated as abysmal. There was no follow-through. Nobody seemed to be keeping track of what was going on. People like Knapp and Keating won important approvals by making promises that didn't get enforced. The examiners complained about Silverado for years, and the supervisors did nothing. All the Texas high fliers looked just like Empire of Mesquite, but the Bank Board didn't set up a system to watch them.

Every single one of the big loss cases could have been held to a small fraction of its cost by prompt supervisory action. As a regulator, you have power to go in and investigate anything you want to investigate. If you don't do it after you have suspicions, it's your own fault. If you don't have suspicions when the red flags are flying, that's your own fault, too. And when you find things that are wrong, you can use a lot of tools, ranging from reading the riot act to going on record with boards of directors to formal enforcement actions to termination-of-insurance proceedings. You don't have to accept "no" for an answer when you direct a regulated entity to change its course of conduct. You just have to be forceful — ask the high flyers who tried to ignore Joe Selby in Texas.

THE LIMITS OF SUPERVISION

Despite regulators' enormous inherent powers, supervisory actions have their limitations. Often they can't prevent banks or S&Ls from failing. And often they can appear to *make* banks or S&Ls fail.

As we have seen, S&L failures result from courses of conduct set in motion years before the failures occur. When an examiner sees a problem early, often he can do little but watch, like a spectator at a Greek tragedy. You know how it ends, but there's nothing you can do about it. Loans committed in year one go bad in year three. You can't prevent the loans from going bad if in year two you discover that the underwriting was flawed in the first place. The best you can do is make sure that the underwriting standards are fixed so that additional bad loans don't compound the problem.

Sometimes examiners and supervisors save banks by seeing the bad lending patterns before it's too late. Sometimes the board of directors can take control and turn the institution around; I've seen it happen. But more often, the slide has gone too far before the lending pattern is stopped. That doesn't mean the regulators blew it. The bankers blew it. The examiners can catch things only periodically.

Moreover, when examiners catch loan problems late in the cycle, they are faced with difficult issues of evaluation and forbearance. When they force write-downs to current market values, they often appear to be causing the failure. Bankers frequently will argue, as the Texas S&L managers did, that temporary regional economic problems have caused a similarly temporary decline in the value of the collateral. The values will turn around with time, they will argue.

Whether they should heed arguments about temporary declines in value is probably the most delicate issue that regulators face. We have said, on the one hand, that capital rules need to be enforced because failing to enforce them leads to moral hazard. On the other hand, the forbearances that FDIC provided to American farm banks seem by and large to have worked. Many of those banks have recovered. The rural towns they serve still have local banks. The effective forbearances that big American banks received when they were allowed to take only gradual losses on their Third World debt also seem to have worked. The American economy is better off for not having seen household name banks like Bank of America and Manufacturers Hanover become insolvent. The human institutions established in the stable postwar world simply couldn't cope with the instability unleashed by free market economic policies in the 1980s.

TO FORBEAR OR NOT TO FORBEAR?

Forbearance has its fashions. In 1982 and 1987 Congress forced forbearance for thrift institutions on reluctant regulators. In 1989 Congress was angry at thrifts and went in the other direction. Today it is fashionable to demand that fixed rules determine when regulators take over banks and S&Ls—and many in Congress support that idea.

However, Congress isn't equipped to make forbearance decisions. Our flexible laws have worked pretty well for the banking system. The FDIC, the Fed, and the Comptroller of the Currency have made subtle forbearance decisions over the years that generally have served the nation well. The FDIC hasn't been endangered by those kinds of decisions, even though for other reasons it now needs to be recapitalized. What happened to the FSLIC doesn't argue for taking away the regulators' discretion about when to close an institution. What happened to the S&Ls and the FSLIC was caused mostly by Congress's first preventing failures from being declared and then not providing enough money because it was unwilling to recognize the problem. Those are not causes which suggest that bank regulators shouldn't be allowed to forbear from taking over a fragile institution if they are prepared to supervise it carefully and try to nurse it back to health.

My plea to Congress would be (1) let regulators be the judges of when failure occurs; (2) give them enough money so that they don't have to make the decision to defer a takeover because of a lack of funds; and (3) insist through the confirmation process that presidents appoint pros. Many scholars whom I respect would disagree with these conclusions because they assert that forbearance almost always is costly and that the regulators have a natural proclivity to overuse their discretion to forbear.

THE LIMITS OF ENFORCEMENT

The S&L debacle has led to predictable "get tough" talk. Institute enforcement actions! Bring criminal prosecutions! Bomb the bastards back to the Stone Age!

Enforcement and criminal sanctions serve three purposes, in order of importance: (1) remedial, (2) deterrent, and (3) retributive.

Remedial actions can save institutions by removing an individual from office or by changing its course of conduct. If remedial actions don't save the institution, at least they will save the insurer money. The remedial process works both formally and informally when regulators get tough. (Regulators can easily get carried away with their power, of course.)

The deterrent effects of criminal sanctions and civil penalties are significant. A board of directors' conduct is more vigilant when members have been reminded of their potential liabilities. Those liabilities don't, however, necessarily have to be criminal in order to be effective. The criminalization of business judgment—except where there is fraudulent intent and personal gain—tends to overdeter, in that it deters responsible people from participating in the activity. Therefore we need to draw a line that says a director can't have criminal responsibility unless he or she does intentional wrong for personal gain.

Retribution is vastly overrated. Its satisfaction is small and, on a broad scale, nobody knows it happened. Nobody knows how many people who defrauded S&Ls have already gone to jail—over 200—or that they have been receiving stiff sentences, topped by the 30 years given to Woody Lemons, who was President of Vernon. We should punish the wrongdoers, of course. Probably another 300–500 convictions will result from all the investigations presently going forward. They will be a sad aftermath that will accomplish little except to cost society more money for incarceration.

An ounce of preventive medicine really would have been worth more than a pound of flesh.

25 Regulation Can't Tame Technology or Market Forces

Those who would regulate financial institutions need to know the difference between building a dike to keep the sea out of the Dutch lowlands and sitting in a grand chair like Canute the Dane and bidding the sea to stand still. Technology and market forces are like the sea. They will wash over and drown anyone foolish enough to think they can be held back.

Technology and market forces overwhelmed the system of interest rate regulation in the late 1970s. They overwhelmed the single-family mortgage business in the mid-1980s. They are overwhelming the intermediary function of commercial banks today.

We have observed, however, that banks need to be regulated, both because of deposit insurance and because of the psychology of money. Regulation can't hold technology back, but it does need to be like the building of protective dikes that permit the sea of technology and market forces to flow elsewhere while the regulated system adjusts. Franklin Savings, we observed for example, probably shouldn't have been permitted to use a hedge until the regulators and its accountants agreed on its treatment. The hedge would have existed and would have been used by others first. Franklin would not have had the benefit of being first in the market. But that's a price one has to pay for being a depository institution, we could say.

On whom should we rely to know the difference between a protective dike and a dangerous, if magisterial, gesture? Reluctantly, I say it has to be the regulators. They are in the best of all the bad positions to judge.

These thoughts put pressure on the professionalism and judgment of the regulators. They have to be given flexible powers, and they have to know when technology can be used safely. The Congress can't make hard and fast rules on these subjects because it can't make adjustments as technology changes.

Technology could make banks obsolete in the next generation or so. We shouldn't try to stop that from happening. We should instead try to let the banks themselves evolve as the needs of commerce dictate, while at the same time protecting ourselves from another disaster like the failure of FSLIC. We botched the S&Ls' transition. That's no reason to play Canute the Dane with the banks.

26 Deposit Insurance Reform

Economists have talked about reforming the federal deposit insurance system almost since the day deposit insurance legislation was passed in 1933. The insurance, they have pointed out ad nauseam, is mispriced, provides incentive to bankers to take unreasonable risks, and, when combined with an accounting system that doesn't tell you when an institution is economically insolvent, is guaranteed to result in big losses for the insurer when institutions get into trouble. Nevertheless, over the years, Congress has done almost nothing to change the system except to multiply the insurers' responsibility by raising the original $2,500 of insurance per account to $5,000 to $10,000 to $20,000 to $40,000, and finally in 1980 to $100,000. The system didn't look broken, so until a federal insurer went broke, Congress and the executive branch didn't have the sense of urgency that's necessary to get major legislation passed. Now, for the first time, it looks like some reforms will be made.

Whatever reforms come about, Congress should try to preserve the two essential roles of deposit insurance that caused it to be enacted and at which it has succeeded: preventing runs on banks and protecting individual depositors from losing their savings. Congress shouldn't deprive the people of the United States of these benefits of stability.

But deposit insurance *is* a problem. It has exposed the government to badly managed risks, and it did cause $150 billion or more of taxpayer losses. The bulk of these losses could have been avoided—and maybe the whole loss could have been avoided—if:

    deposit interest rates hadn't been controlled in 1966

    the insurer had been given enough money to deal with the failed institu-
        tions as they failed

    we had had a reasonable market value accounting system

    we had had capital requirements that weren't so squishy.

Whatever solutions are proposed, they need to deal with these issues, some of which have already been addressed. We don't have interest rate controls (which doesn't mean that we won't have them again when some apparent national priority seems to demand stability when economic forces are producing volatility), and the federal regulatory agencies have increased their capital requirements and the vigor with which they enforce them. We haven't yet dealt with the market value accounting issue, nor has Congress understood yet that the deposit insurance contract obligates the insurer to the people of the country, and that Congress's normal desire to control expenditures can only make the insurer postpone—and therefore almost always increase the cost of—dealing with failed institutions. Just as Treasury bills have to be paid when due, so does deposit insurance.

    The debate about reform has focused on a series of proposals including:

- Private deposit insurance
- Coinsurance by bank syndicates
- Risk-based premiums
- "Narrow bank" proposals
- 100 percent insurance combined with high capital and market value accounting
- Mechanisms that decree a specified percentage of loss for depositors who have over a specified amount on deposit in the failed bank
- Reducing coverage to below $100,000 per account
- Reducing pass-through benefits
- Reducing coverage to a per person multiple of $100,000 in each bank or all banks
- High capital solutions

Each of these proposals would correct some part of the problem, but each also would either generate new risks or deprive society of some of the benefits of the banking system or deposit insurance.

PRIVATE DEPOSIT INSURANCE

These proposals basically would replace federal government deposit insurance with insurance provided by private insurance companies, although most of the proponents concede that a federal safety net under the private insurers would be necessary to prevent runs.

The private insurer, proponents say, will price deposit insurance better than the government can, and will protect itself from bank insolvencies better than the government will. Government regulation inherently can't be efficient. It tends to homogenize the regulated entities and to stifle innovation and competition. With private insurance, we can have a multiplicity of regulatory schemes in competition with each other, which will promote innovation and competition at the bank level.

These very attractive proposals seem to me not to deal well with the practical necessity of the insurer to be able to declare a failure—which in the case of a bank has wide consequences—or with how private insurance companies can manage the billions of dollars of risks inherent in bank insurance or with how the federal government—given that a federal safety net will still be necessary—will regulate the insurers as well as the banks. These issues are likely to create complexity that no one can understand.

I also am not sure that private deposit insurance will deal with the most fundamental deposit insurance issue, which is that depositors can't protect themselves. Except for giant corporations whose finance staffs can do financial analyses of banks and insurers, no one can tell whether a bank is safe. Rumor and innuendo will dominate the public mind. The facts, even if they can be known and assimilated, are difficult to understand. The idea that depositors can provide appropriate market discipline, which was very much in vogue in the early days of deposit interest rate deregulation, doesn't work at all. Indeed, it probably was responsible for some of the regulatory laxity that permitted the mischief.

I would reject private insurance as not being realistic.

COINSURANCE SCHEMES

The coinsurance idea combines banks' guaranteeing each other as a first recourse upon failure with a federal deposit insurance safety net as a last recourse. As advocated by Bert Ely, the concept would allow bank syndicates to create themselves to provide coinsurance of their members. The coinsurers would regulate each other's conduct in the interest of safety.[1]

With all due deference to Mr. Ely's knowledge and insight into the problem, this scheme would invite collusion, discrimination, and complexity that no one would understand.

RISK-BASED PREMIUMS

Imposition of deposit insurance premiums based on risks inherent in a bank's or S&L's assets, liabilities, and capital structure has been attractive to regulators and economists for a long time. Dick Pratt, Ed Gray, and Bill Seidman, for example, all have called for risk-based premiums. Banks won't take undue risks, they reason, if they have to pay for them. The insurer should collect a premium that is appropriate to the risks inherent in the insured, and risk-based premiums would be more like the way a private market would function.

These are attractive concepts. But we already have risk-based capital requirements that attempt to accomplish similar goals by assigning different levels of risk for different types of assets and by requiring different levels of capital to be maintained for the different levels of risk. Do we need to do it twice? Why not do it right once?

Moreover, risk-based insurance premium systems tend to extract larger premiums from banks that have gotten into trouble and therefore need more capital. They therefore have the perverse effect of preventing banks from raising capital when they need it most.

I would put the emphasis on getting the capital regulations right and forgo the risk-based premiums.

"NARROW BANK" PROPOSALS

The "narrow bank" proposal, which can have more and less extreme variations, basically says that if a bank wants to offer the benefits of deposit insurance to its depositors, then it will have to agree to a very limited set of permissible investments. At the extreme, the proposal would permit that narrow bank to invest only in U.S. government securities whose maturities match the maturities of the deposits. The narrow bank would have no credit risk and no interest rate risk, and therefore the insurer wouldn't have any risk. Narrow banks wouldn't fail.[2]

Again, there are attractions to the concept. People would have a safe place to save and we wouldn't have to worry about the deposit insurer losing money.

The narrow bank proposal has several problems, however. One, the narrow banks wouldn't satisfy savers very well because they would be able to pay only low rates of interest. Two, they wouldn't perform an intermediary function, so some kinds of credit, such as small business credit, would need to find new (probably more expensive) sources. And three, uninsured banks that offered higher interest rates would spring up and induce people who couldn't protect themselves to make deposits in them because they would pay 1 percent or 2 percent higher interest. Those uninsured banks would be subject to runs.

I am very attracted to the narrow bank concept because it preserves most of the benefits of deposit insurance while letting the market operate. I don't, however, yet believe that we need a solution as radical as the narrow bank.

100 PERCENT INSURANCE

Inherent in the narrow bank concept is the idea that you can insure all deposits in a bank, regardless of amount, if you make the bank safe enough. Some economists and former regulators—notably Larry White—argue that you can, and should, insure all deposits if you have good enough capital requirements and market value accounting.

White makes a compelling case in his book, *The S&L Debacle: Public Policy Lessons for Bank and Thrift Regulation,* that if you have market value accounting and high capital requirements—and a rule under which you close banks before their capital is exhausted—you can prevent losses by the insurer and can protect all depositors. As an added benefit, he says, you can do away with runs on big banks that now have high levels of uninsured deposits, and therefore you can solve the "too-big-to-fail" problem.

The "too-big-to-fail" problem has haunted politically sensitive regulators and Congressmen at least since the FDIC provided assistance to Continental Illinois Bank in Chicago in 1982 instead of taking it over. Continental, one of America's top ten banks and a favorite of foreign business depositors, got into trouble by participating in energy sector loans, primarily with a little bank called Penn Square in Oklahoma that failed amid charges of fraud. As Continental's involvement came to light, uninsured depositors from all over the world began withdrawing money. Within days, a run by wire surged through the Continental Illinois system.

The Fed provided liquidity to Continental to try to stem the run, but once rumors start that a big bank has lost a lot of money, corporate treasurers all over the world have to protect themselves by taking the uninsured money out. The FDIC was faced with a choice between taking Continental over and selling it with assistance to the buyer or propping it up. Bill Isaac, much against the conventional wisdom, chose to prop it up by injecting liquidity, effectively guaranteeing 100 percent of all deposits, and later providing equity assistance. As part of the process, the FDIC forced out senior management and took about 90 percent of Continental's stock for itself, thereby nationalizing it.

The FDIC's rationale for propping up Continental went something like this: Continental is a symbol of American banking to foreign customers. If we let Continental fail, then we cannot honor the deposits over $100,000. If we do that, we will destroy international confidence in the American banking system. Moreover, Continental has a valuable franchise whose value can't be fully realized by selling it to another bank.

Everyone quickly saw that this rationale would apply to every big bank in the country but couldn't apply to small banks. Congressmen, bankers, people from small towns where banks had failed, all decried the discrimination inherent in the fact that the deposit insurance system made some banks too big to fail. These cries took on more substance in 1990 when the FDIC quickly mirrored its decision not to protect deposits over $100,000 in the failed Freedom National Bank in Harlem with a decision to protect all deposits in Bank of New England after a run of uninsured deposits had started there. The uninsured depositors at Freedom had included minority businesses and churches, as well as the campaign funds of Representative Charles Rangel, one of the ranking members of the House Ways and Means Committee.

The 100 percent insurance proposal would solve the too-big-to-fail problem, White argues, because (1) when all deposits are insured, the impetus toward discrimination is reduced, and (2) with market value accounting and early action on failing institutions, the insurer will be able to deal with large failures in an orderly way without great cost.

The problem with this 100 percent insurance formulation is that it places too much reliance on the ability of market value accounting to accurately value assets at a time when they have to be sold. As we saw in the case of real estate lending in 1986–90, that's not necessarily true. We don't have a system that can accurately value assets in a falling market. We also have a series of laws that make it difficult for lenders to take title to collateral, which tends to exaggerate the falling market problem.

For these reasons, 100 percent insurance won't necessarily solve the too-big-to-fail problem. The insurer will still have pressures and incentives not to declare that prominent institutions have failed. Too-big-to-fail may be just one of those natural problems that can't be eliminated by any sensible mechanism—and that needn't be eliminated. As long as there are big banks, politics will from time to time determine that they can't be allowed to fail, regardless of whether the insurance mechanisms require that.

SPECIFIED PERCENT LOSS

Some of us with less faith in market value accounting than Larry White, who perhaps also have a little bit more belief that corporate treasurers can exercise some level of productive market discipline with respect to big banks, would modify the 100 percent proposal by saying that in any failure, any deposit over some fairly large number, such as $1 million, would be subject to a 2 percent to 4 percent forfeit at the time the failure was declared. The forfeit would be automatic upon declaration by the insurer, regardless of how the insurer dealt with the situation, even if it was by propping up a too-big-to-fail institution. Our hypothesis is that corporate treasurers will be careful, then, not to help weak banks grow out of control and that if corporations suffer losses in big failures, their losses won't be system-threatening.

LOWER INSURANCE COVERAGE

Many writers, noting as we have, that the increase to $100,000 of deposit insurance (1) came right before the S&L losses, (2) increased the amount of insured deposits (and therefore the potential insurance loss), and (3) wasn't the product of thought-out policy, argue that the insurance coverage should be decreased to $50,000 or $40,000 (where it was before 1980), or even lower.

This doesn't make sense because (1) people can't fend for themselves and evaluate an institution's chances of failure very far in advance, (2) we really *don't* want to throw the baby out with the bath water and promote runs, and (3) by now $100,000 is worth not much more than $40,000 was in 1980.

Many writers who favor lowering the insurance amount argue that the fast growth of little S&Ls in 1983–84 couldn't have been accomplished if the insurance limit had stayed at $40,000. They therefore hold the change responsible for a large part of the losses.

That argument is not correct. Those little S&Ls could have grown just as much if the deposit brokers had had to chop deposits into $40,000 chunks rather than $100,000 chunks. Yes, the cost per dollar of deposit would have been marginally higher, but since the high fliers were reporting earnings of 200–1,000 basis points at the time they were growing so fast, a few basis points of cost here or there wouldn't have made any difference to them. Once rates on accounts of under $100,000 had been effectively deregulated, the insurance level became relatively unimportant.

REDUCING PASS-THROUGH BENEFITS

One of the insurance factors that did make a big difference in S&Ls' ability to grow fast was the interpretation of the deposit insurance laws to permit coverage of group funds (such as pension funds and pooled accounts) in amounts of $100,000 per beneficiary. This allowed the managers of those group funds to exercise enormous power over weak S&Ls by being able to place funds with them at high rates without having to evaluate their creditworthiness.

It seemed sound to say that American workers shouldn't have their pension monies threatened by their union representatives having chosen the wrong bank. That argument might have been sound if unions and other pension fund managers were allowed to invest only in government-guaranteed investments. But they aren't limited at all, except by notions of prudence.

This kind of pill would be easier for politicians to sell to the public if it were combined with the "specified percent loss" solution. Of course the problem would go away if we had 100 percent insurance.

PER PERSON TOTAL COVERAGE

In 1990 the Bush administration floated a proposal to limit each person to $100,000 of insurance for all accounts. The individual would have to designate the account or bank that would be insured. Everything else would be uninsured. One hundred thousand dollars, the reasoning went, was all anyone is entitled to have the government protect. Any more, if you have it, you have to protect yourself.[3]

This formulation runs afoul of the same principles as reducing the amount of insurance coverage. In addition, it would make everyone think about a subject—bank strength—for which few have any capacity. Can't you just see Aunt Sadie and Cousin Millie sitting over coffee at the kitchen table in a Florida condominium worrying about what bank's CDs they ought to buy with what their husbands, Harry and Louie, left them? They already talk about this money and the decisions that it puts on them every other night, worrying about whether their money is safe and whether they got the right rate of interest and whether they should have blocked access to their money for a whole six months by buying a CD. If they have to worry about which bank to designate as the protected one, just try to imagine how they'll spread out the Barnett Bank's financial statements and argue about whether the loan loss reserve is high enough.

I don't mean this example to be sexist. Harry and Louie knew just as little— and talked just as aimlessly about money when they were alive. They thought they had to pretend to know more, so they expressed less uncertainty than their wives. Sadie and Millie are demographically more likely to survive to worry about it.

The system can be protected without putting the population through this kind of charade.

More modest proposals to limit the amount that a person can have insured in one bank to $100,000 or a multiple of $100,000, if properly phased in, could have relatively little negative impact, since people can diversify the banks that they use. These proposals also, however, don't seem to accomplish anything.

HIGH CAPITAL SOLUTIONS

A number of the best thinkers about deposit insurance believe that high capital requirements (over 10%), combined with market value accounting and specified capital levels at which the regulators would have to prevent growth, prohibit payment of dividends, or close an institution, would allow the deposit insurance system to work without risk to taypayers.[4] I have to agree that this formulation would practically eliminate the taxpayer risk, even if we insure 100% of the deposits. I would be concerned, however, about three consequences: (1) Would banks be able to be profitable enough at the higher capital levels to be able to attract new capital without contracting the system precipitously? (2) Would American banks be able to compete with foreign banks that had materially lower capital requirements? (3) Would regulatory inflexibility plunge the nation into economic decline if, for example, a problem as large and systemic as the less developed country loan problem were to develop? Hard and fast rules in a volatile world have volatile consequences.

EIGHT POINTS TOWARD SOUND DEPOSIT INSURANCE

Here are my eight points toward sound insurance.

1. People can't protect themselves. A good system won't try to make them do what they can't do.

2. Runs are bad. Deposit insurance successfully prevents most runs. A good system will result in few runs—but it doesn't have to prevent them absolutely.

3. The insurer needs the power and the money to close and liquidate failed institutions. Congress can't hold the purse strings because politics doesn't want banks or S&Ls to fail and doesn't like to spend money for things that people can't see the immediate benefit of. Politics will, therefore, not allocate the money when it is needed. Instead it will defer the problem and temporize. That's what made the S&L problem happen. That's the lesson we *must* learn.

4. We need a market value accounting system for banks and S&Ls. It needs to be developed carefully and comprehensively by a national commission. But we shouldn't put *too much* faith in it. Market value accounting will help, but it's not a panacea. No matter how well designed, it still will be shadows on the wall of the cave, which we shouldn't mistake for absolute reality.

5. Capital rules need to be set at fair but substantial levels and then enforced. This isn't easy, because in doing this the regulator is trying to be a substitute for the market that doesn't exist. The regulator needs to see itself that way, not just as protector of the insurance fund. And the regulator needs flexibility to enforce capital rules as conditions dictate, forbearing from draconian enforcement when the public interest requires forbearance.

6. We need to define exactly what will be protected by the federal safety net. What's in should get full faith and credit. What's out can still be a Chrysler or a Lockheed, but it can't be an FSLIC. (In which category are our pension funds and Ginnie Mae, Fannie Mae, and Freddie Mac? In which should they be?)

7. There's a lot at stake. We can't afford weak, political appointments to bank regulatory positions. Technocrats do the job best. (Yes, I am a technocrat and therefore biased, but after reading this book you should be able to judge for yourself.)

8. We should fix the system as well as we can and then stop tinkering with it for a while. Too many changes distract managements and regulators from doing their jobs.

The hardest thing—and the most important—will be for Congress to give the insurer (the FDIC) power to spend whatever money it needs to do its job. That's unnatural for Congress to do. But if we come away with any lesson, that should be it.

27 The Future of Thrift Institutions

In his July 1990 letter to clients, lobbyist Jim Butera predicted, "One year after FIRREA, the only thing that can be said for certain is that the worst is yet to come, especially for banking institutions that were spared the wrath of last year's legislation." The people of the United States, who, because they instinctively have known the psychological power impulse that motivates people to be bankers, have never loved banks. "The banks are made of marble and their hearts are made of stone" goes a ballad that Pete Seeger used to sing, and even if most Americans didn't buy his left-wing perspective, they could see his point.

So when the S&Ls end up costing hundreds of billions — numbers that most people can't even say, much less imagine — and when Bank of New England has failed and Bank of Boston is said to be in trouble, when the big money center banks like Citicorp and Manufacturers Hanover need to count their loans to foreigners at more than they would fetch on the open market, when Continental Illinois is bailed out by the FDIC, and when you can't pick up a newspaper without reading about some new dumb or heinous thing that a bank or S&L did, the people are mad as hell and Congress knows it. The conditions therefore are ripe for radical legislation — legislation that could be very good or very bad.

As far as the thrift industry, as it used to be called, is concerned, the die has been cast. Although we still need institutions which will originate home loans, we now know that those institutions don't have to be depository institutions. We also know that the secondary market works well enough that homeowners pay no more than a competitive price for the money they borrow. (They pay less than a market price if they qualify for a loan that Ginnie, Fannie, or Freddie will buy.) Today's competitive rate is higher than the regulated rate they would have paid before 1980. But we can't go back to the pre-1980 world because the saver won't pay the freight anymore, and with current technology, the saver can't be forced to.

Soak-the-savers-to-make-homes-affordable is over, but we still have several other ways in which we subsidize home ownership, most prominently (1) through the deduction for interest on home mortgages, (2) through the special bad debt deduction for thrift institutions, (3) through below-market financing for thrifts through the Federal Home Loan Banks, and (4) through the federal safety net under Ginnie Mae, Fannie Mae, and Freddie Mac. All of these should be reexamined.

Not that we don't need a housing policy. But housing policy, family policy, and education policy all should be fitted together. Home ownership is good because it encourages self-esteem, self-reliance, family activities, and local school involvement, and therefore better education, better lives, and a stronger future economy. Repealing inefficient subsidies can help to pay for the more precisely targeted subsidies that can benefit society. We can make some good out of the S&L mess yet, if its impact permits us to look at our society's needs more openly.

For thrift institutions, this means no subsidies, but also no requirement that they lend for housing. Those that are efficient at home lending can, should, and will continue to specialize in that field. Those that aren't efficient will change or fail, if they haven't done so already.

The playing field for banks and thrifts will be level. The local S&Ls and local community banks that survive will look alike. They will finance local home building, local businesses, and local consumers. As in the past, they will have trouble when local economies founder. Our regulatory and deposit insurance systems should give them some leeway as long as they are honest and serve their communities.

The Red Queen from *Alice in Wonderland* is abroad in the land, crying "Off with everybody's head!" We shouldn't let her intimidate us. Whatever her name or power, we have to stand up and remind her that all those little banks and S&Ls helped to make American borrowers feel better because they know the bank officer who decides on their loans. The psychology of money works both ways. The faceless lending institution feels like tyranny to a lot of people.

A higher percentage of the mutual thrifts than of the stock thrifts will survive. The mutuals have tended to be more like community banks, and they don't have to earn a large return on their capital. Their boards of directors are content to provide a service and to preserve their way of life, which, while it looked simplistic to a lot of people in the 1980s, has gained some appeal—indeed even a kind of cachet—in the more sedate 1990s.

The rub-off of all this on bigger American commercial banks is less clear. Like the S&Ls, they overlent and helped to create the boom. Today they, too, are in serious trouble as the real estate loans and LBO loans (more broadly called "highly leveraged transaction" loans or HLTs) run into trouble. Real estate in the Northeast has imitated real estate in Texas: Beginning in 1987, people stopped buying condos, home prices sagged, office building vacancies escalated, and borrowers stopped paying interest to their banks. Northeastern bankers, reminded about overbuilding in Texas in 1986, answered, "That's not what we're doing." But New England bankers weren't much more conservative than their Texas counterparts. Victims of the boom psychology, they kept lending long after the warning signs were up and the red flags were flying.

The banks won't be as badly off as the S&Ls because (1) the banks started with more capital, (2) the banks had better accounting, (3) the banks had better regulatory supervision, (4) the banks lent somewhat recklessly but not totally without underwriting standards, (5) most of the HLTs have junk bonds behind the bank debt, which will absorb most of the losses, (6) the banks have much lower costs of funds, (7) the banks have more fat that can be cut out of their budgets to survive hard times, (8) many banks have nonspread businesses, such as trust business, that can help sustain them while loans aren't paying, and (9) the FDIC fund is bigger than the FSLIC fund was. Nevertheless, the banks are in for a hard time, and so is the FDIC.

What will Congress do to make the banking situation better or worse? One hesitates to expect good things from an institution with Congress's record on banking issues, an institution that is still dominated by pandering. (People in Congress defend by pointing out that they have to get votes.) We can be sure that the panderers will be out in force, declaring against banks and bankers. We can be equally sure that bankers will make the mistake of defending themselves instead of their role in the economy.

The crucial test will be on deposit insurance reform. The various proposals that would require private insurance or that would reduce insurance coverage would radically change American banks in ways that probably would result in many fewer banks and less credit availability over the long term. That would be too bad, because credit does promote growth.

No banking system works perfectly—not any more than any other human institution. What we want from a banking system is a safe place to put money, a mechanism for money to be moved around efficiently, and a place where people and businesses can borrow when they reasonably have the ability to pay it back. Despite some obvious excesses, the American banking system basically has done these things. If it has done them less efficiently than it might have—which it has—that has to be attributed to protectionism, interest rate regulation, misunderstanding the nature of deposit insurance, and the psychology of money and the type of people it has attracted to the banking business.

We can't do anything about the psychology of money. Money not only buys things; it is a talisman, a symbol of who we are, whether we have it or not. Pools of money are power. But precisely because pools of money *are* power, somebody—bankers faute de mieux—has to be allowed to exercise that power by deciding who gets credit. If we have too few credit granters or if we let the government too far into the credit allocation process, we will destroy the benefits of the free market hypothesis. Congress shouldn't do that.

Congress should now want to focus on some long deferred and little understood issues, such as the separation between banking and commerce that the Bank Holding Company Act stands for (but the S&L Holding Company Act doesn't) and the dwindling separation between banking and the securities business that is represented by the Glass–Steagall Act. With the expense of the FSLIC bailout fresh in its collective mind, Congress will be tempted to head back to the 1930s on these issues. That, too, the Congress should resist. Its goals in bank regulation should be to integrate the deposit insurance solution with mechanisms that permit owners of banks to engage in a variety of businesses without giving those businesses the benefits of the federal safety net. The SLHCA basically does that. Nothing that happened in the S&L failures suggests that the SLHCA's permission for industrial companies to own S&Ls caused the problem. American banks will need lots of capital to compete in international commerce. We shouldn't let our bad experience with S&Ls cause us to cripple our banks as well.

Postscript

In the months between completion of the manuscript for this book and the preparation of galleys, the commercial banking world has seemed headed in the same direction that the S&L world went in the 1980s. We have seen an increasing number of failures due to losses on real estate loans and we have seen the regulatory apparatus and the banking industry begin to replicate the pattern of informal forbearance, problem denial, advocacy of accounting shenanigans, and hokey proposals for the industry to pay for its own problems.

The people who run the FDIC have studied the S&L debacle and understand its lessons, but they nevertheless will find it difficult to steer a course between the anger of Congress and the hopelessness of the plight of institutions with large nonperforming loan portfolios. The dilemma involves not only the question of how best to limit the FDIC's losses from banks that fail but also the question of how to reduce the adverse impact that the banks' problems will have on the American economy. Whereas the contraction of the S&Ls looked like it would have only a small impact on the economy because the secondary market could absorb the credit demand for single-family loans, the contraction of the commercial banking system that is accompanying the banks' loan losses is creating serious problems for commercial borrowers because they do not have alternative funding sources to tap as the banking system contracts.

What the FDIC or the Federal Reserve can do about the "credit crunch" that results from banking system contraction is problematical. As we've seen, in a world where capital rules are enforced and accounting rules tell as much of the truth as they can, loan losses force contraction. Capital is the key multiplier and it simply becomes unavailable until risk-adjusted spreads increase sufficiently. The business is perceived as too speculative to justify the relatively skimpy returns that fully capitalized banks reliably can produce on their capital.

What could the regulators do to reverse this trend of contraction? They could repeal the capital rules. They could simply not enforce the capital rules. They could wink at loan losses and permit banks to be under-reserved. They could change the accounting rules and thereby create a new set of regulatory accounting principles—a new "RAP."

Having read about the S&L debacle, you are unlikely to contend that any of these solutions is appropriate. They are all solutions that the FHLBB tried in the S&L context and they all increased the final cost. Basically, the lesson is that growth that is not margined by proper capital is growth that will seek to take unacceptable risks.

If the regulators reason this way—and the FDIC staff is likely to do so—then the contraction of the economy will be significant and the government will pay through reduced tax revenues. The FDIC also will tend to lose, because in a contracting economy more banks will fail and the assets underlying bank loans will be worth less.

For these reasons, the bank problem is different from the S&L problem. Whereas changing technology had made the S&Ls unnecessary for the functioning of the economy, the banks are necessary—at least until alternative lending sources are developed by the private sector. These sources will be developed, but they take time.

Therefore, the FDIC has little choice but to temporize and permit some growth that is not justified by banks' capital positions. They can try to prevent abuses, but abuses there will be. They can hope that insolvent institutions will recover, but more likely they will perform like the broke thrifts that were doomed to lose money forever. They can try to remember the difference between the funny accounting that they have permitted and some notion of better accounting, but numbers have a way of reifying themselves—that is, they have a way of giving the impression that the picture they present is real.

Letting banks lend when their real capital levels suggest that they shouldn't also will tend to delay the formation of the alternative markets that will have to take up the slack from a contracting banking system. The balancing act will be a dangerous one, because if the private systems of finance did not develop during periods of forbearance, then when the regulators repealed the forbearances and finally caused the contraction, the results for the economy would be devastating. The weak banks would be even worse off than they are today; therefore the contraction will be even more acute. If the alternative sources of finance haven't been built up because the weak banks have competed too vigorously, then the economy will be sent into a tailspin.

These delicate decisions will have to be made at a time when Congress is considering fundamental changes in the way that banks and their holding companies are regulated. Subtlety isn't Congress's long suit. It is not likely to understand the impact of its actions on this delicate problem.

One has to be fearful that the forces of volatility and changing technology that defeated the S&Ls will infect the economy for some time to come as they work their way through the banking system. Competent regulators can deal with failing banks on an individual basis, but they aren't necessarily equipped to deal with a systemic economic problem. Regulation and supervision have their limits.

The business cannot attract new capital because the returns aren't very attractive and the Congress has, through legislation concerning the liabilities of bank owners and directors, made the consequences of failure in the banking business disproportionate to the consequences of failure in unregulated businesses. If a business cannot raise new capital, then it must contract until it reaches an equilibrium where its returns justify the risks which the marketplace perceives. Thus new capital will be very expensive to existing shareholders, who will have to give up a part of their returns to beef up the returns to newcomers. Only when spreads widen and banking gets off the congressional agenda will new money be willing to come into the business on an equal basis with old money. Meanwhile, the strong banks will get stronger and the weak banks will get weaker.

Appendix: Dynamics of a Broke S&L

The dynamics that cause a broke S&L to lose money forever work like this: A healthy S&L with $1 million of assets might have a 200-basis point (2 percent) spread, GAAP capital of 5 percent of assets, and very little (maybe 2 percent of assets) invested in nonearning assets, such as bank buildings and machines, that don't pay interest. For this institution the net interest income computation might look like this:

Average interest earned: 10%
Average earning assets for period: $980,000

Average interest paid: 8%
Average paying liabilities for period: $950,000

10% × 980,000 = 98,000
8% × 950,000 = 76,000
Net interest income = 22,000

If this S&L ran efficiently with expenses of 1.5 percent of assets ($15,000) and made some customer service fees of 0.5 percent of assets ($5,000), it would have earnings before taxes of $12,000 (1.2 percent of assets or 120 basis points), which is good.

An S&L's earnings will deteriorate if it suffers a loss (such as by being unable to collect a loan). Moreover, the loss will have a double effect. If the S&L in our example had to write off $50,000, not only would it report a $50,000 loss but its earning assets would decline by that $50,000 while its liabilities remained the same. The net interest income computation now would look like this:

Average interest earned: 10%
Average earning assets for period: $930,000

Average interest paid: 8%
Average paying liabilities for period: $950,000

10% × 930,000 = 93,000
8% × 950,000 = 76,000
Net interest income = 17,000

This S&L can still make a little money ($7,000) so long as it is very careful with its costs (still $15,000) and earns good fee income (still $5,000). But if the S&L had to write off another $100,000, it could not make money without increasing its spread or its fee income very significantly. After losing this $100,000, net interest income would be computed as follows:

Average interest earned: 10%
Average earning assets for period: $830,000

Average interest paid: 8%
Average paying liabilities for period: $950,000

10% × 830,000 = 83,000
8% × 950,000 = 76,000
Net interest income = 7,000

The net interest income is still a positive number, but it is only 0.7 percent (70 basis points) of the liabilities the S&L still has. Even if it continues to be efficient, this S&L will lose money ($3,000 in the first year, in our example) unless it increases its spread or earns extraordinary fees. Moreover, it will lose more money in every succeeding year because each loss will further reduce earning assets without reducing paying liabilities. It cannot make money with a 2 percent spread and normal fees.

In this situation, if the regulators do not take over the institution, management must seek more spread income or more fees or both, and must take whatever risks that entails. If management could increase the spread to 3 percent by increasing the yield on assets from 10 percent to 11 percent, the S&L might be able to recover:

Average interest earned: 11%
Average earning assets for period: $830,000

Average interest paid: 8%
Average paying liabilities for period: $950,000

11% × 830,000 = 91,300
8% × 950,000 = 76,000
Net interest income = 15,300

If expenses stayed at $15,000 and fees stayed at $5,000, the S&L would have a profit of $5,300 and gradually could recover. The problem is that this would require the miracle of the loaves and fishes. You cannot get that additional 1 percent interest on assets without much higher risk or much higher expenses or both. Moreover, almost no S&L has consistently earned a 3 percent spread.

What almost always happens is that in trying to earn that extra 1 percent on assets, the S&L makes risky loans to get the higher rates, and some of those loans turn out to be bad. If we assume that these risky loans will cause another $100,000 of losses, we will see that the S&L will be even worse off than it was before, and will *never again* make money. It will be doomed to lose money *forever.* This is because after losing that next $100,000, the S&L, which still has the hypothetical excellent spread of 3 percent, has too many paying liabilities compared with earning assets *and it can never do anything to correct that imbalance.* It may try by taking more risks (as S&Ls did when the FSLIC didn't do its job in the mid–1980s), but it won't work.

Glossary

Adjustable-Rate Mortgages (ARMs). Used interchangeably with "variable-rate mortgages," although for a time distinctions were made between the two terms. Refers to a mortgage whose interest rate varies in accordance with an index over its term.

Bank Holding Company Act (BHCA). Federal law that requires companies which own banks to register with the Federal Reserve Board. Companies that register may not engage in businesses unrelated to banking.

Capitalized Interest. Interest income that is imputed on direct investments in construction projects. The theory says that during the construction period, the S&L may record interest at its cost-of-funds rate because the project is gaining value as construction proceeds. The theory turned out to be flawed when the projects that were built couldn't be sold for the amount invested plus the capitalized interest.

Collateral. Assets pledged or otherwise set aside to secure repayment of a loan. If the loan is not repaid, the lender can take possession of the collateral and sell it to pay the debt. In the case of real estate loans, the real estate is the collateral.

Commercial Bank Regulatory Agencies. Comptroller of the Currency (chartering authority for national banks), Federal Reserve Board, FDIC, and state chartering authorities.

Commercial Banks. National banks and state-chartered banks that traditionally have offered checking accounts and made business loans. All commercial banks were insured by FDIC, not FSLIC. All national banks are members of the Federal Reserve System. State-chartered commercial bank membership in the Federal Reserve System is voluntary.

Conservator. Person appointed by FSLIC to take charge of and run an institution that is being run improperly. The conservator not only runs the institution but also investigates its financial soundness. Usually appointment of a conservator leads to a sale or liquidation.

Direct Investments. The term that the Bank Board used to denominate equity (as opposed to debt) investments. Direct investments included corporate stocks, non-debt interests in real estate, and debt interests in real estate with equity kickers or characteristics.

Duration-Matched Spreads. Spreads between the cost of funds and the income on loans that are interest-rate-sensitivity matched, so that the lender has no effective interest rate risk. Duration is a sophisticated way of measuring interest rate risk.

Federal Home Loan Banks (FHLBs). Twelve regional banks owned by the S&Ls that are quasi-government agencies. The FHLBs' principal function has been to provide low-cost borrowings to S&Ls that S&Ls then can lend for housing. The FHLBs could accomplish this by borrowing in the public markets with an implied government guarantee. FHLBs also had an important regulatory role before FIRREA.

Federal Home Loan Mortgage Corporation (FHLMC, also known as Freddie Mac). Federal corporation owned by Federal Home Loan Banks. The board of directors consisted of FHLBB members. Still government designated. Guarantees privately issued mortgages for a fee. Obligations have moral U.S. government backing but not full faith and credit.

Federal National Mortgage Association (FNMA, also known as Fannie Mae). Federal corporation owned by private stockholders. Guarantees privately issued mortgages for a fee. Obligations have moral U.S. government backing but not full faith and credit.

Federal Reserve Banks. Twelve regional banks that, as agencies of the U.S. government, act as lenders of last resort for the banking system. They also play a role in commercial bank and bank holding company regulation, and implement Federal Reserve Board monetary policy.

Federal Reserve Board (the Fed). U.S. government agency that makes monetary policy and regulates Federal Reserve member banks (all of which are commercial banks) and bank holding companies under the Bank Holding Company Act.

Financial Accounting Standards Board (FASB). Sets accounting standards for financial reporting by American companies. Its pronouncements are the basic generally accepted accounting principles (GAAP).

First Lien. A security interest in a piece of property—in the case of real property, a mortgage—that comes before any other security interests. Other liens are by definition riskier than first liens.

Government National Mortgage Association (GNMA, also known as Ginnie Mae). U.S. government agency that guarantees and packages government-guaranteed (Veterans Administration or Federal Housing Administration) mortgages. Backed by full faith and credit of U.S. government.

Insider. Senior officer, director, or major stockholder.

Interest Rate Sensitivity. The characteristics of a financial asset or liability that make its interest rate subject to change because of maturity or because of interest rate reset provisions or because of options to prepay or demand prepayment.

Loan-to-Value Tests (LTV). Laws or regulations which say that institutions subject to them are prohibited from making loans secured by real estate unless an appraisal of the property on which the loan is to be made shows a ratio of loan amount to value of not more than a specified percentage.

Mark to Market. Valuing the assets and liabilities of an entity at current market values at a particular point in time rather than carrying them at historical cost.

Mortgage-Based Securities. Securities that provide the owner with an interest in the cash flows from a specified pool of mortgages. They include securities guaranteed by GNMA, FHLMC, and FNMA, as well as securities guaranteed by private mortgage insurers and securities "derived" from these securities by dividing the cash flows among different classes of owners.

Mutual. An institution that is not stockholder-owned. See discussion in Chapter 3.

Net Operating Loss Carryforwards (NOLs). Deductions from income that a corporation may have because it lost money in prior years. Ordinary corporations can carry these deductions forward for fifteen years until they are used up. Banks and S&Ls had only five years to make enough profits to use up their NOLs, and many of them couldn't make enough in five years to use up their losses from 1980–82. Certain NOLs were extended to eight years in 1986.

NOW Accounts. Deposit accounts similar to checking accounts that were developed in New England in the early 1970s to permit thrift institutions to compete with commercial bank checking accounts.

OCC. Office of the Comptroller of the Currency. Charters, regulates, and examines national banks.

OMB. Office of Management and Budget of the White House. Responsible for formulating and enforcing federal budgetary policy.

OTS. Office of Thrift Supervision. Successor to the Federal Home Loan Bank Board under FIRREA. Regulates all federally insured savings associations and charters federally chartered associations.

Principal Supervisory Agent (PSA). The supervisory agent in each of the twelve districts to whom other supervisory agents in the district reported. Often the PSA was also the President of the district FHLB.

Pushdown Purchase Accounting. An extension of purchase accounting theory under which purchase accounting applies not only to the acquiring organization but also to the acquired institution, even though it has not engaged in a business combination. The effect is that a goodwill account is established on the acquired institution's books based on the purchase price.

Resolution Trust Corporation (RTC). Government agency set up under FIRREA to liquidate or otherwise deal with failed S&Ls.

Savings and Loan Holding Company Act (SLHCA). Federal law that requires companies which own S&Ls to register. It does not restrict the activities of companies that own an S&L if they own only one.

Spread Maintenance. An agreement by the deposit insurer to pay the acquirer of a failed institution a guaranteed amount over the institution's cost of funds (or an index of costs of funds) if specified acquired assets don't earn that amount. Typically, the amount of guaranteed spread declines over the term of the agreement.

Straw Borrowers. Persons who are named as borrowers but who in fact never receive the money. They may be paid a fee for use of their names to perpetrate the fraud that gives somebody else most of the money from the loan.

Subordinated Debt. Loans that, in the event of bankruptcy, will not be repaid until other unsecured debt (usually including "senior bank debt") has been repaid. As a consequence of being subordinated, it often is wiped out or loses most of its value if the issuer becomes bankrupt.

Supervisory Agent. Officer of an FHLB responsible for supervising S&Ls. The supervisory agent was the primary interface between the S&L and the Bank Board.

Takeout. A commitment by a long-term lender to a construction lender to make a loan on a project after the project has been constructed in accordance with plans and specifications, regardless of whether the project has sufficient economic value to sustain the loan. Historically, major construction projects were funded by commercial banks, with insurance companies providing takeouts.

Tangible Capital. A bank's or S&L's GAAP capital minus goodwill and similar intangibles. If goodwill exceeds GAAP capital, tangible capital is negative.

Tax-Sharing Agreement. An agreement between affiliated corporations that is common because the tax laws permit or require consolidation of parent and subsidiary corporations for federal income tax purposes. Often the earnings are made by the subsidiary and the parent corporation doesn't have the cash to pay taxes on the subsidiary's earnings even though it is responsible for the taxes under the consolidation rules.

Thin Market. A market in which daily purchases and sales of securities are small. Usually there also are very few "market makers," that is, dealers who are willing to buy at some price in order to make the market orderly.

Thrift Institutions. Usually refers to all savings banks and S&Ls, whether state or federally chartered, whether formerly FSLIC-insured or FDIC-insured.

Vested. Money not subject to forfeiture by the plan participant—that is, the employee. Typically, plans provide several years (five to ten) before participants' interests are fully vested.

Yield. Yield is the composite of current interest paid, interest accrued, deferred fees and interest taken into income currently, and amortization of discount or premium paid for a loan. It is the total current income on the loan for the period.

Notes

In order not to impede the flow of this book, notes have been kept to a minimum.

All unidentified quotations have been taken from interviews conducted by the author. These include interviews of Dick Pratt, Ed Gray, and Danny Wall, all of whom graciously gave their time. In addition, Dick Pratt and Ed Gray made many of their hundreds of speeches and Congressional testimonies while in office available to me. Many FHLBB or OTS staff members and other former directors also submitted to interviews, as did present or former personnel of the banking agencies, White House and legislative staffs, lawyers, accountants, lobbyists, and trade association personnel. Many of these interviews were confidential or off the record. Therefore many quotations are not attributed.

This book contains many references to statutes, bills, regulations, proposed regulations and bills, as well as legislative history materials and hearings. The major regulations and statutes are listed in the bibliography. Individual references generally are not footnoted, but the context should show the law or regulation being referred to.

Descriptions of actions of the Depository Institutions Deregulatory Committee (DIDC) are based on that committee's transcripts and minutes, which are held at the Department of the Treasury.

This book contains a great many statistics, for few of which is a specific citation provided. These statistics generally are based upon FHLBB data, but my source is not always primary. Statistics on individual institutions have been derived from the work of David Cates, now with Ferguson & Co. in Washington, D.C.; from call report data that Salomon Brothers graciously made available from computerized services to which it subscribes; and from annual reports of state S&L commissioners. More general statistics on the industry came from FHLBB sources, from the dozens of GAO publications in the field, and from more than 100 economic studies done for the Bank Board in the 1980s, as well as from books that preceded this one and are included in the bibliography. As much as possible, I have sought corroboration from more than one source. If I have perpetuated other people's mistakes, I apologize. If I have perpetrated some new ones, it was not intentional. The underlying raw data are not good; consequently, mistakes are easy to make.

CHAPTER 1

1. *Report of the Inter-Agency Task Force on Deposit Interest Rate Controls and Housing Credit* (1978).

2. *The Report of the Interagency Task Force on Thrift Institutions* (Washington, D.C.: Department of Treasury, June 30, 1980); *Report of the President's Commission on Financial Structure and Regulation* (1971), known as the Hunt Commission Report; *Financial Institutions and the Nation's Economy, Discussion Principles* (November 1975), known as the FINE Report.

3. Hearing before the Senate Banking Committee, April 6, 1981.

CHAPTER 2

1. This could be the case if, for example, a bank made a thirty-year loan at a fixed rate of 5 percent two years ago and open market interest rates for that kind of loan had increased to 11 percent over the two-year period. We would now have a twenty-eight-year loan paying only 5 percent in an 11 percent world. The loan is a good loan in the sense that the borrower will repay it after twenty-eight years (and therefore it can be shown on the balance sheet at its full original amount), but no one will pay that amount for it because at that price other loans can be bought that will yield 11 percent, rather than 5 percent, for the twenty-eight years.

CHAPTER 3

1. The basic GAAP purchase accounting materials were APB 16, APB 17, and SFAS 72.

2. Additional technical issues arose as to methods of amortization and accretion. This explanation is somewhat simplified.

3. See Federal Reserve Board, *D. H. Baldwin Co.*, February 22, 1977, 42 *Fed. Reg.* 11877, March 1, 1977.

4. John Crockett and A. Thomas King, *The Contribution of New Asset Powers to S&L Earnings: A Comparison of Federal- and State-Chartered Associations in Texas* (Washington, D.C.: Office of Policy and Economic Research, Federal Home Loan Bank Board, July 1982).

5. Federal Home Loan Bank Board, *Agenda for Reform, A Report on Deposit Insurance to the Congress from the Federal Home Loan Bank Board* (Washington, D.C., March 1983), p. 16.

6. Ibid., p. 19.

7. Ibid., p. 29.

8. Ibid., p. 10.

9. Ibid., p. 42.

10. Ibid., p. 73.

11. Ibid., p. 7.

12. Ibid., p. 18.

13. Ibid., p. 78.

CHAPTER 4

1. U.S. League of Savings Institutions, *Homeownership: Celebrating the American Dream* (Chicago: U.S. League of Savings Institutions, 1983).

2. Andrew S. Carron, *The Rescue of the Thrift Industry* (Washington, D.C.: The Brookings Institution, 1983), pp. 1, 31, and 30.

3. The description of Beverly Hills is based principally on the Beverly Hills hearings [hereinafter "Beverly Hills Hearings"] held by the House Committee on Energy and Commerce, June 19, July 15 and 19, September 11, 1985.

4. See, e.g., statement of Richard T. Pratt in Senate Committee on Banking, Housing and Urban Affairs, *Hearings on Financial Institutions Oversight*, April 28, 1981.

CHAPTER 5

1. See, e.g., Edwin Gray, remarks before the Texas Savings and Loan League, Dallas, June 8, 1983.

CHAPTER 6

1. Useful references on these accounting issues include the following: "Notice to Practitioners," *Journal of Accountancy*, November 23, 1983; FASB Emerging Issues Task Force, Issue Summary, Issue Number 84-4, "Acquisition, Development and Construction Loans," July 12, 1984; FASB Emerging Issues Task Force, meeting minutes, July 24, 1984; November 15, 1984; February 14, 1985; March 28, 1985; May 9, 1985; August 8, 1985; February 6, 1986; "Notice to Practitioners on ADC Loans," *CPA Letter*, November 1984; "Accounting for Certain Real Estate Activities," 12 *CFR* Part 571 (proposed October 19, 1984, and adopted April 18, 1985); "Notice to Practitioners," *CPA Letter*, February 10, 1986; AICPA Statement of Position 78-9, "Accounting for Investments in Real Estate Ventures."

2. *New York Times*, May 11, 1990, p. A1.

CHAPTER 7

1. Gray had been at the White House when the Garn–St Germain Act was being formulated; thus he was in a good position to understand its framers' intentions.

2. Edwin J. Gray, remarks at annual meeting of National Savings and Loan League, Maui, Hawaii, October 17, 1983.

3. Paul Horvitz and R. Pettit, "Short-Run Financial Solutions for Troubled Thrift Institutions," in *The Future of the Thrift Industry*, Conference Series No. 24 (Boston: FRB of Boston, Oct. 1981), p. 56.

4. Recommendations of Thrift Industry Study Group on Hedging and Technical Assistance, Applications Processing, and Deposit Insurance Premiums, presented to the Federal Home Loan Bank Board, October 1983.

5. Testimony of John E. Ryan, District Director, and Maria I. Richmond, Deputy District Director, OTS, Atlanta District, before House Committee on Banking, Finance, and Urban Affairs (March 26, 1990).

6. See prepared statement of William K. Black before the House Committee on Banking, Finance, and Urban Affairs, concerning Lincoln Savings and Loan Association, October 26, 1989, p. 43. (Hereinafter "Black Lincoln Testimony.")

7. Testimony of William K. Black before the Subcommittee on Commerce, Consumer, and Monetary Affairs of the House Committee on Government Operations, June 13, 1987, p. 133. (Hereinafter "Black California Testimony.")

CHAPTER 8

1. William J. Schilling, "Savings and Loan Supervision in the '80s . . . the Death of Discretion or Growing Pains?," remarks at North Carolina Savings & Loan League Eastern Secondary Mortgage Market Conference, Raleigh.

2. The description of Mario Renda's activities is largely based on that in Stephen Pizzo, Mary Fricker, and Paul Muolo, *Inside Job: The Looting of America's Savings and Loans* (New York: McGraw-Hill, 1989).

3. E.g., Edwin Gray, remarks to lawyers seminar, National Council of Savings Institutions, Washington, D.C., January 31, 1984.

4. Edwin Gray, testimony before the Subcommittee on Financial Institutions and Consumer Affairs of the Senate Banking Committee, June 5, 1985.

5. *FAIC Securities* v. *United States*, 768 F.2d 352 (1985).

6. The description of Empire of Mesquite and the hearings is based principally on the hearings before the Subcommittee on Commerce, Consumer, and Monetary Affairs of the House Committee on Government Operations, April 25 and August 6, 1984. (Hereinafter "Empire Hearings.")

7. U.S. League, *Washington Notes*, September 6, 1985; see Black California Testimony.

8. Beverly Hills Hearings.

9. Frederick D. Wolf, *Failed Financial Institutions: Reasons, Costs, Remedies and Unresolved Issues* (Washington, D.C.: GAO, 1989).

10. See, e.g., the Empire Hearings and the Beverly Hills Hearings.

11. U.S. League, *Washington Notes*, March 1, 1988.

12. See *Ohio Savings and Loan Crisis and Collapse of E.S.M. Government Securities*,

Inc., hearing before the Subcommittee on Commerce, Consumer, and Monetary Affairs of the House Committee on Government Operations, April 3, 1985.

13. Briefing report to the chairman, Committee on Banking, Housing and Urban Affairs, U.S. Senate, *The Management Consignment Program* (Washington, D.C.: GAO, September 1987).

14. Memorandum from Dennis Jacobe to U.S. League Task Force on FSLIC Issues dated November 1985.

CHAPTER 9

1. See, e.g., Stephen Pizzo, Mary Fricker, and Paul Muolo, *Inside Job* (New York: McGraw-Hill, 1989).

2. Black Lincoln Testimony.

3. Statistics gathered from compilations by Dallas real estate firms.

CHAPTER 11

1. The description of Silverado is based largely on OTS documents, principally the memorandum from Kermit Mowbray, Principal Supervisory Agent, to John M. Buckley, Jr., Secretary of the FHLBB, dated November 9, 1988, "Recommendation for the Appointment of a Receiver for Silverado Banking, Savings and Loan Association."

2. *NTN*, December 12, 1989, p. 25.

3. California information was furnished by the California Department of Savings and Loans and was derived from its annual reports.

4. Information on Lincoln Savings, while derived from a variety of sources, relies principally on the opinion of Judge Sporkin in *Lincoln Savings and Loan Assoc.* v. *M. Danny Wall*, Consolidated Civil Action Nos. 89-1318 and 89-1323, August 2, 1990, and documents introduced into evidence in that case.

5. The description of CenTrust relies primarily on the statement by John E. Ryan, District Director, and Maria I. Richmond, Deputy District Director, OTS, Atlanta District, before the Committee on Banking, Finance, and Urban Affairs, U.S. House of Representatives, March 26, 1990, and other testimony and documents introduced on that date.

CHAPTER 12

1. Sources on S&L junk bond involvement include *High Yield Bonds: Issues Concerning Thrift Investments in High Yield Bonds* (Washington, D.C.: GAO, March 1989); *High Yield Bonds: Nature of the Market and Effect on Federally Insured Institutions* (Washington, D.C.: GAO, May 1988); Jane W. Katz, *Thrift Institutions Investment in Junk Bonds* (Washington, D.C.: Office of Policy and Economic Research, FHLBB, March

1988); Janet Lewis, "How Bad Is the Junk-Bond Backlash?" *Institutional Investor*, October 1989.

CHAPTER 13

1. *Failed Financial Institutions: Reasons, Costs, Remedies and Unresolved Issues* (Washington, D.C.: GAO, 1989).

2. Testimony of Charles A. Deardorff before the Subcommittee on Commerce, Consumer, and Monetary Affairs of the House Committee on Government Operations, June 13, 1987.

CHAPTER 14

1. Information on Franklin is derived from testimony and documents introduced in *Franklin Savings Assoc.* v. *Director*, Case No. 90-4054-S D.KS Saffels, J., September 5, 1990. (Hereinafter the "Franklin Case.")

CHAPTER 15

1. Annual reports of the GAO on FSLIC financial statements.

2. See, e.g., U.S. League, *Savings Institutions*, May 1986, p. 6.

3. See, e.g., U.S. League, *Washington Notes*, March 7, 1986.

4. Ibid., March 14, 1986.

5. *Thrift Industry Problems: Potential Demands on the FSLIC Insurance Fund* (Washington, D.C.: GAO, February 1986).

6. See, e.g., U.S. League, *Savings Institutions*, April 1986.

7. See U.S. League, *Washington Notes*, March 15, 1985.

8. *BNA Washington Financial Reports*, November 11, 1985 (transcript of interview with Peter Stearns).

9. U.S. League, *Washington Notes*, November 8, 1985.

10. Ibid., March 7, 1986.

11. Dennis Jacobe, "Public Perception and Reality Are Often Not the Same," Speech at U.S. League convention, November 4, 1985.

12. U.S. League, *Savings Institutions*, April 1986, p. 56.

13. See, e.g., U.S. League, *Washington Notes*, July 25, 1986.

14. See, e.g., C. Thomas Long, William J. Schilling, and Carol R. Van Cleef, "Enhancing the Value of the Thrift Franchise: A Possible Solution for the Dilemma of the FSLIC?" 37 *Catholic University Law Review*, 385, 419 (1988); Sara Fritz, "Mr. Ed's Revenge," *Los Angeles Times Magazine*, March 25, 1990.

15. See, e.g., U.S. League, *Savings Institutions*, October 1986.

16. See, e.g., U.S. League, *Washington Notes*, October 17, 1986.

17. Black Lincoln Testimony, p. 49.

18. U.S. League, *Washington Notes*, January 23, 1987.

19. Ibid., February 6, 1987.

20. Ibid., March 6, 1987.

21. Bert Ely, *Bailing out the Federal Savings and Loan Insurance Corporation*, July 21, 1986.

22. See Bert Ely, *The Futility of Forbearance*, March 31, 1987.

23. Rep. Stan Parris, "Special Order of the Thrift Industry," speech on floor of House of Representatives, April 1, 1987.

24. See, e.g., U.S. League, *Washington Notes*, March 20, 1987.

25. Ibid., May 1, 1987.

26. Ibid.

27. U.S. League, *Washington Notes*, May 8, 1987.

28. Ibid.

29. Ibid., May 15, 1987.

30. Ibid., August 14, 1987.

31. Ibid.

CHAPTER 16

1. *S&L Reporter*, January 22, 1988.

2. *S&L Reporter*, April 29, 1988.

3. *National Thrift News (NTN)*, February 15, 1988, p. 4.

4. Ibid., October 24, 1988, p. 5A.

5. Ibid., August 8, 1988, p. 1.

6. Ibid., April 25, 1988, p. 36.

7. Ibid., January 3, 1989, p. 27.

8. *New York Times*, July 8, 1990, p. 1.

9. See, e.g., *NTN*, January 23, 1989, p. 41; *NTN*, February 6, 1989, p. 33.

10. *New York Times*, July 22, 1990, p. 1.

11. *NTN*, May 16, 1988, p. 1; *NTN*, August 29, 1988, pp. 30, 32.

12. *S&L Reporter*, July 8, 1988; *NTN*, July 11, 1988, p. 12.

13. *Failed Thrifts: Bank Board's 1988 Texas Resolutions* (Washington, D.C.: GAO, March 1989).

14. *S&L Reporter*, July 15, 1988; *NTN*, July 11, 1988, p. 1.

15. *NTN*, October 10, 1988, p. 10.

16. *NTN*, July 11, 1988, p. 1.

17. See, e.g., *S&L Reporter*, December 1, 1989; *NTN*, October 10, 1988, p. 1.

18. *S&L Reporter*, July 15, 1988.

19. *NTN*, August 8, 1988, pp. 4, 14.

20. Ibid., July 11, 1988, p. 1.

21. Ibid., October 10, 1988, p. 1.

22. Ibid., August 8, 1988, p. 1.

23. See, e.g., *S&L Reporter*, April 29, 1988.

24. Ibid., January 20, 1988.

25. *NTN*, August 15, 1988, p. 1; *NTN*, August 8, 1988, p. 1.

26. See ibid., August 8, 1988, p. 1.

27. Ibid., January 23, 1989, p. 38. For Gonzalez on Wall, see ibid., November 14, 1988, p. 1.

28. See, e.g., Mid-America Institute, *Crisis Resolution in the Thrift Industry* (Boston: Kluwer Academic Publishers, 1989).

29. *New York Times*, September 14, 1990, p. A33; see ibid., p. 1.

30. Memorandum dated July 23, 1987.

31. Memorandum of Understanding dated May 20, 1988.

CHAPTER 17

1. *NTN*, February 13, 1989, p. 4.

2. Ibid., p. 27.

3. Ibid., February 6, 1989, p. 15.

4. Ibid., May 15, 1989, p. 25.

5. Ibid.

6. Ibid., May 1, 1989, p. 25.

PART II

1. Edward Kane, *The S&L Mess* (Washington, D.C.: Urban Institute Press, 1989), p. 1.

2. U.S. League, *Savings Institutions*, June 1986, p. 61.

CHAPTER 20

1. *American Banker*, August 22, 1990, p. 5.

2. Testimony of Bert Ely before the Committee on Banking, Housing, and Urban Affairs of the United States Senate, *Overall Condition of the Thrift Industry*, May 19, 1988.

CHAPTER 21

1. 18 U.S.C. Section 215, Public Law 98–473, Title II, Section 1107(a), 98 Stat. 2145, October 12, 1984; Bank Bribery Amendments Act of 1985, Public Law 99–370, August 4, 1986.

CHAPTER 22

1. See the Franklin Case.

2. *New York Times*, August 16, 1990, p. A25; Edward W. Hill, "New Estimates of the State and Regional Cost of the Savings and Loan Bailout" (May 29, 1990); Edward W. Hill, "The Savings and Loan Bailout One Year Later" (May 24, 1990).

3. *Lincoln Savings and Loan Association* v. *M. Danny Wall,* Consolidated Civil Action Nos. 89-1318 and 89-1323 (Sporkin, J.), August 2, 1990.

CHAPTER 26

1. *American Banker,* August 27–28, 1990, p. 4.
2. See, e.g., Testimony of E. Gerald Corrigan before the Senate Committee on Banking, Housing and Urban Affairs, May 3, 1990.
3. *New York Times,* September 27, 1990, p. D1.
4. See George Benston and George Kaufman, *Risk Insolvency Regulation of Depository Institutions,* New York, NYU Salomon Center Monograph 1988–1.

Selected Bibliography

BOOKS

Adams, James Ring. *The Big Fix: Inside the S&L Scandal.* New York: John Wiley & Sons, 1990.

AICPA. *Audit and Accounting Guide, Savings and Loan Associations.* 1979.

AICPA. *Industry Audit Guide, Audits of Banks.* 1983.

Balderston, Frederick E. *Thrifts in Crisis: Structural Transformation of the Savings and Loan Industry.* Cambridge: Ballinger, 1984.

Benston, George J., Robert A. Eisenbeis, Paul M. Horvitz, Edward J. Kane, and George G. Kaufman. *Perspectives on Safe & Sound Banking: Past, Present, and Future.* Cambridge, Mass.: MIT Press, 1986.

Brumbaugh, R. Dan, Jr. *Thrifts Under Siege: Restoring Order to American Banking.* Cambridge: Ballinger, 1988.

Carron, Andrew S. *The Plight of the Thrift Institutions.* Washington, D.C.: The Brookings Institution, 1982.

Carron, Andrew S. *The Rescue of the Thrift Industry.* Washington, D.C.: The Brookings Institution, 1983.

Eichler, Ned. *The Thrift Debacle.* Berkeley: University of California Press, 1989.

Fabritius, M. Manfred, and William Borges. *Saving the Savings and Loan: The U.S. Thrift Industry and the Texas Experience, 1950–1988.* New York: Praeger, 1989.

Federal Home Loan Bank Board. *Agenda for Reform, A Report on Deposit Insurance to the Congress from the Federal Home Loan Bank Board.* Washington, D.C., March 1983.

Kane, Edward J. *The S&L Mess: How Did It Happen?* Washington, D.C.: The Urban Institute Press, 1989.

Mayer, Martin. *The Greatest-Ever Bank Robbery.* New York: Scribner's, 1990.

Pilzer, Paul Zane, with Robert Deitz. *Other People's Money: The Inside Story of the S&L Mess.* New York: Simon and Schuster, 1989.

Pizzo, Stephen, Mary Fricker, and Paul Muolo. *Inside Job: The Looting of America's Savings and Loans.* New York: McGraw-Hill, 1989.

Robinson, Michael A. *Overdrawn: The Bailout of American Savings.* New York: Dutton, 1990.

Strunk, Norman, and Fred Case. *Where Deregulation Went Wrong: A Look at the Causes Behind the Savings and Loan Failures in the 1980's.* Chicago: U.S. League of Savings Institutions, 1988.

White, Lawrence J. *The S&L Debacle: Public Policy Lessons for Bank and Thrift Regulation.* New York: Oxford University Press, 1991.

FEDERAL HOME LOAN BANK BOARD
RESEARCH PAPERS

For readers who desire a more complete listing of FHLBB research materials and other scholarly papers, White, *The S&L Debacle, supra,* is recommended.

Barth, James R., Philip F. Bartholomew, and Peter J. Elmer. *The Cost of Liquidating Versus Selling Failed Thrift Institutions.* Research Working Paper No. 89-02. Washington, D.C.: Office of Thrift Supervision, November 1989.

Barth, James R., Philip F. Bartholomew, and Carol J. Labich. *Moral Hazard and the Thrift Crisis: An Analysis of 1988 Resolutions.* Research Working Paper No. 160. Washington, D.C.: Office of Policy and Economic Research, Federal Home Loan Bank Board, May 1989.

Barth, James R., and Michael G. Bradley. *Thrift Deregulation and Federal Deposit Insurance.* Research Paper No. 150. Washington, D.C.: Office of Policy and Economic Research, Federal Home Loan Bank Board, October 1986.

Barth, James R., R. Dan Brumbaugh, Jr., and Daniel Sauerhaft. *Failure Costs of Government-Regulated Financial Firms: The Case of Thrift Institutions.* Research Working Paper No. 123. Washington, D.C.: Office of Policy and Economic Research, Federal Home Loan Bank Board, October 1986.

Barth, James R., R. Dan Brumbaugh, Jr., Daniel Sauerhaft, and George H. K. Wang. *Thrift Institution Failures: Causes and Policy Issues.* Research Working Paper No. 117. Washington, D.C.: Office of Policy and Economic Research, Federal Home Loan Bank Board, May 1–3, 1985.

Barth, James R., R. Dan Brumbaugh, Jr., Daniel Sauerhaft, and George H. K. Wang. *Thrift Institution Failures: Estimating the Regulator's Closure Rule.* Research Working Paper No. 125. Washington, D.C.: Office of Policy and Economic Research, Federal Home Loan Bank Board, August 1989.

Bisenius, Donald J., R. Dan Brumbaugh, Jr., and Ronald C. Rogers. *Insolvent Thrift Institutions, Agency Issues, and the Management Consignment Program.* Research Paper No. 141. Washington, D.C.: Office of Policy and Economic Research, Federal Home Loan Bank Board, October 1986.

Cassidy, Henry J. *An Approach for Determining the Capital Requirement for Savings and Loan Associations.* Research Working Paper No. 97. Washington, D.C.: Office of Policy and Economic Research, Federal Home Loan Bank Board, May 1980.

Cassidy, Henry J., Richard G. Marcis, and Dale P. Riordan. *The Savings and Loan Industry in the 1980s.* Research Working Paper No. 100. Washington, D.C.: Office of Policy and Economic Research, Federal Home Loan Bank Board, December 1980.

Edwards, Donald, and Donald J. Bisenius. *Rapid Asset Growth at Thrift Institutions.* Washington, D.C.: Office of Policy and Economic Research, Federal Home Loan Bank Board, April 1988.

Federal Home Loan Bank Board. *A Financial Institution for the Future.* Washington, D.C.: Office of Economic Research, March 1975.

Federal Home Loan Bank Board. *Report of the Expanded Task Force on Current Value Accounting.* Washington, D.C., April 12, 1983.

Katz, Jane W. *Thrift Institution Investment in Junk Bonds.* Washington, D.C.: Office of Policy and Economic Research, Federal Home Loan Bank Board, March 1988.

King, A. Thomas. *The Deposit Rate and the Mortgage Rate: Does Regulation Q Promote Homeownership?* Research Working Paper No. 85. Washington, D.C.: Office of Economic Research, Federal Home Loan Bank Board, September 1979.

Pomeranz, Robert J. *Accounting Standards for the Thrift Industry.* Washington, D.C.: Office of Policy and Economic Research, Federal Home Loan Bank Board, July 1988.

Pomeranz, Robert J. *Understanding Thrift Goodwill.* Washington, D.C.: Office of Policy and Economic Research, Federal Home Loan Bank Board, June 1989.

Riordan, Dale P. *Deregulation and the Future of the Thrift Industry.* Washington, D.C.: Office of Policy and Economic Research, Federal Home Loan Bank Board, September 8, 1980.

Rosen, Kenneth. *The Disintermediation Function: A Gross Flows Model of Savings Flows to Savings and Loan Associations.* Invited Research Working Paper No. 22. Washington, D.C.: Office of Economic Research, Federal Home Loan Bank Board, April 1979.

Thompson, A. Frank, Jr. *An Actuarial Perspective on the Adequacy of the FSLIC Fund.* Research Working Paper No. 102. Washington, D.C.: Office of Policy and Economic Research, Federal Home Loan Bank Board, February 25, 1981.

Wambeke, Carol, and John Duffy. *Thrift Industry Equity-Risk Investment.* Washington, D.C.: Office of Policy and Economic Research, Federal Home Loan Bank Board, November 1988.

U.S. GENERAL ACCOUNTING OFFICE PUBLICATIONS

Federal Savings and Loan Insurance Corporation Financial Statements. Washington, D.C., 1982–89.

Thrift Industry: Cost to FSLIC of Delaying Action on Insolvent Savings Institutions. Washington, D.C., September 1986.

Thrift Industry Problems: Potential Demands on the FSLIC Insurance Fund. Washington, D.C., February 1986.

Briefing Report to the Chairman, Committee on Banking, Housing and Urban Affairs, U.S. Senate, the Management Consignment Program. Washington, D.C., September 1987.

Forbearance for Troubled Institutions 1982–1986. Washington, D.C., May 1987.

Thrift Industry: The Treasury/Federal Home Loan Bank Board Plan for FSLIC Recapitalization. Washington, D.C., March 1987.

Budgetary Implications of the Savings and Loan Crisis. Testimony of Frederick D. Wolf. Washington, D.C., October 5, 1988.

High Yield Bonds: Nature of the Market and Effect on Federally Insured Institutions. Washington, D.C., May 1988.

No Compelling Evidence of a Need for the Federal Asset Disposition Association, Report to Congressional Requesters. Washington, D.C., December 1988.

Bank and Savings and Loan Insurance Funds: Financial Condition and Proposed Reforms. Testimony, Frederick D. Wolf, Asst. Comptroller General. Washington, D.C., March 10, 1989.

CPA Audit Quality: Failure of CPA Audits to Identify and Report Significant Savings and Loan Problems. Washington, D.C., February 2, 1989.

Failed Financial Institutions: Reasons, Costs, Remedies and Unresolved Issues. Testimony, Frederick D. Wolf, Asst. Comptroller General. Washington, D.C., January 13, 1989.

Failed Thrifts: Bank Board's 1988 Texas Resolutions. Washington, D.C., March 1989.

Financial Issues: Information on FSLIC Notes and Assistance Agreements. Washington, D.C., February 1989.

High Yield Bond Market, Testimony. Testimony, Richard L. Fogel, Asst. Comptroller General. Washington, D.C., March 2, 1989.

High Yield Bonds: Issues Concerning Thrift Investments in High Yield Bonds. Washington, D.C., March 1989.

The Need to Improve Auditing in the Savings and Loan Industry. Testimony, Frederick D. Wolf, Asst. Comptroller General. Washington, D.C., February 21, 1989.

Thrift Failures: Costly Failures Resulted from Regulatory Violations and Unsafe Practices. Washington, D.C., June 1989.

Troubled Financial Institutions: Solutions to the Thrift Industry Problem. Washington, D.C., February 1989.

PERIODICALS

American Banker.
BNA Washington Financial Reports.
National Council of Savings Institutions, *Washington Memo.*
National Thrift News.

Savings and Loan Reporter.
U.S. League of Savings Institutions, *Savings Institutions.*
U.S. League of Savings Institutions, *Washington Notes.*

ANNUAL REPORTS

Annual Reports of the Federal Home Loan Bank Board, 1983–89.
Annual Reports of various state S&L Commissioners, 1981–87. U.S. League of
     Savings Institutions, *Sourcebook,* Chicago: 1981–89.

OTHER WORKS

Ferguson & Company. *The Texas Thrifts: Impact of a Depressed Economy* Dallas, Tex.
     May 1987.
Long, C. Thomas, William J. Schilling, and Carol R. Van Cleef. "Enhancing the Value
     of the Thrift Franchise: A Possible Solution for the Dilemma of the FSLIC."
     Catholic University Law Review, 37 (1988).
Silverberg, Stanley C. *The Savings and Loan Problem in the United States.* WPS 351.
     Policy, Research and External Affairs Working Papers. Washington, D.C.: The
     World Bank, March 1990.

MAJOR BANKING LEGISLATION

Financial Institutions Regulatory and Interest Rate Control Act of 1978 (FIRICA).
     Public Law 95-630, 92 Stat. 3641 (1978).
1980 Depository Institutions Deregulation and Monetary Control Act (DIDMCA).
     Public Law 96-221, 94 Stat. 132 (1980).
Garn–St Germain Act. Public Law 97-320, 96 Stat. 1469 (1982).
Competitive Equality Banking Act (CEBA). Public Law 100-86, 101 Stat. 552 (Au-
     gust 10, 1987).
Financial Institutions Reform, Recovery and Enforcement Act (FIRREA). Public Law
     101-73, 103 Stat. 183 (August 9, 1989).

SELECTED SIGNIFICANT FHLBB ACTIONS

Treatment of Goodwill Acquired in Mergers. 12 CFR Parts 546, 561, 563c, and 571.
     Withdrawn August 13, 1981.
Accounting for Gains and Losses Dispositions and for Discounts from Acquisitions of
     Mortgage Loans and Certain Securities. 12 CFR Part 563c. Proposed January
     8, 1982. Adopted May 17, 1982.
Appraised Equity Capital. 12 CFR Parts 541, 561, and 563. Proposed August 26,
     1982. Adopted November 4, 1982.
Industry Conflicts of Interest; Limitations on Loans to One Borrower. 12 CFR Parts

561 and 563. Proposed September 10, 1982. Adopted in part and reproposed in part February 18, 1983. Adopted in part September 28, 1983.

Net Worth Certificates, Regulatory Net Worth, Charter Amendments by Federal Institutions. 12 CFR Parts 552, 561, and 572. Adopted December 8, 1982. Amended February 28, 1983, and March 18, 1983.

Implementation of New Powers, Limitations on Loans to One Borrower. 12 CFR Parts 523, 526, 541, 545, 555, 561, and 563. Proposed December 16, 1982. Reproposed January 19, 1983. Adopted February 18, 1983.

Net Worth Certificates, Regulatory Net Worth. 12 CFR Parts 561 and 572. Adopted February 18, 1983.

Reserve Requirements and Policies Relating to Insurance of Accounts of *De Novo* Institutions. 12 CFR Parts 563 and 571. Proposed November 4, 1983. Adopted December 2, 1983.

Brokered Deposits, Limitations on Deposit Insurance. 12 CFR Part 330. Proposed January 20, 1984. Adopted March 26, 1984.

Accounting for Certain Real Estate Activities. 12 CFR Part 571. Proposed October 19, 1984. Adopted April 18, 1985.

Net-Worth Requirements of Insured Institutions. 12 CFR Part 563. Proposed November 30, 1984. Adopted January 31, 1985.

Regulation of Direct Investments by Insured Institutions. 12 CFR Part 563. Proposed November 30, 1984. Adopted January 31, 1985. Amended February 27, 1987, June 17, 1987.

Index

Acquisition, development and construction (ADC) loans, 78–81, 106, 129
Adjustable-rate mortgages (ARMs), 21, 47, 89, 92
Agenda for Reform, 53–55
All-Savers Act, 46–47
American Continental Corp. (ACC), 97, 146–52, 157
American Diversified Savings, 145
American Institute of Certified Public Accountants (AICPA), 79–80
Anchor Savings Bank, 175
Annunzio, Rep. Frank, 191
Antoce, Mario, 210
Appraisals, 67, 73–75
Appraised equity capital, 44–45

Bad debt deduction, 188, 245, 284
Bank Bribery Act, 76, 253
Bank of New England, 278, 283
Bankers Trust Company, 87
Bank Holding Company Act, 41, 42, 43, 59, 122, 183, 265, 286
Bankruptcy law, 137–38

Barnard, Rep. Doug, 120
Bass, Robert, 209–10
Bear, Stearns & Co., 205
Beesely, Brent 36, 37, 38, 43, 44
Bell Savings (Calif.), 145
Benston, George, 189
Beverly Hills Savings & Loan, 62–63, 119–20, 211
Black, William, 98, 128–29, 148
Blackstone Group, 204
Blain, Spencer, 97
Bluebonnet deal, 207–9
Booz Allen Hamilton, 194
Breeden, Richard, 224
Brokered deposits, 100–105, 108
Bush, Neil, 140–43, 216
Bush, President George, 5, 216, 222–23
Butera, James, 283

California Federal Savings, 42, 175
Capital, defined, 29
Carron, Andrew, 58–59
Carter administration, 17–18

Centennial Savings, 145
CenTrust Savings Bank, 1, 2, 85,
    94–95, 140, 152–54, 155
Change in Control Act, 96–98
Cirona, James, 148–49, 219
Citicorp, 42, 169, 283
Collateralized mortgage obligations
    (CMOs), 167–68
Columbia Savings, 145, 155, 158
Community Reinvestment Act, 144
Competitive Equality Banking Act of
    1987 (CEBA), 177–95
Conflict-of-interest regulations, 56
Congressional Budget Office (CBO),
    183
Connell, Lawrence, 24
Consolidated Savings, 145
Continental Illinois National Bank, 28,
    277
Conversions of S&Ls, 174–75
Coopers & Lybrand, 105–6, 119–20

Daisy chains, 128–29
Deardorff, Charles, 160–61
Deferred loss accounting, 45–46, 123
Deposit insurance limit, 19, 279
Depository Institutions Deregulation
    and Monetary Control Act (1980
    Act), 19–20, 46, 249
Depository Institutions Deregulation
    Committee (DIDC), 19, 22–24, 101,
    247
Deregulation, 17–20, 49–52, 245–49
Dingell, Rep. John, 120
Direct investments, 109–11, 189–90
Dixon, Don, 1, 2, 96–97, 127, 181,
    185, 186, 193, 251
"Douglas Amendment," 42, 122
Downs, Anthony, 242
Drexel Burnham Lambert, 147, 153,
    155–59
Dual banking system, 52
Dukakis, Michael, 216

Ely, Bert, 192, 213, 248, 275
Empire of America, 42, 175
Empire of Mesquite, 97, 105–8, 129,
    229–30, 267
Environmental hazards, 139

Fail, James, 207
Fairbanks, Shannon, 88, 116, 118
FCA/American Savings & Loan,
    95–96, 115–17, 145, 174, 209–10
Federal Asset Disposition Association
    (FADA), 212–13, 238
Federal mortgage agencies, 121, 166,
    245, 281, 283–84
Financial Accounting Standards Board
    (FASB), 79–80, 82, 256
Financial Corporation of Santa Barbara,
    145
Fink, Lawrence, 204, 206
FIRREA, 5, 134, 146, 158, 197, 212,
    218, 222–28, 236, 265–66, 276
First Boston Corporation, 156
First Federal of Arkansas, 175
First Nationwide, 42, 211
First Texas/Gibraltar, 204–6
Fitzpatrick, Dennis, 62
Five-year averaging, 44–45, 108
Fleischer, Ernest, 172–74, 256
Forbearance, 269
Ford, Gerald, 205–6
Ford Motor Company, 42, 211
Franchise value, defined, 37
Franklin Savings, 172–74, 256, 271
Freedom National Bank, 278
FSLIC notes, 202, 215–16

GAO, 123–24, 177–80, 192, 259
Garn, Sen. Jake, 46, 187, 198, 224
Garn–St Germain Act, 47, 49–52, 56,
    89, 91, 157, 174, 247, 249
Gaubert, Tom, 1, 2, 97, 127, 128,
    181, 185, 251
Gibraltar Savings (Calif.), 145

Glass–Steagall Act, 122, 263, 265, 286
Golden Pacific Savings, 145
Gonzalez, Rep. Henry, 177, 187, 201, 217, 228
Goodwill, defined, 39–41
Gould, George, 214
Gravette, Ellis T. (Bud), 199
Gray, Edwin J., 1, 2, 59–60, 63, 88–125, 127, 145, 148, 174, 177–95, 220, 238, 276
Gray Panthers, 18
Great American First Savings & Loan, 60
Great Western Savings, 42, 89, 90, 145
Greenspan, Alan, 82
Greenwich Savings Bank, 13–14, 17, 32
Grigsby, Mary, 60, 115
Gulf Broadcasting, 1, 148

Hall, Craig, 186
Hedging, 170–71, 271
Henkel, Lee, 189–90
Hill, Edward W., 260
Home Federal Savings, 175
Home Savings (Tex.), 131
Home Savings of America, 42, 89, 90, 144, 145
Hovde, Donald, 60, 115, 181

Imperial Savings (Calif.), 145, 155, 158
Independent American, 2, 84, 97, 107, 126, 127, 128, 129, 209, 230
Insider misconduct, 160–63, 233, 250–53
Insolvency, defined, 28–32
Interstate banking, 41
Isaac, William, 23–24, 103–5, 199, 277

Janis, Jay, 182
Johnson, President Lyndon B., 2, 16, 242
Junk bonds, 155–59, 264

Kane, Edward, 242
Kaufman, Henry, 86
Keating, Charles, 1, 2, 97, 110–11, 146–52, 177, 189-90, 251, 267
"Keating Five," 111, 148–49, 242
Knapp, Charles, 95, 115–17, 267
Kohlberg Kravis Roberts (KKR), 156

Lazard Freres, 205
Leach, Rep. Jim, 217
Lemmons, Woody, 270
Levy, Gerald, 190
Lincoln Savings, 1, 2, 97, 110, 140, 144–52, 153, 155, 198, 218–21, 261–62
Loan classifications, 107, 111–15
Loan fee accounting, 81–82, 84, 93–94, 248
Loan loss reserves, 82–84
Loans-to-one borrower regulations, 55–56
Loan-to-value (LTV) regulations, 50, 51, 74–75, 90–91, 107, 108, 248
Lykos, Tom, 205

Management Consignment Program (MCP), 123–24, 127, 182, 238
Manufacturers Hanover Trust Company, 87, 283
Market value accounting, 31–32, 257–59
Martin, Preston, 116
Martin, Roger, 190
McBirney, Ed, 1, 2, 127, 251
McFadden Act, 41
McKenna, William, 88, 93
Merabank, 146
Mercury Savings, 145
Merrill Lynch, 53, 101, 103, 156
Metzenbaum, Sen. Howard, 207
Milken, Michael, 156, 158
Mortgage servicing, 169

Moynihan, Sen. Daniel Patrick, 25
Mutuality, 47–49

National Thrift News, 200, 207
Negative convexity, 168
Net operating loss carryforwards
  (NOLs), 188
Net worth, defined, 29
Net worth certificates, 47
Nolan Act, 52, 92, 145, 232
Non-bank banks, 122, 183
North American Savings, 145
Northeast Savings, 42

Office of Government Ethics, 184
Office of Management and Budget
  (OMB), 22, 36, 144, 112–13, 121
Ohio Deposit Guarantee Fund (ODGF),
  121–22
Overintermediation, 248

PACs, 180
Parris, Rep. Stan, 192
Pass-through benefits, 101–2
Patriarcha, Michael, 148
Paul, David, 1, 2, 94–95
Perelman, Ron, 206
Phoenix plan, 43
Pima Savings, 146
Plato, 254
Popejoy, William, 117
Pratt, Richard, 21–24, 35–57, 59, 60,
  63, 87, 90, 101, 238, 276
Presidio Savings, 145
Proxmire, Sen. William, 183, 187,
  190–95
Prudential-Bache Securities, 116
Psychology of money, 249
Purchase accounting, 38–41

Raiden, Norman, 88, 114, 116, 119
Ramona Savings, 145
Rangel, Rep. Charles, 278
Ranieri, Lewis, 205, 224
Reagan, President Ronald, 2, 20, 49,

58, 59, 90, 189, 195, 242, 247
Reagan administration, 20, 238,
  245–46
Regan, Donald, 20, 22–24, 103, 118
Renda, Mario, 102–3
Riegle, Sen. Donald, 224
Risk-based premiums, 53–54, 276
Root, Stuart, 199
Ryan, John E., 152

Salomon Brothers, 86, 116, 156
San Marino Savings, 145
Savings & Loan Holding Company Act,
  42, 59, 265, 286
Schilling, William, 100, 119
Schumer, Rep. Charles, 213
Seeger, Pete, 283
Seidman, L. William, 225, 276
Selby, H. Joe, 186
Siebert, Muriel, 13–14, 32, 199
Signal Savings, 145
Silverado Banking, Savings & Loan
  Association, 140–43, 198, 211, 216,
  232
Skimming, 84–85, 153
Sooner Federal, 175
Southwest Plan (Tex.), 199–218
Southwest Savings (Tex.), 201
Sporkin, Judge Stanley, 149–52, 219,
  261–62
Sprague, Irvine, 23
Spread, defined, 33
Spread maintenance, defined, 38
State Savings of Lubbock, 126
Stearns, Peter, 181–82
St Germain, Fernand, 177, 183,
  185–88, 190–95, 213–16
Stockman, David, 36, 117, 121
Stockton Savings, 126
Sunbelt Savings, 2, 107, 126, 127,
  128, 129, 209, 237
Supervisory goodwill, 226

Taggert, Lawrence, 145
Tax Act, 1981, 3, 203

Tax Reform Act of 1986, 2, 132–33,
    188–89, 192, 196, 203, 236
Texas Savings & Loan League, 60, 130,
    200
Thomas, Don and Barbara, 175
"Too-big-to-fail," 277
Touche, Ross, 173

U.S. League of Savings Institutions, 21,
    58, 60, 76, 98, 124–25, 130,
    177–94, 200, 214, 253
Usury laws, 19, 137
Utley, Robert, 205–6

Valley National Bank, 147
Vernon Savings, 2, 84, 96–97, 107,
    126, 127, 128, 129, 181, 230, 270

Vesco, Robert, 151
Volcker, Paul, 16, 22–24, 58, 116

Wall, M. Danny, 141, 173, 195,
    198–225, 238
Western Savings (Tex.), 107, 126, 186,
    209, 230
Western Savings (Ariz.), 146
White, Lawrence, 141, 189, 215, 224,
    277, 278
Wise, Michael, 140–43
Wright, Rep. Jim, 177, 185–88, 242
Wylie, Rep. Chalmers, 224

Yang, Linda, 144

ABOUT THE AUTHOR

MARTIN LOWY is a banker and lawyer with twenty-five years of experience in thrift institution law, management, and regulation. As a lawyer he has represented the New York State Superintendent of Banks and the Federal Deposit Insurance Corporation in failing bank situations, and has represented a number of thrift institutions, banks, trade associations, and accounting firms. He served as Vice Chairman of Dollar Dry Dock Bank from 1986 to 1989 and currently is Counsel to the New York law firm Rosenman & Colin.

Mr. Lowy is a graduate of the Yale Law School (where he was managing editor of the *Yale Law Journal*), Amherst College, and the Fieldston School.